Lecture Notes in Artificial Intelligence 4811

Edited by J. G. Carbonell and J. Siekmann

Subseries of Lecture Notes in Computer Science

Olfa Nasraoui   Myra Spiliopoulou
Jaideep Srivastava   Bamshad Mobasher
Brij Masand (Eds.)

Advances in Web Mining and Web Usage Analysis

8th International Workshop
on Knowledge Discovery on the Web, WebKDD 2006
Philadelphia, PA, USA, August 20, 2006
Revised Papers

 Springer

Series Editors

Jaime G. Carbonell, Carnegie Mellon University, Pittsburgh, PA, USA
Jörg Siekmann, University of Saarland, Saarbrücken, Germany

Volume Editors

Olfa Nasraoui
University of Louisville
Louisville, KY 40292, USA
E-mail: olfa.nasraoui@louisville.edu

Myra Spiliopoulou
Otto-von-Guericke-Universität Magdeburg
39106 Magdeburg, Germany
E-mail: myra@iti.cs.uni-magdeburg.de

Jaideep Srivastava
University of Minnesota
Minneapolis, MN 55455, USA
E-mail: srivasta@cs.umn.edu

Bamshad Mobasher
DePaul University
Chicago, IL 60604, USA
E-mail: mobasher@cs.depaul.edu

Brij Masand
Data Miners Inc.
Boston, MA 02114, USA
E-mail: brij@data-miners.com

Library of Congress Control Number: 2007941802

CR Subject Classification (1998): I.2, H.2.8, H.3-5, K.4, C.2

LNCS Sublibrary: SL 7 – Artificial Intelligence

ISSN	0302-9743
ISBN-10	3-540-77484-X Springer Berlin Heidelberg New York
ISBN-13	978-3-540-77484-6 Springer Berlin Heidelberg New York

Springer is a part of Springer Science+Business Media

springer.com

© Springer-Verlag Berlin Heidelberg 2007
Printed in Germany

Typesetting: Camera-ready by author, data conversion by Scientific Publishing Services, Chennai, India
Printed on acid-free paper   SPIN: 12210404   06/3180   5 4 3 2 1 0

Preface

This book contains the postworkshop proceedings with selected revised papers from the 8th international workshop on knowledge discovery from the Web, WEBKDD 2006. The WEBKDD workshop series has taken place as part of the ACM SIGKDD International Conference on Knowledge Discovery and Data Mining (KDD) since 1999.

The discipline of data mining delivers methodologies and tools for the analysis of large data volumes and the extraction of comprehensible and non-trivial insights from them. Web mining, a much younger discipline, concentrates on the analysis of data pertinent to the Web. Web mining methods are applied on usage data and Web site content; they strive to improve our understanding of how the Web is used, to enhance usability and to promote mutual satisfaction between e-business venues and their potential customers.

In the last few years, the interest for the Web as a medium for communication, interaction and business has led to new challenges and to intensive, dedicated research. Many of the infancy problems in Web mining have been solved by now, but the tremendous potential for new and improved uses, as well as misuses, of the Web are leading to new challenges.

The theme of the WebKDD 2006 workshop was "Knowledge Discovery on the Web", encompassing lessons learned over the past few years and new challenges for the years to come. While some of the infancy problems of Web analysis have been solved and proposed methodologies have reached maturity, the reality poses new challenges: The Web is evolving constantly; sites change and user preferences drift. And, most of all, a Web site is more than a see-and-click medium; it is a venue where a user interacts with a site owner or with other users, where group behavior is exhibited, communities are formed and experiences are shared.

The WebKDD 2006 workshop invited research results in all areas of Web mining and Semantic Web mining, with an emphasis on a seven years' update: What are the lessons learned on algorithms, semantics, data preparation, data integration and applications of the Web? How do new technologies, like adaptive mining methods, stream mining algorithms and techniques for the Grid, apply to Web mining? What new challenges are posed by new forms of data, especially flat texts, documents, pictures and streams, as well as the emergence of Web communities? How do we study the evolution of the Web and its effects on searching and browsing behavior? Which lessons have we learned about usability, e-commerce applications, personalization, recommendation engines, Web marketplaces, Web search, Web security, and misuse and abuse of the Web and its services? WebKDD 2006 attempted to address these challenging questions, with an emphasis on expanding the horizon of traditional Web mining to embrace and keep up with recent and emerging trends and emphasis on the Web domain, such as mining search engine queries, mining Web evolution, robustness of recommender systems, and mining blogs for sentiment analysis.

In the first paper, "Adaptive Web site Design using Caching Algorithms", Justin Brickell, Inderjit S. Dhillon, and Dharmendra S. Modha present improved online algorithms for shortcut link selection that are based on a novel analogy drawn between shortcutting and caching. In the same way that cache algorithms predict which memory pages will be accessed in the future, the proposed algorithms predict which Web pages will be accessed in the future. These algorithms are efficient and can consider accesses over a long period of time, but give extra weight to recent accesses. Experiments show significant improvement in the utility of shortcut links selected by the proposed algorithm as compared to those selected by existing algorithms.

In the second paper, "Incorporating Usage Information into Average-Clicks Algorithm", Kalyan Beemanapalli, Ramya Rangarajan, and Jaideep Srivastava present an extension to the Average-Clicks Algorithm, called "Usage Aware Average-Clicks," where the static Web link structure graph is combined with the dynamic Usage Graph (built using the information available from the Web logs) to assign different weights to links on a Web page and hence capture the user's intuition of distance between two Web pages more accurately. This method has been used as a new metric to calculate the page similarities in a recommendation engine to improve its predictive power.

In "Nearest-Biclusters Collaborative Filtering", Panagiotis Symeonidis, Alexandros Nanopoulos, Apostolos Papadopoulos, and Yannis Manolopoulos use biclustering to disclose the duality between users and items in Nearest-neighbor Collaborative Filtering, by grouping them in both dimensions simultaneously. A novel nearest-biclusters algorithm is proposed, that uses a new similarity measure that achieves partial matching of users' preferences. Performance evaluation results are offered, which show that the proposed method improves substantially the performance of the CF process.

In "Fast Categorization of Web Documents Represented by Graphs", Alex Markov, Mark Last, and Abraham Kandel address the limitations of the vector-space model of information retrieval. This traditional model does not capture important structural information, such as the order and proximity of word occurrence, the location of a word within the document, or mark-up information. Three new hybrid approaches to Web document classification are presented, built upon both graph and vector space representations, thus preserving the benefits and discarding the limitations of each. The hybrid methods outperform, in most cases, vector-based models using two model-based classifiers (C4.5 decision-tree algorithm and probabilistic Naïve Bayes) on several benchmark Web document collections.

In "Leveraging Structural Knowledge for Hierarchically Informed Keyword Weight Propagation in the Web," Jong Wook Kim and K. Selcuk Candan elaborate on indexing Web documents that have non-atomic structures, such as navigational/semantic hierarchies on the Web. A novel keyword and keyword weight propagation technique is proposed to properly enrich the data nodes in structured content. The approach first relies on understanding the context provided by the relative content relationships between entries in the structure, and then leveraging this information for relative-content preserving keyword propagation. Experiments show a significant improvement in precision with the proposed keyword propagation algorithm.

In the paper "How to Define Searching Sessions on Web Search Engines," Bernard J. Jansen, Amanda Spink, and Vinish Kathuria investigate three methods for defining a session on Web search engines. The authors examine 2,465,145 interactions from 534, 507 Web searchers, and compare defining sessions using: (1) Internet Protocol address and cookie; (2) Internet Protocol address, cookie, and a temporal limit on intra-session interactions; and (3) Internet Protocol address, cookie, and query reformulation patterns. Research results show that defining sessions by query reformulation along with Internet Protocol address and cookie, provides the best measure, resulting in an 82% increase in the number of sessions; while for all methods, mean session length was fewer than three queries and the mean session duration was less than 30 minutes. Implications are that unique sessions may be a better indicator than the common industry metric of unique visitors for measuring search traffic.

In the paper "Incorporating Concept Hierarchies into Usage Mining Based Recommendations," Amit Bose, Kalyan Beemanapalli, Jaideep Srivastava, and Sigal Sahar address the limitation of most recommendation models in their ability to use domain knowledge in the form of conceptual and structural characteristics of a Web site. Conceptual content organization can play an important role in the quality of recommendations, and forms the basis of resources like Google Directory, Yahoo Directory and Web-content management systems. The authors propose a novel technique to incorporate the conceptual characteristics of a Web site into a usage-based recommendation model. The authors use a framework based on biological sequence alignment. Similarity scores play a crucial role in such a construction, and a scoring system that is generated from the Web site's concept hierarchy is introduced. These scores fit seamlessly with other quantities used in similarity calculation like browsing order and time spent on a page. Additionally they demonstrate a simple, extensible system for assimilating more domain knowledge. Experimental results illustrate the benefits of using a concept hierarchy.

In the paper "A Random-Walk-Based Scoring Algorithm Applied to Recommender Engines," Augusto Pucci, Marco Gori, and Marco Maggini present "ItemRank," a random-walk-based scoring algorithm, which can be used to rank products according to expected user preferences, in order to recommend top-rank items to potentially interested users. The authors tested their algorithm on the MovieLens data set, which contains data collected from a popular recommender system on movies, and compared ItemRank with other state-of-the-art ranking techniques, showing that ItemRank performs better than the other techniques, while being less complex than other algorithms with respect to memory usage and computational cost. The paper also presents an analysis that helps to discover some intriguing properties of the MovieLens data set, that has been widely exploited as a benchmark for evaluating recently proposed approaches to recommender system.

In "Towards a Scalable k-NN CF Algorithm: Exploring Effective Applications of Clustering," Al Mamunur Rashid, Shyong K. Lam, Adam LaPitz, George Karypis, and John Riedl address the need for specially designed CF algorithms that can gracefully cope with the vast size of the data representing customers and items in typical e-commerce systems. Many algorithms proposed thus far, where the principal concern is recommendation quality, may be too expensive to operate in a large-scale system. The authors propose ClustKNN, a simple and intuitive algorithm that is well suited for large data sets. The method first compresses data tremendously by building a straightforward but efficient clustering model. Recommendations are then generated quickly by using a simple Nearest Neighbor-based approach. The feasibility of ClustKNN is demonstrated both analytically and empirically, and a comparison with a number of other popular CF algorithms shows that, apart from being highly scalable and intuitive, ClustKNN provides very good recommendation accuracy.

In "Detecting Profile Injection Attacks in Collaborative Filtering: A Classification-Based Approach," Chad Williams, Bamshad Mobasher, Robin Burke, and Runa Bhaumik address the vulnerability of Collaborative recommender systems to profile injection attacks. By injecting a larger number of biased profiles into a system, attackers can manipulate the predictions of targeted items. To decrease this risk, researchers have begun to study mechanisms for detecting and preventing profile injection attacks. In this paper, the authors extend their previous work that proposed several attributes for attack detection and for classification of attack profiles, through a more detailed analysis of the informativeness of these attributes as well as an evaluation of their impact at improving the robustness of recommender systems.

In "Predicting the Political Sentiment of Web Log Posts Using Supervised Machine Learning Techniques Coupled with Feature Selection", Kathleen T. Durant and Michael D. Smith investigate data mining techniques that can automatically identify the political *sentiment* of Web log posts, and thus help bloggers categorize and filter this exploding information source. They illustrate the effectiveness of supervised learning for sentiment classification on Web log posts, showing that a Naïve Bayes classifier coupled with a forward feature selection technique can on average correctly predict a postings sentiment 89.77% of the time. It significantly outperforms Support Vector Machines at the 95% confidence level with a confidence interval of $[1.5, 2.7]$. The feature selection technique provides on average an 11.84% and a 12.18% increase for Naïve Bayes and Support Vector Machines results, respectively. Previous sentiment classification research achieved an 81% accuracy using Naïve Bayes and 82.9% using SVMs on a movie domain corpus.

In "Analysis of Web Search Engine Query Session and Clicked Documents," David Nettleton, Liliana Calderón-Benavides, and Ricardo Baeza-Yates present the analysis of a Web search engine query log from two different perspectives: the query session and the clicked document. In the query session perspective, they process and analyze a Web search engine query and click data for the query session (query + clicked results) conducted by the user. They initially state some hypotheses for possible user types and quality profiles for the user session, based on descriptive variables of the session. In the clicked document perspective, they repeat the process from the perspective of the documents (URL's) selected. They also initially define possible document categories and select descriptive variables to define the documents. They apply a systematic data mining process to click data, contrasting non- supervised (Kohonen) and supervised (C4.5) methods to cluster and model the data, in order to identify profiles and rules which relate to theoretical user behavior and user session "quality," from the point of view of user session, and to identify document profiles which relate to theoretical user behavior, and document (URL) organization, from the document perspective.

In "Understanding Content Reuse on the Web: Static and Dynamic Analyses", Ricardo Baeza-Yates, Álvaro Pereira, and Nivio Ziviani present static and dynamic studies of duplicate and near-duplicate documents in the Web. The static and dynamic studies involve the analysis of similar content among pages within a given snapshot of the Web and how pages in an old snapshot are reused to compose new documents in a more recent snapshot. With experiments using four snapshots of the Chilean Web, they identify duplicates (in the static study) in both parts of the Web graph – reachable (connected by links) and unreachable components (unconnected) – aiming to identify where duplicates occur more frequently. They show that the number of duplicates in the Web seems to be much higher than previously reported (about 50% higher) and in their data the duplicated in the unreachable Web is 74.6% higher than the number of duplicates in the reachable component of the Web graph. In the dynamic study, they show that some of the old content is used to compose new pages. If a page in a newer snapshot has content of a page in an older snapshot, they consider that the source is a parent of the new page. They state the hypothesis that people use search engines to find pages and republish their content as a new document, and present evidence that this happens for part of the pages that have parents. In this case, part of the Web content is biased by the ranking function of search engines.

We would like to thank the authors of all submitted papers. Their creative efforts have led to a rich set of good contributions for WebKDD 2006. We would also like to express our gratitude to the members of the Program Committee for their vigilant and timely reviews, namely (in alphabetical order): Corin Anderson, Ricardo A. Baeza-Yates, Bettina Berendt, Zheng Chen, Ed H. Chi, Brian D. Davison, Wei Fan, Fabio Grandi, Michael Hahsler, Xin Jin, Thorsten Joachims, George Karypis, Ravi Kumar, Vipin Kumar, Mark Last, Mark Levene, Ee-Peng Lim, Huan Liu, Stefano Lonardi, Alexandros D. Nanopoulos, Georgios Paliouras, Aniruddha G. Pant, Jian Pei, Ellen Spertus, Andrew Tomkins, and Mohammed

Table of Contents

Adaptive Website Design Using Caching Algorithms

Justin Brickell[1], Inderjit S. Dhillon[1], and Dharmendra S. Modha[2]

[1] The University of Texas at Austin, Austin, TX, USA
[2] IBM Almaden Research Center, San Jose, CA, USA

Abstract. Visitors enter a website through a variety of means, including web searches, links from other sites, and personal bookmarks. In some cases the first page loaded satisfies the visitor's needs and no additional navigation is necessary. In other cases, however, the visitor is better served by content located elsewhere on the site found by navigating links. If the path between a user's current location and his eventual goal is circuitous, then the user may never reach that goal or will have to exert considerable effort to reach it. By mining site access logs, we can draw conclusions of the form "users who load page p are likely to later load page q." If there is no direct link from p to q, then it is advantageous to provide one. The process of providing links to users' eventual goals while skipping over the in-between pages is called *shortcutting*. Existing algorithms for shortcutting require substantial offline training, which make them unable to adapt when access patterns change between training sessions. We present improved online algorithms for shortcut link selection that are based on a novel analogy drawn between shortcutting and caching. In the same way that cache algorithms predict which memory pages will be accessed in the future, our algorithms predict which web pages will be accessed in the future. Our algorithms are very efficient and are able to consider accesses over a long period of time, but give extra weight to recent accesses. Our experiments show significant improvement in the utility of shortcut links selected by our algorithm as compared to those selected by existing algorithms.

1 Introduction

As websites increase in complexity, they run headfirst into a fundamental tradeoff: the more information that is available on the website, the more difficult it is for visitors to pinpoint the specific information that they are looking for. A well-designed website limits the impact of this tradeoff, so that even if the amount of information is increased significantly, locating that information becomes only marginally more difficult. Typically, site designers ease information overload by organizing the site content into a hierarchy of topics, and then providing a navigational tree that allows visitors to descend into the hierarchy and find the information they are looking for. In their paper on adaptive website design [12], Perkowitz and Etzioni describe these static, master-designed websites as "fossils cast in HTML." They claim that a site designer's *a priori* expectations for how a

O. Nasraoui et al. (Eds.): WebKDD 2006, LNAI 4811, pp. 1–20, 2007.

site will be used and navigated are likely to inaccurately reflect actual usage patterns, especially as the site adds new content over time. As it is infeasible for even the most dedicated site designer to understand the goals and access patterns of all site visitors, Perkowitz and Etzioni proposed building websites that mine their own access logs in order to automatically determine helpful self-modifications.

One example of a helpful modification is *shortcutting*, in which links are added between unlinked pages in order to allow visitors to reach their intended destinations with fewer clicks. Typically a limit N is imposed on the maximum number of outgoing shortcuts on any one particular page. The shortcutting problem can then be thought of as an optimization problem to choose the N shortcuts per page that minimize the number of clicks needed for future visitors to reach their goal pages. These shortcuts may be modified at any time based on past accesses in order to account for anticipated changes in the access patterns of future visitors. Finding an optimal solution to this problem would require an exact knowledge of the future and a precise way of determining each user's goal. However, shortcutting algorithms must provide shortcuts in an on-line framework, so the shortcuts must be chosen without knowledge of future accesses. Rather than solving the optimization problem exactly, shortcutting algorithms use heuristics and analyze past accesses in order to provide good shortcuts.

In this paper, we draw a novel analogy between shortcutting algorithms, which maintain an active set of shortcuts on each page, and caching algorithms, which maintain an active set of items in cache. The goal of caching algorithms—maximizing the fraction of future memory accesses for items in the cache—is analogous to the goal of shortcutting algorithms. The main contribution of this paper is the CACHECUT algorithm for shortcutting. By using replacement policies developed for caching applications, CACHECUT is able to run with less memory than other shortcutting algorithms, while producing better results. A second contribution is the FRONTCACHE algorithm, which uses similar caching techniques in order to select pages for promotion on the front page.

The remainder of this paper is organized as follows. In Section 2 we discuss related work in adaptive website problems. In Section 3 we give definitions for terms that are used throughout the paper. Section 4 gives a formulation of the shortcutting problem and presents two shortcutting algorithms from existing literature. In Section 5 we detail our CACHECUT algorithm for shortcutting, and in section 6 we describe the FRONTCACHE algorithm for promoting pages with links on the front page. Section 7 describes our experimental setup and the results of our experiments. Finally, in Section 8, we offer some concluding thoughts and suggest directions for future work.

2   Related Work

Perkowitz and Etzioni [11] issued the original challenge to the AI community to build adaptive web sites that learn visitor access patterns from the access log in order to automatically improve their organization and presentation. Their follow-up paper [12] presented several *global* adaptations that affect the presentation of the website to all users. One adaptation from their paper is "index page synthesis," in which new pages are created containing collections of links to related but currently unlinked pages. In his thesis [10], Perkowitz presents the shortcutting problem as a global adaptive problem, in which links are added to each page to ease the browsing experience of all site visitors. Ramakrishnan *et al.* [13] have also done work in global adaptation; they observe that frustrated users who cannot find the content they are looking for are apt to use the "back" button. The authors scan the access log looking for these "backtracks" to identify documents that are misclassified in the site hierarchy, and correct these misclassifications.

Other work has explored adaptations that are *individual*, rather than global; sometimes this is referred to as *personalization*. It is increasingly common for portals to allow users to manually customize portions of their front pages [14]. For instance, a box with local weather information can be provided based on zip code information stored in a client cookie. The Newsjunkie system [7] provides personalized newsfeeds to users based on their news preferences. Personalization is easy when users provide both their identity and their desired customizations, but more difficult when the personalization must take place automatically without explicit management on the part of the user. The research community has made some stabs at the more difficult problem. Anderson and Horvitz [2] automatically generate a personal web page that contains all of the content that the target user visits during a typical day of surfing. Frayling *et al.* [9] improve the "back" button so that it jumps to key pages in the navigation session. Eirinaki and Vazirgiannis [6] give a survey of the use of web mining for personalization.

Operating at a level between global adaptations and individual adaptations are *group* adaptations. The mixture-model variants of the MINPATH algorithm [1] are examples of group-based shortcutting algorithms. When suggesting shortcuts to a website visitor, they first classify that visitor based on browsing behavior, and then provide shortcuts that are thought to be useful to that class of visitors. Classifying users requires examining the "trails" or "clickstreams" in the access log, which are the sequences of pages accessed by individual visitors. Other researchers have investigated trails without the intention of adapting a website. Banerjee and Ghosh [3] use trails to cluster users. Cooley *et al.* [5] discover association rules to find correlations such as "60% of clients who accessed page A also accessed page B." Yang *et al.* [15] conduct temporal event prediction, in which they also estimate *when* the client is likely to access B.

Our work follows the global model of shortcutting [10], in which shortcutting is viewed as a global adaptation that adds links to each page that are the same for every visitor. Like Perkowitz' algorithm, when choosing shortcuts for a page p we pay close attention to the number of times other pages q are accessed *after* p within a trail; however, our algorithm provides improvements in the form of reduced memory requirements and higher-quality shortcuts. A related work by Yang and Zhang [16] sought to create an improved replacement policy for website caching by analyzing the access log. In contrast, our work uses existing caching policies to create an improved website.

3   Definitions

Before describing CACHECUT and other shortcutting algorithms from the literature, we provide some definitions that we will use throughout the paper.

Site Graph. The *site graph* of a website with n unique pages is a directed n-node graph $G = (V, E)$ where $e_{pq} \in E$ if and only if there is a link from page p to page q.

Shortcut. A *shortcut* is a directed connection between web pages p and q that were not linked in the original site graph, *i.e.*, $e_{pq} \notin E$.

Shortcut Set. The *shortcut set* S_p of a page p is a set of pages $\{q_1, ..., q_N\}$ such that there is a shortcut from p to each $q_i \in S_p$.

Access Log. The *access log* records all requests for content on the website. Common webservers like Apache produce an access log automatically. In its raw form, the access log contains information that is not needed by shortcutting algorithms. We strip away this unnecessary information and formally consider the access log to be a sequence of tuples of the form

$$\langle client, page, time, referrer \rangle,$$

where *client* is the identity of the client accessing the website, *page* is the page requested by the client, and *time* is the time of access. Some shortcutting algorithms also use the *referrer* field, which is the last page the client loaded before loading the current page. This information is self-reported by the client and tends to be unreliable, so we prefer not to use it.

Trail. A *trail* is a sequence of pages $\{p_1, p_2, ..., p_k\}$; we also assume there is a function TIME such that $\text{TIME}(p_i)$ returns the time at which page p_i was accessed within the trail. A trail represents a single visit to the website by a single client, starting at page p_1 at time $\text{TIME}(p_1)$ and ending at page p_k at time $\text{TIME}(p_k)$. In order to determine which sequences of page requests constitute a single visit, we require that $\text{TIME}(p_k) - \text{TIME}(p_1) < 10\text{min}$. Of course, it is possible to change the 10 minute value.

Note that there need not necessarily be a link in the original site graph between page p_i and page p_{i+1}. This is in contrast to other definitions of trails, which use the referrer field in order to require that the trail be a sequence of clicks. We adapt the more inclusive definition because there are many ways for a user to navigate from p_i to p_{i+1} without following a direct link. For instance, the user could have navigated to an external site with a link to p_{i+1}, typed in the address for p_{i+1} manually, or followed a link on p_{i-1} after using the "back" button. If visitors to page p often visit q later in the session, this is good evidence that a shortcut from p to q would be useful, regardless of how those visitors found their way from p to q.

Trail-Edge. The set of *trail-edges* E_T of a trail T is the set of forward edges spanned by T. If $T = \{p_1, p_2, ..., p_k\}$, then $E_T = \bigcup_{i=1}^{k-1} \bigcup_{j=i+1}^{k} e_{ij}$; note that $|E_T| = \binom{|T|}{2}$.

In a sense, E_T is the set of edges that *could be useful* to the client in moving from page p_1 to page p_k. Some of these edges are in E, the edge set of the site graph G, while others may become available as shortcuts. A user does not need to have all trail-edges available to successfully navigate a trail, but each edge that is available increases the number of ways to navigate from p_1 to p_k.

4   Shortcutting

Shortcutting adds links to the site graph that allow users to quickly navigate from their current location to their goal page. If a user on page A wishes to visit page E, he may find that there is no way to navigate to E without first loading intermediate pages B, C, and D. Providing a direct link from A to E would save him 3 clicks. If we transformed the site graph G into a complete graph by adding every possible link, then any user could reach any page in a single click. However, this is an impractical transformation because a human visitor cannot make sense of a webpage with hundreds of thousands of links. This is representative of a general tradeoff that we encounter whenever adding links to pages: pages become more accessible when they have more inlinks, but become more confusing when they have more outlinks. We typically address this tradeoff by limiting the number of shortcut links per page to N, a small value such as 5 or 10.

With the restriction of N shortcuts per page in place, an optimal shortcutting algorithm is one that chooses the N shortcuts for each page p that minimize the number of clicks required for site visitors to navigate to their goal page. If we could look into the future and read the minds of site visitors, then each time a visitor loaded a page p, we could choose the shortcuts on p based on that visitor's goal. In this case, only a single shortcut is needed for page p—a shortcut to the visitor's goal page. Since it is not possible to look into the future, algorithms for shortcut selection must instead mine the web access log for access patterns of past visitors, and then provide shortcuts that would have been helpful to past visitors with the assumption that they will also be useful to visitors in the future.

4.1   Evaluating the Quality of a Shortcutting Algorithm

The goal of shortcutting is to reduce the number of clicks that a visitor must make in order to reach his goal page. The shortcutting algorithm must provide shortcuts to the visitor on-line, without any knowledge of where the visitor will go in the future; at the time of suggestion it is impossible to determine whether any of the provided shortcuts will be useful to the visitor. Once a visitor's trail is complete, however, it is possible to examine the trail in its entirety and evaluate the quality of the shortcuts provided at each page in the trail.

Ideally we could evaluate the quality of shortcuts by comparing the number of clicks needed to reach the goal page both before and after shortcutting. Unfortunately, knowledge of an entire trail is not enough to determine which page was the goal. It is possible that the last page of the trail is the goal page, as is the case when visitors leave the web site after reaching their goals. However, it is also possible for visitors to deliberately load several distinct goal pages during their sessions, or to reach their goals midway through their sessions and then browse aimlessly, or to never reach their goals at all.

The shortcut evaluation used by Anderson *et al.* [1] makes the assumption that the last page in a trail is the goal page, even though this assumption may be incorrect for many trails. Rather than make any such assumption about goal pages, we will simply assume that *any* shortcut that allows a visitor to jump ahead in his trail is useful. Then we evaluate the quality of a shortcutting algorithm for a trail T by determining the fraction of trail-edges available to the visitor as shortcuts or links. Formally, let E_T be the set of trail edges of T, let E be the set of edges of the site graph G, and let S_p be the set of shortcuts on page p at the time that page p was visited. Then a trail edge $e_{pq} \in E_T$ is *available* if either $e_{pq} \in E$ or $q \in S_p$. We define the trail-edge hit ratio of a shortcutting algorithm for a trail T as the fraction of trail-edges that are available:

$$HitRatio(T) = \frac{|\text{available trail-edges of } T|}{|\text{trail-edges of } T|}. \tag{1}$$

The hit ratio ranges from 0 (if none of the pages in the trail are linked or shortcutted) to 1 (if every trail-edge is provided as either a link or a shortcut). Note that the hit ratio will generally increase as we increase the number of shortcuts per page, N. To evaluate the overall success of a shortcutting algorithm, we take a suitably large access log with many thousands of trails and compute the average trail edge hit ratio:

$$AverageHitRatio(Trails) = \frac{\sum_{T \in Trails} HitRatio(T)}{|Trails|}, \tag{2}$$

where $Trails$ is the set of trails in the access log.

4.2   Perkowitz' Shortcutting Algorithm

In [10], Perkowitz gives a simple algorithm that we call PERKOWITZSHORTCUT for selecting shortcuts; this algorithm is shown in Algorithm 1. PERKOWITZ-SHORTCUT is periodically run offline to update all of the shortcuts on the website, and these shortcuts remain in place until the next time that an update is performed. For every page p, the algorithm counts the number of times other pages are accessed after p in the same trail, and then it adds shortcuts on p to the N pages most frequently accessed after p. PERKOWITZSHORTCUT is simple and intuitive; however, it theoretically requires n^2 memory, which can be prohibitive. In practice, the memory requirements of Perkowitz are closer to $O(n)$ when a sparse representation of the count array C is used.

Because the shortcuts are updated offline and no information is retained from the previous time the update was run, there is a tradeoff when choosing how frequently to update. If the updates are too frequent, then there is inadequate time for the probability distribution to settle. In particular, pages p that are infrequently accessed may have poorly chosen shortcuts (or no shortcuts at all, if the algorithm never sees a session that loads p). If the updates are too infrequent, then the algorithm will be unable to adapt to changes in visitor access patterns. Our algorithm CACHECUT presented in Section 5 improves on PERKO-WITZSHORTCUT by using less memory and providing higher-quality shortcuts.

Inputs:
$G = (V, E)$ *The $n \times n$ site graph*
L *The access log (divided into trails)*
N *The number of shortcuts per page*
Output:
A shortcut set S_p for each page p

PERKOWITZSHORTCUT(G, L, N)

1: Initialize an $n \times n$ array of counters C. C_{pq} represents how often users who visit page p later go on to visit page q.
2: For each trail T in the access log, and for each page p in T, find all pages q that occur *after p* in T. If $e_{pq} \notin E$, then increment C_{pq}.
3: For each page p, find the N largest values C_{pq}, and select these to be the shortcut set S_p. Output all shortcut sets.

Algorithm 1. A basic shortcutting algorithm for generating shortcuts from the current page to popular destinations

4.3 The MinPath Algorithm

The MINPATH [1] algorithm is a shortcutting algorithm developed to aid wireless devices in navigating complicated websites. Wireless devices benefit from shortcuts more than traditional clients because they have small screens and high latency, so each additional page that must be loaded and scrolled requires substantial effort on the part of the site visitor. Although designed with wireless devices in mind, MINPATH is a general purpose shortcutting algorithm that can suggest shortcuts to any type of client.

Unlike PERKOWITZSHORTCUT and our algorithm CACHECUT, MINPATH does not associate shortcuts with each page on the website. Instead, it examines the *trail prefix* $\langle p_1, ..., p_i \rangle$ that has brought a visitor to the current page p_i. Based on the prefix, MINPATH returns a set of shortcuts specifically chosen for the individual visitor. This approach requires significantly more computation each time that shortcuts are suggested to visitors, but has the potential to provide shortcuts that are more personalized to the individual visitor.

MINPATH works in two stages. In the first stage, which occurs offline, MIN-PATH learns a model of web usage. In the second stage, which occurs offline, MINPATH uses its model to estimate the *expected savings* of web pages, where the expected savings of a page q is the estimated probability that the user will visit page q multiplied by the savings in clicks required to navigate from the current page to q. For example, suppose that a user is currently at page p and the web usage model calculates that there is a 0.3 chance of that user visiting page q. If it takes 3 clicks to navigate from p to q ($e.g. p \rightarrow a \rightarrow b \rightarrow q$), then the expected savings is $0.3 \cdot (3 - 1) = 0.6$ because a shortcut from p to q would reduce the number of clicks from 3 to 1. After computing the expected savings for all possible destinations from the current page, MINPATH presents the user with N shortcuts having the highest expected savings.

The web usage models learned by MINPATH estimate the quantity

$$\Pr(p_i = q | \langle p_0, p_1..., p_{i-1} \rangle),$$

which is the probability that a user currently at page p_{i-1} will click on the link to page q given that he has arrived at p_{i-1} by the trail $\langle p_0, p_1..., p_{i-1} \rangle$. This probability is 0 if there is no direct link from p_{i-1} to q; otherwise, a probability estimate is learned from observed traffic. MINPATH has poor performance in practice, because the evaluation routine calls for a depth-first traversal of the site graph starting at the current page up to a maximum depth d. The MINPATH authors state that during their tests it took MINPATH an average of 0.65 seconds to evaluate the web usage model and return shortcuts each time a visitor loaded a page; if MINPATH were deployed on a web server intended to serve tens of thousands of requests per second the server would struggle to keep up.

5   The CacheCut Algorithm

In this section we present the CACHECUT algorithm, a novel algorithm for the generation of shortcuts on websites which is the main contribution of this paper. In the CACHECUT algorithm, we associate with each page p a cache C_p of size L which stores web pages q that have been accessed *after* p within a trail. It is not possible to store information about every page accessed after p, so CACHECUT must carefully choose which L pages to store in each cache. Our ultimate goal is to select the shortcuts on page p from the contents of cache C_p, so we want to store those pages q which are likely to be accessed after p many times again in the future. When a page q is accessed after p that is *not* currently in C_p, we add it to C_p because it is likely to be accessed again. If C_p is full, then we must select one of its elements to remove and replace with q. We refer to the methodology we use to select the element to be replaced as a *replacement policy*.

The main insight in the CACHECUT algorithm is that replacement policies designed for traditional caching problems are well suited as replacement policies for shortcut caches. We can draw an analogy between traditional caching and shortcut caching:

- Users (site visitors) are analogous to processes.
- Web pages are analogous to pages in memory.
- The shortcut set is analogous to a cache.

Replacement policies for traditional caching applications are heuristics that attempt to throw out the item that is least likely to be accessed in the future, so that the fraction of future accesses that are for objects currently residing in cache is maximized. If we substitute the traditional caching terms for their shortcutting analogs, we see that the goal for cache replacement heuristics is *identical* to the goal for shortcut replacement heuristics, because we want to maximize the fraction of accesses that come after p that are for pages currently in C_p.

Cache replacement policies are evaluated based on their *hit ratio*, which is the fraction of total accesses that are for objects that were in the cache at the time of access. Put in shortcutting terminology, the hit ratio for a trail T with trail-edges E_T becomes:

$$HitRatio(T) = \frac{|\{e_{pq} \in E_T | q \in C_p\}|}{|E_T|}.$$

If we think of the cache C_p as containing the shortcuts for page p in addition to a permanent set of the original links on page p, then this is identical to the evaluation equation for shortcutting algorithms given in equation (1).

5.1   Batched Caching

The simplest way of using a caching algorithm to select shortcuts would be to have the shortcut set for page p directly correspond to the cache C_p for page p. To implement a shortcutting algorithm in this way we would set the cache size L equal to the number of shortcuts N, and each time a page $q \in C_p$ was replaced with a page r, we would immediately replace the shortcut from p to q with a shortcut from p to r. When evaluated based on hit ratio this scheme performs well, but it is impractical as a deployed shortcutting scheme because the shortcut set changes too frequently Each visitor who passes through page p updates the cache C_p with every subsequent page access in the same trail. If there are thousands of site visitors, then the caches may update very frequently, which would be confusing to a visitor expecting the shortcuts to remain the same when he refreshes the page.

Our solution is to *not* have the shortcut sets and the caches be in direct correspondence. We update the cache C_p as usual with every in-trail access that occurs after p. However, instead of immediately updating the shortcuts on p, they are left alone. Periodically (say, once every 2 hours) the contents of C_p become the shortcuts on p. This method allows us to continue using unmodified out-of-the-box cache replacement policies, while relieving site visitors from the annoyance of having the shortcut set change too frequently.

5.2   Increasing the Size of the Underlying Cache

Once we have decided to not have the cache C_p and the set of shortcuts on p in direct correspondence, we are freed from the restriction that they need to be the same size. By allowing the cache size L to be greater than the number of shortcuts N, we may keep track of data (such as hit count) about more than N items, which enables a more intelligent choice of shortcuts. If $L = N$, then any page accessed immediately before the periodic update of shortcuts will become a shortcut for the next time period, even if it's a rarely accessed page. With $L > N$, we can exclude such a page in favor of a page that is more frequently accessed.

Allowing $L > N$ is beneficial, but it adds the additional challenge of choosing which N of the L pages in C_p will become the shortcuts on page p. A simple selection policy that performs well in practice is to maintain a hit count for each item in C_p, and then to choose the N items most frequently accessed during the previous time period. The hit counts are reset each time period, so this selection criteria is based entirely on popularity during the previous time period.

In order to expand the selection criteria to consider accesses during all past time periods, we introduce α-*history selection*. The α-history selection scheme has a parameter $0 \le \alpha < 1$; higher α means that less emphasis is placed on recent popularity, and more emphasis is placed on total past popularity. The scheme works as follows: for a page $q \in C_p$, let $A_p(q)$ be the number of times page q was accessed after page p within a trail during the previous time period. Let $H_p(q)$ be the historical "score" of page q in the shortcut set S_p. Initially, $H_p(q) = 0$ for all $q \in S_p$. At the end of each time period when selecting new shortcuts, first update the scores as:

$$H_p(q) = \begin{cases} \alpha H_p(q) + (1 - \alpha)A_p(q) & \text{for } q \in C_p \\ 0 & \text{for } q \notin C_p \end{cases}.$$

Now when choosing the shortcuts for page p, we pick the top N pages from C_p using the H_p scores. The α-history selection scheme allows us to consider the popularity of pages in past time periods, but exponentially dampens the influence of the old hits based on their age. Note that $H_p(q)$ and $A_p(q)$ information is discarded the moment that a page q is replaced in cache C_p; this ensures that memory usage is still proportional to the cache size when α-history selection is used. As an additional enhancement, we can weight the A_i values by the total number of hits in time period i so that hits that occur during unpopular times (nighttime) are not dominated by hits that occurred earlier during popular times (daytime). All of our experiments use this enhancement. Note that the PERKOWITZSHORTCUT algorithm is equivalent to setting $L = n$, the number of web pages, and $\alpha = 0$.

5.3   CacheCut Implementation

The CACHECUT algorithm, presented in Algorithms 2 and 3 makes use of the following subroutines:

- CACHE(Page p). Returns the cache associated with page p.
- RECORDACCESS(Cache C, page p, time t). Informs the cache C of a request for page p at time t. Page p is then placed in the cache C, and it is the responsibility of C's replacement policy to remove an item if C is already at capacity. The time t is used by some replacement policies, such as least recently used, to determine which item should be replaced.

- SETHITS(Cache C, page p, int x). For a page p assumed to be in cache C, sets the hit count to x.
- GETHITS(Cache C, page p). If p is currently in cache C, returns the hit count of p. Otherwise, returns 0.
- SETSCORE(Cache C, page p, float x). For a page p assumed to be in cache C, sets the score to x.
- GETSCORE(Cache C, page p). If p is currently in cache C, returns the score of p. Otherwise, returns 0.

When CACHECUT is initialized, every page is associated with an empty cache. As visitors complete trails, the caches of pages along the trails are modified; this takes place in the UPDATETRAILCACHES routine given in Algorithm 2. For each trail-edge e_{pq}, two actions are taken. First, the cache C_p is informed of a hit on page q, and the replacement policy chooses an element of C_p to replace with q. Second, a hit count for page q in cache C_p is incremented. Some replacement policies may maintain their own hit counts, but this hit count is used for the α-selection scoring.

Although the caches update with the completion of every trail, the shortcut sets are not updated until a call is made to UPDATESHORTCUTS, which is shown in Algorithm 3. UPDATESHORTCUTS is periodically called in order to choose the shortcut sets S_p from the caches C_p. This is done using α-selection scoring, as described in Section 5.2. The hit counts for each page are reset each time that UPDATESHORTCUTS is called, but some information about prior hit counts is retained in the score.

6   Promoting Pages on the Front Page

In this section we describe the FRONTCACHE algorithm, which is similar to the CACHECUT algorithm but is specifically designed to select shortcuts for only the front page of a website.

6.1   Motivation

Imagine the following scenario: Mount Saint Helens has begun to emit gas and steam, and thousands of worried citizens are anxious for information. They load the United States Geological Survey (USGS) home page at www.usgs.gov, but are frustrated to find that information about Mount Saint Helens is buried several layers deep within a confusing page hierarchy. As a result, visitors to the site wind up loading 5 or 10 pages before finding the page they want, which increases the strain on the server. Of course, this problem would be solved if there were a direct link to the Mount Saint Helens page from the USGS home page, but the site designer can be forgiven for not knowing ahead of time that this page would suddenly become substantially more popular than the thousands of other pages hosted at USGS.

Inputs:
G *The site graph*
T *Observed trail* $\langle p_0, ..., p_k \rangle$

UPDATETRAILCACHES(G, T)

1: **for** $i = 0$ to $k - 1$ **do**
2:   $C_{p_i} \leftarrow$ CACHE(p_i)
3:   **for** $j = i$ to k **do**
4:     **if** there is no link in G from p_i to p_j **then**
5:       RECORDACCESS$(C_{p_i}, p_j, \text{TIME}(p_j))$
6:       $hits = \text{GETHITS}(C_{p_i}, p_j)$
7:       SETHITS$(C_{p_i}, p_j, hits + 1)$
8:     **end if**
9:   **end for**
10: **end for**

Algorithm 2. This routine is called each time a trail completes in the access log, in order to update the caches with the new information from that trail.

The CACHECUT algorithm may be poorly suited to this problem of promoting a link to the suddenly popular page q on the front page. In the worst case, the navigation on the website is so difficult that *nobody* who enters the website through the front page is able to find q. Instead, page q's sudden surge of popularity comes from visitors who find q using a search engine or an external link. In this situation, CACHECUT will never place a shortcut to q on the front page; however, because of the front page's special role in providing navigation for the entire website, it would be advantageous to do so.

Inputs:
P *Set of web pages* $\{p_1, .., p_n\}$
N *Number of shortcuts per page*
α *History weighting parameter*

UPDATESHORTCUTS(P, N, α)

1: **for all** pages p in P **do**
2:   $C_p \leftarrow$ CACHE(p)
3:   **for all** pages q in C_p **do**
4:     $newScore \leftarrow \alpha \cdot \text{GETSCORE}(C_p, q) + (1 - \alpha) \cdot \text{GETHITS}(C_p, q)$
5:     SETSCORE$(C_p, q, newScore)$
6:     SETHITS$(C_p, q, 0)$
7:   **end for**
8:   $S \leftarrow$ top N pages in C_p by GETSCORE(C_p, q)
9:   Set shortcuts of page p to be S
10: **end for**

Algorithm 3. This routine is run periodically to choose the shortcuts for page p_i from the cache C_i. The shortcuts are scored by a combination of their previous score and their number of recent hits, and the top N are chosen.

6.2   The FrontCache Algorithm

The FRONTCACHE algorithm is well suited to scenario described above. It selects shortcuts for the front page with the goal of maximizing the fraction of all page accesses that are for pages linked from the front page. The FRONTCACHE algorithm works in the same way as the CACHECUT algorithm, except that trails (and client identities) are ignored. Instead, a single cache is maintained which is updated when *any* web page in the web site is loaded.

Batched caching and increasing the size of the underlying cache are especially important for the FRONTCACHE algorithm, because the total traffic on the web site is much larger than the traffic conditional on first visiting some page *p*. Without these techniques, the set of shortcuts on the front page would be constantly changing, and high quality shortcuts could be wiped out by bursts of anomalous traffic.

7   Experimental Results

Experimental Setup and Implementation Details

For our experiments, we collected web access log data spanning April 17 to May 16, 2005 from the University of Texas Computer Sciences department website, which has about 120,000 unique web pages. The access log originally included requests for data such as images, movies, and dynamic scripts (asp, jsp, cgi). These data are often loaded as a component to a page rather than as an individual page, which confuses trail analysis because loading a single page can cause multiple sequential requests (such as for the page itself and its 3 images). To address this issue, we removed all requests for content other than html pages, text documents, and Adobe Acrobat documents.

Approximately one-third of the page requests came from automated non-human visitors. These robots and spiders access the website in a distinctly non-human way, often attempting to systematically visit large portions of the website in order to build an index for a search engine or to harvest email addresses for spammers. Because our shortcutting algorithms are intended to assist *human* visitors in navigating the website, we eliminated all requests from robots. This was done in three steps. First, we compared the clients accessing the website with a list of known robots, and removed all matches. Second, we scanned the access files for clients that accessed pages faster than a human normally would, and removed those clients. Finally, we removed all trails that had length greater than 50. Humans are unlikely to access this many web pages from a single website during a 10 minute session, so the majority of remaining trails over length 50 were probably robots that we missed in the previous two passes.

Since trails of length 1 and 2 cannot be improved (assuming that the length 2 trail spans a static link), we restricted our dataset to include only trails of length 3 or greater. Once we performed all the various data cleaning steps, we were left with 89,086 trails with an average length of 7.81 pages. MINPATH requires a separate training and testing set, and the access transactions in the training set should logically occur before the transactions in the test set, so when evaluating MINPATH we made the first two-thirds of the log training data and the last one-third test data. The other algorithms train for their future shortcuts at the same time that they are evaluating their present shortcuts, so we were able to use the entire access log as test data.

The MINPATH algorithm has several parameters; in order to simplify our testing we used a fixed configuration, varying only the number of shortcuts produced. We used the "unconditional model" of web site usage because it was easy to implement. This model had the worst performance of those presented in [1], but its performance was within 20% of the best model, so we feel that it gives a good understanding of the capabilities of MINPATH. We did not group pages together by URL hierarchy (effectively making the URL usage threshold equal to 0%), but our training data had 900,000 page requests, (more than 7 times larger than in [1]), which increased the number of pages with accurate usage estimations.

7.1   Choosing the Best Parameters for CacheCut

The CACHECUT algorithm has several different parameters that can affect performance. They are:

- N, the number of shortcuts per page.
- L, the size of the underlying cache.
- alg, the underlying cache replacement policy.
- α, the history preference parameter.

In this section we examine the tradeoffs allowed by each of these parameters, and investigate how they affect the performance of the CACHECUT algorithm as evaluated by the formula given in equation (2).

The Number of Shortcuts Per Page. In terms of *AverageHitRatio*, it is always beneficial to add more shortcuts. As discussed in the introduction, if we allow N to become arbitrarily large, then *AverageHitRatio* will be 1 since every trail-edge will either be a link or a shortcut. A site designer who wishes to use CACHECUT for automated shortcutting will need to choose a value for N that provides a good tradeoff between shortcutting performance, and the link clutter on each webpage. Figure 1 shows how performance increases with the number of shortcuts. The relationship appears to be slightly less than logarithmic.

The Size of the Underlying Cache. As the size of the underlying cache L increases from N to $2N$, the performance increases substantially. This is because the algorithm is able to retain information about more good pages; when $L = N$ if the algorithm has N good pages in the cache C_p, it is forced to replace one of them with a bad page q when q is accessed after p, and then it loses all of its accumulated data about the good page. The gain as L continues to increase beyond $2N$ is marginal, and it appears that there is little reason to increase L beyond $5N$. Figure 2 shows how performance varies with the size of the cache.

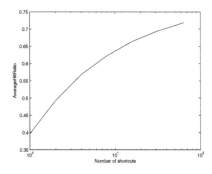

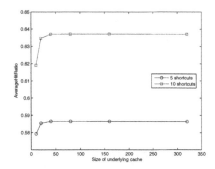

Fig. 1. AverageHitRatio vs. Number of shortcuts. The more shortcuts that are added to each page, the more likely it is that a trail-edge will be available as a link or shortcut. Here GDF is used with $L = 80$ and $\alpha = 0.9$. With no shortcuts (original links only) the hit ratio is 0.23.

Fig. 2. AverageHitRatio vs. Size of cache. Increasing the cache size beyond the size of the shortcut set increases the fraction of trail-edges available as shortcuts. Here GDF is used with $\alpha = 0.9$.

Underlying Cache Replacement Policies. We testted our algorithm on four cache replacement policies: Least Recently Used (LRU), Least Frequently Used (LFU), Adaptive Replacement Cache [8] (ARC), and Greedy Dual Size Frequency [4] (GDF). The latter two policies combine recency and frequency information.

As seen in Figure 3, the greatest variation in performance between cache replacement policies occurs when L is equal to N, or only slightly larger than N. GDF has the best performance, and LRU has the worst. The poor performance of LRU is explained by its lack of consideration of frequency. Because traffic patterns are fairly consistent over time, it's important not to throw out pages that were accessed very often in the past in favor of pages that have been accessed recently, but only infrequently.

The differences between the other three replacement policies are very slight, and become negligible as L increases. Regardless of what replacement policy is used for the cache, the same scoring system is used to choose which N cache elements become shortcuts. As L becomes large, it grows increasingly likely that the N top-scoring pages will be present in all caches, no matter which replacement policy is used. If enough memory is available to support a large L, it would probably be best to use LFU because it is extremely efficient and performs just as well as the more elaborate GDF and ARC policies.

The History Preference Parameter. When choosing the shortcuts on a page p, the history preference parameter α allows us to choose what weight will be given to recent accesses A_p and historic popularity H_p. For a detailed discussion, see Section 5.2. If $\alpha = 0$, then the score is entirely determined by

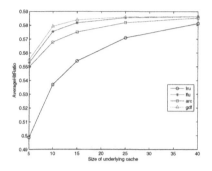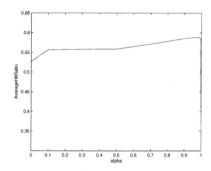

Fig. 3. *AverageHitRatio vs. Replacement policy.* GDF is the best replacement policy, but for large values of L all four policies perform nearly identically. Here $\alpha = 0.9$.

Fig. 4. *AverageHitRatio vs. α.* Increasing α to nearly 1 increases performance, but performance drops off precipitously when α is too close to 1. Here GDF is used with $L = 20$ and $N = 5$.

the recent popularity $H_p(q)$. In this case CACHECUT behaves in the same way as PERKOWITZSHORTCUT, except that it keeps track of counts for a subset of pages rather than for all pages. If $\alpha = 1$ then the algorithm fails to work properly, because the scores will always be equal to 0 since the history, which is initialized to 0, will never be updated. Figure 4 shows how the value of α affects the quality of shortcuts. Values of α very close to 1 do very well, which suggests that usage patterns on the website are somewhat consistent over time.

7.2   Comparing CacheCut to Other Shortcutting Algorithms

We ran several tests to compare CACHECUT to PERKOWITZSHORTCUT, MIN-PATH, and a baseline algorithm that selects N shortcuts for each page entirely at random. In the comparisons we chose the best parameters for CACHECUT that we found in the previous experiments. They were $L = 80$, the GDF replacement policy, and $\alpha = 0.9$. For PERKOWITZSHORTCUT we allowed the time between updates to be quite large, 72 hrs, because doing so produced the best results. Since MINPATH requires separate training and testing phases, we partitioned the data as two-thirds training set and one-third test set.

We evaluate the performance of the 4 shortcutting algorithms using three different criteria:

– **Fraction of trails with at least one useful shortcut.** If a site visitor encounters a single shortcut to a desired destination, then the the short-cutting algorithm was useful to that visitor. Among all trails of length 3 or greater, we find the fraction that have at least one trail-edge available as a shortcut. This comparison is presented in figure 5, and CACHECUT clearly outperforms the other algorithms. Adding random shortcuts is barely more useful than having no shortcuts at all, which is not surprising for a website with 120,000 nodes. It is also noteworthy that with only 5 shortcuts per page, about 75% of visitors that *can* have their trail enhanced (*i.e.*, those with trail lengths of 3 or greater) are provided a useful shortcut by the CACHECUT algorithm.

- **Average fraction of trail-edges available as shortcuts or links.** This is the *AverageHitRatio* criteria motivated in this paper. The results are given in figure 6, and once again CACHECUT shows the best performance.
- **Average trail length after shortcutting.** In [1] when introducing MIN-PATH, the authors state that the goal of their algorithm is to reduce the number of clicks required for a visitor to get from their initial page to their goal page. Because there is no accurate way of determining which page in a trail is the goal page, they assume that the last page in the trail is the goal because after loading it the visitor left the site. Suppose that a visitor's access to the web site is a trail of length $t \geq 3$ pages. By applying short-cutting, we could reduce this length to as few as 2 pages (if there was a direct shortcut from the first page to the last). To determine the length of trails after shortcutting, we assume that at each page, users choose what-ever available shortcut leads furthest along their trail; if there are no trail-edges available as shortcuts then the user goes to the next page in their original trail.

  If a trail has a loop, then evaluating with this scheme may inappropriately attribute a decrease in trail length to the shortcuts. For instance, if a trail of length 7 has page p as both its second page and its seventh page, then regardless of the shortcutting algorithm used we would report the length after shortcutting as 2 for a "savings" of 5 pages. To get around this problem, we removed from consideration all trails with loops. The average trail lengths for the different shortcutting algorithms are shown in figure 7. Even though MINPATH was designed to minimize this value, it is still outperformed by CACHECUT.

Timing Tests. The amount of time that shortcutting algorithms require is just as important as the quality of shortcuts, because a shortcutting algorithm that requires too much time will be impractical to deploy. In order to compare runtimes, we used each algorithm to generate 5 shortcuts per page on the portion of the access log used to test MINPATH; this portion of the log had 29,249 trails and 1,267,921 trail-edges. To complete this task, MINPATH took 8.15 hours, CACHECUT took 32 seconds, and PERKOWITZSHORTCUT took 17 seconds.

PERKOWITZSHORTCUT requires less time than CACHECUT, which is under-standable because CACHECUT must perform a cache replacement for each trail-edge, whereas PERKOWITZSHORTCUT needs only to increment a count in its array. MINPATH required substantially more time than the other two algorithms, because it must evaluate its web-usage model each time a visitor loads a page in order to determine what shortcuts to suggest. The amount of time required to evaluate the model is related to the out-degree of the current page and its offspring, and is very long compared to the constant-time lookup the other al-gorithms need to suggest shortcuts.

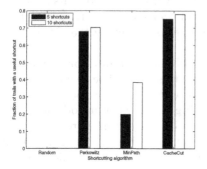
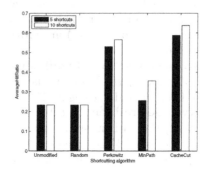

Fig. 5. Trails aided by shortcutting. The fraction of trails that have at least one trail-edge available as a shortcut.

Fig. 6. Edges available as shortcuts. The fraction of trail edges available as shortcuts, averaged over all trails.

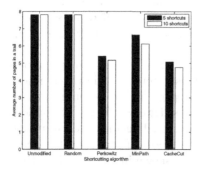
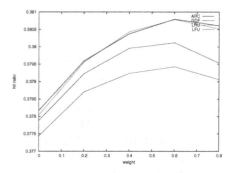

Fig. 7. Length of trails after shortcutting. The average length from the first node in a trail to the last, when the visitor is assumed to take the available shortcut at each node that leads furthest along the trail.

Fig. 8. Hit Ratio of FrontCache vs. α. Values of α around 0.6 give the best performance.

7.3   FrontCache Performance

Our experiments with the FrontCache algorithm were extremely encouraging. By adding only 10 links to the University of Texas at Austin front page, we were able to provide links to nearly 40% of those pages accessed on the web site (including the front page itself). By contrast, the 21 static links provided by the designers represented only 3% of page requests.

We wish to draw attention to the relationship between the FRONTCACHE hit ratio and the α parameter, as it differs from the relationship in the CACHECUT algorithm. As is shown in figure 8, intermediate values of α around 0.6 give the best performance. This is in contrast to CACHECUT, where α nearly equal to 1 gives the best performance. We speculate that this is because of the "bursty popularity" scenarios for which FRONTCACHE is designed. If α becomes too close to 1, then pages which have a sudden surge in popularity will be excluded in favor of shorcuts for pages that have had consistent historical popularity. Lower values of α allow these pages to have shortcuts on the front page for the duration of their popularity surge.

8   Conclusions and Future Work

Shortcutting algorithms add direct links between pages in order to reduce the effort necessary for site visitors to find their desired content. If there was some way to know with absolute certainty what each user's goal page was, then it would be easy to provide a link to that page. Since this is not possible, we instead add a handful of links to each page p that a user is likely to find useful.

In this paper, we introduced the CACHECUT shortcutting algorithm, which uses the predictive power of cache replacement policies to provide website shortcuts that are likely to be useful to site visitors. Compared to other shortcutting algorithms in the literature, CACHECUT is fast and resource efficient. CACHE-CUT can process a month's worth of access logs in a few seconds, so it is suitable for real-time deployment without straining the webserver.

The CACHECUT algorithm is seen to be very effective despite its simplicity. Most visitor trails that can be improved by shortcutting are improved by CACHE-CUT, and in fact a significant fraction of trail-edges are available as shortcuts for the average trail. More complicated shortcutting algorithms such as MIN-PATH consider a visitor's entire trail rather than only the current page, but this added complexity does not improve the quality of shortcuts provided, and the additional computation needed makes them impractical to deploy. Compared to PERKOWITZSHORTCUT, our algorithm produces higher-quality shortcuts and is guaranteed to need only $O(n)$ memory. In some applications this guarantee may be desirable, even though PERKOWITZSHORTCUT uses $O(n)$ memory in practice.

In the future, it would be useful to deploy a shortcutting algorithm on an active website, and observe how it influences the browsing behavior of visitors. Analyzing the performance of shortcutting algorithms offline as done in this paper means that we must ignore the possibility that visitors' browsing trails would be different in the presence of shortcutting links. A deployed version would also need to keep track of how often the presented shortcuts are used, and retain the most utilized shortcuts rather than replace them with new shortcuts. Deploying a shortcutting algorithm requires determining exactly how shortcuts will be added to webpages as links. One possibility is to modify the web server so that when it serves a web page to a visitor, HTML code for the shortcuts are automatically added to the page. The downside of this approach is that it may be difficult to find an appropriate place within the page to add the shortcuts so as to not ruin the page formatting.

Acknowledgments

We would like to thank Albert Chen for his contribution to a preliminary version of this work. This research was supported by NSF grant CCF-0431257, NSF Career Award ACI-0093404, and NSF-ITR award IIS-0325116.

References

1. Anderson, C.R., Domingos, P., Weld, D.S.: Adaptive web navigation for wireless devices. In: Proceedings of the 17th International Joint Conference on Artificial Intelligence (2001)
2. Anderson, C.R., Horvitz, E.: Web montage: A dynamic personalized start page. In: WWW 2002. Proceedings of the eleventh international conference on World Wide Web, pp. 704–712. ACM Press, New York (2002)
3. Banerjee, A., Ghosh, J.: Clickstream clustering using weighted longest common subsequences. In: Proc. of the Workshop on Web Mining, SIAM Conference on Data Mining, pp. 33–40 (2001)
4. Cherkasova, L.: Improving www proxies performance with greedy-dual-size-frequency caching policy. HP Laboratories Report No. HPL-98-69R1 (1998)
5. Cooley, R., Mobasher, B., Srivastava, J.: Web mining: Information and pattern discovery on the world wide web. In: ICTAI 1997. Proceedings of the 9th IEEE International Conference on Tools with Artificial Intelligence, IEEE, Los Alamitos (1997)
6. Eirinaki, M., Vazirgiannis, M.: Web mining for web personalization. ACM Trans. Inter. Tech. 3(1), 1–27 (2003)
7. Gabrilovich, E., Dumais, S., Horvitz, E.: Newsjunkie: Providing personalized news-feeds via analysis of information novelty. In: WWW 2004. Proceedings of the 13th international conference on World Wide Web, pp. 482–490. ACM Press, New York (2004)
8. Megiddo, N., Modha, D.S.: Outperforming LRU with an adaptive replacement cache algorithm. Computer 37(4), 58–65 (2004)
9. Milic-Frayling, N., Jones, R., Rodden, K., Smyth, G., Blackwell, A., Sommerer, R.: Smartback: Supporting users in back navigation. In: WWW 2004. Proceedings of the 13th international conference on World Wide Web, pp. 63–71. ACM Press, New York (2004)
10. Perkowitz, M.: Adaptive Web Sites: Cluster Mining and Conceptual Clustering for Index Page Synthesis. PhD thesis, University of Washington (2001)
11. Perkowitz, M., Etzioni, O.: Adaptive web sites: an ai challenge. In: Proceedings of the 15th International Joint Conference on Artificial Intelligence (1997)
12. Perkowitz, M., Etzioni, O.: Towards adaptive web sites: Conceptual framework and case study. Artificial Intelligence 118(1-2), 245–275 (2000)
13. Srikant, R., Yang, Y.: Mining web logs to improve website organization. In: WWW 2001. Proceedings of the tenth international conference on World Wide Web, pp. 430–437. ACM Press, New York (2001)
14. Yahoo!, Inc. My Yahoo!, http://my.yahoo.com
15. Yang, Q., Wang, H., Zhang, W.: Web-log mining for quantitative temporal-event prediction. IEEE Computational Intelligence Bulletin 1(1), 10–18 (2002)
16. Yang, Q., Zhang, H.H.: Web-log mining for predictive web caching. IEEE Transactions on Knowledge and Data Engineering 15(4), 1050–1053 (2003)

Incorporating Usage Information into Average-Clicks Algorithm

Kalyan Beemanapalli, Ramya Rangarajan, and Jaideep Srivastava

University of Minnesota, 4-192 EE/CS Building,
200 Union Street SE, Minneapolis, MN 55455
{ramya,kalyan,srivastava}@cs.umn.edu

Abstract. A number of methods exists that measure the distance between two web pages. Average-Clicks is a new measure of distance between web pages which fits user's intuition of distance better than the traditional measure of clicks between two pages. Average-Clicks however assumes that the probability of the user following any link on a web page is the same and gives equal weights to each of the out-going links. In our method "Usage Aware Average-Clicks" we have taken the user's browsing behavior into account and assigned different weights to different links on a particular page based on how frequently users follow a particular link. Thus, Usage Aware Average-Clicks is an extension to the Average-Clicks Algorithm where the static web link structure graph is combined with the dynamic Usage Graph (built using the information available from the web logs) to assign different weights to links on a web page and hence capture the user's intuition of distance more accurately. A new distance metric has been designed using this methodology and used to improve the efficiency of a web recommendation engine.

Keywords: Web Mining, Link Analysis, Web Usage Analysis, Recommendation Engines.

1 Introduction

The World Wide Web is an ever growing collection of web pages. Thousands of web sites and millions of pages are being added to this repository every year. The web pages vary widely in their content and format and are very diverse in nature. A lot of useful information is available on the World Wide Web (WWW) and Search Engines help us find what we are looking for. For doing this, Search Engines make extensive use of the Link Structure Graph and a lot of research is going on to ensure that the best set of links are returned to the user based on the search query.

The link structure graph of the web is a digraph where the nodes represent the pages and structure graph to assign different weights to the nodes. The a directed edge from node A to node B implies that page A has a link to Page B. There are important algorithms in the literature like Page Rank [11], HITS [10, 2] and Average-Clicks [18] which use the link structure graph as their basis. These algorithms differ in the way they use link Google [7, 6, 14] search engine uses PageRank algorithm to rank web pages. PageRank is a global ranking algorithm which ranks web pages based

E. Tovar, P. Tsigas, and H. Fouchal (Eds.): OPODIS 2007, LNCS 4878, pp. 21–35, 2007.

solely on the position of the page in the web graph. HITS is another popular algorithm which ranks the web search results. HITS classifies the web pages as Hubs and Authorities. Average-Clicks uses Link Analysis to measure the distance between two pages on the WWW. One inherent problem with all these methods is that all of them are heavily dependent on the link structure graph and hence are static. The dynamic nature of user behavior is not taken into consideration when assigning weights to nodes.

In the Intranet Domain, useful information is available in the form of web logs which record the user sessions. User Sessions track the sequence of web pages visited by the user in addition to a lot of other information like the time spent on each page etc. The user session information is used to alter these algorithms so that they are not biased by the link structure graph and make more accurate weight calculations. Extensions to PageRank and HITS have been proposed in [4] and [9] respectively and they take into consideration the factors from the usage graph as well. These algorithms will be explained in Section 2. Having understood the importance of Usage Behavior data in link analysis, we propose an extension to the Average-Clicks [18] algorithm which measures the distance between two web pages on the WWW.

Our experiments were conducted in the intranet domain where complete and accurate usage data is easily available. On the internet it is difficult to get the usage data as it needs to be heuristically gathered from various external tools like Google Toolbar, Yahoo Toolbar, etc. Data from these sources is incomplete and skewed and needs to be refined using sophisticated algorithms before it can be used. Moreover, the work has been motivated by a recommendation engine that is being built for the intranet. Hence, we confine ourselves to the intranet domain.

The organization of this paper is as follows: Section 2 gives a brief description of some of the algorithms which use Link Analysis and their extensions using Usage Information. Section 3 talks about the Average-Clicks algorithm which forms the basis of our proposed method. Section 4 describes our approach to incorporating usage information into the Average-Clicks algorithm. Section 5 presents experimental results obtained by running the modified algorithm on the cs.umn.edu website. A comparison of the distances obtained by running the new method with that obtained by running the original Average-Clicks algorithm is also made here. Section 6 talks about test cases and evaluation methodologies. Section 7 presents conclusions and potential future work.

2 Related Work

In this section we give a brief description of the PageRank and the HITS algorithms and also their extensions using Usage Information. Our idea of incorporating usage data into the Average-Clicks algorithm has been drawn from these methods. Google uses the PageRank algorithm to rank the web pages. A web page gets a high page rank if it has a large number of backlinks (a lot of pages pointing to it) or if it has backlinks from popular pages (pages that have very high page ranks) [11]. The page rank of a page is the sum of the weights of each of its incoming links and the PageRank of a page is equally distributed among its out links. Figure 1, reproduced from [11] gives an overview of PageRank calculation.

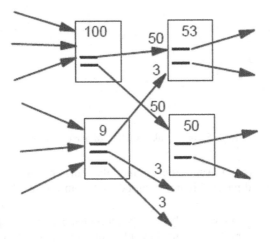

Fig. 1. Simplified PageRank Calculation. Shows the calculation of pagerank using the banklinks on the webpages.

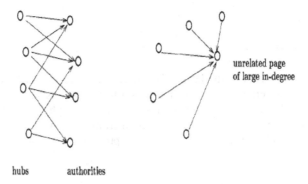

hubs   authorities

Fig. 2. HITS Algorithm – This figure shows the example of Kleinberg's algorithm of calculating hubs and authorities for the webpages

In Usage Aware PageRank (UPR) [4] an extension to the PageRank Algorithm using usage statistics to improve the Rank calculation is suggested. The simple approach taken to incorporate the usage data into Page Ranks algorithm is to use the counts obtained from the web logs. Thus, the weight assigned to each page is based on the page popularity and it has been found that this method, in general, outperforms the original PageRank algorithm. In [13, 16] the authors improve on the PageRank algorithm by using Content information of the web pages. They are probabilistic models of the relevance of the page to a search query.

Kleinberg's HITS is another algorithm which uses Link Structure and HITS ranks the web search results. HITS classifies the web pages as Hubs and Authorities. Good Hubs are pages which have a number of inlinks from good Authorities and good Authorities are the pages which have links to a number of good Hubs for the particular search topic [10]. HITS emphasizes on having a number of incoming links

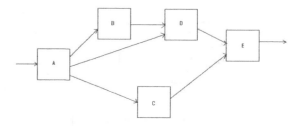

Fig. 3. Sample Link Structure of a Web Graph

from related pages (good Authorities) rather than just having a large number of inlinks from unrelated pages. Figure 3, reproduced from [10] explains the concept of Hubs and Authorities.

In [9] an extension to the Kleinberg's algorithm using Matrix Exponentiation and Web log records is proposed. The key idea of this approach is to replace the adjacency link matrix used by the original algorithm by an exponential matrix using Taylor's Series. The usage graph is combined with this adjacency graph to assign new weights and the preliminary results show that this approach works well and gives improved results.

3 Background

In this section we introduce the basic terms used in this report and also give a brief description of the Average-Clicks method which forms the basis of our approach. As already mentioned, the WWW can be represented as a digraph [8, 1] where the nodes represent the pages and there is a directed edge from node A to node B if the page corresponding to node A has a link to the page represented by node B. The number of

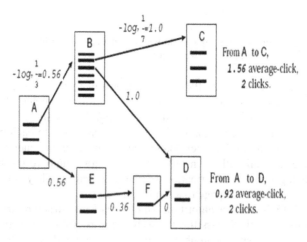

Fig. 4. Average-Clicks and Clicks - example

edges that point to a node (web page) is known as its in-degree (back links) and the number of edges that go out of a node is known as its out-degree (forward links) [11]. For example, in Figure 4, the in-degree of node B is 1 and that of node D is 2 and the out-degree of node B is 1 and that of node D is 2.

3.1 Average-Clicks

The Average-Clicks algorithm calculates the length of the link in a page p as

$$-log_n\left(\alpha/OutDegree(p)\right). \tag{1}$$

Here the probability of clicking each link in page p is a constant given by $\alpha/OutDegree(p)$, where α is the damping factor. Negative log is taken to transform the multiplications while calculating the distances between web pages to additions. One average-click is defined as one click among n links on a page [18]. Extending the definition, one average-click from two pages with n links each is one click among n^2 links. Figure 5 reproduced from [18] shows a sample link graph along with the calculations of Average-Clicks distances.

The distance between two web pages p and q is defined as the shortest path between the nodes representing the pages in the graph. The shortest path can be calculated using any All-Pairs Shortest Path algorithm. Detailed description of the algorithm used in Average-Clicks and the results obtained can be found in [18].

4 Usage Aware Average-Clicks

In this section we give a detailed description of the approach taken by us to incorporate the usage information into the Average-Clicks Algorithm. The usage graph shows the popularity of the pages with users. The link graph analysis provides the importance of the Web pages as designated by the creator of the pages. For example, if there is a link from the Yahoo main page then the link can be considered very important. Similarly, a page might be highly accessed by users even though it is not referenced by important pages in the web domain. Hence, it is important to consider both kinds of information and combine them effectively, so that we are able to determine pages that are popular and also important.

4.1 Usage Graph

As the first step, the usage-graph (U) [15, 5] is constructed from the information available from the web logs. Each node in the graph U represents a page and an edge from node p to node q implies that page q has been accessed from page p. Every edge is assigned a weight and this value is a measure of the co-occurrence pattern of the two pages in the web logs (corresponding to the number of times page q was accessed from page p). Each node is also assigned a numerical value which indicates the number of times the page corresponding to that node occurred in the web logs. Using this graph, an NxN matrix C (holding the conditional probability P(q->p)) is calculated where N is the number of nodes in the graph. Any value C(i,j) indicates the probability of accessing page j from page i. The weight of the edge between each pair of pages p, q is calculated as follows:

$$C(p,q) = (\text{Number of co-occurrences of } p,q)/(\text{Number of occurrences of } p) \quad (2)$$

By co-occurrence of p,q we mean that page q should be accessed immediately after accessing page p. In terms of the usage graph this can be written as follows:

$$C(p,q) = (\text{Weight of the edge from p to q}) / (\text{Weight assigned to node p}) \quad (3)$$

4.2 Link Graph

Next, a link graph is constructed using a web crawler. The Web crawler is run on the website used for testing and a directed graph is generated from the information obtained. Each node is a web page and an edge from node p to node q implies that page p holds a link to page q. Each node is assigned a value which is based only on the number of outgoing links from that page. An NxN link matrix D is calculated where N is the total number of pages in the website. Any value D (i, j) gives the distance of page j from page i. The value of D(i,j) is calculated as follows:

$$D(i,j) = (1/\text{Outdegree}(\text{page i})) \text{ If there is a link from page i to j} \quad (4)$$

We then combine the Link matrix and the Usage matrix to define the new distance between 2 pages as follows:

$$\text{Distance}(p,q) = C(p,q) * \left(-\log_n (\alpha / \text{Outdegree}(p)) \right) \quad (5)$$

where n^1 is the average number of links on a page and α^2 is the damping factor. Using the above distance matrix D, the matrix containing the shortest paths between pairs of pages is calculated using the Floyd Warshall's Algorithm.

4.3 Distance Measure Using Floyd Warshall's Algorithm

Given the web link structure, the shortest distance between any pair of pages can be calculated using any All-Pairs Shortest Path algorithm. The all-pairs shortest-path problem involves finding the shortest path between all pairs of vertices in a graph. Algorithms like Dijkstra's algorithm can be run N times (once for each of the N pages), or Floyd Warshall's algorithm can be used. In our approach we used the Floyd Warshall's algorithm to construct the final NxN distance matrix. Floyd Warshall's Algorithm is very efficient as it uses the concept of Dynamic Programming and hence doesn't make any unnecessary computations.

---

[1] For the World Wide Web the value of n has been identified as 7. A better approach uses 1 external link and 4 internal links.

[2] The damping factor for the World Wide Web is 0.85. For the intranet domain, this can be calculated from the usage data.

4.4 Implementation Issues

The Floyd Warshall's algorithm uses an NxN matrix for distance calculation. As the number of web pages increases, the amount of memory needed to hold the NxN distance matrix increases drastically. Also, the Computation Cost increases exponentially. Thus, this algorithm has poor scalability. To overcome this issue and to make our program highly scalable and memory efficient, we have taken the following approach:

Each page is given a unique page id (starting from 0) and the set of links on a web page is stored as a linked list. The head of each of the linked list is stored in a vector called PageDetail. Thus PageDetail[0] points to the head of the linked list which stores the set of links on page 0. Each node in the linked list for page p stores the PageId of the page q to which it is connected, $C(q\text{->}p)$, Average Clicks distance, Usage Score and the Usage aware Average-Clicks distance between page p and page q. Hence to get the distance between page p and page q, we have to search the list stored at PageDetail[p] for node q. This implementation is highly scalable as adding a new page to a vector is easy and does not require resizing an array each time a new page is added to the list. Also, it is very memory efficient as instead of storing N nodes for each page, we only store a very small number of pages equal to the number of links on that page. These are very important issues because as the number of pages in the domain increases, it is not possible to match the memory requirements of the algorithm. This approach is summarized in Fig 5

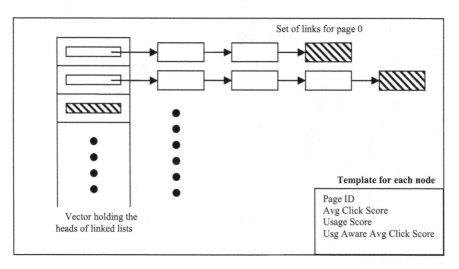

Fig. 5. Data structure for implementing the Floyd-Warshall algorithm

5   Experimental Results

In this section we provide some preliminary results and also provide a comparative study of the distances obtained from the original Average-Clicks Algorithm and our approach.

5.1 Test Data

We have run our experiments on the CS website which is the Computer Science Department website of the University of Minnesota. The website can be accessed at www.cs.umn.edu [17]. The usage data has been collected over a period of 2 weeks in Apr 2006. The data set has been reduced to about 100,000 user sessions by refining and filtering the data. Noise data such as one page sessions, broken sessions etc have been removed to reduce the negative impact on the algorithm. We have implemented a web crawler to spider the website and collect the link information. The crawler has been programmed in such a way that URL's outside of the domain we are interested in are not considered. Also, self links are ignored as it does not make sense to recommend to the user, the same page he is already on.

5.2 Example Distances

Table 1 shows the distances as measured by the original Average-Clicks algorithm and also by Usage Aware Average-Clicks Algorithm between the graduate admissions index page http://www.cs.umn.edu/admissions/graduate/index.php and the links present on the page.

Table 1. Comparison of results from Average-Clicks and Usage Aware Average-Clicks

Destination Page	Average-Clicks	Usage aware Average-Clicks
http://www.cs.umn.edu/index.php	0.0566667	0.000612
http://www.cs.umn.edu/admissions/gradate/evaluation.php	0.0566667	0.002460
http://www.cs.umn.edu/admissions/graduate/procedure.php	0.0566667	0.002460
http://www.cs.umn.edu/admissions/graduate/checklist.php	0.0566667	0.000612
http://www.cs.umn.edu/admissions/graduate/fellowships.php	0.0566667	0.002460
http://www.cs.umn.edu/admissions/graduate/transfers.php	0.0566667	0.056666
http://www.cs.umn.edu/admissions/graduate/application.php	0.0566667	0.003690
http://www.cs.umn.edu/admissions/graduate/faculty.php	0.0566667	0.001228
http://www.cs.umn.edu/about/contact.php	0.0566667	0.000612
http://www.cs.umn.edu/admissions/index.php	0.0566667	0.000612
http://www.cs.umn.edu/degrees/grad/index.php	0.0566667	0.001228

It can be seen that our approach, unlike the Average-Clicks algorithm, gives different weights to different links based on link access frequency. Thus, using the traditional Average-Clicks measure, we will declare that from www.cs.umn.edu/admissions/graduate/index.php it is equally probable to go to any link on the page, whereas, using Usage Aware Average-Clicks measure we can say that users on page www.cs.umn.edu/admissions/graduate/index.php are more likely to go to pages http://www.cs.umn.edu/index.php, http://www.cs.umn.edu/admissions/graduate/check list.php, http://www.cs.umn.edu/about/contact.php or http://www.cs.umn.edu/admissions/index.php than any other page. Similarly, it is also possible to find out the set of pages to which the users are least likely to go to. These results can be very helpful in making recommendations to users. From the user's perspective, the links that have high Usage Aware Average-Clicks scores are nearer to the index page than those that have lower scores. Such results are significant in link analysis.

Distance from http://www.cs.umn.edu/admissions/graduate/index.php[3]

6 Evaluation Methodologies

There are a number of ways of analyzing the results obtained from our method. The significance of the distance between pages can be tested against the Domain Expert's Views or the User's Views. The Domain Expert's view can be obtained by designing test cases that capture the distances between randomly sampled pages. The expert can then be asked to evaluate the distances obtained by using both the approaches. The idea is to be able to verify that the distances obtained by using the Usage Aware Average-Clicks method, match his view of distances (or similarity between pages) more closely than those obtained from the Average-Clicks method.

Two different approaches can be used to evaluate the User Views. In the first approach, we can automate and verify the distances calculated against user logs which are different from the logs used for calculating the distance values. In the second approach, we can evaluate the results by distributing questionnaires to users. This is similar to the approach proposed in the original paper [18]. The idea is to randomly sample web pages from the website and segregate them into groups based on their context. We can then calculate the distances between each of these pages. The users of the website can be asked to rate the pages in a particular context. The two results can be compared for further analysis.

In this report we use its predicting power as a measure of its capability to measure distances accurately. The idea behind using Usage Aware Average-Click scores in a recommender system is that pages that are close (smaller Usage Aware Average-Clicks Dist) to each other are given higher similarity scores than pages that are farther apart (larger Usage Aware Average-Clicks Dist). Hence to recommend a page P_i from $<P_2...P_n>$ to a user who is on page P_1, the Usage Aware Average-Click distance of P_i from P_1 should be the minimum among that from each of $<P_2... P_n>$. We test its predicting capability by incorporating it into a Recommendation Engine which uses both usage

---

[3] Please note that in the tables, the distance values in the two columns are on different scale. Hence comparing columns doesn't make sense. The relative distances within the column can be compared for analysis.

pattern and link structure to make recommendations [3] and measure the quality of recommendations made. Detailed description of the architecture and working of the recommendation can be found in [3].

We followed a similar approach to testing as done in [3]. The performance of this model was compared against the model that uses a '2,-1' scoring model [3] which gives a score of 2 for a match and -1 for a mismatch and the results of the various experiments are shown in the graphs that follow. The only way in which the models differ is in the way similarity scores are calculated between web pages and all the other parameters of the Recommendation Engine remain a constant.

Web logs from the CS server were filtered to get meaningful sessions. A part of the session data was used to train the model and then the model was tested on the remaining sessions. The next page that will be accessed was predicted for the test sessions and if the predicted page was actually accessed later on it the session, it was considered a hit.

The definitions of the various measures used to measure the effectiveness of these models as taken from [3] are restated below:

- *Hit Ratio (HR)*: Percentage of *hits*. If a recommended page is actually requested later in the session, we declare a hit. The hit ratio is thus a measure of how good the model is in making recommendations.

- *Click Reduction (CR)*: Average percentage click reduction. For a test session $(p_1, p_2,..., p_i..., p_j..., p_n)$, if p_j is recommended at page p_i, and p_j is subsequently accessed in the session, then the click reduction due to this recommendation is,

$$Click\ reduction\ =\ \frac{j-i}{i}$$

High hit ratio indicates good quality recommendations.

6.1 Comparison of Results

In the following figures, we refer to the '2,-1' model as Session Similarity Model (SSM) and our model as Link Aware Similarity Model (LASM).

The following box-plots and graphs compare the two models based on the Hit Ratio. The performance of both the models was recorded when the number of required recommendations was set to 3, 5 and 10. Both the models were trained on 1000 sessions and the Clustered Sessions [3] are represented as ClickStreams into 10, 15 and 20 clusters. Once the models were trained, they were tested on a different set of user sessions. Each of these experiments was repeated 5 times (using a different set of training sessions) to check the consistency of the results. Also, a t-test was done in each of the case to show that the results of the two experiments were statistically different. The t-test is a statistical test which computes the probability (p) that two groups of a single parameter are members of the same population. A small (p) value means that the two results are statistically different. The above procedure was repeated for 3000 training sessions as well.

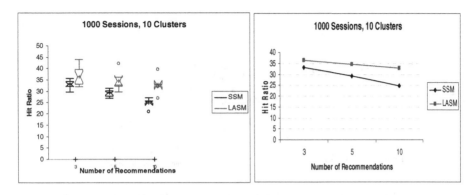

Fig. 6. Hit Ratio vs No. of Recommendations for 1000 sessions, 10 clusters

Table 2. t-test scores for 1000 sessions, 10 clusters

Recommendation	3	5	10
P value	0.123242	0.030262	0.006292

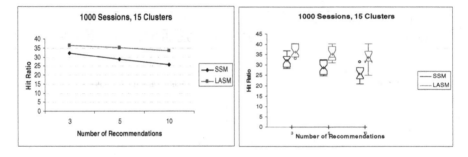

Fig. 7. Hit Ratio vs No. of Recommendations for 1000 sessions, 15 clusters

Table 3. t-test scores for 1000 sessions, 15 clusters

Recommendation	3	5	10
p value	0.053543	0.014464	0.020082

The X-axis of both the box plots and the line graphs shows the number of recommendations made and the Y-axis shows the Hit Ratio corresponding to the number of recommendations made. The box plot shows the distribution of Hit ratio values for different input data. The average value of Hit Ratio across the different experimental runs is used to plot the line graph.

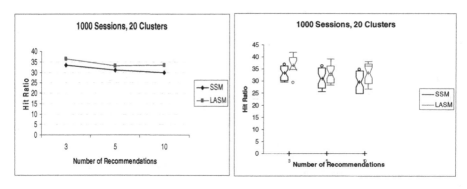

Fig. 8. Hit Ratio vs Number of Recommendations for 1000 sessions 20 clusters

Table 4. t-test scores for 1000 sessions, 20 clusters

Recommendation	3	5	10
p value	0.04985	0.224891	0.125186

Table 5. t-test scores for 3000 sessions, 10 clusters

Recommendation	3	5	10
p value	0.122187	0.055483	0.039619

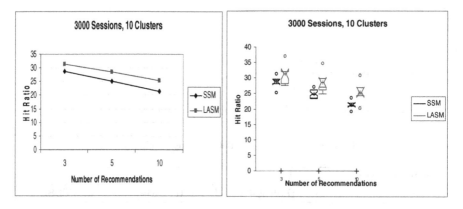

Fig. 9. Hit Ratio vs Number of Recommendations for 3000 sessions 20 clusters

From the graphs and the t-test results it is evident that our model performs better in all the cases. While the '2,-1' method attains a hit ratio of 25% to 30%, the hit ratio obtained for our method is about 40% on an average. This improvement is significant considering the fact, on 100% scale, this is an improvement by 20-25%. Hence, not only our model gives better recommendations but also proves that domain information like link graph is very important in performing usage analysis.

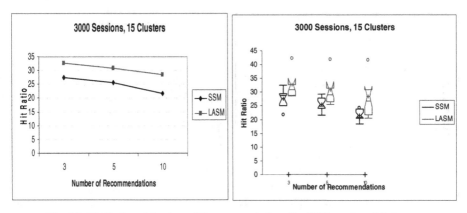

Fig. 10. Hit Ratio vs Number of Recommendations for 3000 sessions 15 clusters

Table 6. t-test scores for 3000 sessions, 15 clusters

Recommendation	3	5	10
p value	0.070035	0.076632	0.078475

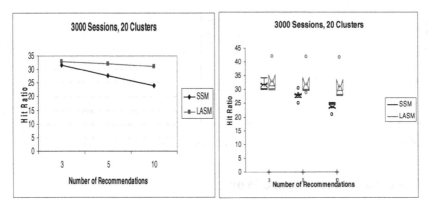

Fig. 11. Hit Ratio vs Number of Recommendations for 3000 sessions 15 clusters

Table 7. t-test scores for 3000 sessions, 20 clusters

Recommendation	3	5	10
p value	0.300533	0.082899	0.02874

Next, we give the improvement obtained for the measure "Path Reduction Ratio". Figures 11 through 13 depict the results. The X-axis corresponds to the number of recommendations made and the Y-axis corresponds to the % Path Reduction. The Average % Path Reduction across the different runs is used to plot the line graphs. Here again we see about a 20% improvement on a relative basis. The box-plots and graphs for the experiments using 1000 training sessions are shown below:

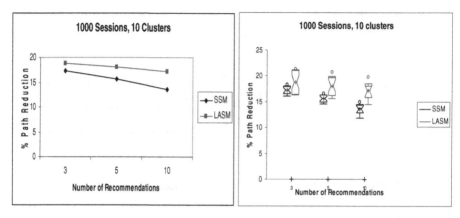

Fig. 12. % Path Reduction vs No. of Recommendations for 1000 sessions, 10 clusters

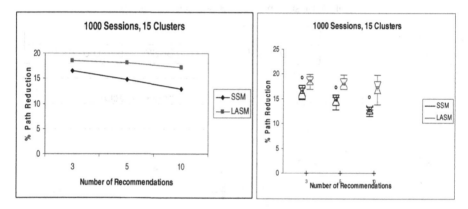

Fig. 13. % Path Reduction vs No. of Recommendations for 1000 sessions, 15 clusters

7   Conclusions and Future Work

In this paper we have proposed an extension to the Average-Clicks Algorithm which uses the Usage Data obtained from the web logs to assign appropriate weights to links on a page. The experiments show that popular links are given higher weights compared to less popular ones rather than just assigning equal static weights to all the links on a page. We used this algorithm in a Recommendation Engine for the Intranet Domain and found that recommendations made using this method were much superior to those made using the '2,-1' scoring method for similarity between web pages.

In the future we plan to verify the accuracy of the results by distributing questionnaires to the web users as well as to the domain experts and evaluating the answers. Verifying with the Domain Experts/User's view is a good idea because the usage logs might not be very representative at all times and the Domain Expert/User's judgment will be better.

Also, we plan to compare the distances obtained from this method with those obtained from an algorithm based on concept hierarchy [12,3] and usage information.

We would also like to fine tune the Recommendation Model to consider domain knowledge in addition to usage information to get higher Hit Ratios. This method if successful will be tested in lab and production environments as part of the larger recommendation engine.

References

1. Broder, A., Kumar, R., Maghoul, F., Raghavan, P., Rajagopalan, S., Stata, R., Tomkins, A., Wiener, J.: Graph Structure in the web. In: Proc. 9th WWW conf. (2000)
2. Borodin, A., Gareth, O., Roberts, J.S., Rosenthal, P.T.: Finding authorities and hubs from link structures on the world wide web. In: World Wide Web, pp. 415–429 (2001)
3. Bose, A., Beemanapalli, K., Srivastava, J., Sahar, S.: Incorporating Concept hierarchies into Usage Mining Based Recommendations. In: Nasraoui, O., Spiliopoulou, M., Srivastava, J., Mobasher, B., Masand, B. (eds.) WebKDD 2006. LNCS (LNAI), vol. 4811, pp. 110–126. Springer, Heidelberg (2007)
4. Oztekin, B.U., Ertoz, L., Kumar, V., Srivastava, J.: Usage Aware PageRank (2003), http://www2003.org
5. Cooley, R., Srivastava, J., Mobasher, B.: Web Mining – Information and Pattern Discovery on the World wide Web. In: 9th IEEE International Conference on Tools with Artificial Intelligence (November 1997)
6. Ward Eric.: How Search Engines Use Link Analysis - A special report from the Search Engine Strategies 2001 Conference, November 14-15, Dallas, TX. (December 2001)
7. Google: http://www.google.com/
8. Kleinberg, J.M., Kumar, R., Raghavan, P., Rajagopalan, S., Tomkins, A.S.: The web as a Graph: measurements, models, and methods. In: Proc. of the International Conference on Combinatorics and Computing (1999)
9. Miller, J.C., Rae, G., Schaefer, F., Ward, L.A., LoFaro, T., Farahat, A.: Modifications of Kleinberg's HITS algorithm using Matrix Exponentiation and Web log Records. In: SIGIR 2001. Proceeding of the 24th annual international ACM SIGIR conference on Research and development in information retrieval, pp. 444–445. ACM Press, New York, NY,USA (2001)
10. Kleinberg, J.M.: Authoritative sources in a hyperlinked environment. Journal of the ACM (JACM) 46(5), 604–632
11. Page, L., Brin, S., Motwani, R., Winograd, T.: The PageRank Citation Ranking: Bringing order to the Web. In: Stanford Digital Library Technologies Project (1998)
12. Lee, J.H., Kim, M.H., Lee, Y.J.: Information retrieval based on conceptual distance in IS-A hierarchies. Journal of Documentation 49(2), 188–207 (1993)
13. Richardson, M., Domingos, P.: The intelligent surfer: Probabilistic combination of link and content information in pagerank. In: Advances in Neural Information Processing Systems, vol. 14, MIT Press, Cambridge, MA (2002)
14. Brin, S., Page, L.: The anatomy of a large-scale hypertextual Web search engine. Computer Networks and ISDN Systems 30(1–7), 107–117 (1998)
15. Srivastava, J., Cooley, R., Deshpande, M.: Web usage mining: Discovery and applications of usage patterns from web data. SIGKDD Explorations 1(2), 12–23 (2000)
16. Haveliwala, T.: Topic-sensitive pagerank: A context-sensitive ranking algorithm for web search. IEEE Transactions on Knowledge and Data Engineering (2003)
17. University of Minnesota, Computer Science Department website, http://www.cs.umn.edu
18. Matsuo, Y., Ohsawa, Y., Ishizuka, M.: Average-Clicks. A New Measure on the World Wide Web-Journal of Intelligent Systems (2003)

Nearest-Biclusters Collaborative Filtering with Constant Values

Panagiotis Symeonidis, Alexandros Nanopoulos, Apostolos Papadopoulos, and Yannis Manolopoulos

Aristotle University, Department of Informatics, Thessaloniki 54124, Greece
{symeon,alex,apostol,manolopo}@delab.csd.auth.gr

Abstract. Collaborative Filtering (CF) Systems have been studied extensively for more than a decade to confront the "information overload" problem. Nearest-neighbor CF is based either on common user or item similarities, to form the user's neighborhood. The effectiveness of the aforementioned approaches would be augmented, if we could combine them. In this paper, we use biclustering to disclose this duality between users and items, by grouping them in both dimensions simultaneously. We propose a novel nearest-biclusters algorithm, which uses a new similarity measure that achieves partial matching of users' preferences. We apply nearest-biclusters in combination with a biclustering algorithm – Bimax – for constant values. Extensively performance evaluations on two real data sets is provided, which show that the proposed method improves the performance of the CF process substantially. We attain more than 30% and 10% improvement in terms of precision and recall, respectively.

1 Introduction

Information Filtering has become a necessary technology to attack the "information overload" problem. In our everyday experience, while searching on a topic (e.g., products, movies, etc.), we often rely on suggestions from others, more experienced in it. In the Web, however, the plethora of available suggestions renders it difficult to detect the trustworthy ones. The solution is to shift from individual to collective suggestions. Collaborative Filtering (CF) applies information retrieval and data mining techniques to provide recommendations based on suggestions of users with similar preferences. CF is a very popular method in recommender systems and e-commerce applications.

1.1 Motivation

Two families of CF algorithms have been proposed in the literature: (a) nearest-neighbors (a.k.a. memory-based) algorithms, which recommend according to the preferences of nearest neighbors; and (b) model-based algorithms, which recommend by first developing a model of user ratings. Related research has reported

O. Nasraoui et al. (Eds.): WebKDD 2006, LNAI 4811, pp. 36–55, 2007.

that nearest-neighbor algorithms present good performance in terms of accuracy. Nevertheless, their main drawback is that they cannot handle scalability to large volumes of data. On the other hand, model-based algorithms, once they have build the model, present good scalability. However, they have the overhead to build and update the model, and they cannot cover as diverse a user range as the nearest-neighbor algorithms do [29]. Therefore, a first goal is to develop nearest-neighbor algorithms that combine good accuracy with the advantage of scalability that model-based algorithms present.

Regarding nearest-neighbor algorithms, there exist two main approaches: (a) *user-based* (UB) CF, which forms neighborhoods based on similarity between users; and (b) *item-based* (IB) CF, which forms neighborhoods based on similarities between items. However, both UB and IB are one-sided approaches, in the sense that they examine similarities either only between users or only between items, respectively. This way, they ignore the clear duality that exists between users and items. Furthermore, UB and IB algorithms cannot detect partial matching of preferences, because their similarity measures consider the entire set of items or users, respectively. However, two users may share similar preferences only for a subset of items. For instance, consider two users that share similar preferences for science-fiction books and differentiate in all other kinds of literature. In this case, their partial matching for science-fiction, which can help to provide useful recommendations between them for this kind of books, will be missed by existing approaches. Therefore, by measuring similarity with respect to the entire set of items, we miss partial matchings between two users, since the differences in the remaining items prevails over the subset of items in which their preferences match. Analogous reasoning applies for the IB case. Thus, a second goal is to develop nearest-neighbor algorithms that will be able to consider the duality between users and items, and at the same time, to capture partial matching of preferences.

Finally, the fact that a user usually has various different preferences, has to be taken into account for the process of assigning him to clusters. Therefore, such a user has to be included in more than one clusters. Notice that this cannot be achieved by most of the traditional clustering algorithms, which place each item/user in exactly one cluster. In conclusion, a third goal is to adopt an approach that does not follow the aforementioned restriction and can cover the entire range of the user's preferences.

1.2 Contribution

To attain the first described goal, i.e., to develop scalable nearest-neighbor algorithms, we propose the grouping of different users or items into a number of clusters, based on their rating patterns. This way, similar searching is performed efficiently, because we use consolidated information (that is, the clusters) and not individual users or items.

To address the second described goal, i.e., to disclose the duality between users and items, we propose the generation of groups of users *and* items at the same time. The simultaneous clustering of users and items discovers *biclusters*, which correspond to groups of users which exhibit highly correlated ratings on groups of items. Biclusters allow the computation of similarity between a test user and a bicluster *only* on the items that are included in the bicluster. Thus, partial matching of preferences is taken into account too. Moreover, a user can be matched with several nearest biclusters, thus to receive recommendations that cover the range of his various preferences.

To face the third described goal, i.e., to include a user in more than one clusters, we allow a degree of overlap between biclusters. Thus, if a user presents different item preferences, by using overlapping biclusters, he can be included in more clusters in order to cover all his different preferences.

The contributions of this paper are summarized as follows:

- To disclose the duality between users and items and to capture the range of the user's preferences, we introduce for the first time, to our knowledge, the application of an exact biclustering algorithm to the CF area.
- We propose a novel nearest-biclusters algorithm, which uses a new similarity measure that achieves partial matching of users' preferences.
- Our extensive experimental results illustrate the effectiveness and efficiency of the proposed algorithm over existing approaches.

The rest of this paper is organized as follows. Section 2 summarizes the related work, whereas Section 3 contains the analysis of the CF issues. The proposed approach is described in Section 4. Experimental results are given in Section 5. Finally, Section 6 concludes this paper.

2   Related Work

In 1992, the Tapestry system [6] introduced Collaborative Filtering (CF). In 1994, the GroupLens system [21] implemented a CF algorithm based on common users preferences. Nowadays, it is known as user-based CF algorithm, because it employs users' similarities for the formation of the neighborhood of nearest users. Since then, many improvements of user-based algorithm have been suggested, e.g., [8,18,23].

In 2001, another CF algorithm was proposed. It is based on the items' similarities for a neighborhood generation [24,13,3]. Now, it is denoted as item-based or item-item CF algorithm, because it employs items' similarities for the formation of the neighborhood of nearest users.

The concept of biclustering has been used in [17] to perform grouping in a matrix by using both rows and columns. However, biclustering has been used previously in [7] under the name *direct clustering*. Recently, biclustering (also known as *co-clustering, two-sided clustering, two-way clustering*) has been exploited by many researchers in diverse scientific fields, towards the discovery of useful knowledge [2,4,5,14,19]. One of these fields is bioinformatics, and more specifically, microarray data analysis. The results of each microarray experiment are represented as a data matrix, with different samples as rows and different genes as columns. Among the proposed biclustering algorithms we highlight the following: (i) Cheng and Churchs algorithm [2] which is based on a mean squared residue score, (ii) the Iterative Signature Algorithm (ISA) which searches for submatrices representing fix points [12], (iii) the Order-Preserving Submatrix Algorithm (OPSM), which tries to identify large submatrices for which the induced linear order of the columns is identical for all rows [1],(iv) the Samba Algorithm, which is a graph theoretic approach in combination with a statistical model [27,26], and (v) the Bimax algorithm, an exact biclustering algorithm based on a divide-and-conquer strategy, that is capable of finding all maximal bicliques in a corresponding graph-based matrix representation [20].

In the CF area, there is no related work that has applied a specific biclustering algorithm to provide recommendations. Madeira and Oliveira [15] have reported in their survey, the existence of works that have used two-sided clustering in the CF field. In these models [28,11], there is a hidden variable for each user and item, respectively, that represents the cluster of that user or item. For each user-item pair, there is a variable that denotes their relation. The existence of the relation depends on the cluster of the person, and the cluster of item, hence the notion of two-sided clustering. These are latent class models using statistical estimation of the model parameters and clustering is performed separately for users and items. In contrast, our approach is based on the application of specific biclustering algorithms[1] that perform simultaneous clustering of users and items.

3   Examined Issues

In this section, we provide details for the issues we examine about CF algorithms. Table 1 summarizes the symbols that are used in the sequel.

Scalability: Scalability is important, because in real-world applications the number of users/items is very large. As the number of users/items grows, CF algorithms face performance problems. Therefore, CF algorithms should be evaluated in terms of their responding time in providing recommendations.

Similarity measure: The most extensively used similarity measures are based on correlation and cosine-similarity [9,24]. Specifically, user-based CF algorithms mainly use Pearson's Correlation (Equation 1), whereas for item-based

---

[1] For implementation issues, we use the Bimax biclustering algorithm, however any other algorithm can be used equally well, as our approach is independent of the specific biclustering algorithm that is used.

Table 1. Symbols and definitions

Symbol	Definition
k	number of nearest neighbors or biclusters
N	size of recommendation list
P_τ	threshold for positive ratings
$\mathcal{I}$	domain of all items
$\mathcal{U}$	domain of all users
u, v	some users
i, j	some items
I_u	set of items rated by user u
U_i	set of users rated item i
$r_{u,i}$	the rating of user u on item i
$\bar{r}_u$	mean rating value for user u
$\bar{r}_i$	mean rating value for item i
n	minimum allowed number of users in a bicluster
m	minimum allowed number of items in a bicluster
$\mathcal{B}$	set of all biclusters
b	a bicluster
I_b	set of items of bicluster b
U_b	set of users of bicluster b

CF algorithms, the Adjusted Cosine Measure is preferred (Equation 2) [16,24]. The Adjusted Cosine Measure is a variation of the simple cosine formula, that normalizes bias from subjective ratings of different users. As default options, for user-based CF we use the Pearson Correlation, whereas for item-based we use the Adjusted Cosine Similarity, because they presented the best behavior overall.

$$\text{sim}(u, v) = \frac{\sum_{\forall i \in S} (r_{u,i} - \bar{r}_u)(r_{v,i} - \bar{r}_v)}{\sqrt{\sum_{\forall i \in S} (r_{u,i} - \bar{r}_u)^2} \sqrt{\sum_{\forall i \in S} (r_{v,i} - \bar{r}_v)^2}}, S = I_u \cap I_v. \quad (1)$$

$$\text{sim}(i, j) = \frac{\sum_{\forall u \in T} (r_{u,i} - \bar{r}_u)(r_{u,j} - \bar{r}_u)}{\sqrt{\sum_{\forall u \in U_i} (r_{u,i} - \bar{r}_u)^2} \sqrt{\sum_{\forall u \in U_j} (r_{u,j} - \bar{r}_u)^2}}, T = U_i \cap U_j. \quad (2)$$

Neighborhood size: The number, k, of nearest neighbors used for the neighborhood formation is important, because it can affect substantially the system's accuracy. In most related works [8,22], k has been examined in the range of values between 10 and 100. The optimum k depends on the data characteristics (e.g., sparsity). Therefore, CF algorithms should be evaluated against varying k, in order to tune it.

Positive rating threshold: Recommendation for a test user is performed by generating the top-N list of items that appear most frequently in his formed neighborhood (this method is denoted as Most-Frequent item-recommendation). Nevertheless, it is evident that recommendations should be "positive", as it is not success to recommend an item that will be rated with, e.g., 1 in 1-5 scale [25]. Thus, "negatively" rated items should not contribute to the increase of accuracy. We use a rating-threshold, P_τ, to recommended items whose rating is not less than this value. If we do not use a P_τ value, then the results become misleading.

Training/Test data size: There is a clear dependence between the training set's size and the accuracy of CF algorithms [24]. Through our experimental study we verified this conclusion. Though most related research uses a size around 80%, there exist works that use significantly smaller sizes [16]. Therefore, CF algorithms should be evaluated against varying training data sizes.

Recommendation list's size: The size, N, of the recommendation list corresponds to a tradeoff: With increasing N, the absolute number of relevant items (i.e., recall) is expected to increase, but their ratio to the total size of the recommendation list (i.e., precision) is expected to decrease. (Recall and precision metrics are detailed in the following.) In related work [13,24], N usually takes values between 10 and 50.

Evaluation Metrics: Several metrics have been used for the evaluation of CF algorithms, for instance the Mean Absolute Error (MAE) or the Receiving Operating Characteristic (ROC) curve [9,10]. MAE represents the absolute differences between the real and the predicted values and is an extensively used metric. From our experimental study (Section 5) we understood that MAE is able to characterize the accuracy of prediction, but is not indicative for the accuracy of recommendation. Since in real-world recommender systems the experience of users mainly depends on the accuracy of recommendation, MAE may not be the preferred measure. For this reason we focus on widely accepted metrics from information retrieval.

For a test user that receives a top-N recommendation list, let R denote the number of *relevant recommended items* (the items of the top-N list that are rated higher than P_τ by the test user). We define the following:

- *Precision* is the ratio of R to N.
- *Recall* is the ratio of R to the total number of relevant items for the test user (all items rated higher than P_τ by him).

Notice that with the previous definitions, when an item in the top-N list is not rated at all by the test user, we consider it as *irrelevant* and it counts negatively to precision (as we divide by N) [16]. In the following we also use F_1, because it combines both the previous metrics:

$$\mathrm{F}_1 = 2 \cdot \mathrm{recall} \cdot \mathrm{precision}/(\mathrm{recall} + \mathrm{precision}).$$

4   Nearest Bicluster Approach

4.1   Outline of the Proposed Approach

Our approach consists of three stages.

- *Stage 1*: the data preprocessing/discretization step.
- *Stage 2*: the biclustering process.
- *Stage 3*: the nearest-biclusters algorithm.

The proposed approach, initially, applies a data preprocessing/discretization step. The motivation is to preserve only the positive ratings. Consequently, we proceed to the biclustering process, where we create simultaneously groups consisting of users and items. Finally, we implement the k nearest-biclusters algorithm. We calculate similarity between each test user and the generated bicluster. Thus, we create the test users' neighborhood, consisted of the k nearest biclusters. Then, we provide for each test user a Top-N recommendation list based on the most frequent items in his neighborhood.

To ease the discussion, we will use the running example illustrated in Figure 1, where I_{1-7} are items and U_{1-9} are users. As shown, the example data set is divided into training and test set. The null cells (no rating) are presented with dash.

	I_1	I_2	I_3	I_4	I_5	I_6	I_7
U_1	5	-	2	-	1	-	-
U_2	2	-	4	1	4	3	-
U_3	4	-	2	-	2	-	5
U_4	-	3	1	4	-	5	2
U_5	-	2	4	2	5	1	-
U_6	5	1	-	1	-	-	3
U_7	-	2	5	-	4	1	-
U_8	1	4	-	5	4	3	-

(a)

	I_1	I_2	I_3	I_4	I_5	I_6	I_7
U_9	5	-	4	-	1	-	2

(b)

Fig. 1. Running example: (a) training Set; (b) test Set

4.2   The Data Preprocessing/Discretization Step

Data preprocessing is applied to make data more suitable for data mining. According to the positive rating threshold, we have introduced in Section 3, recommendations should be "positive", as it is not success to recommend an item that

	I_1	I_2	I_3	I_4	I_5	I_6	I_7
U_1	5	-	-	-	-	-	-
U_2	-	-	4	-	4	3	-
U_3	4	-	-	-	-	-	5
U_4	-	3	-	4	-	5	-
U_5	-	-	4	-	5	-	-
U_6	5	-	-	-	-	-	3
U_7	-	-	5	-	4	-	-
U_8	-	4	-	5	4	3	-

Fig. 2. Training Set with rating values $\geq P_\tau$

	I_1	I_2	I_3	I_4	I_5	I_6	I_7
U_1	1	0	0	0	0	0	0
U_2	0	0	1	0	1	1	0
U_3	1	0	0	0	0	0	1
U_4	0	1	0	1	0	1	0
U_5	0	0	1	0	1	0	0
U_6	1	0	0	0	0	0	1
U_7	0	0	1	0	1	0	0
U_8	0	1	0	1	1	1	0

Fig. 3. Binary discretization of the Training Set

will be rated with, e.g., 1 in 1-5 scale. Thus, "negatively" rated items should not contribute to the increase of accuracy. This is the reason that we are interested only in the positive ratings, as shown in Figure 2.

Furthermore, as biclustering groups items and users simultaneously, it allows to identify sets of users sharing common preferences across subsets of items. In our approach, the main goal is to find the largest possible subsets of users that have rated positively (above P_τ rating threshold) items. Therefore, the problem can be discretized to binary values by setting as discretization threshold the P_τ rating threshold. The binarized data are shown in Figure 3.

Notice that binarization of data is optional and can be omitted, in case we use a biclustering algorithm which discovers biclusters with coherent values on both users and items. In our case, as shown in the next subsection, we use Bimax algorithm which finds clusters with constant values and the binarization step is required. In a future work, we will examine more types of biclustering algorithms, which will omit the preprocessing step.

4.3   The Biclustering Process

The biclustering process on a data matrix involves the determination of a set of clusters taking into account both rows and columns. Each bicluster is defined on

	I_4	I_2	I_6	I_5	I_3	I_1	I_7
U_3	0	0	0	0	0	1	1
U_6	0	0	0	0	0	1	1
U_5	0	0	0	1	1	0	0
U_7	0	0	0	1	1	0	0
U_2	0	0	1	1	1	0	0
U_8	1	1	1	1	0	0	0
U_4	1	1	1	0	0	0	0
U_1	0	0	0	0	0	1	0

Fig. 4. Applying biclustering to the Training Set

a subset of rows and a subset of columns. Moreover, two biclusters may overlap, which means that several rows or columns of the matrix may participate in multiple biclusters. Another important characteristic of biclusters is that each bicluster should be maximal, i.e., it should not be fully contained in another determined bicluster.

For the biclustering step, there are two main bicluster classes that have been proposed: (a) biclusters with constant values and (b) biclusters with coherent values. The first category looks for subsets of rows and subsets of columns with constant values, while the second is interested in biclusters with coherent values. For the biclustering step, we have adopted a simple constant biclustering algorithm denoted as Bimax [20], which is executed off-line. It is an exact biclustering algorithm based on a divide-and-conquer strategy that is capable of finding all maximal biclusters in a corresponding graph-based matrix representation.

For the Bimax algorithm, a bicluster $b(U_b, I_b)$ corresponds to a subset of users $U_b \subseteq \mathcal{U}$ that jointly present positively rating behavior across a subset of items $I_b \subseteq \mathcal{I}$. In other words, the pair (U_b, I_b) defines a submatrix for which all elements equal to 1.

The main goal of the Bimax algorithm is to find all biclusters that are *inclusion-maximal*, i.e, that are not entirely contained in any other bicluster. The required input to Bimax is the minimum number of users and the minimum number of items per bicluster. It is obvious that the Bimax algorithm finds a large number of overlapping biclusters. To avoid this we can perform a secondary filtering procedure to reduce this number to the desired overlapping degree.

In Figure 4, we have applied the Bimax algorithm to the running example. Four biclusters are found (depicted with dashed rectangles), with minimum number of users equal to 2 (i.e., $|U_b| \geq 2$) and the minimum number of items equal to 2 (i.e., $|I_b| \geq 2$). These bilcusters are summarized as follows:

$$b_1 \colon U_{b_1} = \{U_3, U_6\}, \qquad I_{b_1} = \{I_1, I_7\}$$
$$b_2 \colon U_{b_2} = \{U_5, U_7, U_2\}, \, I_{b_2} = \{I_5, I_3\}$$
$$b_3 \colon U_{b_3} = \{U_2, U_8\}, \qquad I_{b_3} = \{I_6, I_5\}$$
$$b_4 \colon U_{b_4} = \{U_8, U_4\}, \qquad I_{b_4} = \{I_4, I_2, I_6\}$$

We have to notice that there is overlap between biclusters. Specifically, between biclusters 2 and 3 in item I_5. Also, we have overlapping between biclusters 3 and 4 in item I_6. We can allow this overlapping (it reaches 16,6%) or we can forbid it. If we forbid it, then we will abolish the existence of the third bicluster because it is smaller than the other two. In order not to miss important biclusters, we allow overlapping. However, overlapping introduces a trade-off: (a) with few biclusters the effectiveness reduces, as several biclusters may be missed; (b) with a high number of biclusters efficiency reduces; as we have to examine many possible matchings. In our experimental results we show the tuning of the allowed overlapping factor.

4.4   The Nearest Bicluster Algorithm

In order to provide recommendations, we have to find the biclusters containing users with preferences that have strong partial similarity with the test user. This stage is executed on-line and consists of two basic operations:

- The formation of the test user's neighborhood, i.e., to find the k nearest biclusters.
- The generation of the top-N recommendation list.

```
Array k-NearestBiclusters(nB, IB[nB][nI], UI[nI])
begin
//int nI number of items
//int nB number of biclusters
//int cI, ncI common items/items not in common
//Array IB[nB][nI] stores items per bicluster (binary)
//Array UI[nI] stores the user ratings
//Array SIM[nB] stores user-biclusters similarities
for b=1 to nB
    cI=0; ncI=0; SIM[b] = 0;

    for i=1 to nI
        if (IB[b][i] = 1) and (UI[i] ≥ Pτ)
            cI = cI + 1;
        if (IB[b][i] = 1) and (UI[i] < Pτ)
            ncI=ncI+1;
        SIM[b] = cI/ (cI + ncI);

sort(SIM); //descending order
return (SIM[0..k-1]);
end
```

Fig. 5. The algorithm for the formation of a test user's biclusters neighborhood

To find the k nearest biclusters, we measure the similarity of the test user and each of the biclusters. The central difference with the past work is that we are interested in the similarity of test user and a bicluster *only* on the items that are included in the bicluster and not on all items that he has rated. As described, this allows for the detection of partial similarities. The similarity between the test user and each bicluster is calculated by dividing the items they have in common to the sum of items they have in common and not in common. In Equation 3, we calculate the similarity between a user u and bicluster b as follows:

$$sim(u,b) = \frac{|I_u \bigcap I_b|}{|I_u \bigcap I_b| + |I_b - I_u|} \qquad (3)$$

It is obvious that similarity values range between [0,1]. The algorithm for the formation of the similarity matrix between a test user and the biclusters is shown in Figure 5.

```
Array TOPN(nI, nnB, topN, UB[nB], SIM[k])
begin
//int nI number of test users/items
//int topN number of items in recommendation list
//int nnB number of nearest biclusters
//Array IB[nB][nI] stores items per bicluster(binary)
//Array WF[nI] stores items' Weighted Frequency
//Array SIM[nB] stores users-biclusters similarities
//Array UB[nB] stores the number of users per bicluster
//Array TOPN[topN] stores the recommendation list
    for j=1 to nI
        WF[j].value = 0;
        WF[j].position = j;

    for b=1 to nnB

        for j=1 to nI
            //if an item belongs to the bicluster
            if (IB[SIM[b].position][j] > 0)
                WF[j].value += UB[b] * SIM[b];

    sort(WF); //descending order of WF values

    for i=1 to topN
        if (WF[i].value > 0)
            TOPN[i]= WF[i].position;
end
```

Fig. 6. Generation of top-N recommendation list

In the next phase, we proceed to the generation of the top-N recommendation list. For this purpose, we have to find the appearance frequency of each item and recommend the N most frequent. In Equation 4, we define as *Weighted Frequency* (WF) of an item i in a bicluster b, the product between $|U_b|$ and the similarity $sim(u, b)$. This way we weight the contribution of each bicluster with its size in addition to its similarity with the test user:

$$WF(i, b) = sim(u, b) * |U_b| \qquad (4)$$

Finally, we apply the Most Frequent Item Recommendation (proposing those items that appear most frequently in the test user's formed neighborhood). Thus, we add the item weighted frequencies, we sort them, and propose the top-N items in the constructed list, which is customized to each test user preferences. The algorithm for the top-N generation list, is shown in Figure 6.

In our running example, assume that we keep all four biclusters (allow overlapping) and we are interested in 2 nearest biclusters ($k = 2$). As it is shown, U_9 has rated positively only two items (I_1, I_3). So, his similarity with each of the biclusters is (0.5, 0.5, 0, 0), respectively. Thus, test user's nearest neighbors come from the first two biclusters, and the recommended items for him will be items I_7 and I_5.

5   Experimental Configuration

In the sequel, we study the performance of the described nearest bicluster approach, against existing CF algorithms, by means of a thorough experimental evaluation. Henceforth, the proposed algorithm is denoted as Nearest Biclusters, the user-based algorithm as UB and the item-based algorithm as IB. Factors that are treated as parameters, are the following: the neighborhood size (k, default value 20), the size of the recommendation list (N, default value 20), and the size of training set and the test data set (default value 75% and 25%, respectively). The metrics we use are precision, recall, and F_1.

We performed experiments with several real data sets that have been used as benchmark in prior work. In particular, we examined two MovieLens data sets: (i) the first one with 100,000 ratings assigned by 943 users on 1,682 movies, denoted 100K data set (this is the default data set) and (ii) the second one with about 1 million ratings for 3,592 movies by 6,040 users, denoted 1M data set. The range of ratings is between 1(bad)-5(excellent) of the numerical scale, the P_τ threshold is set to 3 and the value of an unrated item is considered equal to zero. Moreover, we consider the division between not hidden and hidden data. For each transaction of a test user we keep the 75% as hidden data (the data we want to predict) and use the rest 25% as not hidden data (the data for modeling new users).

5.1   Results for Tuning Nearest Biclusters

As already discussed in Section 4.3, the only input of the Bimax algorithm is the minimum allowed number of users in a bicluster, n, and the minimum allowed number of items in a bicluster, m. In order to discover the best biclusters (in terms of effectiveness and efficiency), it is important to fine-tune these two input variables. So, we examine the performance of F_1 metric vs. different values for n and m.

Figure 7a illustrates F_1 for varying n (in this measurement we set $m = 10$). As n is the minimum allowed number of users in a bicluster, Figure 7a also depicts (through the numbers over the bars) the average numbers of users in a bicluster, which as expected increase with increasing n. As shown, the best performance is attained for $n = 4$. In the following, we keep this as the default value. Nevertheless, notice that performance is, in general, robust against varying n. In particular, for $n \leq 6$ the resulting F_1 is high. In contrast, for higher n, F_1 decreases. The reason is that with higher n we result with an inadequate number of biclusters to provide qualitative recommendations. The conclusion is that, small values for n are preferred, a fact that eases the tuning process.

Similarly, we examined F_1 for varying m. The results for F_1 are depicted in Figure 7b ($n = 4$). As previously, in the same figure we also illustrate the resulting average numbers of items in a bilcuster. The best performance is attained for $m = 10$ (henceforth kept as default value), whereas F_1 decreases for higher or lower m values. The reason is as follows: for very small values of m, there are not enough items in each bicluster to capture the similarity of users' preferences (i.e., matching is easily attained), thus the quality of recommendation decreases; on the other hand, for very large values of m, the number of discovered biclusters is not adequate to provide recommendations.

In Section 4.3, we mentioned that Bimax finds all biclusters that are not entirely contained in any other bicluster. It is obvious that this characteristic generates overlapping biclusters. The number of overlapping biclusters can be

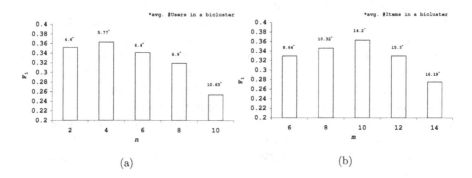

(a)   (b)

Fig. 7. F_1 vs. tuning number of (a) users, (b) items

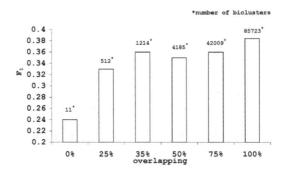

Fig. 8. F_1 vs. overlapping percentage between the biclusters

enormously large. To avoid this, we can perform a secondary filtering procedure to reduce the number of biclusters with respect to the desired overlapping degree. In Figure 8 we can see F_1 vs. varying overlapping degree (given as a percentage of common items/users between the biclusters). The figure also depicts (numbers over the bars) the resulting number of biclusters for each overlapping degree. With decreasing overlapping degree, F_1 decreases too. On the other hand, by keeping a high level of overlap between the biclusters, we harm efficiency –in terms of execution time– of the Nearest Biclusters algorithm (for its on-line part). As shown, by permitting 100% of overlapping, the number of generated biclusters is 85,723. It is obvious that this number impacts the efficiency of the recommendation process. The best combination of effectiveness and efficiency can be attained by having an overlapping equal to 35% (results to 1,214 biclusters), where the resulting F_1 is 0.36 (very close to the 100% overlapping result).

For the 1M data set, we follow the same tuning procedure and we resulted to the following values which have the best results in our experiments in terms of F1 measure : n=3, m=6, overlapping = 10%, which results to 2126 biclusters.

5.2   Comparative Results for Effectiveness

We now move on to the comparison of Nearest Bicluster algorithm with the UB and IB. The results for precision and recall vs. k are displayed in Figure 9a and b, respectively. As shown, the UB performs worst than IB for small values of k. The performance of the two algorithms converges to the same value as k increases. The reason is that with a high k, the resulting neighborhoods for both UB and IB are similar, since they include almost all items. Thus, the top-N recommendation lists are about the same, as they are formed just by the most frequent items. In particular, both UB and IB reach an optimum performance for a specific k. In the examined range of k values, the performance of UB and IB increases with increasing k and outside this range (not displayed), it stabilizes and never exceeds 40% precision and 15% recall.

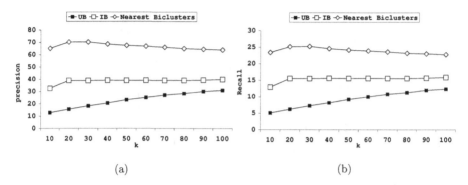

(a)   (b)

Fig. 9. Comparison between UB , IB and Bicluster CF in terms of (a) precision (b) recall

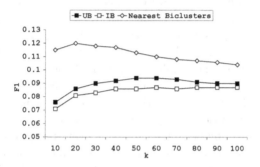

Fig. 10. Comparison between UB, IB, and Nearest Biclusters algorithm in terms of F1 measure for the 1M data set

Nearest Biclusters significantly outperforms UB and IB. The difference in precision is larger than 30%, whereas with respect to recall, it exceeds 10% (we refer to the optimum values resulting from the tuning of k). The reason is that Nearest Biclusters takes into account partial matching of preferences between users and the possibility of overlapping between their interests. In contrast, UB and IB are based on individual users and items, respectively, and do not consider the aforementioned characteristics.

For the 1M data set, the results for F1 measure vs. k are displayed in Figure 10. As shown, Nearest Biclusters outperforms UB and IB. The difference is analogous to the 100K data set. The reason again is that Nearest Biclusters takes into account partial matching of the users' preferences.

5.3   Comparative Results for Efficiency

Regarding efficiency, we measured the wall-clock time for the on-line parts of UB, IB and Nearest Biclusters algorithms. The on-line parts concern the time it takes to create a recommendation list, given what is known about a user. Notice

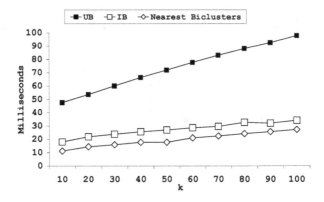

Fig. 11. Comparison between UB , IB and Nearest Biclusters in terms of execution time

that there is an off-line part for the IB and Nearest Biclusters, which demands additional computational time, needed to build the items' similarity matrix and find the biclusters, respectively. However, these computations are executed off-line. Thus, we do not count them in the recommendation time. Our experiments were performed on a 3 GHz Pentium IV with 1 GB of memory running the Windows XP operating system. The results vs. k are presented in Figure 11. In particular, we present the average time in milliseconds that takes to provide recommendations to a test user.

As shown, IB needs less time to provide recommendations than UB. Notice that the required time for IB to provide recommendation for a test user is almost stable, whereas the time for UB increases with increasing k. The reason is that UB finds, firstly, user neighbors in the neighborhood matrix and then counts presences of items in the user-item matrix. In contrast, with IB, the whole task is completed in the item-neighborhood matrix, which is generated off-line. Thus, in terms of execution time, IB is superior to UB.

In all cases, however, Nearest Biclusters needs even less time than IB to provide recommendations. This is due to the fact that the biclusters are also created off-line and, secondly, the number of biclusters in our experiment (1,214) is less than the number (1,682) of items' of the similarity matrix in the IB case. As it is already presented in Section 5.1, by decreasing the percentages of overlap between biclusters, accuracy decreases too. On the other hand, by keeping a high level of overlap between biclusters, we harm the efficiency. Thus, to combine effectiveness and efficiency, a prerequisite is a fine-tuning of the overlapping biclusters.

5.4 Examination of Additional Factors

In this section we examine the impact of additional factors. In our measurements we again consider UB, IB, and Nearest Biclusters algorithms.

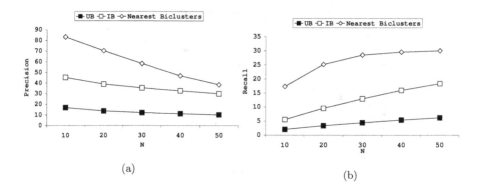

(a)

(b)

Fig. 12. Comparison vs. N: (a) precision, (b) recall

Recommendation list's size: We examine the impact of N. The results of our experiments are depicted in Figure 12. As expected, with increasing N, recall increases and precision decreases. Notice that the best performance of UB and IB corresponds to the worst performance of Nearest Biclusters. The relative differences between the algorithms are coherent with those in our previous measurements. We have to mentioned that in real applications, N should be kept low, because it is impractical for a user to see all recommendations when their number is large.

Training/Test data size: Now we test the impact of the size of the training set, which is expressed as percentage of the total data set size. The results for F_1 are given in Figure 13. As expected, when the training set is small, performance downgrades for all algorithms. Therefore, we should be careful enough when we evaluate CF algorithms so as to use an adequately large training sets. Similar to the previous measurements, in all cases Nearest Biclusters is better than IB and UB. The performance of both UB and IB reaches a peak around 75%,

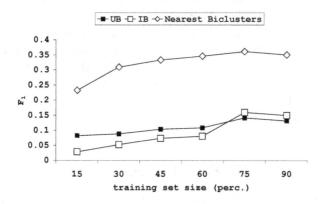

Fig. 13. Comparison vs. training set size

after which it reduces. It is outstanding that Nearest Biclusters trained with the 15% of the data set, attains much better F_1 than UB and IB when they are trained with 75%. Also, we see that after a threshold of the training set size, the increase in accuracy for algorithms is less steep. However, the effect of overfitting is less significant compared to general classification problems. In contrast, low training set sizes negatively impact accuracy. Therefore, the fair evaluation of CF algorithms should be based on adequately large training sets.

6   Conclusions

We proposed the application of an exact biclustering algorithm in the CF area, to disclose the duality between users and items and to capture the range of the user's preferences. In addition, we propose a novel nearest-biclusters algorithm, which uses a new similarity measure that achieves partial matching of users' preferences and allows overlapping interests between users.

We performed experimental comparison of the nearest biclusters algorithm against well known CF algorithms, like user-based or item-based methods. Our extensive experimental results illustrate the effectiveness and efficiency of the proposed algorithm over the existing approaches.

We highlight the following conclusions from our examination:

- Our approach shows significant improvements over existing CF algorithms, in terms of effectiveness, because it exploits the duality of users and items through biclustering and partial matching of users' preferences. In particular, we attain more than 30% improvement and recall more than 10% in terms of precision and recall, respectively.
- Our approach shows improvements over existing CF algorithms, in terms of efficiency. The Nearest Biclusters algorithm needs even less time than item based approach to provide recommendations.
- In our experiments we have seen that only a 15% of the training set is adequate to provide accurate results.
- We introduced a similarity measure for the biclusters' neighborhood formation and proposed the Weighted Frequency for the generation of the top-N recommendation list of items.

Summarizing the aforementioned conclusions, we see that, the proposed Nearest Biclusters algorithm through a simple, yet effective, biclustering algorithms (Bimax) and the partial matching of users' preferences, achieves better results in terms of effectiveness and efficiency than traditional CF algorithms. For this reason, in our future work we will compare biclusters with constant values with other categories of biclusters (i.e biclusters with coherent values). The first category looks for subsets of rows and subsets of columns with constant values, while the second is interested in biclusters with coherent values. Moreover, we will also examine different similarity measures between a user and a bicluster based on the items that are included in the bicluster or based on features characteristics of those items.

References

1. Ben-Dor, A., Chor, B., Karp, R., Yakhini, Z.: Discovering local structure in gene expression data: The order-preserving submatrix problem. Journal of Computational Biology 10(3/4), 373–384 (2003)
2. Cheng, Y., Church, G.: Biclustering of expression data. In: Proceedings of the ISMB Conference, pp. 93–103 (2000)
3. Deshpande, M., Karypis, G.: Item-based top-n recommendation algorithms. ACM Transactions on Information Systems 22(1), 143–177 (2004)
4. Dhillon, I.S.: Co-clustering documents and words using bipartite spectral graph partitioning. In: Proceedings of the ACM SIGKDD Conference (2001)
5. Dhillon, I.S., Mallela, D.S., Modha, S.: Information theoretic co-clustering. In: Proceedings of the ACM SIGKDD Conference (2003)
6. Goldberg, D., Nichols, D., Brian, M., Terry, D.: Using collaborative filtering to weave an information tapestry. ACM Communications 35(12), 61–70 (1992)
7. Hartigan, J.A.: Direct clustering of a data matrix. Journal of the American Statistical Association 67(337), 123–129 (1972)
8. Herlocker, J., Konstan, J., Borchers, A., Riedl, J.: An algorithmic framework for performing collaborative filtering. In: Proceedings of the ACM SIGIR Conference, pp. 230–237 (1999)
9. Herlocker, J., Konstan, J., Riedl, J.: An empirical analysis of design choices in neighborhood-based collaborative filtering algorithms. Information Retrieval 5(4), 287–310 (2002)
10. Herlocker, J., Konstan, J., Terveen, L., Riedl, J.: Evaluating collaborative filtering recommender systems. ACM Transactions on Information Systems 22(1), 5–53 (2004)
11. Hofmann, T., Puzicha, J.: Latent class models for collaborative filtering. In: Proceedings of the IJCAI Conference (1999)
12. Ihmels, J., Bergmann, S., Barkai, N.: Defining transcription modules using large-scale gene expression data. Bioinformatics 20(13), 1993–2003 (2004)
13. Karypis, G.: Evaluation of item-based top-n recommendation algorithms. In: Proceedings of the ACM CIKM Conference, pp. 247–254 (2001)
14. Long, B., Zhang(Mark), Z., Yu, P.S.: Co-clustering by block value decomposition. In: KDD 2005. Proceeding of the eleventh ACM SIGKDD international conference on Knowledge discovery in data mining, pp. 635–640. ACM Press, New York (2005)
15. Madeira, S., Oliveira, A.: Biclustering algorithms for biological data analysis: a survey. ACM Transactions on Computational Biology and Bioinformatics 1, 24–45 (2004)
16. McLauglin, R., Herlocher, J.: A collaborative filtering algorithm and evaluation metric that accurately model the user experience. In: Proceedings of the ACM SIGIR Conference, pp. 329–336 (2004)
17. Mirkin, B.: Mathematical classification and clustering. Kluwer Academic Publishers, Dordrecht (1996)

18. Mobasher, B., Dai, H., Luo, T., Nakagawa, M.: Improving the effectiveness of collaborative filtering on anonymous web usage data. In: Proceedings of the Workshop Intelligent Techniques for Web Personalization, pp. 53–60 (2001)

19. Murali, T., Kasif, S.: Extracting conserved gene expression motifs from gene expression data. In: Proceedings of the Pacific Symposim on Biocompomputing Conference, vol. 8, pp. 77–88 (2003)

20. Prelic, A., et al.: A systematic comparison and evaluation of biclustering methods for gene expression data. Technical Report (2005)

21. Resnick, P., Iacovou, N., Suchak, M., Bergstrom, P., Riedl, J.: Grouplens: An open architecture for collaborative filtering on netnews. In: Proceedings of the Computer Supported Collaborative Work Conference, pp. 175–186 (1994)

22. Sarwar, B., Karypis, G., Konstan, J., Riedl, J.: Analysis of recommendation algorithms for e-commerce. In: Proceedings of the ACM Electronic Commerce Conference, pp. 158–167 (2000)

23. Sarwar, B., Karypis, G., Konstan, J., Riedl, J.: Application of dimensionality reduction in recommender system-a case study. In: ACM WebKDD Workshop (2000)

24. Sarwar, B., Karypis, G., Konstan, J., Riedl, J.: Item-based collaborative filtering recommendation algorithms. In: Proceedings of the WWW Conference, pp. 285–295 (2001)

25. Symeonidis, P., Nanopoulos, A., Papadopoulos, A., Manolopoulos, Y.: Collaborative filtering process in a whole new light. In: Proc. IDEAS conf., pp. 29–36 (2006)

26. Tanay, A., Sharan, R., Kupiec, M., Shamir, R.: Revealing modularity and organization in the yeast molecular network by integrated analysis of highly heterogeneous genomewide data. In: Proceedings of the National Academy of Science conference, pp. 2981–2986 (2004)

27. Tanay, A., Sharan, R., Shamir, R.: Discovering statistically signifnicant biclusters in gene expression data. In: Proceedings of the ISMB conference (2002)

28. Ungar, L., Foster, D.: A formal statistical approach to collaborative filtering. In: Proceedings of the CONALD Conference (1998)

29. Xue, G., Lin, C., Yang, Q., et al.: Scalable collaborative filtering using cluster-based smoothing. In: Proceedings of the ACM SIGIR Conference, pp. 114–121 (2005)

Fast Categorization of Web Documents Represented by Graphs

A. Markov[1], M. Last[1], and A. Kandel[2]

[1] Department of Information Systems Engineering
Ben-Gurion University of the Negev
Beer-Sheva 84105, Israel
a.i.markov@gmail.com, mlast@bgu.ac.il
[2] Department of Computer Science and Engineering
University of South Florida
Tampa, FL 33620, USA
kandel@csee.usf.edu

Abstract. Most text categorization methods are based on the vector-space model of information retrieval. One of the important advantages of this representation model is that it can be used by both instance-based and model-based classifiers for categorization. However, this popular method of document representation does not capture important structural information, such as the order and proximity of word occurrence or the location of a word within the document. It also makes no use of the mark-up information that is available from web document HTML tags.

A recently developed graph-based representation of web documents can preserve the structural information. The new document model was shown to outperform the traditional vector representation, using the k-Nearest Neighbor (k-NN) classification algorithm. The problem, however, is that the eager (model-based) classifiers cannot work with this representation directly. In this chapter, three new, hybrid approaches to web document categorization are presented, built upon both graph and vector space representations, thus preserving the benefits and overcoming the limitations of each. The hybrid methods presented here are compared to vector-based models using two model-based classifiers (C4.5 decision-tree algorithm and probabilistic Naïve Bayes) and several benchmark web document collections. The results demonstrate that the hybrid methods outperform, in most cases, existing approaches in terms of classification accuracy, and in addition, achieve a significant increase in the categorization speed.

1 Introduction

Document classification (a.k.a. *document categorization* or *topic spotting*) is the task of labeling documents with a set of predefined thematic categories. The first document classification approaches belonged to the so-called knowledge engineering domain. Categorization according to these techniques was based on rules generated by knowledge experts for each one of the categories separately. Such a rule generation process was very expensive and its prediction capability was quite low. Nowadays

O. Nasraoui et al. (Eds.): WebKDD 2006, LNAI 4811, pp. 56–71, 2007.

machine learning and data mining techniques are most commonly used for inducing a classification model from a training set of labeled documents. This model can later be used to classify documents belonging to unknown categories.

In information retrieval techniques, the vector-space model [20] is typically used for document representation. A set of terms (features) $T(t_1,...,t_{|T|})$ that occurred at least once in at least one document of the training corpus serves as a feature set and each document d_j is represented as a vector $\overline{d_j} = (w_1,...,w_{|T|})$, where each w_i is a significance weight of a term t_i in a document d_j. The set T is usually called vocabulary or dictionary[1]. The differences between the various approaches are in the method used to define the term and the method used to calculate the weight of each term.

In traditional information retrieval techniques single words are used as terms. This method is called 'set' or 'bag-of-words' and it is widely used in document categorization research studies and applications. Some examples can be found in [5, 14. 17, and 25]. According to this approach, vocabulary is constructed from either all or N most important (having the highest weight) words that appear in the training set of documents. Though this simple representation provides relatively good results in terms of predictive accuracy, its limitations are obvious. This popular method of document representation does not capture important structural information, such as the order and the proximity of term occurrence or the location of a term within the document.

As to term weight calculation, the TF × IDF (term frequency × inverse document frequency) measure [21, 22] is most frequently used. Such a calculation gives the highest weight to terms that occur frequently in a few documents but do not appear at all in most other documents. The Boolean model is also very popular and it usually produces good accuracy results [1, 11]. Here a document is represented as a vector where dimension values are Boolean with zero indicating the absence and one indicating the presence of the corresponding dictionary term in a document. In a number of works [6 ,7 ,8 ,13] more complicated text representation techniques were presented and evaluated. These representations did not yield better results compared to the bag-of-words in [21].

Web document classification became a very important sub-field of document categorization in the last decade due to the rapid growth of the Internet. Most web categorization methods originated in traditional text classification techniques that use only the plain text for documents representation and classification model induction. Such an approach is not optimal for web documents, since it completely ignores the fact that web documents contain markup elements (HTML tags), which are an additional source of information. These tags can be used for identification of hyperlinks, title, underlined, or bold text, etc. Major document representation techniques also give no weight to the order and combination of words in the text. We believe that this kind of structural information may be critical for accurate web page classification. An enhanced document representation can deal with these issues.

The Graph-Theoretic web document representation technique was recently developed [23]. The strength of the graph approach is in its ability to capture important structural information hidden in a web document and its HTML tags. The graph-theoretic similarity measures between two graphs [3, 4] allow to classify graphs using some

---

[1] The difference between *dictionary* and *bag/set of words* is that in the first, a *term* is not defined and can be anything, while in the second, a *term* is a single word.

distance-based ("lazy") algorithms such as k-NN; the online computational complexity of such kinds of algorithms is, however, very high. It is obvious, therefore, that lazy algorithms cannot be used for massive and online document classification. The major limitation of the graph representation is that model-based classification algorithms, such as C4.5 [19] Naïve Bayes [9] and others cannot work with it directly. This fact prevents quick document categorization based on a pre-induced classification model.

In this chapter, we present detailed experimental results for our recently developed hybrid methods [15, 16] of web document representation. These methods are based on frequent sub-graph extraction that can help us to overcome the problems of traditional bag-of-words [20] and graph [23] techniques. Our hybrid methodology has two main benefits: (1) we keep important structural web page information by extracting relevant sub-graphs from a graph that represents this page; (2) we can use most eager classification algorithms for inducing a classification model because, eventually, a web document is converted into a simple vector with Boolean values. In this chapter, we evaluate the hybrid representation methodology using two model-based classifiers (C4.5 decision-tree algorithm and probabilistic Naïve Bayes) and two benchmark web document collections.

2   Graph Document Models: An Overview

In this section, we briefly describe a novel, graph-based methodology that is designed especially for web document representation [23]. The main benefit of graph-based techniques is that they allow keeping the inherent structural information of the original document. Before presenting the graph-based methodology, the definition of a graph, subgraph and graph isomorphism should be given.

A graph G is a 4-tuple: $G=(V, E, \alpha, \beta)$, where V is a set of nodes (vertices), $E \subseteq V \times V$ is a set of edges connecting the nodes, $\alpha : V \rightarrow \Sigma v$ is a function labeling the nodes, and $\beta : V \times V \rightarrow \Sigma e$ is a function labeling the edges (Σv and Σe being the sets of labels that can appear on the nodes and edges, respectively). For brevity, we may refer to G as $G=(V, E)$ by omitting the labeling functions. A graph $G1=(V_1, E_1, \alpha_1, \beta_1)$ is a *subgraph* of a graph $G_2=(V_2, E_2, \alpha_2, \beta_2)$, denoted $G_1 \subseteq G_2$, if $V_1 \subseteq V_2$, $E_1 \subseteq E_2 \cap (V_1 \times V_1)$, $\alpha_1(x) = \alpha_2(x) \ \forall x \in V_1$ and $\beta_1(x, y) = \beta_2(x, y) \ \forall (x, y) \in E_1$. Conversely, graph G_2 is also called a *supergraph* of G_1.

All graph representations proposed in [23] are based on the position and the co-location of terms in an HTML document. Under the standard method, the most frequent unique terms (keywords) appearing in the document become nodes in the graph representing that document. Distinct terms (stems, lemmas, etc.) can be identified by a stemming algorithm and other language-specific normalization techniques. Each node is labeled with the term it represents. The node labels in a document graph are unique, since a single node is created for each keyword even if a term appears more than once in the text. Second, if word a immediately precedes word b somewhere in a "section" s of the document, then there is a directed edge from the node corresponding to term a to the node corresponding to term b with an edge label s. An edge is not created between two words if they are separated by certain punctuation marks (such as periods). Sections defined for the standard representation are: title (TL), which contains the text related to the document's title and any provided keywords (meta-data);

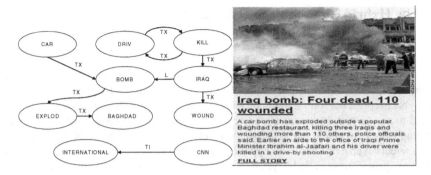

Fig. 1. *Standard* Graph-based Document Representation. The original web page is shown on the right.

link (L), which is the anchor text that appears in hyper-links on the document; and text (TX), which comprises any of the visible text in the document (this includes hyperlinked text, but not text in the document's title and keywords). Graph representations are language-independent: they can be applied to a normalized text in any language. Fig. 1 presents an example of a standard graph representation based on 10 most frequent words extracted from a short English web document.

Other graph representations introduced in [23] include:

- *Simple Representation.* It is basically the same as the standard representation, except that we look at only the visible text on the page (no title or metadata is examined) and we do not label the edges between nodes.
- *N-distance Representation.* Under this model, there is a user-provided parameter, n. Instead of considering only terms immediately following a given term in a web document, we look up to n terms ahead and connect the succeeding terms with an edge that is labeled with the distance between them (unless the words are separated by certain punctuation marks).
- *N-simple Distance.* This model is identical to n-distance, but the edges are not labeled, which means we only know that the distance between two connected terms is not more than n.
- *Absolute Frequency Representation.* This is similar to the simple representation (adjacent words, no section-related information) but each node and edge is labeled with an additional frequency measure.
- *Relative Frequency Representation.* This approach is the same as the absolute frequency representation but with normalized frequency values associated with the nodes and edges.

The ability to calculate similarity between two graphs allows to classify graphs with some distance-based lazy algorithms like k-NN, but available eager algorithms (like *ID3, C4.5, NBC* etc) work only with vectors and cannot induce even a simple classification model from a graph structure. On the other hand, lazy algorithms are very problematic in terms of classification speed and cannot be used for massive online classification of web documents represented by graphs. The *hybrid approach* to document representation aims to solve this problem.

3   The Hybrid Methodology Overview

3.1   Term Definition

In order to represent a web document, a document term has to be defined first. The proposed hybrid methodology is based on the graph document representation [23]. In the hybrid representation methods presented here, terms are defined as subgraphs selected to represent a document already converted into a graph form. Since all possible subgraphs in a document graph cannot be taken as attributes because of their quantity, some selection criteria should be applied. In this work, we present three optional term selection procedures, called Hybrid Naïve, Hybrid Smart, and Hybrid Smart with Fixed Threshold.

3.2   Categorization Model Induction Based on a Hybrid Document Representation

The process for inducing a classification model from labeled web documents represented by graphs is shown in Figure 2.

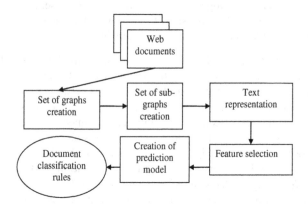

Fig. 2. Classification Model Induction

First we obtain a training corpus of labeled web documents $D = (d_1,..., d_{|D|})$ and a set of categories $C = (c_1, ..., c_{|C|})$, where each document $d_i \in D$; $1 \leq i \leq |D|$ belongs to one and only one category $c_v \in C$; $1 \leq v \leq |C|$. Then graph representation of each document is generated (Section 3) and a set of labeled graphs $G = (g_1, ..., g_{|D|})$ is obtained. Now we are able to extract predictive features (subgraphs in this case) by identifying the subgraphs, which are most relevant for classification in a set of training graphs. Naïve, Smart or Smart with Fixed Threshold subgraph extraction methods can be used (see sub-sections 3.3, 3.4, and 3.5 respectively). A set of terms or vocabulary $T = (t_1, ..., t_{|T|})$ is the output of this stage.

Using T we can now represent all document graphs in a corpus as binary vectors (one – a subgraph from the set T created in the previous stage appears in the graph,

zero - otherwise). Subsequently, *feature selection* techniques may be applied to identify a subset of best attributes (Boolean features) for classification.

Then prediction model creation and extraction of classification rules can be performed using one of the "eager" classification algorithms. Naïve Bayes and C4.5 were
used for evaluation purposes in this particular research study.

3.3 The Hybrid Naïve Approach

All graphs representing the web documents in the training corpus are labeled by their
class attribute value. Then the frequent sub-graphs extraction algorithm (see subsection 3.6 below) is activated on each class (category) with a user-specified threshold
value $0 < t_{min} < 1$. Every sub-graph more frequent than the t_{min} threshold is chosen by
the algorithm to be a term (classification feature) and stored in the vocabulary. All accepted groups of classification-relevant sub-graphs are combined into one set.

The Naive method is based on a simple postulate that an attribute explains the
category best if it is frequent in that category but in real-world situations it is not necessarily the case. For example if a sub-graph g is frequent in more than one category it
can be chosen to be an attribute but it cannot help us to discriminate instances belonging to those categories. The "smart" extraction method has been developed by us to
overcome this problem.

3.4 The Hybrid Smart Approach

As in the Naïve representation, all graphs representing the web documents should be
divided into groups by class attribute value. In order to extract classification-relevant
subgraphs we defined a measure called Classification Rate (*CR*) [16]. The *CR* measure maximizes the weight of subgraphs that are frequent in some specific category
and infrequent in other categories. In order to extract subgraphs, which are relevant
for classification, some measures are defined, as follows:

SCF – Sub-graph Class Frequency:

$$SCF\left(g'_k(c_i)\right) = \frac{g'_k f(c_i)}{N(c_i)}$$

Where
$SCF\left(g'_k(c_i)\right)$ - Frequency of sub-graph g'_k in category c_i.

$g'_k f(c_i)$ - Number of graphs containing a sub-graph g'_k in category c_i.

$N(c_i)$ - Number of graphs in category c_i.

ISF - Inverse Sub-graph Frequency:

$$ISF\left(g'_k(c_i)\right) = \begin{cases} \log_2\left(\dfrac{\sum N(c_j)}{\sum g'_k f(c_j)}\right) & \text{if } \sum g'_k f(c_j) > 0 \\ \log_2\left(2 \times \sum N(c_j)\right) & \text{if } \sum g'_k f(c_j) = 0 \end{cases} \quad \{\forall c_j \in C;\ j \neq i\}$$

$ISF(g'_k(c_i))$ - Measure for inverse frequency of sub-graph g'_k in category Ci.

$N(c_j)$ - Number of graphs in category c_j.

$g'_kf(cj)$ - Number of graphs containing g'_k in category c_j.

And finally we calculate the *CR – Classification Rate*:

$$CR(g'_k(c_i)) = SCF(g'_k(c_i)) \times ISF(g'_k(c_i))$$

$CR(g'_k(c_i))$ - Classification Rate of sub-graph g'_k in category Ci. The interpretation of this measure is how well g'_k explains category Ci. $CR(g'_k(c_i))$ reaches its maximum value when every graph in category Ci contains g'_k and graphs in other categories do not contain it at all.

According to the Smart method, CR_{min} (minimum classification rate) is defined by the user and only sub-graphs with CR value higher than CR_{min} are selected as terms and entered into the vocabulary. The calculation of the Classification Rate for each candidate subgraph is a slightly more complicated and time-consuming procedure in the Smart approach than finding only the subgraph frequency because of the *ISF* (Inverse Sub-graph Frequency) calculation where graphs from other categories are taken into account. Nevertheless, as can be seen from the results of our experiments, in some cases using the Smart representation produces better results in terms of accuracy.

3.5 The Hybrid Smart Approach with Fixed Threshold

In this type of extraction we define a minimal classification rate CR_{min} together with the minimal frequency threshold t_{min}. In order to select a subgraph g'_k as relevant for classification, two conditions should be met:

- $SCF(g'_k(c_i)) > t_{min}$
- $CR(g'_k(c_i)) > CR_{min}$

The first condition was added because, in some cases, when a subgraph is infrequent in some category but even less frequent or non-existent in other categories it can still pass the CR_{min} threshold. This hypothesis is theoretically logical, but in practice it did not provide a significant improvement in classification accuracy. However, introduction of a fixed threshold for additional elimination of non-relevant subgraphs should reduce the computation time. The extraction process is similar to the Smart extraction with one small difference – when Sub-graph Class Frequency *(SCF)* is calculated for a specific term, it is compared to t_{min}. If $SCF < t_{min}$ – the subgraph is dropped, otherwise we proceed with calculating the classification rate *CR*.

3.6 Frequent Sub-graph Extraction Problem

The input of the sub-graph discovery problem is, in our case, a set of labeled, directed graphs and threshold parameters t_{min} and/or CR_{min}. The goal of the frequent sub-graph discovery is to find all connected sub-graphs that satisfy the classification relevancy constraints defined above. Additional property of our graphs is that a labeled vertex is

Table 1. Notations Used in the Algorithm

Notation	Description
G	Set of document graphs
t_{min}	Subgraph frequency threshold
K	Number of edges in the graph
G	Single graph
sg	Single subgraph
sg^k	Subgraph with k edges
F^k	Set of frequent subgraphs with k edges
E^k	Set of extension subgraphs with k edges
C^k	Set of candidate subgraphs with k edges

BFS Subgraph Extraction (G, t_{min})
1: $F^0 \leftarrow$ Detect all frequent 1 node subgraphs (vertexes) in G
2: $k \leftarrow 1$
3: **While** $F^{k-1} \neq \emptyset$ **Do**
4:      **For Each** subgraph $sg^{k-1} \in F^{k-1}$ **Do**
5:            **For Each** graph $g \in G$ **Do**
6:                  **If** $sg^{k-1} \subseteq g$ **Then**
7:                        $E^k \leftarrow$ Detect all possible k edge extensions of sg^{k-1} in g
8:            **For Each** subgraph $sg^k \in E^k$ **Do**
9:                  **If** sg^k already a member of C^k **Then**
10:                      $\{sg^k \in C^k\}.Count++$
11:            **Else**
12:                      $sg^k.Count \leftarrow 1$
13:                      $C^k \leftarrow sg^k$
14:      $F^k \leftarrow \{sg^k$ in $C^k \mid sg^k.Count > t_{min} * |G|\}$
15:      $k++$
16: **Return** $F^1, F^2, ...F^{k-2}$

Algorithm 1. The Naïve Approach to Frequent Subgraph Extraction

unique in each graph. This fact makes our problem much easier than the standard sub-graph discovery case [12] where such restriction does not exist. The most complex task in frequent sub-graph discovery problem is the *sub-graph isomorphism identifi-cation*[2]. It is known as an NP-complete problem when nodes in the graph are not uniquely labeled but in our case it has a polynomial $O(n^2)$ complexity. We use *breadth first search* (BFS) approach and simplify the FSG algorithm given in [12] for sub-graph detection.

---

[2] Means that a graph is isomorphic to a part of another graph.

Our Naïve algorithm for frequent subgraph extraction and its notations are presented in Algorithm 1 and Table 1 respectively. First, all frequent nodes in the input set of graphs are detected and inserted into the frequent subgraph set. At each iteration of the *While* loop (Row 3), we try to extend each frequent subgraph of size k by finding subgraph isomorphism between it and the graphs from the input set and adding outgoing edge to the subgraph (Row 7). Then we construct a set C^k of all possible candidate subgraphs (Rows 8 to 13). We store frequent candidates in the frequent set F^k (Row 14) and return the union of all frequent subgraph sets obtained after each iteration (Row 16).

4 Comparative Evaluation

4.1 Description of Benchmark Data Sets

In order to evaluate the performance of the methods studied in this work, two experiments were performed using two different collections of web documents, called the K-series [2] and the U-series [7]. These data sets were selected for two major reasons. First, all of the original HTML documents are available for these data sets, which is necessary if the web documents are to be represented using the proposed hybrid methodology. Many other document collections only provide a pre-processed vector representation, which is unsuitable for use with these methods. Second, ground truth classifications are provided for each data set, and there are multiple classes (categories) representing easily understandable groupings that relate to the content of the documents. Most other benchmark collections of web document are not labeled or stored with some other task in mind than content-related classification (e.g., question answering or building a predictive model based on user preferences).

The K-series consists of 2,340 documents and 20 categories: *business, health, politics, sports, technology, entertainment, art, cable, culture, film, industry, media, multimedia, music, online, people, review, stage, television,* and *variety*. The last 14 categories are subcategories related to entertainment, while the entertainment category refers to entertainment in general. Experiments on this data set are presented in [24]. These were originally news pages hosted at Yahoo! (www.yahoo.com). The K-series dataset can be downloaded from the following FTP directory: ftp:// ftp.cs.umn.edu/ dept/ users/ boley/ PDDPdata.

The U-series contains 4,167 documents taken from the computer science department of four different universities: Cornell, Texas, Washington, and Wisconsin. Initially, documents were divided into seven different categories: *course, faculty, students, project, staff, department* and *other* that refers to all remaining documents. For the classification experiments, only four of these classes were used: *course, faculty, students,* and *project,* and pool the remaining examples into a single *other* class. This collection can be found and downloaded here - http://www.cs.cmu.edu/~webkb.

The bag-of-words representation was compared with our hybrid techniques using two model-based classifiers: Naïve Bayes and C4.5.

4.2 Preprocessing and Representation

In this section a comparison of Hybrid and bag-of-words representation techniques is presented. Some preprocessing steps were done before representation:

Table 2. Dictionary sizes per collection and N

Series	N				
	20	30	40	50	100
K	6553	7988	9258	10663	16874
U	9313	11814	13911	15594	21463

- All redundant words (stopwords) were removed from every document
- Stemming was done using the Porter stemmer [18].

To construct a dictionary for the bag-of-words representation, N most frequent words were selected from each document. Unique words were inserted in the dictionary. The different values of N which were used in these experiments together with the dictionary sizes obtained can be found in Table 2. Each document was then represented as a vector of Boolean values, one for presence and zero for absence of a dictionary word in the document. As can be understood from Table 2, the longest vector (21,463 words) was obtained using the U-series data set and $N = 100$. After the representation stage, documents were randomly partitioned into a training set and a validation set. The documents in the validation set were classified using the classification model induced from the training set. Since in some cases the accuracy gap between two different cross validation runs with the same dictionary can reach $1.5 - 2\%$, the average of ten runs of a ten-fold cross validation was used as the final accuracy value for each collection and dictionary size.

As for Hybrid techniques, the same N most frequent words in each document were taken for graph construction, that is, exactly the same words in each document were used for both the graph-based and the bag-of-words representations. Subgraphs relevant for classification were then extracted using the Naïve and the Smart approaches. A dictionary containing subgraphs instead of simple words was constructed. Each document was then represented as a vector of Boolean values, one for presence and zero for absence of a dictionary term (subgraph) in the document. Hundreds of experiments were performed, with N being varied together with t_{min} and CR_{min} for Naïve and Smart approaches, respectively. Exactly the same values of N were taken as in the bag-of-words representation. The Smart extraction was also applied with the fixed frequency threshold of $t_{min} = 0.1$ together with CR_{min}. The value of t_{min} was not chosen arbitrarily. The assumption was that subgraphs that appear in less than 10% of the graphs in a given category cannot be predictive features even if they do not appear at all in other categories.

4.3 Comparison of Hybrid and Bag-of-Words Representations Using the C4.5 Classifier

Only the best results for each technique are presented here. Classification results for K and U-series are given in Figure 3 and Figure 4, respectively.

As can be seen from the figures, in all cases Hybrid approaches achieved better classification results than did the regular Vector Space Model (bag-of-words) representation, especially in the U-series dataset where all Hybrid representations showed much better results for all values of N. In the K-series data set case (Figure 3), the bag-of-words representation outperformed the Hybrid Smart and the combined

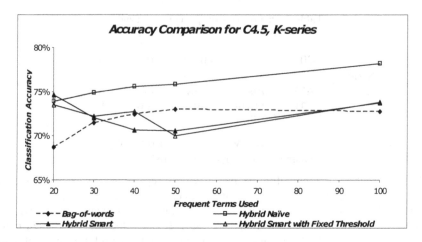

Fig. 3. Comparative results for K-series with C4.5 classifier

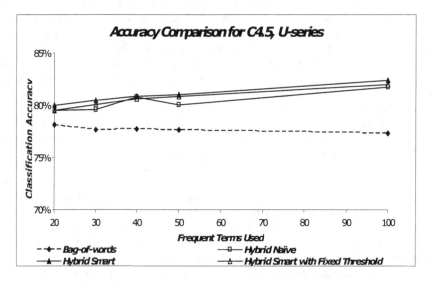

Fig. 4. Comparative results for U-series with C4.5 classifier

approach for some values of N. However, the best classification accuracy was still found to belong to the Hybrid Naïve method. Absolute best accuracy results for each data set are emphasized in bold, and it can easily be seen that they were all produced by the Hybrid techniques.

The times needed to build a classification model and categorize one document in the U-series data set, which was the most time-consuming task in each method, were also measured and compared. The time required for each procedure was measured on the same computer under the same operation conditions: a 2GHz Pentium 4 processor with one Gigabyte of RAM. Execution time was measured for the most accurate cases of each approach. The total time span needed to create a classification model in each case

Table 3. Total time needed to create classification model (C4.5) – U Dataset

Method	Time to Build Graphs (sec)	Time to Build Dictionary (sec)	Time to Construct Vectors (sec)	Time to Build Classification Model (sec)	Total Time Offline (sec)
Hybrid Smart	223.2	2628.56	5.59	4.36	2861.71
Hybrid Naïve	223.2	43.4	31.16	76.59	374.35
Hybrid with Fixed Threshold	223.2	66.35	7.47	6.09	303.11
Bag-of-words	n/a	300.9	133.2	330.32	764.42

is given in Table 3. It is called the offline classification time because the classification model is usually constructed before the start of the categorization stage, and does not change during it[3]. The model preparation stage consists of several steps, so the total offline time is broken down into windows according to the steps which were done:

- *Time to Build Graphs* – time needed to build graphs of 100 nodes from each document in the collection (not relevant for the bag-of-words representation)
- *Time to Build Dictionary* – for the Hybrid techniques this is the time needed to extract relevant subgraphs, while for the bag-of-words it is the time needed to find and combine the 20 (in the highest accuracy case) most frequent words from every document
- *Time to Construct Vectors* – time required for document representation in the vector format
- *Time to Induce Classification Model* – building a model with C4.5

It is noteworthy that the extraction process using the Smart method took much more time than the Naive Hybrid technique. Such a difference occurred because an infrequent subgraph cannot be dropped without calculating its *CR*. Another fact which catches one's attention is that creating a dictionary using Hybrid approaches (subgraphs extraction) with fixed thresholds is faster than creating one for bag-of-words, even for relatively small N (20 in this case). All Hybrid techniques also demonstrated better data representation and model creation time than did bag-of-words representation. This fact can be easily explained by the size of the relevant sub-graph dictionary obtained using Hybrid approaches, which is smaller than the dictionary used with the bag-of-words representation. Finally, the shortest total time is reached with Hybrid Smart using the fixed threshold approach, where the highest accuracy is also reached.

The average time needed to classify one document, or *online classification time*, for current cases is presented in Table 4. This parameter is usually much more important than the model creation time. As can be seen, documents represented by Hybrid techniques are classified much faster. This is due to the relatively small dictionary size and the resultant smaller decision tree.

---

[3] *Incremental* induction of classification models is beyond the scope of this research.

Table 4. Average time to classify one document (C4.5) – U Dataset

Method	Average Time to Classify One Document (sec)
Hybrid Smart	2.88×10^{-4}
Hybrid Naïve	4.56×10^{-4}
Hybrid with Fixed Threshold	3.12×10^{-4}
Bag-of-words	1.68×10^{-3}

4.4 Comparison of Hybrid and Bag-of-Words Representations Using Probabilistic Naïve Bayes Classifier

In the experiments using the Naïve Bayes classifier the same preprocessing stages as in the previous section were performed. Exactly the same input parameter values and document representation were used in the empirical evaluation. Since the document representation stage remained unchanged, the dictionaries used for the C4.5 experiments stayed exactly the same. Accuracy results for available K and U-series collections are presented in Figure 5 and Figure 6 respectively.

As shown in Figure 6, with the Naïve Bayes Classifier (NBC), Hybrid techniques are also better than the bag-of-words representation for the U-series dataset. However, in the K-series collection (see Figure 5), the bag-of-words representation achieved better accuracy results for most values of N. This can be explained by NBC's ability to perform well with a large number of features.

Comparative timing results for classification model construction and single document categorization are given in Table 5 and Table 6, respectively. Model creation took more time with Hybrid Smart extraction than with bag-of-words, but other Hybrid techniques succeeded in performing faster. Computational time reduction in other

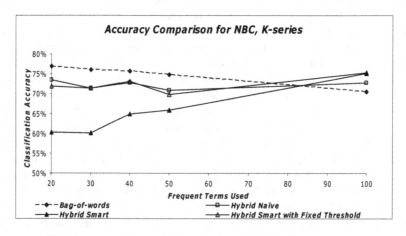

Fig. 5. Comparative results for K-series with Naïve Bayes classifier

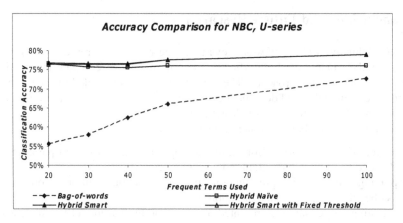

Fig. 6. Comparative results for U-series with Naïve Bayes classifier

Table 5. Total time needed to create classification model (NBC) – U Dataset

Method	Time to Build Graphs (sec)	Time to Build Dictionary (sec)	Time to Construct Vectors (sec)	Time to Build Classification Model (sec)	Total Time Offline (sec)
Hybrid Smart	223.2	2460.87	4.21	0.12	2688.4
Hybrid Naïve	283.64	1.46	0.5	0.08	285.68
Hybrid with Fixed Threshold	223.2	62.3	4.19	0.12	289.81
Bag-of-words	n/a	51.55	286.34	42.46	380.51

Table 6. Average time to classify one document (NBC) – U Dataset

Method	Average Time to Classify One Document (sec)
Hybrid Smart	1.2×10^{-3}
Hybrid Naïve	6.49×10^{-4}
Hybrid with Fixed Threshold	5.7×10^{-4}
Bag-of-words	0.125

than Smart hybrid approaches is explained by the presence of a fixed frequency threshold that helps to remit number of candidate subgraphs in each iteration. A significant improvement is also seen in the average time required to classify one document using all Hybrid approaches vs. bag-of-words which, of course, results from a smaller dictionary size reached by the Hybrid methods.

5   Conclusions and Future Research

The goal of this research study was to evaluate a new document representation model on two popular model-based classification algorithms and to compare this model to existing representation approaches. The hybrid model has succeeded in improving the performance of model-based document classifiers in terms of classification time while preserving nearly the same level of classification accuracy.

As for future research, some issues are still open.

1. Developing some heuristic for finding the optimal values of input parameters N, CR_{min} and t_{min}, which will attain more accurate classification results.
2. Applying the Hybrid representation approaches to other information retrieval tasks beyond document categorization.
3. Evaluating the techniques presented here with additional model-based classifiers and graph-based document representations.

Acknowledgment

This work was partially supported by the National Institute for Systems Test and Productivity at the University of South Florida under the USA Space and Naval Warfare Systems Command Grant No. N00039-01-1-2248.

References

1. Apté, C., Damerau, F.J., Weiss, S.M.: Automated learning of decision rules for text categorization. ACM Transactions on Information Systems 12(3), 233–251 (1994)
2. Boley, D., Gini, M., Gross, R., Han, E.-H., Hastings, K., Karypis, G., Kumar, V., Mobasher, B., Moore, J.: Document Categorization and Query Generation on the World Wide Web Using WebACE. AI Review 13, 365–391 (1999)
3. Bunke, H.: On a relation between graph edit distance and maximum common subgraph. Pattern Recognition Letters 18, 689–694 (1997)
4. Bunke, H.: Error Correcting Graph Matching: On the Influence of the Underlying Cost Function. IEEE Transactions on Pattern Analysis and Machine Intelligence 21(9), 917–922 (1999)
5. Carreira, R., Crato, J.M., Goncalves, D., Jorge, J.A.: Evaluating Adaptive User Profiles for News Classification. In: Proc 9th International Conference on Intelligent User Interface, pp. 206–212 (2004)
6. Cohen, W.W.: Learning to classify English text with ILP methods. In: De Raedt, L. (ed.) Advances in Inductive Logic Programming, pp. 124–143. IOS Press, Amsterdam (1995)
7. Craven, M., DiPasquo, D., Freitag, D., McCallum, A., Mitchell, T., Nigam, K., Slattery, S.: Learning to extract symbolic knowledge from the World Wide Web. In: AAAI 1998. Proceedings of the Fifteenth National Conference on Artificial Intelligence, pp. 509–516 (1998)
8. Fagan, J.: Experiments in Automatic Phrase Indexing for Document Retrieval: A Comparison of Syntactic and Non-Syntactic Methods. PhD thesis, Dept of Computer Science, Cornell University (1987)

9. John, G.H., Langley, P.: Estimating Continuous Distributions in Bayesian Classifiers. In: Proceedings of the Eleventh Conference on Uncertainty in Artificial Intelligence, pp. 338–345. Morgan Kaufmann, San Francisco (1995)
10. Hall, H.: Networked information: dealing with overload. In: Proceedings of Information (Strathclyde Business School, November 1997), Library Association CIG Scotland, Paisley, pp. 37–44 (1997)
11. Koller, D., Sahami, M.: Hierarchically classifying documents using very few words. In: ICML 1997. Proceedings of 14th International Conference on Machine Learning, Nashville, US, pp. 170–178 (1997)
12. Kuramochi, M., Karypis, G.: An Efficient Algorithm for Discovering Frequent Subgraphs. IEEE Transactions on Knowledge and Data Engineering 16(9), 1038–1051 (2004)
13. Lewis, D.D.: An evaluation of phrasal and clustered representations on a text categorization task. In: SIGIR 1992. Proceedings of 15th ACM International Conference on Research and Development in Information Retrieval, pp. 37–50. ACM Press, New York (1992)
14. Maria, N., Silva, M.J.: Theme-based Retrieval of Web news. In: Proc. 23rd Annual International ACM SIGIR Conference on Research and Development in Information Retrieval, pp. 354–356. ACM Press, New York (2000)
15. Markov, A., Last, M.: A Simple, Structure-Sensitive Approach for Web Document Classification. In: Szczepaniak, P.S., Kacprzyk, J., Niewiadomski, A. (eds.) AWIC 2005. LNCS (LNAI), vol. 3528, pp. 293–298. Springer, Heidelberg (2005)
16. Markov, A., Last, M.: Efficient Graph-Based Representation of Web Documents. In: MGTS 2005. Proceedings of the Third International Workshop on Mining Graphs, Trees and Sequences, pp. 52–62 (2005)
17. McCallum, A., Nigam, K.: A Comparison of Event Models for Naive Bayes Text Classification. In: AAAI 1998. Workshop on Learning for Text Categorization, pp. 41–48 (1998)
18. Porter, M.: An algorithm for suffix stripping. Program 14(3), 130–137 (1980)
19. Quinlan, J.R.: C4.5: Programs for Machine Learning. Morgan Kaufmann Publishers Inc., San Francisco (1993)
20. Salton, G., Wong, A., Yang, C.C.: A Vector Space Model for Automatic Indexing. J. Communications of the ACM 18(11), 613–620 (1975)
21. Salton, G., Buckley, C.: Term Weighting Approaches in Automatic Text Retrieval. Technical Report: TR87-881, Cornell University (1988)
22. Salton, G., McGill, M.: Introduction to Modern Information Retrieval. McGraw-Hill, New York (1983)
23. Schenker, A., Bunke, H., Last, M., Kandel, A.: Graph-Theoretic Techniques for Web Content Mining. Series in Machine Perception and Artificial Intelligence, vol. 62. World Scientific, Singapore (2005)
24. Strehl, A., Ghosh, J., Mooney, R.J.: Impact of similarity measures on web-page clustering. In: AAAI 2000. Proc. AAAI Workshop on AI for Web Search, Austin, pp. 58–64. AAAI/MIT Press, Cambridge (2000)
25. Weiss, S.M., Apte, C., Damerau, F.J., Johnson, D.E., Oles, F.J., Goetz, T., Hampp, T.: Maximizing Text-Mining Performance. J. IEEE Intelligent Systems 14(4), 63–69 (1999)

Leveraging Structural Knowledge for Hierarchically-Informed Keyword Weight Propagation in the Web*

Jong Wook Kim and K. Selçuk Candan

Comp. Sci. and Eng. Dept., Arizona State University, Tempe, AZ 85287
{jong,candan}@asu.edu

Abstract. Although web navigation hierarchies, such as *Yahoo.com* and *Open Directory Project*, enable effective browsing, their individual nodes cannot be indexed for search independently. This is because contents of the individual nodes in a hierarchy are related to the contents of their neighbors, ancestors, and descendants in the structure. In this paper, we show that significant improvements in precision can be obtained by leveraging knowledge about the structure of hierarchical web content. In particular, we propose a novel keyword weight propagation technique to properly enrich the data nodes in web hierarchies. Our approach relies on leveraging the context provided by neighbor entries in a given structure. We leverage this information for developing *relative-content* preserving keyword propagation schemes. We compare the results obtained through proposed hierarchically-informed keyword weight (pre-) propagation schemes to existing state-of-the-art score and keyword propagation techniques and show that our approach significantly improves the precision.

1 Introduction

Many web sites and portals, such as *Yahoo.com* [29] and *Open Directory Project* [11], organize their content in terms of navigation hierarchies. In most cases, these navigation hierarchies reflect the semantic relationships (such as generality and specialization) between the data content: nodes closer to the root are more general than those deeper in the navigation hierarchy (e.g., Figure 1). Although these are effective when users are browsing with the aim of locating a specific content, they provide challenges for effective indexing. Since intermediate nodes are there to cluster relevant material together and redirect the users to the lower levels in the hierarchy, the keyword contents of these nodes themselves

---

* This is an extended version of a work originally published at the *WebKDD*'2006 workshop [15]. This work is supported by an NSF ITR Grant, ITR-0326544; "*ILearn: IT-enabled Ubiquitous Access for Educational Opportunities for Blind Individuals*" and an RSA Grant "*Ubiquitous Environment to Facilitate Access to Textbooks and Related Materials for Adults and School Age Children who are Blind or Visually Impaired*".

O. Nasraoui et al. (Eds.): WebKDD 2006, LNAI 4811, pp. 72–91, 2007.

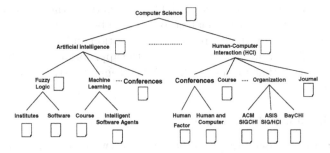

Fig. 1. The Yahoo CS hierarchy: the contents of the individual nodes do not state unambiguously their places in the semantic hierarchy (e.g.,"Conferences")

may not describe *unambiguously* their places in the underlying semantic hierarchy (Figure 1). As a result keyword searches are usually directed to the root of the hierarchy (causing an undesirable topic drift) or to the leaves (which individually may not be enough to satisfy the query). Thus, it is important to identify the appropriate intermediary node/page in the hierarchy to direct the user.

To address this shortcoming, in this paper *we develop a keyword and keyword weight propagation technique*[1], *which exploits the context provided by the relative contents of the neighboring entries to propagate keywords along a structure to enrich the individual nodes for effective searches.* This keyword propagation technique enables keyword based indexing of hierarchical web data.

Given a navigation hierarchy, a naive solution to keyword propagation would be to treat an entire sub-structure (the node and all the descendant nodes) as a single atomic document and use all the corresponding keywords. However, as shown in the evaluation section, this naive solution does not necessarily associate the correct set of keywords with the intermediary nodes as it ignores the fact that a node can inherit content both from its ancestors in the hierarchy and its descendants.

As one moves up in the navigational hierarchy, the nodes get more *generalized* and subsume the content of their descendant nodes. As one moves down in a navigational/semantic hierarchy, the nodes get more *specialized* and focus on specific content. It is important that the keyword content of the nodes reflect this specialization/generalization behavior, while still acting as appropriate discriminators. For instance, in Figure 1, the nodes labeled "Artificial Intelligence" and "Human Computer Interaction" are good discriminators, but their children labeled "Conferences" may not be if the parent labels are not appropriately reflected in the children nodes. A pertinent question is whether the children should inherit keywords from their parents or whether parents should inherit keywords from their children. We propose that a node should inherit content from both its ancestor as well as its descendants in the hierarchy; except that the keyword inheritance should not cause the flattening of the semantic hierarchy. In other

---

[1] In the rest of the paper, we use the terms "keyword weight propagation" and "keyword propagation" interchangeably.

words, while keywords and keywords weights are inherited, the original semantic structure (i.e., generalization/specialization) should be preserved. The challenge of course is to be quantify the degrees of generalization and specialization inherent in the original structure and to determine the appropriate degree of keyword inheritance in a way that preserves the original semantic structure inherent in the hierarchy.

1.1 Contributions of the Paper

Based on the above observations, we propose a keyword-propagation algorithm which leverages the relationships between the entries in a structure. In particular,

- we develop a method for discovering and *quantifying* the inherent generalization/specialization relationship between entries in a navigation hierarchy, based on their relative content (Section 3.1),
- we introduce a novel keyword propagation algorithm, which uses this relationship between a pair of neighboring entries to propagate keywords and keyword weights between them (Section 4.1), and
- we show how to extend this pairwise technique to the indexing of more complex structures (Section 4.2).

We then experimentally evaluate the proposed techniques in Section 5. Results show that the proposed techniques provide upto 15% improvement in precision and capture the domain context better than alternative solutions.

2   Related Work

Various techniques have been proposed to leverage the web structure in identifying document associations, such as the companion and co-citation algorithms proposed by Dean and Henzinger [9]. One approach to organizing web query results based on available web structure is *topic distillation* proposed in [17]. The basic idea in topic-distillation and related work is to use random walks on the structure of the Web to propagate scores between pages in a way to organize topic spaces in terms of smaller sets of hub and authoritative pages. PageRank [4] computes single scores as opposed to hub and authority scores. [20] applied random walk approach to solve the reverse problem of *"finding on which topic a given page is reputable"*. A related problem of *"finding why two given pages are related"* is addressed by [5,6] again using a random walk based score propagation. Unlike these works, instead of basing score propagation on a "random surfer", we aim to understand the semantic structure of the web content and preserve it during keyword weight propagation.

Bharat and Henzinger [3] showed that the hubs and authorities having the high score may deviate from the original topic, which is called topic drift. To prevent the topic drift in multitopic pages, Chakrabarti et al. [7] presented an algorithm which accumulates the hub score along the frontier nodes. These techniques are usually general purpose and are not explicitly designed to leverage the semantically-supported structures of navigation hierarchies.

2.1   Score and Keyword Frequency Propagation

Recently, there has been growing interest in integrating keyword search into graph-structured databases. BANKS [2] tries to find the rooted subtree connecting all the nodes that match a keyword in the query. It proposes a *backward expansion* search that starts from the nodes matching a keyword in the query and finds a common node from which there exist paths to the starting nodes. Kacholia et al. [13] introduces a *bidirectional expansion* search method, where besides backward search, forward search is done from nodes that might be potential root nodes. XRank [12] and ObjectRank [1] propose algorithms, similar to PageRank [4], to compute ranking results for keyword-style database queries. XSEarch [8], a semantic search engine for XML data, relies on extended information retrieval techniques in ranking results.

Unlike the above approaches which propagate scores representing structural properties of the pages, others propagate the term frequency values or (given a query) the relevance score itself. For instance, given a query, [26] propagates the relevance score between web pages connected with hyperlinks. [27,25] show that the term frequency values can be propagated between neighboring pages. Recently, Qin et al. [18] propose a generic relevance propagation framework, which brings together techniques from [26] and [27]. Next, we describe [18] and [27] in more detail:

Keyword Propagation. *Song et al.* [27] propose a keyword weight propagation method. Their propagation algorithm is based on a sitemap, which is created through a URL analysis. Given user query keyword, k, the weight of keyword k in a page p is computed using the following equation:

$$w'_k(p) = (1 + \theta)w_k(p) + \frac{(1 - \theta)}{|Child(p)|} \sum_{p_{child} \in Child(p)} w_k(p_{child}),$$

where $w_k(p)$ is keyword weight in page p before propagation, $w'_k(p)$ is keyword weight in page p after propagation, and $Child(p)$ is the set of children of page p based on the sitemap. Keyword propagation in [27] is done through a one-step iteration.

Qin et al. [18] extend this approach to an iterative algorithm using

$$w_k^{t+1}(p) = \theta w_k^0(p) + \frac{(1 - \theta)}{|Child(p)|} \sum_{p_{child} \in Child(p)} w_k^t(p_{child}),$$

where $w_k^0(p)$ is the original keyword weight in page p and $w_k^{t+1}(p)$ is the keyword weight in page p after $(t + 1) - th$ iterations.

Score Propagation. In the same paper, *Qin et al.* [18] use a similar formulation to propose a score propagation scheme as well. Given a user query, the sitemap tree is exploited to propagate a relevance score for each page:

$$s^{t+1}(p) = \theta s^0(p) + \frac{(1 - \theta)}{|Child(p)|} \sum_{p_{child} \in Child(p)} s^t(p_{child}),$$

where $s^0(p)$ is the initial relevance score of page p, and $s^{t+1}(p)$ is the relevance score of page p after $(t+1) - th$ iterations.

Note that, although *Qin et al.* [18] propose other propagation techniques based on the hyperlink structure, according to their experiments, sitemap-based propagation algorithms outperform the hyperlink-based models. Thus, in Section 5, we will compare our propagation technique to the results obtained through the above two propagation methods on sitemap. The approach we present in this paper is also a term-frequency-propagation technique; however, unlike the above methods, the techniques we introduce explicitly quantify the context provided by entries in the structures in terms of degree of generalization and specialization.

2.2   Measuring the Degree of Generalization/Specialization in a Hierarchy

There have been a number of proposals for measuring semantic similarities between keywords in a taxonomy. These approaches can be classified into two categories: structure-based or information-based methods. [19] proposes that the conceptual distance between two concept-nodes should be defined as the shortest path between two nodes in the taxonomy and that this should satisfy metric distance properties. This approach proved to be very useful in small and specific domains, such as medical semantic nets. However, it ignores that (a) the semantic distance between neighboring nodes are not always equal and that (b) the varying local densities in the taxonomy can have strong impacts on the semantic distance between concept-nodes. To overcome these shortcomings, [22] associate weights to the edges in the hierarchy: the edge weight is affected both by its depth in the hierarchy and the local density in the taxonomy. To capture the effect of the depth, [28] estimates the conceptual distance between two concepts, c_1 and c_2, by counting the number of edges between them, and normalizing this value using the number of edges from the root of the hierarchy to the closest common ancestor of c_1 and c_2.

Note that the above approaches try to measure the semantic relationships in a given concept hierarchy, without the help of any supporting text associated to each node. We, on the other hand, note that pages in navigation hierarchies and portals contain supporting text that can be leveraged for more informed measurement of generalization and specialization. Thus, we next introduce the concept of *relative content* of entries in a navigation structure.

3   Relative Content

As discussed in the introduction, in this paper we develop a *hierarchically-informed* keyword propagation technique which leverages the context inherent in navigation structures. Naturally, to implement a hierarchically-informed propagation, we first have to quantify the semantic relationship between entries in a given structure.

In this paper, we base our approach on the observation that in a navigation hierarchy, the semantic relationships between various entries are usually in the form of *specializations* and *generalization* [14]:

- A specialized entry corresponds to a more focussed (or constrained) concept, while
- a general entry is less constrained.

For instance, in the CS hierarchy shown in Figure 1, "Machine Learning" is more *general* than its child "Intelligent Software Agents", but more *specialized* than its parent "Artificial Intelligence". Thus, discovering the degree of semantic relationship between two neighboring nodes in a structure involves identifying the *specialization* and *generalization* direction and degrees between these two nodes.

In concept (IS-A) hierarchies, the direction of generalization/specialization is usually implied by the parent/child (ancestor/descendant) relationships: an entry closer to the root is more general than a descendant deeper in the hierarchy. However, quantifying *how general* one entry is relative to another one is not trivial. Identifying semantic similarity/dissimilarity between entries in a semantic hierarchy is a well studied problem [21,19,22,16]. Most existing techniques extract these relationships either (a) from the information content of the terms in an ontology (computed over a large corpus) [21,16] or (b) from the structure (eg., density, depth) in the hierarchy itself [19,22]. In this paper, we note that, when we consider hierarchies of text or navigation structures, there is a third and complementary piece of information (i.e., the textual content of the entries themselves) which can be exploited to extract the relationships between entries.

In this section, we discuss how to measure the relative content of a pair of parent/child entries.

3.1   Intuition

Let us consider two entries, A and B, in a navigation hierarchy. Let us further assume that keyword vectors, $\boldsymbol{A}$ and $\boldsymbol{B}$, represent the node contents quantitatively. Depending on which data representation model is used, the keyword weights in these vectors could be TF/IDF values or some other feature importance measures.

One way to think of relative content of these two data entries is in terms of constraints imposed on them by their keyword compositions: the statement that *"entry A is more general than B"* can be interpreted as A being less constrained than B by its keywords.

Example 1. Let us consider two entries, A and B, where A is an ancestor of B in the navigation hierarchy. Let us assume that A has three independent keywords, k_1, k_2 and k_3, and B has only two keywords, k_2 and k_3:

- Since the ancestor, A, is more general than the descendant, B, in the navigation hierarchy, the extra keyword, k_1, must render A less constrained. In a sense, **if** B is interpreted as $k_2 \vee k_3$, **then** A should be interpreted as $k_1 \vee k_2 \vee k_3$ (less constraining than $k_2 \vee k_3$).

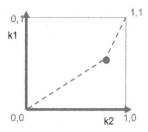

Fig. 2. An entry with two keywords, k_1 and k_2

In order to be able to benefit from this observation in measuring degrees of generality, we need to be able to *quantify* how well a given entry can be interpreted as the disjunction of the corresponding keywords.

3.2   Quantifying the Degree of "OR"ness of a Keyword Vector

Extended boolean model [23] of vector spaces associates well defined disjunctive and conjunctive semantics to a document in order to be able to answer boolean queries on vector data. For example, consider an entry, e, with two keywords k_1 and k_2 in Figure 2. The extended boolean model interprets the point $(1,1)$ as a (hypothetical) entry which contains both k_1 and k_2; i.e, $k_1 \wedge k_2$; in contrast, the origin, $\mathcal{O} = \langle 0, 0 \rangle$ is interpreted as an entry which contains neither k_1 nor k_2; i.e, $\neg k_1 \wedge \neg k_2 = \neg(k_1 \vee k_2)$. Thus, in extended boolean model, the and-ness of this entry can be measured as its similarity to the entry $(1,1)$; i.e., an entry closer to $(1,1)$ better matches the statement $k_1 \wedge k_2$ than an entry further away. The or-ness of an entry, on the other hand, can be measured as its dissimilarity from the entry $(0,0)$; in other words, an entry further away from $(0,0)$ better matches the statement $k_1 \vee k_2$ than an entry closer to $(0,0)$.

We can apply this observation to our example, Example 1, as follows:

Example 2. In Example 1, let the origin point, $\mathcal{O} = \langle 0, 0, 0 \rangle$, correspond to a (hypothetical) entry which does not contain k_1, k_2 and k_3. In other words, $\mathcal{O}$ can be interpreted as $(\neg k_1 \wedge \neg k_2 \wedge \neg k_3)$ or equivalently as $\neg(k_1 \vee k_2 \vee k_3)$. Since $\mathcal{O}$ corresponds to $\neg(k_1 \vee k_2 \vee k_3)$, how much a entry A represents a disjunct can be measured by $|A - \mathcal{O}|$; i.e., the length, $|A|$, of the vector A. In a similar way, $|B|$ (in the same space) measures the degree of or-ness for entry B, consisting of keywords k_2 and k_3.

If A is said to be more general than B, then $|A - \mathcal{O}|$ needs to be larger than $|B - \mathcal{O}|$.

Note that, although this example illustrates the special case where one entry contains three keywords (k_1, k_2, k_3) and the other contains two (k_2, k_3) of these three, it also illustrates the underlying mechanism we will exploit to evaluate the relative degree of generality between a pair of entries.

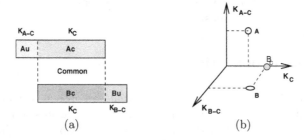

Fig. 3. (a) Visual representation of the keyword contents of two data entries: they share a common keyword base, but they also have their own individual keyword content; (b) vector space representation of A, B, and B_C (B projected onto the common keyword space)

3.3   Evaluating the Relative Generality

As shown in Figure 3(a), given A and B in the navigation hierarchy, we can split each one into two fragments (Figure 3): the two entries will have a common keyword base, K_C[2] (set of keywords). The entries will also have their own individual sets of keywords, K_{A-C} and K_{B-C}. We denote the fragments of the entries, A and B, corresponding to the common base K_C, as A_C and B_C (and corresponding keyword vectors, $\boldsymbol{A_C}$ and $\boldsymbol{B_C}$), respectively. We also denote the un-common fragments of the two entries, as A_U and B_U (and corresponding keyword vectors, $\boldsymbol{A_U}$ and $\boldsymbol{B_U}$[3]). Thus, these two entries (and their fragments) can be represented as vectors in a vector space, where the dimensions correspond to keyword sets K_{A-C}, K_{B-C}, and K_C, as shown in Figure 3(b)[4].

Definition 1 (Relative-Content). Given two entries, A and B, we can define the degree of *generality* of A relative to (the common base of A and) B as

$$R_{AB} = \frac{|\boldsymbol{A}|}{|\boldsymbol{B_C}|} = \frac{|\boldsymbol{A_U} + \boldsymbol{A_C}|}{|\boldsymbol{B_C}|}.$$

This essentially measures whether the additional keywords $\boldsymbol{A_U}$ that do not appear in B render A more general or less general (more specialized) than $\boldsymbol{B_C}$. We also refer this as the relative-content *of A vs. (the common base of A and) B. R_{BA} is similarly defined.*

Note that, when available, additional information-theoretic [21,16] and structural information [19,22] (commonly used for evaluating semantic similarity when nodes do not have text associated with them) can also be used in supporting the degree of generality and the relative-content values computed based

---

[2] C stands for *common*.

[3] U stands for *uncommon*.

[4] Note that, although this figure represents the vectors in a 3-dimensional space for ease of visualization, common and un-common bases are in reality collections of keywords.

on the text associated to the nodes in the navigation hierarchy. In this paper, we do not consider such extensions.

4 Keyword Propagation

Proper keyword-based retrieval of entries that fall into a semantically-based structure requires identification of the appropriate keywords representing each entry in this structure. When the entries themselves do not originally contain all appropriate keywords, then these keywords (and keyword weights) need to be propagated among the entries.

In this section, we first discuss how to propagate keywords (and their weights) between a neighboring pair of entries using the knowledge of the relative-content relationship between them. Note that, for our purposes, it is sufficient to concentrate initially only on parent/child entries as the keyword propagation in the hierarchy will follow edges between individual parent/child pairs. Thus, we can extend the keyword propagation between parent/child pairs to the propagation of keywords in more complex structures as described in Section 4.2.

4.1 Relative-Content Preserving Keyword Propagation Between a Pair of Entries

The main purpose of keyword propagation is to enrich the entries in a navigation hierarchy by keywords inherited from their neighbors. Naturally, such a propagation of keywords should change the composition of the keyword vectors of the entries, yet *after the keyword propagation the semantic hierarchy should not end up being flattened due to the shared keywords*; thus, the original semantic properties (i.e., relative generality) of the pair of entries should be preserved, despite the fact that there is larger keyword sharing between the entries.

Based on this observation, we compute a pairwise propagation degree between two neighboring entries as follows:

Definition 2 (Pairwise Propagation Degree, α). Given two entries, A and B, where a_i is the weight associated with keywords $k_i \in K_A$ and b_j is the weight for $k_j \in K_B$, the degree of pairwise keyword propagation is a parameter, α, such that, after the propagation, we obtain two enriched entries, A' and B', such that

- for all $k_i \in K_{A'}$,
  - if $k_i \in (K_A - K_B)$, then $a_i' = a_i$,
  - if $k_i \in (K_A \cap K_B)$, then $a_i' = a_i + \alpha b_i$, and
  - if $k_i \in (K_B - K_A)$, then $a_i' = \alpha b_i$
- similarly, for all $k_i \in K_{B'}$,
  - if $k_i \in (K_B - K_A)$, then $b_i' = b_i$,
  - if $k_i \in (K_B \cap K_A)$, then $b_i' = b_i + \alpha a_i$, and
  - if $k_i \in (K_A - K_B)$, then $b_i' = \alpha a_i$.

Note that after the keyword propagation, these two entries are located in a common keyword space, K_C, where

$$K_C = K_{A'} = K_{B'} = K_A \cup K_B.$$

In other words, the keyword propagation degree, α, governs how much content these two pairs of entries will exchange. Naturally, if we would like for the keyword propagation to be relative-content preserving, we need to ensure that

$$R_{A'B'} = R_{AB}.$$

Since after enrichment K_C will be equal to $K_{B'}$, we can restate this requirement as

$$R_{AB} = \frac{|A|}{|B_C|} = \frac{|A'|}{|B'|} = R_{A'B'}$$

Thus, we compute the appropriate propagation degree, by solving the resulting equation for α.

When to Apply Propagation? One critical observation is that keyword propagation is applicable only when A and B have at least one uncommon keyword (i.e., $K_A \neq K_B$). To see this, let us also consider the special case where the two document entries A and B have originally the same keyword content (i.e., $K_A = K_B = K_C$ and $K_{A-C} = K_{B-C} = \emptyset$). In this particular case,

$$R_{AB} = \frac{|A|}{|B_C|} = \frac{|A|}{|B|} = \left(\frac{\sum_{k_i \in K_A = K_C} a_i^p}{\sum_{k_i \in K_A = K_C} b_i^p} \right)^{\frac{1}{p}},$$

and

$$R_{A'B'} = \frac{|A'|}{|B'|} = \left(\frac{\sum_{k_i \in K_{A'} = K_C} (a_i + \alpha b_i)^p}{\sum_{k_i \in K_{A'} = K_C} (b_i + \alpha a_i)^p} \right)^{\frac{1}{p}}.$$

If we try to solve for $R_{AB} = R_{A'B'}$, we will get $\alpha = 0$ as a solution. Consequently, keyword propagation is not applicable when two entries, A and B, have the same set of keywords. As discussed in the next section, this provides a stopping condition for the keyword propagation process on more complex structures.

4.2   Keyword Propagation Across a Complex Structure

By propagating keywords between a given pair of entries, we enable both entries to get enriched based on their contexts relative to each other. However, in a more complex structure, considering only pairs of contents is not sufficient. Therefore, the propagation process should not be limited to pairs of entries.

Propagation Adjacency Matrix. Let $\mathcal{H}(N, E)$ denote a navigation hierarchy, where N is the set of nodes (corresponding to the entries in the hierarchy) and E is the set of edges (corresponding to the navigational links) between these pairs of nodes in N.

Definition 3 (Propagation Adjacency Matrix). *Given a navigation hierarchy, $\mathcal{H}(N, E)$, its corresponding propagation adjacency metric, M, is defined as follows:*

- *if there is an edge $e_{ij} \in E$, then both (i, j) and (j, i) of M is equal to α_{ij} (i.e., the pairwise propagation degree between the corresponding nodes);*
- *otherwise, both (i, j) and (j, i) of M are equal to 0.*   ◇

Note that M is symmetric and the diagonal values of M are equal to 0.

Keyword Propagation Operator. Given a navigation hierarchy, $\mathcal{H}(N, E)$, let T be the corresponding term-node (or term-document) matrix, where (t, i) of T is the weight of term k_t in node $n_i \in N$.

Furthermore, let P denote the term propagation matrix, where (t, i) is the propagation weight of term k_t in node n_i being inherited from its neighbors in the adjacency matrix, M. Thus, the keyword propagation matrix, P, can be computed as follows:

Definition 4 (Keyword Propagation Operator). *The keyword propagation operator, $\oplus$, is such that, given a term-node matrix T and a propagation adjacency matrix M, $P = T \oplus M$ is the keyword propagation matrix. Note that, based on the definition of pairwise propagation, the entry (t,i) of P is computed as follows:*

$$P_{t,i} = \sum_h T_{t,h} \times M_{i,h}.$$

Furthermore, since M is symmetric,

$$P_{t,i} = \sum_h T_{t,h} \times M_{h,i}.$$

Thus, we can see that the semantics of the keyword propagation operator is that of matrix multiplication:

$$P = T \oplus M = TM,$$

where TM is the matrix multiplication of T and M.

Thus, the new *enriched* term-node matrix is equal to

$$T' = T + P = T + (T \oplus M) = T + TM = T(I + M) = TM_I$$

where I is the identity matrix. Note that since all diagonal values in M are zero, $M_I = I + M$ is such that all diagonal values are 1 and all non-diagonal entries are those in M.

Keyword Propagation Process. After the application of $\oplus$, each node in the structure has not only its original keywords, but also keywords inherited from its immediate neighbors. Therefore, after the first application of the keyword propagation operator, $T' = TM_I$ is the first-level enrichment (T_1) of T.

Since, during propagation, at least one node inherited keywords from its neighbors, the columns of T_1 have fewer zeros than the columns of T. This process is visualized in Figures 4 (a,b,c) with an example:

1. Initially, the three nodes in the example each have a different keyword set (Figure 4 (a));
2. After the first keyword propagation step, the middle node (which has two neighbors) has all possible keywords, whereas the left- and the right-most nodes did not receive each others' keywords yet (Figure 4(b)).
3. Thus, the process has to be repeated (Figure 4 (c)).
4. After the second iteration, all nodes received all keywords (but with different weights). Since the keyword sets of all the nodes are the same, the pairwise propagation degrees are all 0s, and the keyword propagation process stops.

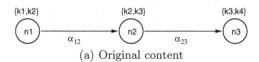

(a) Original content

(b) After the first keyword propagation

(c) After the second keyword propagation

Fig. 4. Keyword propagation across a structure: since the maximum distance between any pair of nodes is two, it takes two propagation cycles to propagate all the keywords across the structure; note that after the last phase, the value of the pairwise keyword propagation degree for all edges is 0, and the process stops

Note that, since at each iteration the keyword composition of the nodes changes, the pairwise keyword propagation degrees may need to be recomputed in a way to preserve the relative generality values.

We can generalize this process as follows: Let d be the diameter (the greatest number of edges between any nodes) in the navigation hierarchy, $\mathcal{H}$. Then, the final enriched term-node matrix is equal to

$$\mathbf{T}_{final} = \mathbf{T}\mathbf{M}_{\mathbf{I}1}\mathbf{M}_{\mathbf{I}2}\mathbf{M}_{\mathbf{I}2}\dots\mathbf{M}_{\mathbf{I}d},$$

where $\mathbf{M}_{\mathbf{I}m}$ is the propagation adjacency matrix computed for the mth iteration. Since, after the dth iteration, the keyword sets of all nodes in the structure are going to be the same, all pairwise keyword propagation degrees are 0. Thus, the process naturally stops after d steps.

5   Experiments

We evaluated the effectiveness of the keyword (weight) propagation technique through a user study. First we describe the experimental setup and then discuss the results.

Table 1. Data set properties

	CS.	Math.	Movie
Average Depth	3.05	3.224	3.514
Maximum Depth	5	5	7
Num. of Categories	107	138	335

Table 2. The relevance weight ($\mathbf{r}$) of labels under three interpretations: Relaxed, Differentiated, and Strict

$\mathbf{r}$	Relaxed	Differentiated	Strict
irrelevant	0	0	0
partially relevant	1	0.5	0
fully relevant	1	1	1

5.1   Setup

Data: We used Yahoo Computer Science, Mathematics, and Movie directories [29]. *Yahoo Directory* has a structure which follows a class-hierarchy. Each page in the Yahoo directory contains not only the description of itself, but also the description of the web sites listed in the page. The characteristics of the data collected from these directories are shown in Table 1.

Ground truth: We used 10 sample keyword queries, with logical operators *AND* and *OR*, which can be answered using the collected data. Given these queries, we established the ground truth by asking 8 users, not involved in the project, to assess the available data relative to the queries. During the ground truth establishment process, assessors were asked to assign them labels: irrelevant, partially-relevant, or relevant. These labels are used to evaluate the relevance ($\mathbf{r}$) under three different interpretations: *relaxed, differentiated,* and *strict* (Table 2). We evaluate the statistical significance of the ground truth on Section 5.6.

Query processing alternatives: The similarity, $sim(n, q)$, between a query q and a data entry, n, is computed using the extended boolean model [23].

In order to verify that keyword propagation algorithm can indeed successfully capture the implicit context in the hierarchical data, we also used alternative context discovery mechanisms, where the hierarchy is split into domains and keywords for the nodes in each domain are merged (keyword weights are averaged) to create a collective *domain* context. In the experiments, we defined the *domain* of a given node n by using two alternative score propagation schemes:

- *whole subtree as the domain:* in this case, the *domain* of a given node n is defined as the sub-tree that contains node n and is rooted at a child of the root. For example, in Figure 1, *domain* of "Fuzzy Logic" is the subtree, whose root is "Artificial Intelligence"; note that entries "Fuzzy Logic" and "Intelligent Software Agents" have the same *domain.*
- *neighborhood as the domain:* node n obtains its domain context from its parent and children.

Given a node n and a query q, we refer to the similarity between a query q and the *domain* of the node n as $sim(domain(n), q)$. In the experiments, given a node n and a query q we computed the corresponding score using the following alternative methods:

- **case** N; *no keyword propagation or other context discovery:* $score(n, q) = sim(n, q)$, i.e., each data node is considered individually without any contextual help.
- **cases** D_t **and** D_n; *no keyword propagation, but context extracted from the domain is used:* in these cases, similarity of the query to $domain(n)$ is included in varying degrees to the basic node-only similarity; i.e,
  $score(n, q) = \beta \times sim(n, q) + \gamma \times sim(domain(n), q)$, where $\beta + \gamma = 1$.
  Note that D_t corresponds to the case where $domain(n)$ is the whole subtree under n and D_n corresponds to the case where the domain of the node is its immediate neighborhood.
- **case** SP; *score propagation based on the sitemap [18]:* in this case, similarity of the query to the node, n, is computed based on iterative score propagation using [18]; i.e.,
  $score^{t+1}(n, q) = \theta sim(n, q) + \frac{(1-\theta)}{Child(n)} \sum_{c \in Child(n)} score^t(c, q)$
- **case** KP; *keyword propagation based on the sitemap [18]:* in this case, similarity of the query to the node, n, is computed based on keyword propagated version of the data node, n_{kp}, using the approach in [18]; i.e.,
  $score(n, q) = sim(n_{kp}, q)$.
- **case** HKP; *hierarchically-informed keyword propagation:* in this case, similarity of the query to the node, n, is computed based on hierarchically-informed keyword propagated version of the data node, n_{hkp}, presented in this paper; i.e.,
  $score(n, q) = sim(n_{hkp}, q)$.
- **cases** $HKP + D_t$ **and** $HKP + D_n$; *hierarchically-informed keyword propagation further augmented with* domain-*provided context:* in these cases, similarity of the query to the node is computed by combining the similarity of the hierarchically-informed keyword propagated version of the data node, n_{hkp}, and the similarity of the domain of the data node:
  $score(n, q) = \beta \times sim(n_{hkp}, q) + \gamma \times sim(domain(n), q)$, where $\beta + \gamma = 1$.

Evaluation measures: Given the ground truth, in order to evaluate various algorithms, we used (a) **P@10** $= \sum_{i=1}^{10} \frac{r_i}{10}$, where r_i is the relevance of the i-th result (weighted according to Table 2) and (b) **paired t-Test**. The *paired*

Table 3. P@10 for N, HKP, SP, and KP

	N	SP [18]		KP [18]		HKP
		$\theta = 0.2$	$\theta = 0.8$	$\theta = 0.2$	$\theta = 0.8$	
Relaxed	0.670	0.693	0.690	0.693	0.717	**0.753**
Differentiated	0.542	0.546	0.552	0.547	0.568	**0.612**
Strict	0.415	0.399	0.415	0.401	0.419	**0.469**

t-Test evaluates the significance of the difference between means of two small independent data sets [24].

5.2 Hierarchically-Informed Keyword Propagation vs. No Propagation

Table 3 shows the impact of hierarchically-informed keyword propagation on the precision. We see that the improvement provided by hierarchically-informed keyword propagation (HKP) over a non-keyword propagation based scheme (N) is around 15% under all three precision measures.

The first row of Table 4 shows the *p-values* computed by comparing HKP and N results using the t-Test. The fact that the p-values are all smaller than the baseline value 0.05 indicates that we can be $\geq$ **95%** certain that HKP functions better than N.

5.3 Hierarchically-Informed Keyword Propagation vs. State-of-the-Art Propagation Techniques

We compare the results obtained through HKS to existing score (SP [18]) and keyword (KP [18]) propagation techniques, which were described in Section 2.1. In the experiments, θ value for KP and SP were varied between 0.2 and 0.8 (Note that $\theta = 1$ corresponds to no propagation case). As can be seen in Table 3, we observed that although both KP and SP can boost precision compared with N, the best results are still obtained when HKP is used. Table 4 shows the *p-values* computed by comparing HKP against KP and SP using the t-Test. The p-values from the t-Test are all smaller than 0.1; that is, we can be $\geq$ **90%** confident that HKP functions better than KP and SP. This implies that the HKP approach shows better search performance than SP and KP on hierarchical web data.

5.4 Hierarchically-Informed Keyword Propagation vs. Non-Propagation-Based Context Representation Schemes

We also evaluated the relative impact of HKP against more traditional non-propagation-based context representation schemes D_t and D_n described in Section 5.1. For these experiments, we varied the β and γ values as shown in Table 5. The results show that, although non-propagation-base context representation

Table 4. The p-values from the t-Test for HKP vs. N, SP, and KP

p-values for		Relaxed	Differentiated	Strict	Statistical Confidence on HKP's superiority
HKP vs. N		0.029	0.031	0.047	95%
HKP vs. SP [18]	$\theta = 0.2$	0.055	0.027	0.020	90%
	$\theta = 0.8$	0.042	0.032	0.040	95%
HKP vs. KP [18]	$\theta = 0.2$	0.021	0.004	0.001	95%
	$\theta = 0.8$	0.085	0.018	0.005	90%

Table 5. HKP provides the best results. Additional domain knowledge does not improve HKP's result.

Relaxed; P@10						
β/γ	1/0	0.8/0.2	0.6/0.4	0.4/0.6	0.2/0.8	0/1
N	0.670	-	-	-	-	-
D_t	-	0.682	0.683	0.717	0.694	NA
D_n	-	0.658	0.672	0.675	0.699	0.706
HKP	**0.753**	-	-	-	-	-
$HKP + D_t$	-	0.752	0.750	0.750	0.733	NA
$HKP + D_n$	-	0.753	0.752	0.736	0.718	0.706

(a) Relaxed P@10

Differentiated; P@10						
β/γ	1/0	0.8/0.2	0.6/0.4	0.4/0.6	0.2/0.8	0/1
N	0.542	-	-	-	-	-
D_t	-	0.539	0.545	0.579	0.558	NA
D_n	-	0.532	0.542	0.547	0.564	0.572
HKP	**0.612**	-	-	-	-	-
$HKP + D_t$	-	0.606	0.607	0.607	0.597	NA
$HKP + D_n$	-	0.611	0.612	0.596	0.584	0.572

(b) Differentiated P@10

Strict; P@10						
β/γ	1/0	0.8/0.2	0.6/0.4	0.4/0.6	0.2/0.8	0/1
N	0.415	-	-	-	-	-
D_t	-	0.396	0.407	0.439	0.422	NA
D_n	-	0.405	0.412	0.419	0.429	0.436
HKP	**0.469**	-	-	-	-	-
$HKP + D_t$	-	0.461	0.464	0.464	0.460	NA
$HKP + D_n$	-	0.469	0.469	0.457	0.449	0.436

(c) Strict P@10

Table 6. Confidence associated with performance (relative to N, no-keyword propagation) evaluated by t-Test

	Differentiated; t-Test					
β/γ	1/0	0.8/0.2	0.6/0.4	0.4/0.6	0.2/0.8	0/1
D_t vs. N	-	worse	55.1%	84.4%	63.5%	NA
D_n vs. N	-	worse	54.0%	65.2%	81.1%	90.5%
HKP vs. N	**96.9%**	-	-	-	-	-
$HKP + D_t$ vs. N	-	96.2%	95.7%	95.7%	90.0%	NA
$HKP + D_n$ vs. N	-	96.7%	96.8%	91.8%	86.5%	90.5%

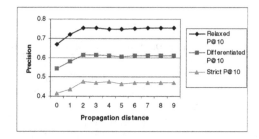

Fig. 5. The effect of propagation distance for HKP: there is a significant improvement at 1- and 2-distances; the performance becomes stable after 3-distance

methods are better than not using anything, the best results are obtained when HKP is used.

(D_t/D_n vs. N). Table 5 shows that domain context (denoted by D_t and D_n) could improve the precision when compared against the case where no context-information is used (denoted by N). With the sub-tree based alternative D_t, the best-result is obtained when the γ value is set to 0.6. Beyond this point, this approach loses the individuality of the nodes and starts under-performing. On the contrary, the best results with the neighborhood-based alternative D_n are obtained when the γ value is set high.

(HKP vs. HKP + D). More importantly, Table 5 shows that the **best** results are obtained when hierarchically-informed keyword propagation is used (HKP) instead of non-propagation-based context representation schemes. Furthermore, providing additional domain information ($HKP + D$) does not improve the results; in fact, such an augment actually hurts the precision provided by HKP. This means that the HKP approach is sufficient (and better than the alternative ways) for capturing data context.

Table 6 verifies these results using the alternative t-Test metric for differentiated interpretation of relevance labels (results for the other interpretations are similar). As this table shows, *HKP alone provides the largest confidence value when compared to N, i.e., no keyword propagation.*

5.5   Effect of the Structural Distance

In order to observe the effects of the distances between the entries in the structure, we artificially varied the maximum allowed propagation distance. Results are reported in Figure 5: the first value in the curves corresponds to 0-distance (no propagation); the next value (1-distance) corresponds to the immediate neighbor propagation, and so on. As can be seen in this figure, we observed significant improvements at both 1-distance and 2-distance propagation cases. Beyond 3-distance the precision becomes stable. This means that HKP improves the precision, but when the entries in the structures are far apart, their impacts on each others are not discernable.

5.6   Statistical Validation of the Ground Truth

Finally, we ran a statistical test to observe the agreement between the assessors used for creating the ground truth for the experiments. For this purpose, we ran an ANOVA test [10], which measures the difference between the means of two or more groups (evaluator label judgments in our case). The ANOVA test provides an F value which needs to be smaller than an $F_{critical}$ value to ensure that none of the observations is significantly different from the others. In our experiments, the F value returned by the ANOVA test was 6.89 against a $F_{critical}$ value of 2.13 for 95% confidence. This implies there was a disagreement among evaluator label judgments. In particular, we identified two evaluators whose judgments were significantly different from the others.

When the ANOVA test was rerun excluding these two evaluators, the new F value was computed as 1.55 against an $F_{critical}$ value of 2.39, highlighting that the evaluator judgments for the remaining core group were in agreement. Therefore, we also computed precision and t-Test evaluations against the judgments of this core group alone. The results for differentiated interpretation of relevance labels are presented in Table 7 and Table 8 (results for the other interpretations are similar). Most importantly, HKP still provides the best (in fact, further improved) results when the judgements provided by the core group is considered.

Table 7. When the judgements provided by the core group is considered, HKP still provides the best precision

		Differentiated; P@10				
β/γ	1/0	0.8/0.2	0.6/0.4	0.4/0.6	0.2/0.8	0/1
N	0.538	-	-	-	-	-
D_t	-	0.547	0.556	0.594	0.571	NA
D_n	-	0.525	0.537	0.544	0.565	0.573
HKP	**0.628**	-	-	-	-	-
$HKP + D_t$	-	0.625	0.624	0.624	0.608	NA
$HKP + D_n$	-	0.625	0.625	0.614	0.601	0.573

Table 8. Confidence associated with performance (relative to N) evaluated by t-Test with the judgements provided by the core group

	Differentiated; t-Test					
β/γ	1/0	0.8/0.2	0.6/0.4	0.4/0.6	0.2/0.8	0/1
D_t vs. N	-	62.0%	71.3%	80.4%	72.1%	NA
D_n vs. N	-	worse	worse	69.9%	74.9%	91.8%
HKP vs. N	**97.3%**	-	-	-	-	-
$HKP + D_t$ vs. N	-	96.4%	96.6%	96.6%	90.5%	NA
$HKP + D_n$ vs. N	-	96.4%	96.4%	93.8%	90.5%	91.8%

6   Conclusion

In structured web content, entries get their context implicitly from their neighbors, ancestors, as well as their descendants. In this paper, we first presented a technique to identify contextual relationships between entries through their relative-contents. We then presented a relative-content preserving keyword propagation technique to enrich entries in a given structure. The novel hierarchically-informed keyword weight propagation technique enables effective keyword based indexing of hierarchical web data. The experiments showed that the hierarchically-informed keyword propagation algorithm described in this paper provides a significant improvement in results and captures the domain context better than alternative solutions.

References

1. Balmin, A., Hristidis, V., Papakonstantinou, Y.: ObjectRank: Authority-based keyword search in databases. In: VLDB 2004 (2004)
2. Bhalotia, G., Hulgeri, A., Nakhe, C., Chakrabarti, S.: Keyword Searching and Browsing in Databases using BANKS. In: ICDE 2002 (2002)
3. Bharat, K., Henzinger, M.: Improved algorithms for topic distillation in a hyperlinked environment. In: SIGIR 1998 (1998)
4. Brin, S., Page, L.: The anatomy of a large scale hypertextual web search engine. In: WWW 1998 (1998)
5. Candan, K.S., Li, W.S.: Using Random Walks for Mining Web Document Associations. In: Terano, T., Chen, A.L.P. (eds.) PAKDD 2000. LNCS, vol. 1805, Springer, Heidelberg (2000)
6. Candan, K.S., Li, W.S.: Reasoning for Web Document Associations and its Applications in Site Map Construction. DKE 43(2), 121–150 (2002)
7. Chakrabarti, S., Josdhi, M., Tawde, V.: Enhanced Topic Distillation using Text, Markup Tag, and Hyperlink. In: SIGIR 2001 (2001)
8. Cohen, S., Mamou, J., Kanza, Y., Sagiv, Y.: XSEarch: A semantic search engine for XML. In: VLDB 2003 (2003)
9. Dean, J., Henzinger, M.: Finding related pages in the World Wide Web. In: WWW 1999 (1999)
10. Faraway, J.: Practical Regression and Anova using R,
   http://www.stat.lsa.umich.edu/~faraway/book

11. Open Directory Project, http://www.dmoz.org/
12. Guo, L., Shao, F., Botev, C., Shanmugasundaram, J.: XRANK: Ranked keyword search over XML documents. In: SIGMOD 2003 (2003)
13. Kacholia, V., Pandit, S., Chakrabarti, S., Sudarshan, S.: Bidirectional Expansion For Keyword Search on Graph Databases. In: VLDB 2005 (2005)
14. Kim, J.W., Candan, K.S., Donderler, M.E.: Topic segmentation of message hierarchies for indexing and navigation support. In: WWW 2005 (2005)
15. Kim, J.W., Candan, K.S.: Keyword Weight Propagation for Indexing Structured Web Content. In: WebKDD 2006 (2006)
16. Lin, D.: An Information-Theoretic Definition of Similarity. In: ICML 1998 (1998)
17. Kleinberg, J.: Authoritative sources in a hyperlinked environment. Journal of the ACM 46, 604–632 (1999)
18. Qin, T., Liu, T., Zhang, X., Chen, Z., Ma, W.: A Study of Relevance Propagation for Web Search. In: SIGIR 2005 (2005)
19. Rada, R., Mili, H., Bicknell, E., Blettner, M.: Development and Application of a Metric on Semantic Nets. In: IEEE Transactions on Systems, Man and Cybernetics, pp. 17–30 (1989)
20. Rafiei, D., Mendelzon, A.: What is this page known for? Computing web page reputations. In: WWW 2000 (2000)
21. Resnik, P.: Semantic Similarity in a Taxonomy: An Information-Based Measure and Its Application to Problems of Ambiguity in Natural Language. Journal of Artificial Intelligence Research 11, 95–130 (1999)
22. Richardson, R., Smeaton, A.F., Murphy, J.: Using WordNet as a Knowledge Base for Measuring Semantic Similarity, Dublin City Univ (1994)
23. Salton, G., Fox, E.A., Wu, H.: Extended Boolean information retrieval. Communications of the ACM 26(11), 1022–1036 (1983)
24. Sanderson, M., Zobel, J.: Information Retrieval System Evaluation: Effort, Sensitivity, and Reliability. In: SIGIR 2005 (2005)
25. Savoy, J., Xue, G., Ma, W.: Ranking Schemes in Hybrid Boolean Systems: A New Approach. Issue 49(3), 223–253 (1997)
26. Shakery, A., Zhai, C.: Relevance Propagation for Topic Distillation UIUC TREC-2003 Web Track Experiments. In: Text REtrieval Conferences (2003)
27. Song, R., Wen, J.R., Shi, S., Xin, G., Liu, T.Y., Qin, T., Zheng, X., Zhang, J., Xue, G., Ma, W.Y.: Microsoft Research Asia at Web Track and Terabyte Track of TREC 2004. In: Text REtrieval Conferences (2004)
28. Wu, Z., Palmer, M.: Verb Semantics and Lexical Selection. In: Annual Meeting of the Association for Computational Linguistics (1994)
29. Yahoo Directory, http://dir.yahoo.com/

How to Define Searching Sessions on Web Search Engines

Bernard J. Jansen[1], Amanda Spink[2], and Vinish Kathuria[3]

[1] College of Information Sciences and Technology, The Pennsylvania State University,
University Park, Pennsylvania, 16802, USA
[2] Faculty of Information Technology, Queensland University of Technology,
Gardens Point Campus, Brisbane QLD 4001 Australia
[3] Search Engineer, Infospace, Inc. – Search & Directory, Bellevue, WA 98004 USA
{jjansen@acm.org,ah.spink@qut.edu.au,
Vinish.Kathuria}@infospace.com

Abstract. In this research, we investigate three techniques for defining user sessions on Web search engines. We analyze 2,465,145 interactions from 534,507 Web searchers. We compare three methods for defining sessions using: 1) Internet Protocol address and cookie; 2) Internet Protocol address, cookie, and a temporal limit on intra-session interactions; and 3) Internet Protocol address, cookie, and query reformulation patterns. Research results shows that defining sessions by query reformulation provides the best measure of session identification, with a nearly 95% accuracy. This method also results in an 82% increase in the number of sessions compared to Internet Protocol address and cookie alone. Regardless of the method, mean session length was fewer than three queries and the mean session duration was less than 30 minutes. Implications are that unique sessions may be a better indicator than the common industry metric of unique visitors for measuring search traffic. Results of this research may lead to tools to better support Web searching.

Keywords: Web sessions, Web queries, query reformulation, Markov states.

1 Introduction

The querying methods and tactics that a user employs to locate relevant information can shed light on the searcher's underlying need. Detecting query reformulations by a Web searcher during a search episode is an important area of research for designing helpful searching systems, recommender systems, personalization, and targeting content to particular users. One can define a search episode on a Web search engine as a temporal series of interactions among a searcher, a Web system, and the content provided by that system within a specific period. During a Web search episode, the user may take several actions including submitting a query, viewing result pages, clicking on uniform resource locators (URLs), viewing Web documents, and returning to the Web search engine for query reformulation. However, it is possible that one searching episode will be composed of one or more sessions.

O. Nasraoui et al. (Eds.): WebKDD 2006, LNAI 4811, pp. 92–109, 2007.

We define a session from a contextual viewpoint as a series of interactions by the user towards addressing a single information need. As such, the session is the critical level of analysis in determining the success or failure of a Web information system. If the user's information need from the session is satisfied, then one can say that the system (or perhaps the user – system team) was successful. Additionally, an understanding of the contextual information need of a session is key to the development of tools to support Web searching, especially for more complex information needs such as health, e-commerce, and exploratory searching.

As such, the session level is a primary level of analysis for much research. Numerous researchers have analyzed Web searching sessions with the goal of using the information about users' activities to improve the performance of Web search engines. Methods explored by these researchers include both qualitative (i.e., the use of human judges to manually analyze query patterns on usually small samples) and nondeterministic algorithms, typically using large amounts of training data to predict sessions boundaries [19, 26].

Several researchers have highlighted the benefit of identifying the user's underlying need or goal. Shneiderman, Byrd and Croft [27] present recommendations for designing Web search engine interfaces that support the searching session strategies of users. Also, Hansen and Shriver [7] examined navigation data using a session-level analysis to cluster search sessions.

Results from such research can aid in the design of effective information searching systems. Efforts relying on session-level data have taken a variety of approaches. CiteSeer [20] utilizes an agent paradigm to recommend computer science and computer science-related articles based on a user profile. CiteSeer (http://citeseer. ist.psu.edu/) offers a variety of searching assistance based on searcher interactions during the session. Jansen and Pooch [12] developed an application for Web search engines that provided targeted searching assistance based on the user interactions during a session. The researchers noted that there are predictable patterns of when searchers seek and implement assistance from the system [9, 10]. These patterns may designate when the searcher is open to assistance from the system, thereby avoiding task interruptions.

Given the ability of searching systems to record interactions, researchers have explored methods to use these records of interactions to improve the system. Using transaction logs, Anick [1] studied the interactive query reformulation support of the AltaVista search engine for searchers. The researcher used a control group of AltaVista searchers given no query feedback and a feedback group offered twelve refinement terms along with the search results. There was no significant difference in searching performance between the two groups. Conversely, Belkin, Cool, Kelly, Lee, Muresan, Tang, and Yuan [3] reported that query expansion assistance from the system may be helpful and improve searching performance.

An obstacle with all of these applications relying on searching data is determining "exactly what is the session" in practical terms. That is, what is the set of interactions by the user that relates to a single information need? With traditional IR or library systems, one could usually distinguish one user from another user based on a logon. In the Web and Internet environment, how to determine a session between a searcher and a Web search engines is an open question. The difficulty related to both technical and contextual issues.

2 Related Studies

The technological difficulty of how to define a search session (or even a single user or searcher) on the Web is due in part to the stateless nature of the client-server relationship of the underlying Internet. Most Web search engines servers have used the Internet Protocol (IP) address of the client machine to identify *unique visitors*. With referral sites, Internet service providers (ISP), dynamic IP addressing, and common user terminals it is not always easy to identify or define a single user session on a Web search engine. Therefore, a single IP address does not always correspond to a single user. However, this approach is commonly used for marketing purposes and Web site traffic reporting (see for example, Nielsen Netranking and iProspect).

The developers of Web search engines have explored other methods of user identification. In reaction to the dynamically allocated IP's situations, Web search engine researchers have moved to the use of cookies, along with IP addresses, for identification of searchers. The use of cookies minimizes the user identification problem somewhat, but with common access computers (i.e., computers at libraries, schools, labs, office shops, and manufacturing floors which many people share) along with spyware, and cookie management software, one computer may not correspond to one searcher. Additionally, a single searcher may engage a search engine with multiple information needs simultaneously or in rapid succession [32, 33] during a single searching episode. To consider these multiple information needs together presents significant problems for recommender systems and personalized online content.

As a result, some search engines also use a temporal boundary along with cookies to help address this problem. The idea is that this temporal boundary helps minimize the common user terminal issue, and it also helps delineate repeat searchers to a Web search engine who have returned but with a new information need. However, this approach does not address the users with multiple information needs during a single searching episode issue. These methods (*IP address; IP and cookie;* and *IP, cookie, and temporal boundary*) all employ a mechanical definition of a session rather than a conceptual or contextual definition that defines a searching session within an information seeking task.

In response to these technical constraints, there has been some research into using the query context to help define the session. However, this is difficult to do given that the user is typically not available or unwilling to provide deep contextual elaboration.

He, Göker and Harper [8] used contextual information from a Reuters transaction log and a version of the Dempster–Shafer theory in an attempt to identify search engine session boundaries. Using transaction log IP codes and query context, the researchers determined the average Web user session duration was about 12 minutes. Jansen and Spink [13] reported a mean session length of about 15 minutes but with a sizeable percentage of sessions being less than 5 minutes.

Continuing this line of study, Özmutlu and Cavdur [23] attempted to duplicate the findings of [8], but the researchers reported that there were issues relating to implementation, algorithm parameters, and fitness function. Özmutlu, Cavdur, Spink and Özmutlu [24] and Özmutlu and Cavdur [23] investigated the use of neural networks to automatically identify topic changes in sessions, reporting high percentages (72% to 97%) of correct identifications of topic shifts and topic continuations. Özmutlu, Cavdur, Spink, and Özmutlu [24] report that neural networks were effective at topic identification, even if the neural network application was trained with data from another search engine transaction log. This line of research involved the use of sophisticated algorithmic approaches or extensive amounts of training data for topic identification. Whether one could obtain comparable results with simpler approaches was not investigated. In addition, these research studies did not contrast the findings of their approaches with other methods of session identification or reformulation classifications.

In this study, we examine three methods of session identification. For real time identification of sessions, one desires the method that is most relatively straightforward but also as accurate as possible. With a method of low computational costs and high accuracy, one could implement such an algorithm for real time identification of sessions in Web searching systems.

In the pursuit of this research goal, we compare the results among these three methods of session identification. We also examine quantitative techniques of identifying query reformulations within sessions and investigate the accuracy of our methods. We compare the results from our dataset to results reported in other research.

3 Research Questions

The research question driving this investigation is: *What are the differences in results when using alterative methods for identification of Web search engines sessions?*

We compare three methods for session identification. The methods we use are (1) *IP address and cookie*; (2) *IP address, cookie, and a temporal cut-off*; and (3) *IP address, cookie, and query context changes*. Although there may be other techniques, these three methods represent the major approaches to session identification. We do not evaluate the sole use of an IP address for session identification, as it is commonly known to be inferior to the use of both IP address and cookie.

In this research, we used data from real traffic submitted by real users to an operational Web search engine, Dogpile.com. We explain our data analysis methods in the following section.

3.1 Research Design

3.1.1 Web Data
We collected search data from Dogpile.com for this research. Dogpile.com (http://www.dogpile.com/) is a meta-search engine, owned by Infospace, Inc. Meta-search engines provide a unique service by presenting the alternate results provided by the various search engines, which have a low rate of overlap [30]. When a searcher submits a query, Dogpile.com simultaneously submits the query to multiple other Web search engines, collects the results from each, removes duplicate results, and aggregates the remaining results into a combined ranked listing using a proprietary algorithm. Dogpile.com integrates the results of the four leading Web search indices (i.e., Ask Jeeves, Google, MSN, and Yahoo!) along with other search engines into its search results listing.

Dogpile has various federated indices or verticals, offering users a variety of content collections to search. Dogpile.com has indexes for searching the *Web*, *Images*, *Audio*, and *Video* content, which searchers can access via tabs off the Dogpile.com interface. Dogpile.com also offers query reformulation assistance with alternate query suggestions listed in an *Are You Looking for?* area of the interface. See Figure 1 for an illustration of the Dogpile.com interface.

3.1.2 Data Collection

For data collection, we recorded searcher – system interactions in a transaction log that represents a portion of the searches executed on Dogpile.com on 6 May 2005. The original general transaction log contained 4,056,374 records, each containing seven fields:

- *User Identification*: a code to identify a particular computer
- *Cookie*: an anonymous cookie automatically assigned by the Dogpile.com server to identify unique users on a particular computer.
- *Time of Day*: measured in hours, minutes, and seconds as recorded by the Dogpile.com server on the date of the interaction.
- *Query Terms*: the terms exactly as entered by the given user.
- *Location*: a code representing the geographic location of the user's computer as denoted by the computer's IP address.
- *Source*: the content collection that the user selects to search (e.g., *Web, Images, Audio, News,* or *Video*), with *Web* being the default.
- *Feedback*: a binary code denoting whether or not the query was generated by the *Are You Looking for?* query reformulation assistance provided by Dogpile.com (see Figure 1).

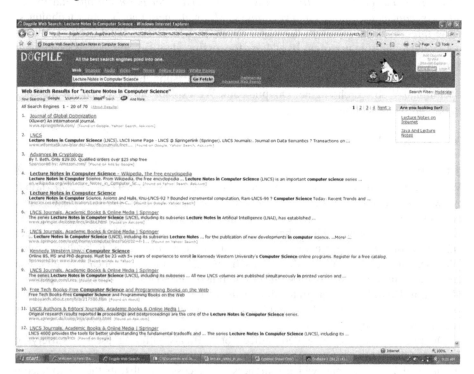

Fig. 1. Dogpile.com Web Search Engine Interface

Then, we imported the original flat ASCII transaction log file of 4,056,374 records into a relational database. We generated a unique identifier for each record. We used four fields (*Time of Day, User Identification, Cookie,* and *Query*) to locate the initial query and then recreate the sequential series of actions from a particular user, determined by *User Identification* and *Cookie*. An analysis of the dataset shows that the interactions of Dogpile.com searchers was generally similar to Web searching on other Web search engines [16], so we expect the results to be generalizeable.

3.1.3 Data Preparation

An accurate definition of terms is important in any research project. The terminology that we use in this research is similar to that used in other Web transaction log studies [c.f., 12, 25] for directed searching on Web search engines.

- *Term:* a series of characters within a query separated by white space or other separator.
- *Query:* string of terms submitted by a searcher in a given instance of interaction with the search engine.

  o *Initial query:* first query submitted in a session by a given user.
  o *Subsequent query:* a query within a session that is not the *initial query*.

However, we deviate from earlier work at the session level. In prior studies [c.f., 2, 25], researchers generally defined a *session* as a *series of queries submitted by a user during one episode of interaction between the user and the Web search engine.* Researchers have added certain operational constraints to this definition including Web pages [7] and temporal cut-offs between query submissions [28]. Each of these constraints, or lack of constraints, affects what is a *session*. We investigate the effect of some of these constraints in this paper.

How to define a session affects other metrics concerning sessions, namely:

o *Session Length*: the number of queries submitted by a searcher during a defined period of interaction with the search engine.
  How one defines the session boundaries is critically important in determining session length.
o *Sessions Duration*: the period from the submission of the *initial query* through the submission of *final query*.

Determining the *initial query* is relatively straightforward. Determining the *final query* again depends on how one defines the session boundary conditions. For example, if one uses only IP address with no other conditions, then the session duration is the period from the *initial query* until the searcher departed the search engine for the last time (i.e., does not return to the search engine) during the period of data collection. If one includes other constraints, then there may be multiple sessions by a single searcher within a given episode. However, all are constrained by the recording ability of the Web server.

There are limits to server-side data collection. Unless one has client-side data, search engine logs can only measure the total user time on the search engine, defined as the time spent viewing the first and subsequent result lists and documents, except the final Web document regardless of any other constraints on the session. This final viewing time is not available since the search engine servers record the time stamp. Naturally, the time between visits from the Web document to the server may not have been entirely spent viewing the Web document or interacting with the search engine.

Conceptually, we are examining only the directed searching sessions, such as on Web search engines or searching on individual Websites. This view of directed search on the Web certainly ignores browsing for information, which one could also include within the session. Bodoff [5] defines b*rowsing* as "actively looking through information (active) or keeping one's eyes open for information (passive), without a particular problem to solve or question to answer (unfocused need)" [p. 70]. Bodoff [5] also provides a nice review of browsing definitions within certain contents and contrasts browsing with directed search, such as that on a Web search engine. However, our focus in this research is on directed searching.

3.2 Data Analysis

3.2.1 Session Analysis Using Multiple Methods
Referring to our research question (*What are the differences in results when using alterative methods for identification of Web search engines sessions?*), we investigated defining sessions using three approaches.

Method 1: IP and Cookie

For the first method of session identification, we defined the session as the period from the first interaction by the searcher with Dogpile.com thorough the last interaction as recorded in the transaction log. We used the searcher's IP address and the browser cookie to determine the *initial query* and all *subsequent queries* to establish *session length*. The *session duration* was the period from the time of the *initial query* to time of the last interaction with the search engine. A change in either IP address or cookie always identified a new session. The algorithm for method 1 is shown in Algorithm 1.

Algorithm 1. Method for Identifying sessions using IP and cookies

```
Algorithm: IP and Cookie Session Identification
Assumptions:
1. Null queries and page request queries are removed.
2. Transaction log is sorted by IP address, cookie, and
time (ascending order by time).
Input: Record R_i with IP address (IP_i) and cookie (K_i), and
record R_{i+1} with IP address (IP_{i+1}) and cookie (K_{i+1}).
Variables: S_x = count of sessions

Output: Session Identification, S_x
begin
Move to R_i

Store values for IP_i, and K_i,

S_x = 1
```

```
While not end of file
   Move to R_{i+1}

   If (IP_i = IP_{i+1} and K_i, = K_{i+1}) then S_x

   Elseif
   S_x = S_x + 1

(R_{i+1} now becomes R_i)

Store values for R_{i+1} as IP_i, and K_i
end loop
end
```

Method 2: IP, Cookie, and Temporal Cut-off

For the second method to session identification, we again used the searcher's IP address and the browser cookie to determine the *initial query* and *subsequent queries*. However, in this method, we used a 30-minute period between interactions as session boundary. For example, if a searcher submitted two queries within a 30 minute period, this searching episode would be one counted as one session. However, if a searcher submitted two queries and the interaction period between each query was longer than 30 minutes, this episode would be counted as two sessions.

For this method, we selected the 30-minute period based on the industry standard view of a session (e.g., see OneClick.com and Nielsen Netranking). This 30-minute norm is most likely based on Catledge and Pitkow's reporting that the typical Web session duration was 25.5 minutes on average [6], although this session metric included browsing activities. However, other temporal metrics have been used. Silverstein, Henzinger, Marais and Moricz [28] assigned a temporal cut-off of 5 minutes between interactions as the maximum session duration. Montgomery and Faloutsos [22] used a 125 minute session period, stating that various temporal cut-offs did not substantially affect results. Additionally, Jansen and Spink [13] and He, Göker, and Harper [8] report that the average search engine is about 15 minute based on IP address alone. The approach for method 2 is shown in Algorithm 2.

Algorithm 2. Method for Identifying sessions using IP, cookies, and duration

```
Algorithm: IP, Cookie, and Time Identification
Assumptions:
1. Null queries and page request queries are removed.
2. Transaction log is sorted by IP address, cookie, and
time (ascending order by time).
Input: Record R_i with IP address (IP_i), cookie (K_i), and
time T_i, and record R_{i+1} with IP address (IP_i), cookie (K_i),
and time T_i.

Variables:
D = serial time for 30 minutes
```

S_x = count of sessions

Output: Search pattern, *SP*

begin
Move to R_i

Store values for IP_i, K_i, *and* T_i

S_x = 1

While not end of file
    Move to R_{i+1}*If* $(IP_i = IP_{i+1}$ *and* K_i, $= K_{i+1}$ *and* $T_{i+1} < T_i + D)$
then S_x

    Elseif

    $S_x = S_x + 1$

$(R_{i+1}$ *now becomes* $R_i)$

Store values for R_{i+1} *as* IP_i,, K_i *and* T_i
end loop
end

Method 3: IP, Cookie, and Content Change

For the third approach for session identification, we used a contextual method to identify sessions. We once again used the searcher's IP address and the browser cookie to determine the *initial query* and *subsequent queries*. However, instead of using a temporal cut-off, we used changes in the content of the user queries.

In this method, we assigned each query into a mutually exclusive group based on an IP address, cookie, query content, use of the feedback feature, and query length. The classifications are:

- *Assistance:* the current query was generated by the searcher's selection of an *Are You Looking For?* query.
- *Content Change*: the current query is identical but executed on another content collection.
- *Generalization:* the current query is on the same topic as the searcher's previous query, but the searcher is now seeking more general information.
- *New:* the query is on a new topic.
- *Reformulation:* the current query is on the same topic as the searcher's previous query and both queries contain common terms.
- *Specialization*: the current query is on the same topic as the searcher's previous query, but the searcher is now seeking more specific information.

For this method, the *initial query* (Q_i) from a unique IP address and cookie always identified a new session. In addition, if a *subsequent query* (Q_{i+1}) by a searcher contained no terms in common with the previous query (Q_i), we also deemed this the start of a new session. Naturally, from an information need perspective, these sessions may be related at some level of abstraction. However, with no terms in common, one can also make the case that the information state of the of the user changed, either based on the results from the Web search engine or from other sources [4]. In addition, from a system perspective, two queries with no terms in common represent different executions to the inverted file index and content collection.

To identify the query reformulations, we classified each query using an application that evaluated each record in the database. Building from He, Göker, and Harper [8], the algorithm for the application is shown in Algorithm 3.

Algorithm 3. Method for Identifying Sessions using IP, cookie, and Query Reformulations

```
Algorithm: Search Pattern Identification
Assumptions:
1. Null queries and page request queries are removed.
2. Transaction log is sorted by IP address, cookie, and
time (ascending order by time).
Input: Record Rᵢ with IP address (IPᵢ), cookies (Kᵢ), query
Qᵢ, feedback Fᵢ, and query QLᵢ; and record Rᵢ₊₁ with IP
address (IPᵢ₊₁), cookies (Kᵢ₊₁), query Qᵢ₊₁, feedback Fᵢ₊₁, and
query QLᵢ₊₁.
Variables:
B = {t|t ∈ Qᵢ ∧ t ∈ Qᵢ₊₁} // terms in common
    C = {t|t ∈ Qᵢ ∧ t ∉ Qᵢ₊₁} // terms that appear in Qᵢ
only
    D = {t|t ∉ Qᵢ ∧ t ∈ Qᵢ₊₁} // terms that appear in Qᵢ₊₁
only
    E = {1 if QLᵢ = QLᵢ₊₁} // queries QLᵢ and QLᵢ₊₁ are the
same length; default is 0.
    G = {1 if QLᵢ > QLᵢ₊₁} // query QLᵢ has more terms
than QLᵢ₊₁; default is 0.
    H = {1 if QLᵢ < QLᵢ₊₁} // query QLᵢ has less terms
than QLᵢ₊₁; default is 0.

Output: Search pattern, SP
begin

Move to Rᵢ

Store values for IPᵢ, Kᵢ, Qᵢ, Fi, and QLᵢ

SP = New //default value for first Rᵢ in record set

While not end of file
Move to Rᵢ₊₁
If (IPᵢ ≠ IPᵢ₊₁ and Kᵢ, ≠ Kᵢ₊₁) then SP = New
Elseif
    Calculate values for B, C, D, F, G, and H
    If Fᵢ₊₁ = 1 then SP = Assistance
```

```
Elseif (B ≠ ∅ , C ≠ ∅ , D = ∅ , E = 0 , G = 1 , H = 0)
then SP = Generalization
Elseif (B ≠∅ , C ≠ ∅ , D ≠ ∅ , E = 0 , G = 1 , H = 0)
then SP = Generalization with Reformulation
Elseif (B ≠ ∅ , C = ∅ , D ≠ ∅ , E =0 , G =0 , H=1) then
SP = Specialization
Elseif (B ≠ ∅ , C ≠ ∅ , D ≠ ∅ , E =0 , G =0 , H=1) then
SP = Specialization with Reformulation
Elseif (B ≠ ∅ , C ≠ ∅ , D ≠ ∅ , E =1 , G = 0 , H = 0)
then SP = Reformulation
Elseif (B ≠ ∅ , C = ∅ , D = ∅ , E =1 , G = 0 , H = 0)
then SP = Content Change
Elseif SP = New
```

$(R_{i+1}$ now becomes $R_i)$

```
Store values for R_{i+1} as IP_i, K_i, Q_i ,F_i, and QL_i
end loop

Move to R_i
S_x = 0

While not end of file

    If SP = New Then (S_x = S_x + 1)

end loop
end
```

4   Results

We now discuss our results, relating to our research question, focusing on both session length and session duration.

4.1   Session Lengths

We begin by examining differences in session lengths, displayed in Table 1.

Focusing on the first algorithm, method 1 is the approach used to define a session in many Web searching studies [29]. Table 1 shows that more than 79% of the sessions identified using method 1 were three or fewer queries. By means of method 1, the mean session length was 2.85 queries with a standard deviation of 4.43 queries. The maximum session length was 99 and the minimum was 1 query. This finding is similar to other analyses of Web search engines trends. For example, Spink and Jansen [31] reported short sessions during Web searching sessions. Jansen and Spink [14], in their analysis of European searching, noted a similar inclination for short sessions as measured by number of queries submitted. However, AltaVista users conducted slightly longer sessions [17]. Koshman, et al., [18] found that one in five Vivisimo users entered only two queries during their session. Koshman, et al. [18] used IP and cookie on given days to define sessions.

Moving to the next approach, method 2 has been used by various researchers [c.f., 21, 22, 25, 28], although most employed various time limits, ranging from 5 to 120 minutes. Using method 2, 97% of the sessions were three or fewer queries, which is an 18 %-point increase over method 1. The mean session length was 2.31 queries (15.4% decrease) with a standard deviation of 3.18 queries. The maximum session length was 99 and the minimum was 1 query, which is no change from method 1.

With these method, the results parallel more directly the percentage reported by Silverstein, Henzinger, Marais and Moricz [28] that 95% of queries were three queries or fewer using a 5 minute limit between query submissions. Montgomery and Faloutsos [22] defined a session as less than 120 minutes of inactivity between viewings, although they dealt primarily with browsing activity rather than searching. The researchers report that they tried several cutoff values, but the choice did not substantially alter the findings [21]. Catledge and Pitkow [6] report that mean between each user interface events was 9.3 minutes, and they used a session boundaries of 25.5 minutes between events, although it is unclear where this temporal boundary came from. Catledge and Pitkow [6] also include browsing activities in their session activities.

With method 3, we see from Table 1 that 93% of the sessions were three or fewer queries. Using method 3 to denote a session, the mean session length was 2.31 queries with a standard deviation of 1.56 queries. The maximum session length was 57 and the minimum was 1 query. Note that the mean session length was the same as for method 2, although the standard deviation was about half. Generally, it appears that

Table 1. Comparing session lengths

Session Length	Method 1: IP and Cookie		Method 2: IP, Cookie, and 30 min. Time Limit		Method 3: IP, Cookie, and Query Content	
	Occurrences	%	Occurrences	%	Occurrences	%
1	288,231	53.92%	533,950	81.15%	691,672	71.64%
2	88,875	16.63%	81,224	12.34%	153,056	15.85%
3	47,664	8.92%	24,840	3.78%	58,537	6.06%
4	29,345	5.49%	9,219	1.40%	27,134	2.81%
5	19,655	3.68%	3,822	0.58%	14,168	1.47%
6	13,325	2.49%	1,755	0.27%	7,745	0.80%
7	9,549	1.79%	944	0.14%	4,430	0.46%
8	7,169	1.34%	622	0.09%	2,791	0.29%
9	5,497	1.03%	442	0.07%	1,769	0.18%
10	4,130	0.77%	331	0.05%	1,193	0.12%
> 10	21,067	3.94%	871	0.13%	2,944	0.30%
	534,507	100%	658,020	100%	965,439	100%

method 3 provides a more granular definition of the session based on the reduced variance in the number of queries per session. Using 534,507 sessions as the base, method 2 resulted in a 23% increase in the number of sessions, and method 3 resulted an 82% increase in sessions.

Do these methods result in different classifications of sessions? We investigated whether these three methods produced significantly different results by performing a chi square test. The chi-square is a non-parametric test of statistical significance. The chi-square test tells us whether or not samples are different enough in some characteristic from which we can generalize that the populations are also different.

A chi-square goodness of fit shows that the three methods are statistically different, ($\chi^2(10)$ = 29.73, p<0.01; critical value of χ^2 = 23.209). So, the methods are significantly dissimilar in their classification of sessions by number of queries.

4.2 Session Durations

The analysis presented above focused on session length (i.e., number of queries in a session). What is the effect of these methods on session duration? Examining session durations, we see in Table 2 that method 1 shows a large percentage of very short session durations.

Table 2. Comparing session durations

Session Duration	Method 1: IP and Cookie		Method 2: IP, Cookie, and 30 min. Time Limit		Method 3: IP, Cookie, and Query Content	
	Occurrences	%	Occurrences	%	Occurrences	%
< 1 minute	302,653	56.62%	372,983	56.68%	794,765	82.32%
1 to < 5 minutes	83,236	15.57%	93,251	14.17%	86,358	8.94%
5 to < 10 minutes	36,347	6.80%	55,956	8.50%	28,044	2.90%
10 to < 15 minutes	19,806	3.71%	36,020	5.47%	12,277	1.27%
15 to < 30 minutes	27,210	5.09%	61,767	9.39%	13,752	1.42%
30 to < 60 minutes	18,441	3.45%	30,790	4.68%	12,628	1.31%
60 to < 120 minutes	14,236	2.66%	6,615	1.01%	7,524	0.78%
120 to < 180 minutes	8,262	1.55%	506	0.08%	3,320	0.34%
180 to < 240 minutes	5,901	1.10%	76	0.01%	1,919	0.20%
> 240 minutes	18,415	3.45%	56	0.01%	4,852	0.50%
	534,507	100%	658,020	100%	965,439	100%

For method 1, the mean session duration was 26 minutes and 32 seconds, with a standard deviation of 1 hour, 36 minutes and 25 seconds. The maximum session was just under 24 hours (23:57:51), and the minimum session was 0 (i.e., the user submitted one query and performed no other search activity on the search engine during the session). This is more than twice that reported by He et al [8], who reported a session duration of 12 minutes.

With method 2, the absolute numbers have increased, but the percentages of very short session durations remains relatively stable. However, the mean session duration was 6 minutes and 36 seconds, with a standard deviation of 16 minutes and 5 seconds. This is closer to the large number of sessions at approximately 5 minutes reported by Jansen and Spink [13]. The maximum session was just under 24 hours (23:57:24).

Just as with method 1, the maximum session length using method 2 is cause for concern, as it seems highly unlikely that a single searcher would spend 24 hours submitting queries to a search engine. More than likely, these methods are inadvertently combining sessions or the database still contains agent submissions.

Examining method 3, the percentages of very short session durations again remains relatively stable. The mean session duration was 5 minutes and 15 seconds, with a standard deviation of 39 minutes and 22 seconds. The maximum session duration was again just under 24 hours (23:41:53).

In comparing the mean session durations, the mean using method 1 is 333% greater than the mean session duration using method 2 and 420% greater than the mean session duration using method 3. This outcome is in contrast to that reported by [22] where changes in temporal cut-offs for the session boundaries did not substantially alter results.

5 Discussion

In this research, we explored three alternative methods for detection of session boundaries using 2,465,145 interactions from 534,507 users of Dogpile.com recorded on 6 May 2005. We compared three methods of session identification (1) *using IP address and cookie*, (2) *IP address, cookie, and a temporal limit on intra-session interactions*, and (3) *IP address, cookie, and query reformulation patterns*.

From our research, the results show that defining sessions by query content as outline in method 3 provides the best session identification with an extremely high level of granularity when compared to method 1. Comparatively, method 1 appears to artificially extend both session length and duration. Method 2 appears to shorten artificially session length and duration. By relying on IP address and cookie as a basis, plus content changes between queries, method 3 provides the best contextual identification of Web sessions within a user episode on a Web search engine.

Overall, method 3, using IP address, cookie, and query content changes, appears to provide the most detailed method for session identification with both session length and session duration. Since the method does not rely on probability methods, it can be calculated real time with near total accuracy of new session identification. Using this content approach, Web search systems can develop automated assistance interfaces, such as reported in [11] that provide session level searching assistance to Web engine users.

Table 3. Query reformulation

Search Patterns	Occurrence	%	Occurrence (excluding *New*)	% (excluding *New*)
New	964,780	63.34%	-	-
Reformulation	126,901	8.33%	126,901	22.73%
Assistance	124,195	8.15%	124,195	22.25%
Specialization	90,893	5.97%	90,893	16.28%
Content change	65,949	4.33%	65,949	11.81%
Specialization with reformulation	55,531	3.65%	55,531	9.95%
Generalization with reformulation	54,637	3.59%	54,637	9.78%
Generalization	40,186	2.64%	40,186	7.20%
	1,523,072	100.00%	558,292	100.00%

There are several possible avenues to explore in this regard. As an example, Table 3 presents the query modifications executed by searchers during their searching episodes as identified by the algorithm used in method 3. We see from Table 3 that more than 8% of the query modifications were for *Reformulation*, with another approximately 8% of query modifications resulting from system *Assistance*. If we exclude the *New* queries, *Reformulation* and *Assistance* account for nearly 45% of all query modifications. This finding would seem to indicate that a substantial portion of searchers go through a process of defining their information need by exploring various terms and system feedback to modify the query as an expression of their information need. Another 16% of query modifications are *Specialization*, supporting prior reports that precision is a primary concern for Web searchers [15]. With this tighter view of a session, Web search engines can more effective personalize for searching assistance, content, or online advertising.

Table 4. Classification of 551 Queries

Reformulation	299	54.3%
Specialization	76	13.8%
Parallel	63	11.4%
Generalization	34	6.2%
Specialization with reformulation	34	6.2%
Parallel with Reformulation	22	4.0%
Related	12	2.2%
Generalization with reformulation	6	1.1%
Hierarchical	5	0.9%
	551	100.0%

Certainly though, any improvements in Web search engines is based on the accuracy of the session classification. In order to evaluate the session classification algorithm, we manually classified 10,000 queries that our algorithm in method 3 labeled as the start of a new session. Using the preceding and subsequent queries, we determined if the query actually was the start of a new session. Based on our analysis, 94.5 percent (9,449) were correctly identified as the start of a new session. However, 5.5 percent (551) were incorrectly identified as the start of a new session. Instead of beginning new sessions, these queries were session continuations.

In order to shed light on the misclassifications, we investigated the 551 misclassifications and identified what transition was actually occurring. We report the results of our analysis in Table 4.

We define the classifications as:

- *Generalization:* the current query is on the same topic as the searcher's previous query, but the searcher is now seeking more general information.
- *Hierarchical:* the current query is on the same topic as the as the searcher's previous query, but the searcher is looking for a subject related to the previous topic by some hierarchy (i.e., was searching for a musical artist and is now looking for a song by that artist).
- *Parallel:* the current query is on the same topic as the as the searcher's previous query, but the searcher is looking for other related information (i.e., another song by the same artist).
- *Reformulation:* the current query is on the same topic as the searcher's previous query, but the searcher reformulated the query in some manner (i.e., usually correcting a misspelling or using a synonym).
- *Specialization:* the current query is on the same topic as the searcher's previous query, but the searcher is now seeking more specific information.

As shown in Table 4, more than 54 percent of the "new session" misclassifications were actually *Reformulation*, where the searcher has reformulated the query but on the same topic. *Specialization* was the next most common occurrence. *Parallel* (i.e., the query was on a similar topic) occurred approximately 11 percent.

This research has important results for the design of future Web searching systems. The detection of Web searching sessions is a critical area of research for developing more supportive searching systems, especially in the more complex searching environments of exploratory searching and multitasking. The method presented in this research relies on the content of searchers' queries, along with other data collected by the search engine, to identify searching sessions. The method is advantageous for real-time system implementation.

6 Conclusion

In future research, these algorithms may be used as models to facilitate cross-system investigations. An attempt to standardize session detection would also enhance comparative transaction log analyses. We are currently conducting qualitative analysis of Dogpile users' query reformulation that we will compare with the results reported in this paper. Also, several searcher – system interactions can be recorded by the Web search engine server. However, there are other actions, such as Back, Forward, Bookmark, Scrolling, among others, that occur on the client-side computer.

The server does not record these actions. We are investigating the development of server-client tools that can monitor the entire set of searcher actions during a session.

Acknowledgments. We thank Infospace, Inc. for providing the Web search engine transaction log data without which we could not have conducted this research. We encourage other search engine companies to explore ways to collaborate with the academic research community. We also thank Ms. Danielle Booth for coding the algorithm presented in this manuscript. Portions of this research funded by the U.S. Department of the Air Force, FA9550-60-10328.

References

[1] Anick, P.: Using Terminological Feedback for Web Search Refinement - a Log-Based Study. In: Twenty-Sixth Annual International ACM SIGIR Conference on Research and Development in Information Retrieval, Toronto, Canada, pp. 88–95. ACM, New York (2003)

[2] Beitzel, S.M., Jensen, E.C., Chowdhury, A., Grossman, D., Frieder, O.: Hourly Analysis of a Very Large Topically Categorized Web Query Log. In: 27th annual international conference on Research and development in information retrieval, Sheffield, U.K., pp. 321–328 (2004)

[3] Belkin, N., Cool, C., Kelly, D., Lee, H.-J., Muresan, G., Tang, M.-C., Yuan, X.-J.: Query Length in Interactive Information Retrieval. In: 26th Annual international ACM Conference on Research and Development in Information Retrieval, Toronto, Canada, pp. 205–212. ACM Press, New York (2003)

[4] Belkin, N., Oddy, R., Brooks, H.: Ask for Information Retrieval, Parts 1 & 2. Journal of Documentation 38, 61–7, 145-164 (1982)

[5] Bodoff, D.: Relevance for Browsing, Relevance for Searching. Journal of the American Society of Information Science and Technology 57, 69–86 (2006)

[6] Catledge, L.D., Pitkow, J.E.: Characterizing Browsing Strategies in the World Wide Web. Computer Network and ISDN Systems 27, 1065–1073 (1995)

[7] Hansen, M.H., Shriver, E.: Using Navigation Data to Improve Ir Functions in the Context of Web Search. In: Tenth International Conference on Information and Knowledge Management, Atlanta, Georgia, USA, pp. 135–142 (2001)

[8] He, D., Göker, A., Harper, D.J.: Combining Evidence for Automatic Web Session Identification. Information Processing & Management 38, 727–742 (2002)

[9] Jansen, B.J.: Seeking and Implementing Automated Assistance During the Search Process. Information Processing & Management 41, 909–928 (2005)

[10] Jansen, B.J.: Using Temporal Patterns of Interactions to Design Effective Automated Searching Assistance Systems. Communications of the ACM 49, 72–74 (2006)

[11] Jansen, B.J., McNeese, M.D.: Evaluating the Effectiveness of and Patterns of Interactions with Automated Searching Assistance. Journal of the American Society for Information Science and Technology 56, 1480–1503 (2005)

[12] Jansen, B.J., Pooch, U.: Web User Studies: A Review and Framework for Future Work. Journal of the American Society of Information Science and Technology 52, 235–246 (2001)

[13] Jansen, B.J., Spink, A.: An Analysis of Web Information Seeking and Use: Documents Retrieved Versus Documents Viewed. In: 4th International Conference on Internet Computing, Las Vegas, Nevada, pp. 65–69 (2003)

[14] Jansen, B.J., Spink, A.: An Analysis of Web Searching by European Alltheweb. Information Processing & Management 41, 361–381 (2005)

[15] Jansen, B.J., Spink, A.: How Are We Searching the World Wide Web? A Comparison of Nine Search Engine Transaction Logs. Information Processing & Management 42, 248–263 (2005)

[16] Jansen, B.J., Spink, A., Blakely, C., Koshman, S.: Web Searcher Interaction with the Dogpile. Com Meta-Search Engine. Journal of the American Society for Information Science and Technology (forthcoming)

[17] Jansen, B.J., Spink, A., Pedersen, J.: Trend Analysis of Altavista Web Searching. Journal of the American Society for Information Science and Technology 56, 559–570 (2005)

[18] [18] Koshman, S., Spink, A., Jansen, B.J., Park, M., Field, C.: Web Searching on the Vivisimo Search Engine. Journal of the American Society of Information Science and Technology (forthcoming)

[19] Lau, T., Horvitz, E.: Patterns of Search: Analyzing and Modeling Web Query Refinement. In: 7th International Conference on User Modeling, Banff, Canada, pp. 119–128 (1999)

[20] Lawrence, S., Giles, C.L., Bollacker, K.: Digital Libraries and Autonomous Citation Indexing. IEEE Computer 32, 67–71 (1999)

[21] Montgomery, A., Faloutsos, C.: Trends and Patterns of Www Browsing Behaviour. In: Ziarko, W., Yao, Y. (eds.) RSCTC 2000. LNCS (LNAI), vol. 2005, Springer, Heidelberg (2001)

[22] Montgomery, A., Faloutsos, C.: Identifying Web Browsing Trends and Patterns. IEEE Computer 34, 94–95 (2001)

[23] Özmutlu, H.C., Cavdur, F.: Application of Automatic Topic Identification on Excite Web Search Engine Data Logs. Information Processing & Management 41, 1243–1262 (2005)

[24] Özmutlu, H.C., Çavdur, F., Spink, A., Özmutlu, S.: Cross Validation of Neural Network Applications for Automatic New Topic Identification. In: ASIST 2005. Association for the American Society of Information Science and Technology, Charlotte, NC, pp. 1–10 (2005)

[25] Park, S., Bae, H., Lee, J.: End User Searching: A Web Log Analysis of Naver, a Korean Web Search Engine. Library & Information Science Research 27, 203–221 (2005)

[26] Radlinski, F., Joachims, T.: Query Chains: Learning to Rank from Implicit Feedback. In: KDD 2005. Eleventh ACM SIGKDD international conference on Knowledge discovery in data mining, Chicago, Illinois, pp. 239–248 (2005)

[27] Shneiderman, B., Byrd, D., Croft, W.B.: Sorting out Searching: A User-Interface Framework for Text Searches. Communications of the ACM 41, 95–98 (1998)

[28] Silverstein, C., Henzinger, M., Marais, H., Moricz, M.: Analysis of a Very Large Web Search Engine Query Log. SIGIR Forum 33, 6–12 (1999)

[29] Spink, A., Jansen, B.J.: Web Search: Public Searching of the Web. Kluwer, New York (2004)

[30] Spink, A., Jansen, B.J., Blakely, C., Koshman, S.: A Study of Results Overlap and Uniqueness among Major Web Search Engines. In: Information Processing & Management (forthcoming)

[31] Spink, A., Jansen, B.J., Wolfram, D., Saracevic, T.: From E-Sex to E-Commerce: Web Search Changes. IEEE Computer 35, 107–111 (2002)

[32] Spink, A., Özmutlu, H.C., Özmutlu, S.: Multitasking Information Seeking and Searching Processes. Journal of the American Society for Information Science and Technology 53, 639–652 (2002)

[33] Spink, A., Park, M., Jansen, B.J., Pedersen, J.: Multitasking During Web Search Sessions. Information Processing & Management 42, 264–275 (2005)

Incorporating Concept Hierarchies into Usage Mining Based Recommendations

Amit Bose[1], Kalyan Beemanapalli[1],
Jaideep Srivastava[1], and Sigal Sahar[2]

[1] University of Minnesota, 4-192 EE/CS Building,
200 Union Street SE, Minneapolis, MN 55455, USA
{abose,kalyan,srivasta}@cs.umn.edu
[2] Intel Corporation, FM1-56, 1900 Prairie City Road
Folsom, CA 95630, USA
sigal.louchheim@intel.com

Abstract. Recent studies have shown that conceptual and structural characteristics of a website can play an important role in the quality of recommendations provided by a recommendation system. Resources like Google Directory, Yahoo! Directory and web-content management systems attempt to organize content conceptually. Most recommendation models are limited in their ability to use this domain knowledge. We propose a novel technique to incorporate the conceptual characteristics of a website into a usage-based recommendation model. We use a framework based on biological sequence alignment. Similarity scores play a crucial role in such a construction and we introduce a scoring system that is generated from the website's concept hierarchy. These scores fit seamlessly with other quantities used in similarity calculation like browsing order and time spent on a page. Additionally they demonstrate a simple, extensible system for assimilating more domain knowledge. We provide experimental results to illustrate the benefits of using concept hierarchy.

1 Introduction

Web Mining is described as the application of data mining techniques to extract patterns from usage information [5]. Internet usage continues to grow at a tremendous pace as an increasing number of activities are performed online. Computers on the Internet that host websites, the web servers, are capable of collecting information about website usage. Given the popularity of the Internet the volume of such data is enormous. The rapid increase in secondary storage size and decrease in their cost has made it feasible to store all this information. This information is a valuable repository for mining and discovering interesting patterns. Researchers have focused on using the extracted patterns to predict the next user request during an online session with the website. Such systems are called *Recommender Systems* and are useful tools to predict user requests. This predictive ability has application in areas like pre-fetching of pages, increase in overall usability of the website, etc [26].

Various data mining methods have been used to generate models of usage patterns. Models based on association rules [16], clustering algorithms [15], sequential analysis

O. Nasraoui et al. (Eds.): WebKDD 2006, LNAI 4811, pp. 110–126, 2007.

[17] and Markov Models [2, 28] have been well studied in the literature. All these models are predominantly based on usage information from web-logs alone. They are not easily extensible to include other pieces of information that may be available. Gündüz et al [12], for instance, use a new technique which combines usage behavior with the time spent by the user on each of the pages visited. The inclusion of the additional dimension, time spent on page, appears to improve the recommendations made. Significant improvement can also be achieved by making use of domain knowledge, which is usually available from domain experts, content providers, web designers and the web-pages themselves.

Few recommendation models have been suggested which make use of the domain knowledge [1]. Nakagawa et al [19] propose a recommendation model based on website topology. Here the emphasis is on the link structure of the website and the degree of connectivity. The paper argues that these characteristics of the website have a profound impact on the behavior of the recommendation models. Jia et al [13] discuss a new recommendation model based on usage data, content data and structure data in a website for generating better user navigational models. It is appropriate to mention the contribution of Sieg et al [25] which makes use of concept hierarchy of a website for information retrieval. Nasraoui et al [20] assume that the URLs of web-pages convey an implicit hierarchical relationship between pages. They quantify this relationship as a distance measure and use it for clustering. Pierrakos and Paliouras [21] create Community Directories from web directories through the use of usage information by viewing the web directory as a concept hierarchy. Nakagawa et al [18] give a detailed evaluation of the impact of website characteristics on the recommendation models. Though a few methods have been proposed to incorporate knowledge of the website's target domain, very few techniques exist which use a combination of usage behavior and domain knowledge to make recommendations. Domain knowledge can exist in various forms: concept hierarchy, website topology and semantic classification. This knowledge in conjunction with usage behavior data can be used to improve the performance of the recommendation engine.

In this paper we introduce a new model that effectively combines usage information with information from the conceptual structure of the website to generate our recommendations. Such a structure is termed the *concept hierarchy* of the website. It is important to emphasize here that we limit ourselves only to the hierarchy of pages of an individual website and do not deal with a hierarchy of the entire web. A suitable analog of web directory like Google Directory [10] or Yahoo! Directory [29] for a website, or the information from content-management systems could be used to approximate the concept hierarchy. Overall, the dimensions that are considered for making recommendations are the sequences of web pages browsed in sessions, time spent on these web pages and the position of pages in the concept hierarchy. Experimental results show that incorporating the concept hierarchy to make recommendations indeed improves the efficiency of the recommendation engine. Moreover, our model is flexible enough to be extended to incorporate other kinds of domain information like website topology and semantic classification of documents of the website.

The remaining paper is organized as follows: in Section 2 we briefly review the model proposed by Gündüz et al [12] which provides the framework for our proposition. In Section 3 we detail the methods used for incorporating concept hierarchy into the model. In Section 4 we describe the experiments we performed and discuss the results. We conclude in Section 5 and discuss future work. Finally in section 6 we acknowledge other people who contributed to this work.

2 Background

In this section we briefly describe the method proposed by [12] which forms the basis for our model. The proposed method is based on optimal sequence alignment of two user sessions. The remaining part of the section covers the sequence alignment method for defining session similarity and the prediction model using clickstream tree representation of data.

2.1 Optimal Sequence Alignment Based Session Similarity

Optimal sequence alignment is defined as the optimal alignment of two sequences such that their alignment score is maximized. Algorithms for finding such optimal alignments are well studied and are based on dynamic programming. A user session can be represented as a sequence of pairs, each pair containing the web page accessed and the normalized time spent on that page. For instance a user session S can be represented as:

$$S = (<P_1, T_1>, <P_2, T_2>, <P_3, T_3>, ..., <P_n, T_n>)$$

where, P_1, P_2, P_3, P_4,... are the pages in the session, and T_1, T_2, T_3, T_4,... are the respective normalized times.

	P1	P2	P3	P4	P5	-
P2	1	2	1	1	-2	-4
P4	-1	0	1	2	-1	-3
P5	-4	-3	-2	-1	0	-2
P6	-5	-4	-3	-1	-1	-1
-	-5	-4	-3	-2	-1	0

Fig. 1. Calculation of similarity score between sequences using dynamic programming

Given two such user sessions, using dynamic programming one can calculate the optimal alignment of the sessions. A scoring method is employed to denote matching and mismatching of pages. A simple method would be to use a score of 2 for a match and -1 for a mismatch. For instance, consider the following two sequences of web-pages Q_1 and Q_2:

$$Q_1 = (P_1, P_2, P_3, P_4, P_5)$$
$$Q_2 = (P_2, P_4, P_5, P_6)$$

Using dynamic programming and applying the simple scoring method [11], the alignment matrix for these two sequences would look like Figure 1.

The highest score in this table is defined as the alignment score of the sessions. Using another table for backtracking, the optimal alignment obtained is:

$$\_\_\ P_2\ \_\_\ P_4\ P_5\ P_6$$

$$P_1\ P_2\ P_3\ P_4\ P_5\ \_\_$$

Intuitively, we are finding sessions that are similar in terms of their order of occurrence in the pages in the two sessions. The similarity score between the two sessions is determined using the optimal alignment score calculated in this manner by additionally considering the time spent on these web pages. The formulae used for calculating the similarity score are detailed in [12]. Every distinct pair of sessions is aligned in this fashion, and the resulting alignment scores form a *session similarity matrix*. Value in cell *(i,j)* of this matrix gives the similarity score for sessions *i* and *j*.

2.2 Clustering of Sessions

The session similarity matrix is the input to a clustering algorithm based on graph partitioning. The algorithm creates a graph in which the vertices are the sessions and the edge between every pair of vertices is weighted by the similarity score between the corresponding two sessions. The problem of clustering user sessions is formulated as partitioning the graph into sub-graphs by minimizing the Min-MaxCut function [8]. The sub-graphs are generated such that similarity between inter-cluster sessions is minimized and similarity between intra-cluster sessions is maximized. We make use of the clustering package *Cluto* [3] to achieve this.

2.3 Prediction Model Using Clickstream Trees

The clusters of user sessions can be efficiently represented using a data structure called the clickstream tree [12]. The tree is indexed by a *data table* for easy look-up of nodes in the tree while searching. Each node in the tree consists of three components: page identifier, normalized time spent on the page and a count variable. Each page in the web-site is identified uniquely through the page identifier. Time spent on a page is indicative of the importance of the page within a session and it is normalized as mentioned in [12]. The purpose of the count variable is to keep track of how many sessions in the cluster have traversed the path to that node. The data table holds the pointers to the nodes in the tree. Hence, to find a particular node in the tree, we search the data table to find the pointer to the node and use this to access the actual node in the tree. Each node in the tree also points to a similar node (having same page number and normalized time) existing in the different part of the tree. This link helps us to navigate efficiently and quickly through all the nodes in the tree which match the search criteria.

Figure 2 shows an example clickstream representation for the following sessions:

$$S_1 = (<P_1,1>,\ <P_7,2>,\ <P_3,1>,\ <P_6,3>)$$

$$S_2 = (<P_1,1>,\ <P_2,1>,\ <P_3,1>,\ <P_4,1>,\ <P_5,3>)$$

$$S_3 = (<P_2,1>, < P_4,2>, <P_3,1>, < P_6,3>)$$
$$S_4 = (<P_2,1>, <P_4,2>, <P_7,1>, <P_6,2>)$$

During the online phase, a user's session is matched against the sessions in the clusters and a recommendation score is assigned to each such match. A session from the cluster with highest recommendation score is generated and the next page from this session is recommended to the user.

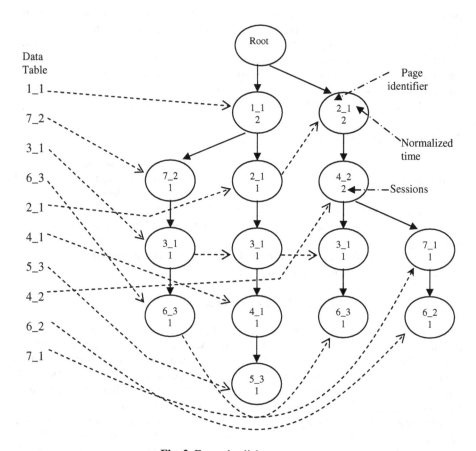

Fig. 2. Example clickstream tree

3 Concept Hierarchy and Recommendations

In this section we explain the role of a concept hierarchy for measuring similarity between user sessions, and then introduce a method for calculating this similarity value. Finally, the overall workflow of the system is described to show how the different components fit together.

3.1 Motivation

The method of sequence alignment is based on the idea of quantifying similarity between pages. To calculate this similarity, a distance measure is required that scores similar pages with lower values and dissimilar pages with larger values. There are two related challenges in defining a distance measure:

(a) on what basis do we decide that two given pages are similar or dissimilar, and,
(b) what is the procedure for calculating a metric that expresses the strength of this similarity.

The model for calculating distances should be such that it captures notions of similarity in terms of quantities that can be actually measured and manipulated.

The semantics of aligning sequences (of web-pages, proteins, etc) provides a suitable starting point in the quest for a good model. In the context of web-usage mining, the string of web-pages that we call a sequence is actually a *session* of usage of the website. It is reasonable to assume that each session is guided by the user's need to achieve specific goal(s) during the browsing session. The session is therefore representative of the intent of the user browsing the website. We can expect the pages viewed in a session to be focused around a particular intent. This interpretation of a session is fundamental in trying to align sequences of web-pages. When we try to align sessions optimally, we are searching for the best matching of user intents. The best match is obtained by aligning pages that are the same or are strongly correlated in the context of user's intent. With only the usage logs for one's perusal, it is difficult to correctly discover the user's intent. This is where domain knowledge is handy.

3.2 Concept Hierarchy

Websites of any reasonable size usually are organized and structured in ways that reflect the functional characteristics of the website. A natural form of organization is a hierarchical arrangement. Work in the field of document retrieval suggests that relations between documents, based on semantic similarity, can be considered to be taxonomic or hierarchical [23]. That is, the relationship forms a directed acyclic graph, with documents forming the leaves, and internal nodes of the tree representing instances of some dimension that relates the documents. This hierarchy is a collection of domain concepts and documents organized according to an "IS-A" relationship. Such an abstract hierarchical organization of content is called *Concept Hierarchy*: it structures content into units which are formal abstractions of concepts of human thought, allowing meaningful comprehensible interpretation [9, 25]. Figure 3 illustrates an example concept hierarchy for a student services website in a university.

Each part of the hierarchy is usually designed to address a particular functionality, or more generally, to address an idea or a concept. The intent of a user browsing the website is directly influenced by the website's functionality. This would suggest that all the different concepts in the website's concept hierarchy are a reflection of probable user intents, as expected by the content designer. In other words, one can make an informed guess about the user's intent during a session by determining the

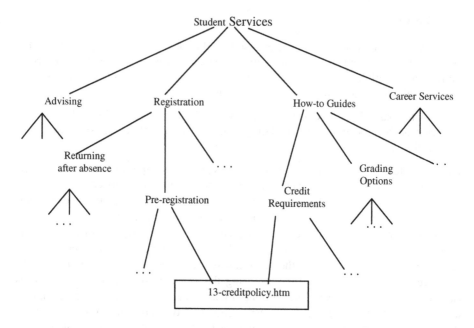

Fig. 3. Example concept hierarchy for a university student-services website

concept(s) in the hierarchy that subsume pages viewed in that session. Similarity between sessions can then be deduced by measuring the similarity between subsuming concepts. Determining page similarity now becomes equivalent to determining concept similarity within the concept hierarchy.

3.3 Similarity Model

An obvious and widely used method to calculate distance between nodes of a hierarchy is edge counting [14, 22, 23]. Here one tries to find the shortest number of edges required to reach one concept from the other; the smaller the number of edges, the smaller the distance and the greater the similarity between the concepts. If there are multiple paths, the distance is the shortest of all possible paths. Edge counting assumes that concepts are farther apart from each other if one needs to ascend the hierarchy significantly in an attempt to go from one node to the other. However, edge counting also assumes that all links in the hierarchy represent the same distance semantically [24]. In actual hierarchies, there may be wide variation in the distance covered by a link. For example, a concept that has many "child"-concepts is more distant to each one of its children than another concept that has fewer children. This makes sense because the concept having many children is much more generalized and is therefore conceptually farther from its children who are specialized concepts and documents. Resnik [24] proposes a model to calculate similarity between words in a language from a word-taxonomy using ideas from information theory. The model we propose here for similarity calculation is an adaptation of the aforementioned model to the context of the web documents. This method does not assume all links to represent the same distance. It also combines the hierarchy with probability estimates. The concept hierarchy of a website is fairly static, and changes only when the site undergoes a major overhaul. Page content changes frequently, and so one could expect the popularity of pages (and hence their probabilities) to vary quite a bit over time. The model we describe here allows us to use relatively static concept information in such a dynamic environment while limiting the changes needed due to content updates.

Suppose we have the concept hierarchy of a website, with concepts and pages represented by particular nodes. Each node is assigned a probability value that measures the strength of the concept or page that it represents. That is, a node having a high probability signifies that the corresponding concept or page is popular and occurs very often. Nodes in the concept hierarchy can belong to different subsuming concepts simultaneously, and thus the hierarchy is really a directed acyclic graph, instead of a tree. Any node in the graph represents a union of concepts represented by its children, and so any instance of a child concept is also an instance of the parent concept. This constrains probability values to be monotonically non-decreasing as we ascend the hierarchy. The nodes at the upper levels of the hierarchy have high probabilities, with the root node having a probability of 1, if one exists. Using principles on information theory, the *information content* of a node is defined as the negative logarithm of its probability. Let $I(n)$ denote the information content of a node n in the hierarchy. Then,

$$I(n) = -\log p(n)$$

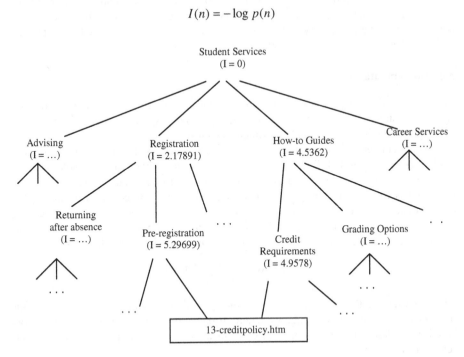

Fig. 4. Annotated concept hierarchy for student-services example

In the above formula, $p(n)$ is the probability assigned to node n. One can see that as probability of a node increases, the amount of information that one gets from it decreases. This directly results in higher level nodes having lesser information content than the lower ones, with the root node providing no information at all.

Defining information content in this manner makes sense when we consider the closest subsuming node for a given pair of nodes: the higher the *subsumer* in the hierarchy, the higher its probability and hence the lesser the similarity is between the nodes. Formally, let $S(n_1,n_2)$ represent the similarity between two nodes n_1 and n_2, both of which represent pages of the website. Since a particular page can belong to multiple concepts, it is possible that n_1 and n_2 may have more than one parent node, and hence more than one path to the root of sub-graph to which they belong to. Let A represent the set of *least common ancestors* of n_1 and n_2 for all possible combinations of such paths for the two nodes. The least common ancestor on a path combination is that node which appears in both paths and that is as far away as possible from the root. Set A will thus contain one ancestor node for every pair of paths-to-root that has at least one node in common. The overall similarity can be obtained from the maximum value of the information content of nodes in A. Thus,

$$S(n_1,n_2) = \max_{a_i \in A} \{ I(a_i) \}$$

Resnik [24] mentions that a more faithful way to calculate $S(n_1,n_2)$ would be to weight each candidate common ancestor according to some measure and take a weighted average of information contents as the similarity value. In this paper, however, we do not explore such a possibility. Figure 4 shows a portion of the annotated concept hierarchy for the student services website.

3.4 Implementation

The concept hierarchy for a website can be obtained directly from its content designers. Many sites nowadays use a content management system to store their content. Concept hierarchies can be readily extracted from such systems.

Given a concept hierarchy, the task that remains in the realization of this similarity model is to assign probabilities (and hence information content values) to the nodes of the hierarchy. We rely on the actual usage of pages to calculate probabilities. Each page that is found in the usage log of the website is considered as an occurrence of every concept that it belongs to, taking care to do so exactly once. Owing to the IS-A property of the hierarchy, these concepts are not just the immediate parents of a node, but include each one of the node's ancestors in the hierarchy. Formally,

$$freq(c) = \sum_{n \in pages(c)} count(n)$$

where *pages(c)* is the set of pages that a concept node c subsumes, and *count(n)* is the number of occurrences of a page n. When all pages in the usage log have been processed, the relative frequency of each concept node c gives the probability of occurrence of that node:

$$\hat{p}(c) = \frac{freq(c)}{N}$$

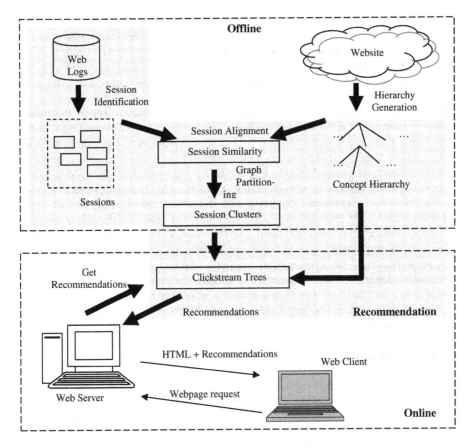

Fig. 5. The Recommender System

where N is the total number of pages encountered in the log, excluding those that were not part of the given hierarchy. A more detailed discussion on this general method can be found in [24].

Information content of a node, being a logarithm, lies in the range 0 to ∞. This range needs to be normalized if information values are to be used for calculating alignment scores of sessions. In addition, the notion of penalizing mismatching alignments needs to be accommodated in the similarity values. Thus, we normalize the similarity value calculated from information content of nodes so that it lies in the range -1 (maximum penalty) to 1 (maximum reward). Thus, normalized similarity between page nodes n_1 and n_2 is given as

$$Sim(n_1, n_2) = \begin{cases} \dfrac{S(n_1, n_2)}{I_M} - 1 & \text{if } S(n_1, n_2) \leq I_M \\[2ex] \dfrac{S(n_1, n_2) - I_M}{I_{MAX} - I_M} & \text{otherwise} \end{cases}$$

where I_M and I_{MAX} are the median and maximum values of the information contents of all concept nodes of the hierarchy. Normalized similarities calculated in this way are used directly in calculating alignment metrics like alignment score component and local similarity component. Remaining tasks in the offline analysis of web logs (similarity matrix generation, clustering and clickstream tree generation) are described in [12].

The online component of the recommendation engine finds a set of the best k-pages for every page requested by the user. To do this, the recommendation engine keeps track of the user's online session by storing the pages accessed and times spent on them. Then it finds all occurrences of the current page in the clickstream trees. For each occurrence, an upward traversal of the tree is performed till the root to extract the partial session associated with that clickstream branch. Once a set of such sessions has been obtained, a pair-wise alignment with the online session is performed and an alignment score is obtained for each partial session. We designate the alignment score as our recommendation score, although a more complex measure could be devised by combining the alignment score with the number of occurrences of the page across all clusters and size of the cluster. The recommendation scores are ranked in non-increasing order and the top k-sessions are selected for making the recommendations. By doing so, we have found the top k-sessions which are the best match for the current user session. Hence the next page from each of these k-sessions is given as a recommended page to the user.

3.5 Overall Workflow

Figure 5 provides a schematic description of the recommendation process. The inputs to the system are the web-usage logs from the web-servers and the concept hierarchy of the website content. Usage logs are cleaned, pre-processed and structured into user sessions using heuristic techniques described in [4]. Simultaneously, the concept hierarchy is annotated with information content values using the web-usage logs. User sessions and concept hierarchy are utilized to generate a similarity score for each session pair based on optimal sequence alignment using the similarity model described before. The sessions are then clustered based on their similarity scores using graph partitioning. We use the clustering tool Cluto [3] for this purpose. These clusters are represented as clickstream trees. During an online session, the web-server receives requests for web-pages. The request is then passed to the recommendation system to generate recommendations for the currently requested page. The system tries to align the pages visited so far optimally with clickstream sessions. Best alignments are ranked and form the basis for recommendations. The recommendations are then assimilated into the web-page that was requested, and the combined document is sent back to the client for display.

4 Experiments and Results

We call our method of page and session similarity calculation, described in Section 3, *concept-aware similarity model* (CASM). We carried out a series of experiments to evaluate the performance of this model as compared to other methods: one that assigns a score of 2 to a match and -1 to a mismatch (the "2,-1" scoring system), as described in [12], and the other that assigns similarity values randomly. We call the first comparative model, *simple similarity model* (SSM), and the second one, *random similarity model* (RSM). In carrying out these tests, the only variation across these methods was the manner of calculating similarity between pages; all other steps, including clustering and recommendation generation were identical in all three methods.

4.1 Experimental Setup

The experiments were carried out on web-server logs obtained from the College of Liberal Arts of University of Minnesota [27]. The College of Liberal Arts is the largest college at the University of Minnesota, serving over 14,500 students in nearly 70 majors. In particular, we used the Student Services website as the data source, which contains over 1,500 web pages and other documents. The usage logs available had over 200,000 sessions with majority of them being one-page sessions. Such sessions are not useful in making predictions, and therefore were disregarded leaving 20,000 sessions as useful data. In addition, the classification of the documents into topics/subtopics was available [7]. This classification, in combination with (human) expert knowledge about the website and topology of the website was used to manually create a concept hierarchy that represented Student Services as well as possible.

The general method for testing used was as follows: from the cleaned logs, we used a portion of the logs to train the recommendation system. The remaining sessions were treated as test sessions, for which we predicted the next page that will be requested at every stage of the session using the clickstream trees constructed. Intuitively, if predicted pages were actually accessed by the user in the session later on, it would mean that the clickstream trees were indeed capable of making sensible recommendations. The performance of various models for similarity can then be compared quantitatively on the basis of the "success rate" of their predictions.

The following measures were used to assess the success of predictions based on different models:

- *Predictive Ability (PA)*: Percentage of pages in the test sessions for which the model was able to make recommendations. This is a measure of how useful the model is.
- *Prediction Strength (PS)*: Average number of recommendations made for a page.
- *Hit Ratio (HR)*: Percentage of *hits*. If a recommended page is actually requested later in the session, we declare a hit. The hit ratio is thus a measure of how good the model is in making recommendations.
- *Click Reduction (CR)*: Average percentage click reduction. For a test session $(p_1, p_2,..., p_i..., p_j..., p_n)$, if p_j is recommended at page p_i, and p_j is subsequently accessed in the session, then the click reduction due to this recommendation is,

$$Click\ reduction\ = \frac{j-i}{i}$$

- *Recommendation Quality (RQ)*: Average rank of a hit. Recommendations made for a page are ranked as described in Section 3.4. If a recommendation is a hit, then the rank of the recommendation is the rank of that hit. The lower the rank of a hit, the better the quality of recommendation.

The first two measures simply validate the utility of the system as a predictive tool. A good hit ratio indicates that the model was able to successfully learn usage patterns from the training data. In defining a hit, we do not restrict ourselves to testing only against the next requested page, as in [6]. This is because the recommendations are made after the user has browsed the website. Recommendations are thus "passive" and cannot influence the user's choice of next page. Similarly, in getting to the target page(s), the user is likely to browse other navigational pages that are not necessarily desired. Recommendations can reduce the number of clicks needed to reach the intended page. Click reduction measures the usefulness of recommendations from this point of view.

4.2 Comparison on number of recommendations made

Table 1 compares the three similarity models by varying the maximum number of recommendations generated. The recommendation size is limited to these typical values: 3, 5 and 10. The models were trained on data containing 5,000 user sessions, with clickstream trees grouped into 10 clusters. The remaining 15,000 sessions were used for testing.

The predictive ability of all three models is fairly good, although not 100%. This happened because we were working with an incomplete data-set - test sessions contained pages that were not present either in the training sessions or in the concept hierarchy (The concept hierarchy available was not for the same time-span as covered by the available usage logs). The system is clueless about these pages, and is therefore unable to make predictions for them. All three models have good prediction strength and can produce a desired number of recommendations. Comparisons on hit ratio and click reduction indicate that CASM outperforms the other two models in all three cases, with the disparity increasing with the number of recommendations. An interesting point to be noted is that RSM performs better than the SSM on hit ratio and click reduction. This is an indication of the fact that a naïve scoring method of assigning 2

Table 1. Comparison of different models for various recommendation sizes

Model	Metric				
	PA	PS	HR	CR	RQ
Maximum number of recommendations = 3					
RSM	93.42	2.99	31.23	21.67	2.11
SSM	97.50	2.99	33.98	21.67	2.20
CASM	97.27	2.99	34.50	23.49	2.26
Maximum number of recommendations = 5					
RSM	93.42	4.96	38.13	27.09	3.12
SSM	97.50	4.96	37.93	24.50	3.59
CASM	97.27	4.96	40.20	27.65	3.41
Maximum number of recommendations = 10					
RSM	93.42	9.82	45.22	32.98	6.23
SSM	97.50	9.81	42.17	27.38	6.28
CASM	97.27	9.80	54.08	38.89	6.38

for match and -1 for mismatch is not a good idea and it should be substituted by a more sophisticated scoring method. CASM performs the best when we try to make a larger number of recommendations. This is an indication of the power of the model not only to capture the top recommendations but also recommendations which are lower in the order. CASM however performs slightly worse on the recommendation quality aspect, and the difference is more pronounced with more recommendations. This probably is due to the manner in which recommendations are ranked: we used domain knowledge only during the process of session alignment and therefore for the generation of candidate recommendations. Ranking within the candidates does not make use of any domain knowledge but instead relies solely on usage information (implicitly contained in the clickstream construction). The recommendation model needs to be improved, and using domain information is one way of doing that. In our future work, we intend to find out ways in which the concept hierarchy may be used for ranking as well. Generalizing this idea to include other forms of domain knowledge should also be helpful.

Table 2. Comparison of different models for various cluster sizes

Model	Metric				
	PA	**PS**	**HR**	**CR**	**RQ**
Number of clusters = 5					
RSM	94.40	4.96	38.20	27.00	3.03
SSM	97.46	4.96	43.68	29.37	3.50
CASM	96.67	4.96	43.88	29.34	3.37
Number of clusters = 10					
RSM	93.42	4.96	38.13	27.09	3.12
SSM	97.50	4.96	37.93	24.50	3.59
CASM	97.27	4.96	40.20	27.65	3.41
Number of clusters = 20					
RSM	91.81	4.96	23.56	15.50	3.95
SSM	97.82	4.96	34.70	23.20	3.40
CASM	96.83	4.96	34.67	23.71	3.69

4.3 Comparison on number of clusters

Table 2 compares the similarity models by varying the number of clusters used while building the clickstream trees.

The cluster sizes used were 5, 10 and 20. The models were trained on data containing 5000 user sessions and the remaining 15,000 sessions were used for testing. Recommendations were limited to 5. The results show that our recommendation model outperforms the other two models when the number of clusters is limited to 10.

The overall trend in the measurements shows that CASM performs at least as good as SSM if not better. For the College of Liberal Arts data-set that we used, it appears that a smaller number of clusters is more representative of the actual clustering pattern that exists in the data. Currently the cluster count is a parameter that needs to be externally supplied. However, here again one can estimate the likely number of clusters by using other information, e.g. the number of nodes in the concept hierarchy at a pre-defined level can be one such estimate. Devising such estimators is another aspect that we will work on.

5 Conclusions and Future Work

Recommendation models based only on usage information are inherently incomplete because they neglect domain knowledge. Better predictions can be made by modeling and incorporating context dependent information: concept hierarchy, link structure and semantic classification allow us to do so. In this paper, we have described a method to combine usage information and domain knowledge based on ideas from bioinformatics and information retrieval. The results are promising and are indicative of the utility of domain knowledge. We believe that more improvement can be achieved, and therefore intend to enhance and augment the method described here in several ways:

Investigate similarity calculations that use information content values weighted by context that could provide better estimates for similarity. There is a substantial scope for improvement in the ranking of recommendations: domain knowledge can again be used along with the local sequence alignment. In fact, we believe that the similarity model should incorporate link structure and semantics of documents, appropriately weighted, to provide a composite similarity score that can be used in alignment. Testing and evaluation of the system also presents opportunities for improvement: testing with domain experts or average users should verify the ultimate usefulness of recommendations that use a concept hierarchy. Devising better metrics for performance comparison is another area that we intend to work on. Finally, creating the concept hierarchy from scratch may be a very tedious task. Automating this will increase the applicability of methods like ours to a wider class of websites.

Acknowledgements

This work is supported by research grants from Intel IT Research towards development of a recommender system for internal use. In particular we would like to thank Amy Auler, Bill Draven, Brandon Bohling, Brian Quiner, Jerzy Bilchuk, Sri Canakapalli from Intel for their inputs on implementing the proposed system. We also thank Colin DeLong from University of Minnesota College of Liberal Arts for providing the data sources.

References

1. Adomavicius, G., Tuzhilin, A.: Towards the Next Generation of Recommender Systems: A Survey of the State-of-the-Art and Possible Extensions. IEEE Transactions on Knowledge and Data Engineering 17 (June 2005)
2. Anderson, C., Domingos, P., Weld, D.: Relational Markov models and their application to adaptive Web navigation. In: Proceedings of 8th ACM SIGKDD Intl. Conf. on Knowledge Discovery and Data Mining, Edmonton, Canada, pp. 143–152. ACM Press, New York (2002)

3. Cluto, http://www-users.cs.umn.edu/karypis/cluto/index.html
4. Cooley, R., Mobasher, B., Srivastava, J.: Data preparation for mining World Wide Web browsing patterns. Journal of Knowledge and Information Systems 1(1) (1999)
5. Cooley, R., Srivastava, J., Mobasher, B.: Web Mining: Information and pattern discovery on the world-wide web. In: 9th IEEE International Conference on Tools with Artificial Intelligence (November 1997)
6. Cosley, D., Lawrence, S., Pennock, D.M.: REFEREE: An open framework for practical testing of recommender systems using research index. In: Bressan, S., Chaudhri, A.B., Lee, M.L., Yu, J.X., Lacroix, Z. (eds.) CAiSE 2002 and VLDB 2002. LNCS, vol. 2590, Springer, Heidelberg (2003)
7. DeLong, C., Desikan, P., Srivastava, J. (User Sensitive Expert Recommendation): What Non-Experts NEED to Know, WebKDD 2005 Workshop. In: Nasraoui, O., Zaïane, O., Spiliopoulou, M., Mobasher, B., Masand, B., Yu, P.S. (eds.) WebKDD 2005. LNCS (LNAI), vol. 4198, Springer, Heidelberg (2006)
8. Ding, C., He, X., Zha, H., Gu, M., Simon, H.: Spectral min-max cut for graph partitioning and data clustering. Technical Report TR-2001-XX, Lawrence Berkeley National Laboratory, University of California, Berkeley, CA (2001)
9. Ganter, B., Wille, R.: Formal Concept Analysis - Mathematical Foundations. Springer, Heidelberg (1999)
10. Google Directory, http://directory.google.com
11. Gusfield, D.: Algorithms on Strings, Trees and Sequences: Computer Science and Computational Biology. Cambridge University Press, Cambridge (1997)
12. Gündüz, S., Ozsu, M.T.A.: Web Page Prediction Model Based on Click-Stream Tree Representation of User Behavior. In: Proceedings of the 9th ACM SIGKDD International Conference on Knowledge Discovery and Data Mining, pp. 535–540. ACM Press, New York (2003)
13. Jia, L., Zaïane, O.R.: Combining Usage, Content, and Structure Data to Improve Web Site Recommendation. In: Bauknecht, K., Bichler, M., Pröll, B. (eds.) EC-Web 2004. LNCS, vol. 3182, pp. 305–315. Springer, Heidelberg (2004)
14. Lee, J.H., Kim, M.H., Lee, Y.J.: Information retrieval based on conceptual distance in IS-A hierarchies. Journal of Documentation 49(2), 188–207 (1993)
15. Mobasher, B., Cooley, R., Srivastava, J.: Creating adaptive web sites through usage-based clustering of URLs. In: Knowledge and Data Engineering workshop (1999)
16. Mobasher, B., Dai, H., Luo, T., Nakagawa, M.: Effective Personalization Based on Association Rule Discovery from Web Usage Data. In: Proceedings of the 3rd ACM Workshop on Web Information and Data Management (WIDM 2001)/International Conference on Information and Knowledge Management (CIKM 2001), Atlanta GA (November 2001)
17. Mobasher, B., Dai, H., Luo, T., Nakagawa, M.: Using sequential and non-sequential patterns for predictive web usage mining tasks. In: ICDM 2002. Proceedings of the IEEE International Conference on Data Mining, Maebashi City, Japan (December 2002)
18. Nakagawa, M., Mobasher, B.: Impact of site characteristics on recommendation models based on association rules and sequential patterns. In: Proceedings of the IJCAI (2003)
19. Nakagawa, M., Mobasher, M.: A hybrid web personalization model based on site connectivity. In: Zaïane, O.R., Srivastava, J., Spiliopoulou, M., Masand, B. (eds.) WEBKDD 2002 - Mining Web Data for Discovering Usage Patterns and Profiles. LNCS (LNAI), vol. 2703, pp. 59–70. Springer, Heidelberg (2003)
20. Nasraoui, O., Frigui, H., Joshi, A., Krishnapuram, R.: Mining Web Access Logs Using Relational Competitive Fuzzy Clustering. In: IFSA 1999. Proceedings of the 8th International Fuzzy Systems Association World Congress, Taipei (August 1999)

21. Pierrakos, D., Paliouras, G.: Exploiting Probabilistic Latent Information for the Construction of Community Web Directories. In: Ardissono, L., Brna, P., Mitrović, A. (eds.) UM 2005. LNCS (LNAI), vol. 3538, pp. 89–98. Springer, Heidelberg (2005)
22. Rada, R., Bicknell, E.: Ranking documents with a thesaurus. JASIS 40(5), 304–310 (1989)
23. Rada, R., Mili, H., Bicknell, E., Blettner, M.: Development and application of a metric on semantic nets. IEEE Transaction on Systems, Man, and Cybernetics 19(1), 17–30 (1989)
24. Resnik, P.: Semantic Similarity in a Taxonomy: An Information-Based Measure and its Application to Problems of Ambiguity in Natural Language. Journal of Artificial Intelligence Research 11, 95–130 (1999)
25. Sieg, A., Mobasher, B., Burke, R.: Inferring User's Information Context: Integrating User Profiles and Concept Hierarchies. In: Proceedings of the 2004 Meeting of the International Federation of Classification Societies, Chicago IL (2004)
26. Srivastava, J., Cooley, R., Deshpande, M., Tan, P.N.: Web usage mining: Discovery and applications of usage patterns from web data. SIGKDD Explorations 1(2), 12–23 (2000)
27. University of Minnesota College of Liberal Arts, http://www.class.umn.edu
28. Zhu, J., Hong, J., Hughes, J.G.: Using Markov Models for website link prediction. In: Proceedings of the 13th ACM Conference on Hypertext and Hypermedia, pp. 169–170. ACM Press, New York (2002)
29. Yahoo! Directory, http://dir.yahoo.com

A Random-Walk Based Scoring Algorithm
Applied to Recommender Engines

A. Pucci, M. Gori, and M. Maggini

Dipartimento di Ingegneria dell'Informazione, University of Siena,
Via Roma, 56. Siena, Italy
{augusto,marco,maggini}@dii.unisi.it

Abstract. Recommender systems are an emerging technology that helps consumers find interesting products and useful resources. A recommender system makes personalized product suggestions by extracting knowledge from the previous users' interactions. In this paper, we present "Item-Rank", a random–walk based scoring algorithm, which can be used to rank products according to expected user preferences, in order to recommend top–rank items to potentially interested users. We tested our algorithm on a standard database, the MovieLens data set, which contains data collected from a popular recommender system on movies and that has been widely exploited as a benchmark for evaluating recently proposed approaches to recommender systems (e.g. [1,2]). We compared ItemRank with other state-of-the-art ranking techniques on this task. Our experiments show that ItemRank performs better than the other algorithms we compared to and, at the same time, it is less complex with respect to memory usage and computational cost too. The presentation of the method is accompanied by an analysis of the MovieLens data set main properties.

1   Introduction

The modern electronic marketplace offers an unprecedented range of products. Such a huge quantity of possibilities for consumers is a value in itself but also a source of difficulties in the choosing process. Recommender systems are automatic tools able to make personalized product suggestions by extracting knowledge from the previous user interactions with the system. Such services are particularly useful in the new marketplace scenario we introduced. In fact a recommender system represents an added value both for consumers, who can easily find products they really like, and for sellers, who can focus their offers and advertising efforts. The electronic marketplace offers a strongly heterogeneous collection of products, so several recommender systems have been developed that cope with different class of items or services, e.g. MovieLens for movies (see [3]), GroupLens for usenet news [4], Ringo for music [5], Jester for jokes [6] and many other (see e.g. [7] for a review). In a general framework a recommender system constructs a user profile on the basis of explicit or implicit interactions of the user with the system. The profile is used to find products to recommend to the user. Many different solutions and approaches have been proposed in literature. In the simplest paradigm, the profile is constructed using only features

O. Nasraoui et al. (Eds.): WebKDD 2006, LNAI 4811, pp. 127–146, 2007.

that are related to the user under evaluation and to the products he/she has already considered. In those cases, the profile consists of a parametric model that is adapted according to the customer's behavior. Scalability and quality of the results are key issues of collaborative filtering approach. In fact, real life large–scale E–commerce applications must efficiently challenge with hundreds of thousands of users. Moreover, the accuracy of the recommendation is crucial in order to offer a service that is appreciated and used by customers. In this paper, we present "ItemRank", a random–walk based scoring algorithm, which can be used to rank products according to expected user preferences, in order to recommend top–rank items to potentially interested users. We tested our algorithm on a popular database, the MovieLens dataset[1] by the GroupLens Research group at University of Minnesota and we compared ItemRank with other state-of-the-art ranking techniques (in particular the algorithms described in [1,8]). This database contains data collected from a popular recommender system on movies that has been widely exploited as a benchmark for evaluating recently proposed approaches to recommender system (e.g. [1,2]). The schema of this archive resembles the structure of the data of many other collaborative filtering applications. Our experiments show that ItemRank performs better than the other algorithms we compared to and, at the same time, it is less complex than other proposed algorithms with respect to both memory usage and computational cost too. Finally, the presentation of the method is accompanied by an analysis that helps to discover some intriguing properties of the MovieLens dataset, that are evidenced by a direct statistical analysis of the data set. The paper is organized as follows. In the next subsection (1.1) we revise the related literature with a special focus on other graph based similarity measure and scoring algorithms applied to recommender systems. Section 2 describes the MovieLens data set (in subsection 2.1) and illustrates the data model we adopted (in subsection 2.2). Section 3 discusses ItemRank algorithm in details and we address ItemRank algorithm complexity issues in subsection 3.1 and convergence in subsection 3.2. Section 4 contains the details of the experimentation, while Section 5 draws some conclusions and addresses future aspects of this research.

1.1 Related Work

Many different recommending algorithms have been proposed in the literature, for example there are techniques based on singular value decomposition [9], Bayesian networks [10], Support Vector Machines [11] and factor analysis [12]. On the other hand, the most successful and well–known approach to recommender system design is based on collaborative filtering [13,3,5]. In collaborative filtering, each user collaborates with others to establish the quality of products by providing his/her opinion on a set of products. Also, a similarity measure between users is defined by comparing the profiles of different users. In order to suggest a product to an "active user", the recommender system selects the items among those scored by similar customers. The similarity measure is often

---

[1] http://www.movielens.umn.edu

computed using the Pearson–r correlation coefficient between users (e.g. in [3]). Recently a graph based approach has been proposed in [8,1]. Authors compared different scoring algorithm to compute a preference ranking of products (in that case movies) to suggest to a group of users. In these papers the problem has been modeled as a bipartite graph, where nodes are users (**people_node**) and movies (**movie_node**), and there is a link connecting a people_node u_i to a movie_node m_j if and only if u_i watched movie m_j, in this case arcs are undirected and can be weighted according to user preferences expressed about watched movies. Authors tested many different algorithms using a wide range of similarity measures in order to rank movies according to user preferences, some of the most interesting methods are:

Average first-passage time (One-way). This is a similarity measure between a pair of nodes i and j in a graph, we denote it as $m(i, j)$, it is defined as the average number of steps that a random walker[2] going across a given graph, starting in the state corresponding to node i, will take to enter state j for the first time, that is the reason why this similarity score is also called *one-way time*. Obviously one-way time is not symmetrical in a directed graph, that is $m(i, j) \neq m(j, i)$.

Average first-passage time (Return). This score measures the similarity between node i and node j as $m(j, i)$, that is the transpose of $m(i, j)$). It correspond to the average time needed to a random walker in node j to come back to node i. We can refer to this measure as *return time*. Return time, as one-way time, is not symmetrical.

Average Commute Time (CT). This is a distance measure between a pair of nodes i and j in a graph, we denote it as $n(i, j)$, it is defined as the average number of steps that a random walker going across a given graph, starting in the state corresponding to node i, will take to enter state j for the first time and go back to i. So commute time depends on one-way and return time, in fact $n(i, j) = m(i, j) + m(j, i)$. It clearly states that CT is symmetrical. If we measure this distance between people and movie nodes in the given bipartite graph, we can use this score to perform the movie ranking.

Principal Component Analysis based on Euclidean Commute Time Distance (PCA CT). From the eigenvector decomposition of $\mathbf{L}^+$, that is the pseudoinverse of the Laplacian matrix ($\mathbf{L}$) corresponding to the graph, it is possible to map nodes into a new Euclidean space (with more than 2600 dimensions in this case) that preserves the Euclidean Commute Time Distance, it is also possible to project to a m-dimensional subspace by performing a PCA and keeping a given number of principal components. Then distances computed between nodes in the reduced space can be used to rank the movies for each person.

Pseudoinverse of the Laplacian Matrix ($\mathbf{L}^+$). Matrix $\mathbf{L}^+$ is the matrix containing the inner products of the node vectors in the Euclidean space where the nodes are exactly separated by the ECTD, so $l_{i,j}^+$ can be used as the simi-

---

[2] See [14,15] for more details.

larity measure between node i and j, in order to rank movies according to their similarity with the person.

Katz. This is a similarity index [16] typical of the social sciences field. It has been applied to collaborative recommendation [17] and it is also known as the von Neumann kernel [18]. This method computes similarities between nodes taking into account the number of direct and indirect links between items. The Katz matrix is defined as: $K = \alpha A + \alpha^2 A^2 + \cdots + \alpha^n A^n + \cdots = (I - \alpha A)^{-1} - I$ where A is the graph adjacency matrix and α is a positive attenuation factor which dumps the effectiveness of n-step paths connecting two nodes. The series converge if α is less than the inverse of the spectral radius of A. The similarity between a node pair i and j, according to Katz definition, will be $sim(i,j) = k_{i,j} = [K]_{i,j}$.

Dijkstra. This is a classical algorithm for the shortest path problem for a directed and connected graph with nonnegative edge weights. This score can be used as a distance between two nodes. This algorithm does not take into account multiple paths connecting a node pair, that is the reason why its performance is really poor in a collaborative recommendation task (close to a random algorithm).

In literature there are many other examples of algorithms using graphical structures in order to discover relationships between items. Chebotarev and Shamis proposed in [19] and [20] a similarity measure between nodes of a graph integrating indirect paths, based on the matrix-forest theorem. Similarity measures based on random-walk models have been considered in [21] and in [22], where average first-passage time has been used as a similarity measure between nodes. More recently, Newman [23] suggested a random-walk model to compute a "betweenness centrality" of a given node in a graph, that is the number of times a node is traversed during a random walk between two other nodes: the average of this quantity provides a general measure of betweenness [24] associated to each node. Moreover a continuous-time diffusion process based model has been illustrated in [25]. In collaborative recommendation field, it is also interesting to consider different metrics described in [26]. The Random-walk model on a graph is also closely related to spectral-clustering and spectral-embedding techniques (see for example [27] and [28]).

2   The Problem

There are different philosophies and design criteria that can be applied to recommender systems, so first of all it is necessary to define the general framework and problem scenario we wish to face. Formally, a recommender system deals with a set of users u_i, $i = 1, \ldots, U_n$ and a set of products p_j, $j = 1, \ldots, P_n$, and its goal consists of computing, for each pair: u_i, p_j, a score $\hat{r}_{i,j}$ that measures the expected interest of users u_i for product p_j on the basis of a knowledge base containing a set of preferences expressed by some users about products. So we need a scoring algorithm to rank products/items for every given user according to its expected preferences, then a recommender system will suggest to a user

top-ranked items with respect to personalized ordering. A different, but complementary approach would be to consider the suggestion problem as a regression
task for a function which assigns a preference score to products, but we reckon
the ranking point of view is more general. In this section, we present the data
model we adopted and the MovieLens data set, that is a widely used benchmark
to evaluate scoring algorithms applied to recommender systems. Our choice with
respect to the data model and the data set is not restrictive since it reflect a very
common scenario while dealing with recommender systems. In the following we
will indifferently make use of terms such as *item*, *product* and *movie* depending
on the context, but obviously the proposed algorithm is a general purpose scoring algorithm and it does not matter which kind of items we are ranking in a
particular scenario, moreover we will also use the notation m_j to refer a product
p_j in the particular case of movies to be ranked.

2.1 MovieLens Data Set

MovieLens site has over $50,000$ users who have expressed opinions on more than
$3,000$ different movies. The MovieLens dataset is a standard dataset constructed
from the homonym site archive, by considering only users who rated 20 or more
movies, in order to achieve a greater reliability for user profiling. The dataset
contains over $100,000$ ratings from 943 users for $1,682$ movies. Every opinion
is represented using a tuple: $t_{i,j} = (u_i, m_j, r_{i,j})$, where $t_{i,j}$ is the considered
tuple, $u_i \in \mathcal{U}$ is a user, $m_j \in \mathcal{M}$ is a movie, and $r_{i,j}$ is an integer score between
1 (bad movie) and 5 (good movie). The database provides a set of features
characterizing users and movies which include: the category of the movie, the
age, gender, and occupation of the user, and so on. The dataset comes with five
predefined splittings, each uses 80% of the ratings for the training set and 20%
for the test set (as described in [2]). For every standard splitting we call $\mathcal{L}$ and
$\mathcal{T}$ respectively the set of tuples used for training and for testing, moreover we
refer the set of movies in the training set rated by user u_i as $\mathcal{L}_{u_i}$ and we write
$\mathcal{T}_{u_i}$ for movies in the test set. More formally:

$$\mathcal{L}_{u_i} = \{t_{k,j} \in \mathcal{L} : k = i\}$$

and

$$\mathcal{T}_{u_i} = \{t_{k,j} \in \mathcal{T} : k = i\}$$

In order to clarify some properties of the dataset, a statistical analysis has been
carried out. Figure 1 shows respectively the probability distribution of the number of movies rated by a user (on the left) and the probability distribution of
the number of ratings received by a movie (on the right).

It is worth noting that the distributions clearly follow a power law[3]. In fact,
it is likely that the number of ratings received by a movie increases proportionally to its popularity, i.e. the ratings already received; similarly, the number of
ratings given by a user increases proportionally to its previous experience with

---

[3] Relationships between two variables $x, y \in \mathcal{R}$ follow a power law if it can be written
as $y = x^b$, where $b \in \mathcal{R}$.

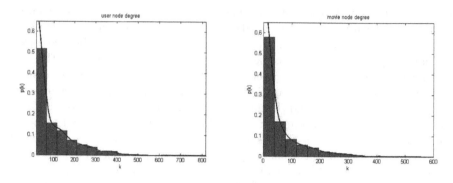

Fig. 1. Probability distribution of the number of movies rated by a user (left) and probability distribution of the number of ratings received by a movie (right)

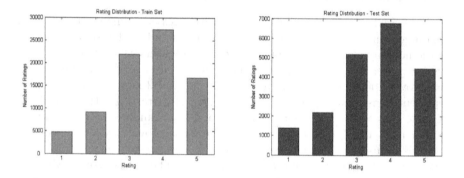

Fig. 2. Number of ratings for each score in the training data set (left) and the testing data set (right)

the system, i.e. the current number of opinions the user has provided. It is also useful to have a look at the features of user/movie pairs involved in each rating.

Figure 2 displays the distribution of the ratings in a training data set and in the corresponding testing data set, respectively. The histogram presents the number of ratings with the admissible scores 1, 2, 3, 4, 5. It is observed that most of the ratings correspond to the scores 3 and 4, while 1 is the least selected rate. Such a trend is confirmed by the average of the ratings over all the archive being 3.53. It is interesting to note that the ratings are quite biased and their distributions are not uniform.

2.2   Data Model: Correlation Graph

Even from a superficial analysis of the proposed problem, it seems to be clear that there is a different correlation degree between movies. Different kinds of relationships can exist between a pair of movies, for example due to movie category similarities or the presence of the same actor as a main character, these are all feature based similarity but we are not interested in such a property. We desire to extract a notion of correlation directly from user preferences as an aggregate. In fact a single user tends to have quite homogeneous preferences about movies, so we can reasonably think that if movie m_i and movie m_j tend to appear together in many preference lists for different users, then m_i and m_j are related. So the correlation we look for is linked to a co-occurrence criterion. If we could exploit this information from the training set then it would be quite easy to compute user dependent preferences. We define $\mathcal{U}_{i,j} \subseteq \mathcal{U}$ the set of users who watched (according to the training set) both movie m_i and movie m_j, so:

$$\mathcal{U}_{i,j} = \begin{cases} \{u_k : (t_{k,i} \in \mathcal{L}_{u_k}) \wedge (t_{k,j} \in \mathcal{L}_{u_k})\} & \text{if } i \neq j \\ \emptyset & \text{if } i = j \end{cases}$$

Now we compute the ($|M| \times |M|$) matrix containing the number of users who watched each pair of movies:

$$\tilde{\mathcal{C}}_{i,j} = |\mathcal{U}_{i,j}|$$

where $| \cdot |$ denotes the cardinality of a set. Obviously $\forall i$, $\tilde{\mathcal{C}}_{i,i} = 0$ and $\tilde{\mathcal{C}}$ is a symmetric matrix. We normalize matrix $\tilde{\mathcal{C}}$ in order to obtain a stochastic matrix[4] $\mathcal{C}_{i,j} = \frac{\tilde{\mathcal{C}}_{i,j}}{\omega_j}$ where ω_j is the sum of entries in $j-th$ column of $\tilde{\mathcal{C}}$. $\mathcal{C}$ is the *Correlation Matrix*, every entry contains the correlation index between movie pairs. The Correlation Matrix can also be considered as a weighted connectivity matrix for the *Correlation Graph* $\mathcal{G_C}$. Nodes in graph $\mathcal{G_C}$ correspond to movies in $\mathcal{M}$ and there will be an edge (m_i, m_j) if and only if $\mathcal{C}_{i,j} > 0$. Moreover the weight associated to link (m_i, m_j) will be $\mathcal{C}_{i,j}$, note that while $\tilde{\mathcal{C}}$ is symmetrical, $\mathcal{C}$ is not, so the weight associated to (m_i, m_j) can differ from (m_j, m_i) weight. The Correlation Graph is a valuable graphical model useful to exploit correlation between movies, weights associated to links provide an approximate measure of movie/movie relative correlation, according to information extracted from ratings expressed by users in the training set. Anyway it has to be clear that graph $\mathcal{G_C}$ is only the "static ingredient" of the proposed algorithm (see section 3 for details), in fact the Correlation Graph captures only the similarity among movies as extracted from aggregated user preferences in $\mathcal{L}$, but it is also necessary to take into account any single user preference list $\mathcal{L}_{u_i}$ in order to create the personalized movie ranking for user u_i, that is the "dynamic ingredient" of ItemRank algorithm (a user dependent preference vector d_{u_i}). In order to clarify the meaning and building process of the Correlation Graph, we can consider a simple example. In table 1 we report a small learning set $\mathcal{L}$, in every row of the table there is the listing of movies watched (Y) and not-watched (-) by the corresponding user.

---

[4] Stochastic matrices are non-negative matrices having all columns that sum up to one.

Table 1. Listing of movies rated by users

	m_1	m_2	m_3	m_4	m_5
u_1	Y	Y	-	-	-
u_2	-	Y	Y	Y	-
u_3	Y	-	Y	-	-
u_4	Y	-	-	Y	Y
u_5	Y	Y	Y	Y	-
u_6	Y	-	Y	-	-
u_7	Y	-	Y	Y	-
u_8	Y	Y	-	Y	-
u_9	Y	-	-	-	Y
u_{10}	Y	-	-	-	Y
u_{11}	-	Y	-	Y	-
u_{12}	-	-	Y	Y	-

The resulting $\tilde{C}$ matrix is:

$$\tilde{C} = \begin{pmatrix} 0 & 3 & 4 & 4 & 3 \\ 3 & 0 & 2 & 4 & 0 \\ 4 & 2 & 0 & 4 & 0 \\ 4 & 4 & 4 & 0 & 1 \\ 3 & 0 & 0 & 1 & 0 \end{pmatrix}$$

So the corresponding Correlation Matrix C is:

$$C = \begin{pmatrix} 0 & 0.333 & 0.400 & 0.307 & 0.750 \\ 0.214 & 0 & 0.200 & 0.307 & 0 \\ 0.285 & 0.222 & 0 & 0.307 & 0 \\ 0.285 & 0.444 & 0.400 & 0 & 0.250 \\ 0.214 & 0 & 0 & 0.076 & 0 \end{pmatrix}$$

The Correlation Graph associated to the previous Correlation Matrix is shown in figure 3.

3   ItemRank Algorithm

The idea underlying the ItemRank algorithm is that we can use the model expressed by the Correlation Graph to forecast user preferences. For every user in the training set we know the ratings he assigned to a certain number of movies, that is $\mathcal{L}_{u_i}$, so, thanks to the graph $\mathcal{G}_C$ we can "spread" user u_i's preferences through the Correlation Graph. This process has to be repeated for every user and it involves graph $\mathcal{G}_C$ as a static user independent part and user u_i preferences as a dynamic user dependent part. Obviously we have to properly control the *preference flow* in order to transfer high score values to movies that are strongly related to movies with good ratings. The spreading algorithm that we apply has to possess two key properties: propagation and attenuation. These properties reflect two key assumptions. First of all if a movie m_k is related to one or more good movies, with respect to a given user u_i, then movie m_k will also be a good suggestion for user u_i , if we analyse the Correlation Graph we can easily discover relationships between movies and also the strength of these connections, that is the weight associated to every link connecting two movies. The second important factor we have to take into account is attenuation. Good movies have to transfer their positive influence through the Correlation Graph, but this effect decreases its power if we move further and further away from good movies, moreover if a good movie m_i is connected to two or more nodes, these have to share the boosting effect from m_i according to the weights of their connections as computed in matrix C. PageRank algorithm (see [29]) has both the propagation and the attenuation properties that we need, furthermore thanks to significant research efforts we can compute PageRank in a very efficient way (see [30,31]). Consider a generic graph $\mathcal{G} = (\mathcal{V}, \mathcal{E})$, where $\mathcal{V}$ is the set of nodes connected by directed links in $\mathcal{E}$, the classic PageRank algorithm computes an importance score $PR(n)$ for every node $n \in \mathcal{V}$ according to graph connectivity: a node will be important if it is connected to important nodes with a low out-degree. So the PageRank score for node n is defined as:

$$PR(n) = \alpha \cdot \sum_{q:(q,n)\in\mathcal{E}} \frac{PR(q)}{\omega_q} + (1-\alpha) \cdot \frac{1}{|\mathcal{V}|} \tag{1}$$

where ω_q is the out-degree of node q, α is a decay factor[5]. The equivalent matrix form of equation 1 is:

$$\mathbf{PR} = \alpha \cdot \mathbf{C} \cdot \mathbf{PR} + (1-\alpha) \cdot \frac{1}{|\mathcal{V}|} \cdot \mathbf{1}_{|\mathcal{V}|} \tag{2}$$

where $\mathbf{C}$ is the normalized connectivity matrix for graph $\mathcal{G}$ and $\mathbf{1}_{|\mathcal{V}|}$ is a $|\mathcal{V}|$ long vector of ones. PageRank can also be computed iterating equation 2, for example by applying the Jacobi method [32], even if iteration should be run until PageRank values convergence, we can also use a fixed number I of iterations. Classic PageRank can be extended by generalizing equation 2:

$$\mathbf{PR} = \alpha \cdot \mathbf{M} \cdot \mathbf{PR} + (1-\alpha) \cdot \mathbf{d} \tag{3}$$

where $\mathbf{M}$ is a stochastic matrix, its non-negative entries has to sum up to 1 for every column, and vector $\mathbf{d}$ has non-negative entries summing up to 1. Vector $\mathbf{d}$ can be tuned in order to bias the PageRank by boosting nodes corresponding to high value entries and matrix $\mathbf{M}$ controls the propagation and attenuation mode. Biased PageRank has been analysed in [33,34] and custom static score distribution vectors $\mathbf{d}$ have been applied to compute topic-sensitive PageRank [35], reputation of a node in a peer-to-peer network [36] and for combating web spam [37]. We present the *ItemRank* algorithm, that is a biased version of PageRank designed to be applied to a recommender system.

---

[5] A common choice for α is 0.85.

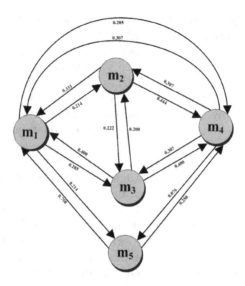

Fig. 3. A simple Correlation Graph

ItemRank equation can be easily derived from equation 3. We use graph $\mathcal{G}_C$ to compute an ItemRank value IR_{u_i} for every movie node and for every user profile. In this case the stochastic matrix $\mathbf{M}$ will be the Correlation Matrix $\mathcal{C}$ and for every user u_i we compute a different IR_{u_i} by simply choosing a different $\mathbf{d}_{u_i}$ static score distribution vector. The resulting equation is:

$$\mathbf{IR}_{u_i} = \alpha \cdot \mathcal{C} \cdot \mathbf{IR}_{u_i} + (1-\alpha) \cdot \mathbf{d}_{u_i} \tag{4}$$

where $\mathbf{d}_{u_i}$ has been build according to user u_i's preferences as recorded in training set $\mathcal{L}_{u_i}$. The unnormalized $\tilde{\mathbf{d}}_{u_i}$, with respect to the $j-th$ component, is defined as:

$$\tilde{d}_{u_i}^j = \begin{cases} 0 & \text{if } t_{i,j} \notin \mathcal{L}_{u_i} \\ r_{i,j} & \text{if } t_{i,j} \in \mathcal{L}_{u_i} \wedge t_{i,j} = (u_i, m_j, r_{i,j}) \end{cases}$$

So the normalized $\mathbf{d}_{u_i}$ vector will simply be $\mathbf{d}_{u_i} = \dfrac{\tilde{\mathbf{d}}_{u_i}}{|\tilde{\mathbf{d}}_{u_i}|}$. ItemRank, as defined in equation 4, can be computed also iteratively in this way:

$$\begin{cases} \mathbf{IR}_{u_i}(0) = \frac{1}{|\mathcal{M}|} \cdot \mathbf{1}_{|\mathcal{M}|} \\ \mathbf{IR}_{u_i}(t+1) = \alpha \cdot \mathcal{C} \cdot \mathbf{IR}_{u_i}(t) + (1-\alpha) \cdot \mathbf{d}_{u_i} \end{cases} \tag{5}$$

This dynamic system has to be run for every user, luckily it only needs on average about 20 iterations to converge (see section 4 for details). The interpretation of $\mathbf{IR}_{u_i}$ score vector for user u_i is straightforward, ItemRank scores induce a sorting of movies according to their expected liking for a given user. The higher is the ItemRank for a movie, the higher is the probability that a given user will prefer it to a lower score movie. In order to better explain how ItemRank algorithm works, we come back to the example discussed in subsection 2.2. We

Table 2. User u_1 preferences

	m_1	m_2	m_3	m_4	m_5
u_1	0.8	0.4	0	0	0

can compute preferences for user u_1 according to graph $\mathcal{G}_C$ in figure 3, suppose user u_1 expressed opinions as summarized in table 2.

Static score vector for user u_1 is $\mathbf{d}_{u_1} = (0.66, 0.33, 0, 0, 0)$, then the iteration of system 5 produces an ItemRank $\mathbf{IR}_{u_1} = (0.3175, 0.1952, 0.1723, 0.2245, 0.0723)$.

3.1   Complexity Issues

Algorithm scalability is a key issue for recommender systems, so any proposed technique has to be reasonably fast and able handling large amounts of user preferences and products. The ItemRank algorithm is be very efficient from both computational and memory resource usage points of view. When implemented it needs to store an $|M|$ nodes graph with a limited number of edges, representing the data model and it uses an extremely sparse preference vector (with few non-zero components) for every user. The interesting fact is that graph $\mathcal{G}_C$ contains edges (m_i, m_j) and (m_j, m_i) if and only if $\exists u_k : t_{k,i} \in L_{u_k} \wedge t_{k,j} \in L_{u_k}$, so no matter the number of users satisfying the previous condition, ratings information will be compressed in just a couple of links anyway. Obviously user preferences will not be lost, because preference vectors are the user-based ingredient we combine to the data model. It is interesting to note that the data structure we use scale very well with the increase of the number of users, in fact $\mathcal{G}_C$ node set cardinality is independent from $|\mathcal{U}|$ and also the number of edges tend to increase very slowly after $|\mathcal{U}|$ has exceeded a certain threshold $\bar{U}$. That is a very useful property, because in a real applicative scenario the number of users for a certain e-commerce service and the number of expressed preferences about products will rise much faster than the total number of offered products. Moreover ItemRank computation is very efficient, thanks to its strong relationship with PageRank algorithm, in fact the Correlation Matrix $\mathcal{C}$ is usually quite sparse, so that we can compute the ItemRank score in a very fast way by exploiting such a property (see [30,31] for example). In section 3.2 we show an alternative way to compute ItemRank that can scale also better than the iterative approach when the number of products we consider is not huge, that is a different (but equivalent) version of the same algorithm worth to be considered in many recommender system scenarios. It is also important to consider that we only need about 20 iterations of system 5 for every user in order to rank every movie according to every user taste, so if we have $|\mathcal{U}|$ users we have to run the algorithm $|\mathcal{U}|$ different times. In some time critical scenarios ItemRank can be combined with a user preference clustering, in that case we use preference vectors representing preferences for a cluster of users (something like a cluster centroid). But we need to recall that user profile clustering decreases performance from the recommendation quality point of view, while increasing a system scalability, as proved in [9]. So, in case we adopt user preference clustering, we need to tune for a proper trade-off between speed and accuracy. ItemRank is also faster than similar Random-Walk based approach such as CT and L^+ (already introduced in subsection 1.1, see [8,1] for details), in fact both CT and L^+ require to handle a graph containing nodes representing users and products and edges referred to user preferences. So in this graph there are $|\mathcal{U}|+|\mathcal{M}|$ nodes and two edges $(u_i, m_j),(m_j, u_i)$ for every opinion $(u_i, m_j, r_{i,j})$, while in the case of ItemRank you have only $|\mathcal{M}|$ nodes and ratings information is compressed. CT is used to rank every movie with respect to every system user, so the average commute time (CT) $n(u_i, m_j)$ referring to any user-movie couple u_i, m_j has to be computed, but $n(u_i, m_j) = m(u_i|m_j) + m(m_j|u_i)$ where $m(u_i|m_j)$ denotes the average first-passage time from node u_i to node m_j. So CT needs $2 \cdot |\mathcal{U}| \cdot |\mathcal{M}|$ average first-passage time computations, while ItemRank has to be applied only $|\mathcal{U}|$ times to rank every movie with respect to its similarity to every user. The situation is similar also if we consider L^+ algorithm, in this case, as stated in [8,1], the direct computation of the pseudoinverse of the Laplacian matrix L becomes intractable if the number of nodes becomes large (that could easy happen as the number of users increase), some optimized methods to partially overcome these limitations has been proposed in [26,38]

3.2   ItemRank as a Linear Operator and Convergence

In section 3 we presented ItemRank algorithm as an iterative method to compute a user preference dependent score for items according to equation 5, we also discussed complexity and efficiency issues in section 3.1. In the present section we wish to formulate the algorithm in a different way which allows us to discuss the convergence problem. This point of view can also be used to implement ItemRank in a more efficient way, depending on applicative scenario specific features. Starting from equation 5 we initialize the ItemRank value as $\mathbf{IR}_{u_i}(0) = \frac{1}{|\mathcal{M}|} \cdot \mathbf{1}_{|\mathcal{M}|}$, for simplicity we write $\mathbf{IR}_{u_i}(0) = \mathbf{IR}_0$, now it is possible to compute the first $T + 1$ steps of iteration 5 obtaining:

$$
\begin{cases}
\mathbf{IR}_{u_i}(0) = \mathbf{IR}_0 \\
\mathbf{IR}_{u_i}(1) = \alpha \cdot \mathcal{C} \cdot \mathbf{IR}_0 + (1 - \alpha) \cdot \mathbf{d}_{u_i} \\
\mathbf{IR}_{u_i}(2) = \alpha^2 \cdot \mathcal{C}^2 \cdot \mathbf{IR}_0 + \alpha \cdot \mathcal{C} \cdot (1 - \alpha) \cdot \mathbf{d}_{u_i} + (1 - \alpha) \cdot \mathbf{d}_{u_i} \\
\mathbf{IR}_{u_i}(3) = \alpha^3 \cdot \mathcal{C}^3 \cdot \mathbf{IR}_0 + \alpha^2 \cdot \mathcal{C}^2 \cdot (1 - \alpha) \cdot \mathbf{d}_{u_i} + \alpha \cdot \mathcal{C} \cdot (1 - \alpha) \cdot \mathbf{d}_{u_i} + (1 - \alpha) \cdot \mathbf{d}_{u_i} \\
\cdots \\
\mathbf{IR}_{u_i}(T + 1) = \alpha^{T+1} \cdot \mathcal{C}^{T+1} \cdot \mathbf{IR}_0 + (\sum_{t=0}^{T} \alpha^T \cdot \mathcal{C}^T) \cdots (1 - \alpha) \cdot \mathbf{d}_{u_i}
\end{cases}
$$

(6)

We are interested in studying the convergence of the sequence 6 when $T \to +\infty$. So we analyse:

$$
\mathbf{IR}_{u_i} = \lim_{T \to \infty} \left(\alpha^{T+1} \cdot \mathcal{C}^{T+1} \cdot \mathbf{IR}_0 + \left(\sum_{t=0}^{T} \alpha^t \cdot \mathcal{C}^t \right) \cdot (1 - \alpha) \cdot \mathbf{d}_{u_i} \right) \qquad (7)
$$

We recall that $\alpha \in (0, 1)$, moreover since matrix $\mathcal{C}$ is stochastic, then (according to Frobenius theorem) its maximum eigenvalue $\rho_{\mathcal{C}}$ is less than or equal 1. These facts result in:

$$\lim_{k \to \infty} \alpha^k \cdot \mathcal{C}^k \cdot \mathbf{x}_0 = \mathbf{0} \ \forall \mathbf{x}_0 \tag{8}$$

So the left part in equation 7 has value:

$$\lim_{T \to \infty} \alpha^{T+1} \cdot \mathcal{C}^{T+1} \cdot \mathbf{IR}_0 = 0$$

and we can ignore this term, that is also the reason why ItemRank score does not depend on its initialization $\mathbf{IR}_0$. It remains to deal with the series obtained from the right part of equation 7:

$$\mathbf{IR}_{u_i} = (\sum_{t=0}^{\infty} \alpha^t \cdot \mathcal{C}^t) \cdot (1 - \alpha) \cdot \mathbf{d}_{u_i}$$

but $\sum_{t=0}^{\infty} \alpha^t \cdot \mathcal{C}^t$ is guaranteed to converge due to the same considerations for equation 8.

If we denote $\tilde{IR} = \sum_{t=0}^{\infty} \alpha^T \cdot \mathcal{C}^T$, we note that ItemRank is just a linear operator. We use $\tilde{IR}$ linear operator to compute ItemRank score given a user preference vector $\mathbf{d}_{u_i}$ as:

$$\mathbf{IR}_{u_i} = \tilde{IR} \cdot (1 - \alpha) \cdot \mathbf{d}_{u_i}$$

It is important to consider that, while ItemRank score $\mathbf{IR}_{u_i}$ depends on user u_i preferences (through preference vector $\mathbf{d}_{u_i}$), $\tilde{IR}$ is user independent and it can be also precomputed off-line and applied to user preferences for every user on-line when required. So, even if ItemRank score requires to be recomputed for every system user, we can avoid equation 5 iteration by precomputing $\tilde{IR} = \sum_{t=0}^{\infty} \alpha^T \cdot \mathcal{C}^T$ off-line only one time and then we multiply $\tilde{IR}$ by every user preference vector $\mathbf{d}_{u_i}$ in order to obtain $\mathbf{IR}_{u_i}$. From a theoretical point of view this approach is equivalent to iterating equation 5, but its practical feasibility strongly depends on matrix $\mathcal{C}$ dimensionality. Depending on the application scenario we can decide to use the linear operator formulation for ItemRank, that is the case in many recommender system application, whenever the number of items to be suggested to users is big but not huge. A counter example is the case of PageRank computation (see [29]), PageRank can be obtained as a special case from ItemRank by properly setting vector $\mathbf{d}_{u_i}$ and matrix $\mathcal{C}$, as previously shown, so it is also possible to obtain a linear operator form for PageRank using the same procedure we applied in this section for ItemRank. Unluckily in that case computing the convergence value of the series $\sum_{t=0}^{\infty} \alpha^T \cdot \mathcal{C}^T$ is unfeasible due to the dimensionality of matrix $\mathcal{C}$. This dimension scales with the number of the considered web pages and it is obviously huge.

For the sake of completeness it is worth to recall some convergence speed properties that has been shown to be true for PageRank in [34], this property also states for ItemRank as a generalization of PageRank. Let $|\delta(t)|_1$ be the 1 norm of the relative error made in the computation of ItemRank with respect to its actual value at time t, so:

$$|\delta(t)|_1 = \frac{||\mathbf{IR}_{u_i}(t) - \mathbf{IR}_{u_i}||_1}{||\mathbf{IR}_{u_i}||_1} \tag{9}$$

In [34] it has been proved that:

$$|\delta(t)|_1 \le \alpha^t \cdot |\delta(0)|_1$$

If we call P_n the number of items to be considered by the system to be suggested (the dimensionality of vector $\mathbf{IR}_{u_i}$) it is obvious that

$$||\mathbf{IR}_{u_i}(t) - \mathbf{IR}_{u_i}||_1 \le P_n$$

and

$$||\mathbf{IR}_{u_i}||_1 \ge P_n \cdot (1 - \alpha)$$

so if we recall equation 9 we obtain:

$$|\delta(t)|_1 \le \frac{\alpha^t}{1 - \alpha} \tag{10}$$

If we want the desired error to be under a given threshold ϵ, it is simply possible to derive the condition from:

$$\frac{\alpha^t}{1 - \alpha} \le \epsilon$$

obtaining:

$$t \ge \frac{\log((1 - \alpha)\epsilon)}{\log d}$$

With respect to the experiment we ran (see section 4), we observed a reasonable convergence after only 20 iterations. From a theoretical point of view it is sufficient to apply equation 10 by setting $\alpha = 0.85$ and $t = 20$ to obtain $|\delta(20)|_1 = 0.2583$, since $P_n = 1,682$ for the considered dataset (see section 2.1) the average δ on every $\mathbf{IR}_{u_i}$ vector component is $1,5362e^{-4}$, that is a really reasonable convergence error.

4   Experimental Results

The experimental evaluation is one of the most crucial aspects for a recommender engine, since after all the only really valuable evaluation method would be to measure the satisfaction of a wide user group for an operative system that has been deployed and used for a long time. Unluckily that is not something so easy to do, then we need to try our systems on some popular benchmark before implementing it as a real system. To evaluate the performances of the ItemRank algorithm, we ran a set of experiments on the MovieLens data set, described in subsection 2.1. The choice of this particular data set is not restrictive, since it is a widely used standard benchmark for recommender system techniques and its structure is typical of the most common applicative scenarios. In fact we can apply ItemRank every time we have a set of users ($\mathcal{U}$) rating a set of items or products ($\mathcal{I}$ that is the generic notation for $\mathcal{M}$), if we can model our recommendation problem this way (or in any equivalent form) it will be possible to use ItemRank to rank items according to user preferences. It is possible to measure a recommender system's performance in many different ways such as using MAE, MSE, DOA and so on, but in this context we are not interested in using the state-of-the-art quality index because we wish to compare ItemRank with other graph based algorithms. So we chose an experimental setup and performance index that is the same as used in [8,1], this way we can directly compare our algorithm with some of the most promising scoring algorithms we found in related literature (CT, L^+ and so on), having many points in common with ItemRank "philosophy". In fact these algorithms, like ItemRank, use graphs to model the dataset, and our target was to develop a system able to use in an optimal way this kind of representation because we believe the graphical data model is a very intuitive, simple and easy way to describe the data in a recommender system. We split the MovieLens data set as described in [2], in order to obtain 5 different subsets, then we applied ItemRank 5 times (5-fold cross validation). Each time, one of the 5 subsets is used as the test set and the remaining 4 subsets have been merged to form a training set. At the end we computed the average result across all 5 trials. So we have 5 splittings, each uses 80% of the ratings for the training set (that is $80,000$ ratings) and 20% for the test set (the remaining $20,000$ ratings), that is exactly the same way tests have been performed in [8,1]. The performance index we used is the *degree of agreement* (DOA), which is a variant of Somers'D (see [39] for further details). DOA is a way of measuring how good is an item ranking (movie ranking in MovieLens case) for any given user. To compute DOA for a single user u_i we need to define a set of movies $\mathcal{NW}_{u_i} \subset \mathcal{M}$ ("Not Watched" by user u_i) that is the set of movies that are not in the training set for user u_i, nor in the test set for user u_i, so:

$$\mathcal{NW}_{u_i} = \mathcal{M} \setminus (\mathcal{L}_{u_i} \cup \mathcal{T}_{u_i})$$

We need to remark that $\mathcal{NW}_{u_i}$ refers to user u_i and it is not empty. In fact the movie set $\mathcal{M}$ contains every movie referred inside the system no matter the user who rated it, so a generic movie $m_k \in \mathcal{NW}_{u_i}$ belongs to $\mathcal{L}_{u_h}$ and/or $\mathcal{T}_{u_h}$ for at least one user $u_h \neq u_i$. Now we define the boolean function *check_order* as:

$$check\_order_{u_i}(m_j, m_k) = \begin{cases} 1 \text{ if } IR_{u_i}^{m_j} \geq IR_{u_i}^{m_k} \\ 0 \text{ if } IR_{u_i}^{m_j} < IR_{u_i}^{m_k} \end{cases}$$

where $IR_{u_i}^{m_j}$ is the score assigned to movie m_j with respect to user u_i preferences, by the algorithm we are testing. Then we can compute individual DOA for user u_i, that is:

$$\text{DOA}_{u_i} = \frac{\sum_{(j \in \mathcal{T}_{u_i}, \, k \in \mathcal{NW}_{u_i})} check\_order_{u_i}(m_j, m_k)}{|\mathcal{T}_{u_i}| \cdot |\mathcal{NW}_{u_i}|}$$

So DOA_{u_i} measures for user u_i the percentage of movie pairs ranked in the correct order with respect to the total number of pairs, in fact a good scoring algorithm should rank the movies that have indeed been watched in higher positions than movies that have not been watched. A random ranking produces a degree of agreement of 50%, half of all the pairs are in correct order and the other half in bad order. An ideal ranking correspond to a 100% DOA. Two different global degree of agreement can be computed considering ranking for individual users: Macro-averaged DOA and micro-averaged DOA. The Macro-averaged DOA (or shortly Macro DOA) will be the average of individual degree of agreement for every user, so:

$$\text{Macro DOA} = \frac{\sum_{u_i \in U} \text{DOA}_{u_i}}{|\mathcal{U}|}$$

The micro-averaged DOA (or shortly micro DOA) is the ratio between the number of movie pairs in the right order (for every user) and the total number of movie pairs checked (for every user), so it can be computed as:

$$\text{micro DOA} = \frac{\sum_{u_i \in \mathcal{U}} \left(\sum_{(j \in \mathcal{T}_{u_i}, \, k \in \mathcal{NW}_{u_i})} check\_order_{u_i}(m_j, m_k) \right)}{\sum_{u_i \in \mathcal{U}} \left(|\mathcal{T}_{u_i}| \cdot |\mathcal{NW}_{u_i}| \right)}$$

Then micro DOA is something like a weighted averaging of individual DOA values. In fact the bigger is set $\mathcal{T}_{u_i}$ for a given user u_i, the more important is the individual DOA_{u_i} contribution to micro DOA global computation. Macro DOA and micro DOA have been evaluated for every experiment we ran. We summarize experimental results in table 3, 4 and 5. In table 3 we compare ItemRank performances to a simplified version of the same algorithm, in order to highlight the importance of the information hidden in the Correlation Matrix $\mathcal{C}$. ItemRank with the binary graph is identical to classical ItemRank (described in section 3) but there is a key difference in the way we build matrix $\mathcal{C}$ (we denote the simplified version as $\mathcal{C}^{bin}$), in this case it is obtained by normalizing a binary version of $\tilde{\mathcal{C}}$ ($\tilde{\mathcal{C}}^{bin}$), so we have: $\mathcal{C}_{i,j}^{bin} = \frac{\tilde{c}_{i,j}^{bin}}{\omega_j}$ where $\tilde{\mathcal{C}}_{i,j}^{bin}$ can be computed as:

$$\tilde{c}_{i,j}^{bin} = \begin{cases} 1 \text{ if } \mathcal{U}_{i,j} > 0 \\ 0 \text{ if } \mathcal{U}_{i,j} = 0 \end{cases}$$

In other words if we compute ItemRank with binary graph, we are weighting every correlation edge connecting two items in the same way, no matter the number of co-occurrences in user preference lists fro these items, since $\mathcal{C}^{bin_{i,j}}$

Table 3. Performance comparison between ItemRank and its simplified version with binary Correlation Graph

	ItemRank		ItemRank (binary graph)	
	micro DOA	Macro DOA	micro DOA	Macro DOA
SPLIT 1	87.14	87.73	71.00	72.48
SPLIT 2	86.98	87.61	70.94	72.91
SPLIT 3	87.20	87.69	71.17	72.98
SPLIT 4	87.08	87.47	70.05	71.51
SPLIT 5	86.91	88.28	70.00	71.78
Mean	**87.06**	**87.76**	**70.63**	**72.33**

Table 4. Comparison among different scoring algorithm applied to MovieLens data set

	MaxF	CT	PCA CT	One-way	Return
Macro DOA	84.07	84.09	84.04	84.08	72.63
difference with MaxF (in %)	0	+0.02	-0.03	+0.01	-11.43

Table 5. Comparison among different scoring algorithm applied to MovieLens data set (second part)

	L^+	ItemRank	Katz	Dijkstra
Macro DOA	87.23	**87.76**	85.83	49.96
difference with MaxF (in %)	+3.16	**+3.69**	+1.76	-34.11

correspond to the weight of edge (m_i, m_j) in the Correlation Graph $\mathcal{G}_C$ we use for information propagation.

Table 3 clearly shows the usefulness of a properly weighted Correlation Matrix $\mathcal{C}$ compared to $\mathcal{C}^{bin}$. This table provides both Macro and micro DOA for every split and for ItemRank and its simplified version with binary graph: ItemRank clearly works much better when we use a proper Correlation Matrix. For example, if we look at Macro DOA mean values, ItemRank with Correlation Matrix $\mathcal{C}$ obtain +15.43 points (in %) with respect to $\mathcal{C}^{bin}$ version. These are interesting results because they confirm our main hypothesis: ItemRank algorithm ranks items according to the information extracted from the Correlation Matrix (that is equivalent to the weighted Correlation Graph) and the way we compute $\mathcal{C}$ entries is really able to properly model relationships among evaluated items.

Finally table 4 and table 5 show a performance comparison among different scoring algorithm applied to the MovieLens data set. We briefly described some of these algorithms in subsection 1.1, for further details see [8,1]. For every tested algorithm we provide Macro DOA index, that has been computed for every technique as the average result across all 5 trials of 5-fold cross-validation. Moreover we provide the difference (in %) with performance obtained by the trivial MaxF algorithm. MaxF is our baseline for the task, it is a user independent scoring algorithm, it simply ranks the movies by the number of persons who watched them, movies are suggested to each person in order of decreasing popularity. So MaxF produces the same ranking for all the users. ItemRank performs better than any other considered technique obtaining **+3.69** with respect to the baseline. In this test ItemRank also perform better than L^+ algorithm by obtaining a Macro DOA value of **87.76** versus 87.23 for L^+. In addition it is worth to note that ItemRank is less complex than other proposed algorithms with respect to memory usage and computational cost too, as already argued in subsection 3.1.

5 Conclusions

In this paper, we presented a random–walk based scoring algorithm, which can be used to recommend products according to user preferences. We compared our algorithm with other state-of-the-art ranking techniques on a standard benchmark (MovieLens data set). ItemRank performs better than the other algorithms we compared to and, at the same time, it is less complex than other proposed algorithms with respect to memory usage and computational cost too. A theoretical analysis of convergence properties for the algorithm is also included. Future research topics include the experimentation of the algorithm on different applications. We are now working on an extension of ItemRank. The version presented so far is able to handle the recommendation task as an item scoring/ranking problem. But we can face the problem from the regression point of view too. So we expect ItemRank 2.0 will also be able to produce expected satisfaction prediction for a given recommendation, other than product ranking.

References

1. Fouss, F., Pirotte, A., Sarens, M.: A novel way of computing dissimilarities between nodes of a graph, with application to collaborative filtering. In: Boulicaut, J.-F., Esposito, F., Giannotti, F., Pedreschi, D. (eds.) ECML 2004. LNCS (LNAI), vol. 3201, pp. 26–37. Springer, Heidelberg (2004)
2. Sarwar, B.M., Karypis, G., Konstan, J., Riedl, J.: Recommender systems for large-scale e-commerce: Scalable neighborhood formation using clustering. In: Fifth International Conference on Computer and Information Technology (2002)
3. Sarwar, B.M., Karypis, G., Konstan, J.A., Riedl, J.: Item-based collaborative filtering recommendation algorithms. In (WWW10). 10th International World Wide Web Conference (May 2001)
4. Miller, B., Riedl, J., Konstan, J.: Grouplens for usenet: Experiences in applying collaborative filtering to a social information system. In: Leug, C., Fisher, D. (eds.) From Usenet to CoWebs: Interacting with Social Information Spaces, Springer, Heidelberg (2002)
5. Shardanand, U., Maes, P.: Social information filtering: Algorithms for automating "word of mouth". In: CHI 1995 (1995)
6. Goldberg, K., Roeder, T., Gupta, D., Perkins, C.: Eigentaste: A constant time collaborative filtering algorithm. Information Retrieval 4(2), 133–151 (2001)

7. Schafer, J., Konstan, J., Riedl, J.: Electronic commerce recommender applications. Journal of Data Mining and Knowledge Discovery (January 2001)
8. Fouss, F., Pirotte, A., Renders, J.M., Sarens, M.: A novel way of computing dissimilarities between nodes of a graph, with application to collaborative filtering. In: IEEE / WIC / ACM International Joint Conference on Web Intelligence, pp. 550–556. IEEE Computer Society Press, Los Alamitos (2005)
9. Sarwar, B.M., Karypis, G., Konstan, J.A., Riedl, J.: Application of dimensionality reduction in recommender system a case study. In: ACM WebKDD 2000 Web Mining for E-Commerce Workshop, ACM Press, New York (2000)
10. Breese, J.S., Heckerman, D., Kadie, C.: Empirical analysis of predictive algorithms for collaborative filtering. In: 14th Conference on Uncertainty in Artificial Intelligence (UAI-98), pp. 43–52 (July 1998)
11. Grcar, M., Fortuna, B., Mladenic, D., Grobelnik, M.: Knn versus svm in the collaborative filtering framework. In: Nasraoui, O., Zaïane, O., Spiliopoulou, M., Mobasher, B., Masand, B., Yu, P.S. (eds.) WebKDD 2005. LNCS (LNAI), vol. 4198, Springer, Heidelberg (2006)
12. Canny, J.: Collaborative filtering with privacy via factor analysis. In: IEEE Conference on Security and Privacy, IEEE Computer Society Press, Los Alamitos (2002)
13. Herlocker, J., Konstan, J., Borchers, A., Riedl, J.: An algorithmic framework for performing collaborative filtering. In: ACM SIGIR 1999, ACM Press, ACM SIGIR (1999)
14. Kemeny, J.G., Snell, J.L.: Finite Markov Chains. Springer, Heidelberg (1976)
15. Norris, J.: Markov Chains. Cambridge University Press, Cambridge (1997)
16. Katz, L.: A new status index derived from sociometric analysis. Psychmetrika 18(1), 39–43 (1953)
17. Huang, Z., Chen, H., Zeng, D.: Applying associative retrieval techniques to alleviate the sparsity problem in collaborative filtering. ACM Transactions on Information Systems 22(1), 116–142 (2004)
18. Scholkopf, B., Smola, A.: Learning with kernels. MIT Press, Cambridge (2002)
19. Chebotarev, P., Shamis, E.: The matrix-forest theorem and measuring relations in small social groups. Automation and Remote Control 58(9), 1505–1514 (1997)
20. Chebotarev, P., Shamis, E.: On proximity measures for graph vertices. Automation and Remote Control 59(10), 1443–1459 (1998)
21. Harel, D., Koren, Y.: On clustering using random walks. In: Conference on the Foundations of Software Technology and Theoretical Computer Science, pp. 18–41 (2001)
22. White, S., Smyth, P.: Algorithms for estimating relative importance in networks. In: Ninth ACM SIGKDD International Conference on Knowledge Discovery and Data mining, pp. 227–266. ACM Press, New York (2003)
23. Newman, M.: A measure of betweenness centrality based on random walks. Social Networks 27(1), 39–54 (2005)
24. Wasserman, S., Faust, K.: Social Network Analysis: Methods and Applications. Cambridge University Press, Cambridge (1994)
25. Nadler, B., Lafon, S., Coifman, R., Kevrekidis, I.: Diffusion maps, spectral clustering and eigenfunctions of fokker-planck operators. In: Advances in Neural Information Processing Systems (2005)
26. Brand, M.: A random walks perspective on maximizing satisfaction and profit. In: 2005 SIAM International Conference on Data Mining (2005)
27. Ding, C.: Tutorial on spectral clustering. In: Gama, J., Camacho, R., Brazdil, P.B., Jorge, A.M., Torgo, L. (eds.) ECML 2005. LNCS (LNAI), vol. 3720, Springer, Heidelberg (2005)

28. Saerens, M., Fouss, F., Yen, L., Dupont, P.: The principal components analysis of a graph, and its relationships to spectral clustering. In: Boulicaut, J.-F., Esposito, F., Giannotti, F., Pedreschi, D. (eds.) ECML 2004. LNCS (LNAI), vol. 3201, Springer, Heidelberg (2004)
29. Page, L., Brin, S., Motwani, R., Winograd, T.: The pagerank citation ranking: Bringing order to the web. Technical report, Stanford University (1998)
30. Haveliwala, T.: Efficient computation of pagerank. Technical report, Stanford University (1999)
31. Kamvar, S., Haveliwala, T., Manning, C., Golub, G.: Extrapolation methods for accelerating pagerank computations. In: Twelfth International Conference on World Wide Web (2003)
32. Golub, G., Loan, C.V.: Matrix Computations, 3rd edn., The Johns Hopkins University Press (1996)
33. Langville, A., Meyer, C.: Deeper inside pagerank. Internet Mathematics 1(3), 335–380 (2003)
34. Bianchini, M., Gori, M., Scarselli, F.: Inside pagerank. ACM Transactions on Internet Technology 5(1), 92–128 (2005)
35. Haveliwala, T.: Topic-sensitive pagerank. In: Eleventh International Conference on World Wide Web (2002)
36. Kamvar, S., Schlosser, M., Garcia-Molina, H.: The eigentrust algorithm for reputation management in p2p networks. In: Twelfth International Conference on World Wide Web (2003)
37. Gyongyi, Z., Garcia-Molina, H., Pedersen, J.: Combating web spam with trustrank. Technical report, Stanford University (2004)
38. Ho, N., Dooren, P.V.: On the pseudo-inverse of the laplacian of a bipartite graph. Applied Mathematics Letters 18(8), 917–922 (2005)
39. Siegel, S., Castellan, J.: Nonparametric Statistics for the Behavioral Sciences. McGraw-Hill, New York (1988)

Towards a Scalable *k*NN CF Algorithm: Exploring Effective Applications of Clustering

Al Mamunur Rashid, Shyong K. Lam, Adam LaPitz, George Karypis, and John Riedl

Computer Science and Engineering
University of Minnesota
Minneapolis, MN 55455
{arashid,lam,lapitz,karypis,riedl}@cs.umn.edu

Abstract. Collaborative Filtering (CF)-based recommender systems bring mutual benefits to both users and the operators of the sites with too much information. Users benefit as they are able to find items of interest from an unmanageable number of available items. On the other hand, e-commerce sites that employ recommender systems can increase sales revenue in at least two ways: a) by drawing customers' attention to items that they are likely to buy, and b) by cross-selling items. However, the sheer number of customers and items typical in e-commerce systems demand specially designed CF algorithms that can gracefully cope with the vast size of the data. Many algorithms proposed thus far, where the principal concern is recommendation quality, may be too expensive to operate in a large-scale system. We propose CLUSTKNN, a simple and intuitive algorithm that is well suited for large data sets. The method first compresses data tremendously by building a straightforward but efficient clustering model. Recommendations are then generated quickly by using a simple NEAREST NEIGHBOR-based approach. We demonstrate the feasibility of CLUSTKNN both analytically and empirically. We also show, by comparing with a number of other popular CF algorithms that, apart from being highly scalable and intuitive, CLUSTKNN provides very good recommendation accuracy as well.

1   Introduction

The amount of content available on the web today is tremendous. The English version of the online encyclopedia Wikipedia contains more than 1.1 million articles. Flickr, a popular photo sharing service, has about 130 million photos[1]. The blog search engine Technorati has over 41 million blogs and 2.5 billion links in its index. This is far too much content for any person to consume, and is, in a nutshell, the problem of *information overload*. To help solve this problem, people need tools to help them decide what items might be worthwhile to look at. One effective tool for this task is a *recommender system*. These systems suggest items that a user might be interested based on her preferences, observed behaviors, and information about the items themselves.

---

[1] *http://time.com/time/magazine/article/ 0,9171,1186931,00.html*

O. Nasraoui et al. (Eds.): WebKDD 2006, LNAI 4811, pp. 147–166, 2007.

An example of a recommender system in use is the personalized internet radio station last.fm[2], which chooses songs to play for a user based on the songs and artists that she has listened to and expressed opinions about in the past. Another example is MovieLens[3], a movie recommender that uses peoples' opinions about movies to recommend other movies that users might enjoy watching.

Collaborative Filtering. Recommender systems are often implemented using an *automated collaborative filtering* (ACF, or CF) algorithm. These algorithms produce recommendations based on the intuition that similar users have similar tastes. That is, people who you share common likes and dislikes with are likely to be a good source for recommendations. Numerous CF algorithms have been developed over the past fifteen years, each of which approach the problem from a different angle, including similarity between users[20], similarity between items[23], personality diagnosis[19], Bayesian networks[2], singular value decomposition[25], and neural networks[18]. These algorithms have distinguishing qualities with respect to evaluation metrics such as recommendation accuracy, speed, and level of personalization.

When deciding which algorithm to use in a system, one key factor to consider is the algorithm's ability to scale given the size of the data. In systems with millions of items and possibly tens of millions of users, the number of CF algorithms that are practically able to produce quality recommendations in real time is limited. Even with costs of commodity hardware falling rapidly, a brute-force approach may be prohibitively expensive. Tradeoffs between speed and recommendation accuracy often need to be made, and the problem of developing highly scalable algorithms continues to be an interesting problem.

Efficient and Scalable CF Algorithms. Yu et al. note in [32] that there has been relatively little work in studying the efficiency of CF algorithms and developing algorithms that do not have either extremely expensive precomputation time or slow online performance. Linden et al. explore the suitability of several algorithms for use on the Amazon.com web site and conclude that algorithms based on similarity between items are the best choice for a system of their size[14]. They consider algorithms based on clustering techniques, but dismiss those algorithms on the premise that they produce poor recommendation quality. However, other researchers have found that using clustering techniques can indeed lead to good recommendations[4,30,22,13]. The algorithm proposed in this paper is based on classical clustering methods, and based on our results, we also believe that using clustering is a viable way to increase efficiency and scalability while maintaining good recommendation quality. A more in-depth summary of previous work in applying clustering methods to collaborative filtering can be found in [13].

Contributions. In this paper, we propose CLUSTKNN, a hybrid memory and model-based CF algorithm based on clustering techniques, as a way to overcome this scalability challenge. By applying complexity analysis, we analyically

---

[2] *http://last.fm*
[3] *http://www.movielens.umn.edu*

demonstrate the performance advantages that CLUSTKNN has over traditional CF algorithms. In addition, we present empirical measurements of the performance and recommendation accuracy of CLUSTKNN and several other algorithms.

The remainder of this paper is organized as follows. Section 2 introduces the general framework in which CF algorithms operate in, and further discusses the problem that we are solving. Section 3 describes our proposed approach in detail. Section 4 outlines several other well-known CF algorithms that we compare our approach to. The results of our comparison are presented in section 5 and discussed in section 6. Finally, we conclude in section 7 with a brief discussion of future work.

2   The Problem Domain

A collaborative filtering domain consists of a set of n customers or users $\{u_1, u_2, \ldots, u_n\}$, a set of m products or items $\{a_1, a_2, \ldots, a_m\}$, and users' preferences on items. Typically, each user only expresses her preferences for a small number of items. In other words, the corresponding *user* × *item* matrix is very sparse.

Users' preferences can be in terms of *explicit* ratings on some scale including a binary like/dislike, or they can be *implicit*—for example, a customer's purchase history, or her browsing patterns. A recommender system may also maintain demographic and other information about the users, and information about item features such as actors, directors, and genres in the case of a movie. This additional content information can be used to create *content-based filtering* [16,21], which can help improve a CF system, particularly where rating data is limited or absent (e.g., newly introduced items). In this paper we consider CF systems consisting of explicit numerical ratings and no content information.

Next we address two semantically different types of recommendations. A CF recommender system can produce two forms of recommendations on the items the target user has not already rated: a) predicted ratings on the items, and b) an ordered list of items the user might like the most. The latter type of recommendations is sometimes referred to as *top-N* recommendations [25,23]. Note that a *top-N* list can be trivially constructed by first computing rating predictions on all items not yet rated, and then sorting the result and keeping the top N. We study both types of recommendation in this paper.

We now turn to the problem statement. An e-commerce recommender system may easily involve millions of customers and products [14]. This amount of data poses a great challenge to the CF algorithms in that the recommendations need to be generated in real-time. Furthermore, the algorithm also has to cope with a steady influx of new users *and* items. For the majority of the algorithms proposed to date, the primary emphasis has been given into improving recommendation accuracy. While accuracy is certainly important and can affect the profitability of the company, the operator simply cannot deploy the system if it does not scale to the vast data of the site.

3   Proposed Approach

In [2], Breese et al. introduce a classification of CF algorithms that divides them into two broad classes: *memory-based* algorithms and *model-based* algorithms. Here, we briefly discuss each of these and describe how our approach leverages the advantages of both types of algorithms.

A memory-based algorithm such as User-based KNN [20] utilizes the entire database of user preferences when computing recommendations. These algorithms tend to be simple to implement and require little to no training cost. They can also easily take new preference data into account. However, their online performance tends to be slow as the size of the user and item sets grow, which makes these algorithms as stated in the literature unsuitable in large systems. One workaround is to only consider a subset of the preference data in the calculation, but doing this can reduce both recommendation quality and the number of items that can be recommended due to data being omitted from the calculation. Another workaround is to perform as much of the computation as possible in an offline setting. However, this may make it difficult to add new users to the system on a real-time basis, which is a basic necessity of most online systems. Furthermore, the storage requirements for the pre-computed data could be high.

On the other hand, a model-based algorithm such as one based on Bayesian networks [2] or singular value decomposition (SVD) [25] computes a model of the preference data and uses it to produce recommendations. Often, the model-building process is time-consuming and is only done periodically. The models are compact and can generate recommendations very quickly. The disadvantage to model-based algorithms is that adding new users, items, or preferences can be tantamount to recomputing the entire model.

CLUSTKNN, our proposed approach is a hybrid of the *model* and *memory* based approaches and has the advantages from both types. One of our primary goals is to maintain simplicity and intuitiveness throughout the approach. We believe this is important in a recommender algorithm because the ability to succintly explain to users how recommendations are made is a major factor in providing a good user experience [29]. We achieve this by utilizing a straightforward *partitional clustering* algorithm [12] for modeling users. To generate recommendations from the learned model, we use a nearest-neighbor algorithm similar to the one described in [20]. However, since the data is greatly compressed after the model is built, recommendations can be computed quickly, which solves the scalability challenge discussed previously.

One interesting property of CLUSTKNN is its tunable nature. We show later in the paper that a tunable parameter, the number of clusters k in the model, can be adjusted to trade off accuracy for time and space requirements. This makes CLUSTKNN adaptable to systems of different sizes and allows it to be useful throughout the life of a system as it grows.

We now provide the details of the algorithm. First we give an outline, and following that we provide explanations of the key points. The algorithm has two phases: model building (offline) and generation of predictions or recommendations (online).

Model Building

- Select the number of user-clusters k, considering the effect on the recommendation accuracy and resource requirements.
- Perform BISECTING k-MEANS clustering on the user-preference data.
- Build the model with k *surrogate* users, directly derived from the k *centroids*: $\{c_1, c_2, \ldots, c_k\}$, where each c_i is a vector of size m, the number of items. That is, $c_i = (\tilde{R}_{c_i,a_1}, \tilde{R}_{c_i,a_2}, \ldots, \tilde{R}_{c_i,a_m})$, where $\tilde{R}_{c_i,a_j}$ is the element in the centroid vector c_i corresponding to the item a_j. Further, since $\tilde{R}_{c_i,a_j}$ is essentially an average value, it is 0 if nobody in the i-th cluster has rated a_j.

Prediction Generation

In order to compute the rating prediction $\hat{R}_{u_t,a_t}$ for the target (user, item) pair (u_t, a_t), the following steps are taken.

- Compute similarity of the target user with each of the surrogate model users who have rated a_t using the Pearson correlation coefficient:

$$w_{u_t,c_i} = \frac{\sum_{a \in \mathcal{I}}(R_{u_t,a} - \overline{R}_{u_t})(\tilde{R}_{c_i,a} - \overline{R}_{c_i})}{\sqrt{\sum_{a \in \mathcal{I}}(R_{u_t,a} - \overline{R}_{u_t})^2 \sum_{a \in I}(\tilde{R}_{c_i,a} - \overline{R}_{c_i})^2}}$$

where $\mathcal{I}$ is the set of items rated by both the target user and i-th surrogate user.
- Find up to l surrogate users most similar to the target user.
- Compute prediction using the adjusted weighted average:

$$\hat{R}_{u_t,a_t} = \overline{R}_{u_t} + \frac{\sum_{i=1}^{l}(\tilde{R}_{c_i,a_t} - \overline{R}_{c_i})w_{u_t,c_i}}{\sum_{i=1}^{l} w_{u_t,c_i}}$$

Note that any *partitional clustering* [12] technique can used for model-building in CLUSTKNN. We selected the BISECTING k-MEANS algorithm, which we describe below.

BISECTING k-MEANS is an extension to and an improved version of the basic k-MEANS algorithm [12]. The algorithm starts by considering all data points (rating-profiles of all users, in our case) as a single cluster. Then it repeats the following steps $(k-1)$ times to produce k clusters.

1. Pick the largest cluster to split.
2. Apply the basic k-MEANS (2-MEANS, to be exact) clustering to produce 2 sub-clusters.
3. Repeat step 2 for j times and take the best split, one way of determining which is looking for the best *intra*-cluster similarity.

At this stage, it is straightforward to derive the time-complexity of CLUSTKNN. Note that the time complexity of CF algorithms can be divided into two parts: one for the offline model-building, and the other for the online generation of recommendations.

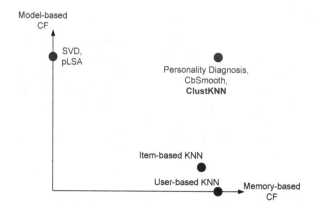

Fig. 1. The space encompassed by the CF algorithms we studied

The time-complexity of the basic k-MEANS is reported to be $O(n)$ in [12]; however, this is assuming the cost of computing the *similarity* or *distance* between the data points and centroids as a constant. However, in CLUSTKNN, this cost is $O(m)$, so the k-MEANS time-complexity becomes $O(mn)$. Therefore, the complexity of the BISECTING k-MEANS becomes $O((k-1)jmn) \simeq O(mn)$, which is the offline complexity of CLUSTKNN.

During the online stage, $O(k)$ similarity weight calculations are needed for the target user, each of which takes $O(m)$ time; therefore, online time-complexity is $O(km) \simeq O(m)$.

In their work on document clustering [28], Steinbach et al. empirically showed that BISECTING k-MEANS performed the best on a set of text datasets. Furthermore, the authors noted a nice property of BISECTING k-MEANS—the produced clusters tended to be of relatively uniform size. Whereas, in regular k-MEANS, the cluster sizes may vary significantly, producing poorer quality clusters.

4   Other CF Algorithms Considered

Xue et al [31] took the same idea of using clustering to transform a k-NN-based CF algorithm scalable. We study this algorithm side by side with our approach. In order to investigate how CLUSTKNN compares with other CF algorithms, we selected several other algorithms shown in figure 1. Our criteria for picking the algorithms include a) how frequently the algorithms are cited in the literature, and b) whether the algorithms span the classification space introduced by Breese et al [2]. In the following, we provide a brief overview of each of the selected algorithms.

pLSA

Probabilistic Latent Semantic Analysis (pLSA) for collaborative filtering is an elegant *generative* model proposed by Hofmann et al [11]. pLSA is a *three-way aspect* model adapted from their earlier contribution of *two-way aspect* models applied to text analysis [10].

At the heart of the pLSA approach is the notion of the *latent* class variable Z. The number of states of Z is an input to the model, and each state z can be interpreted as a different *user-type*. Each user belongs to these user-types with a unique probability distribution $P(z|u)$. Recall that this type of probabilistic assignment of entities to groups is similar in principle to the so-called *soft-clustering* approach.

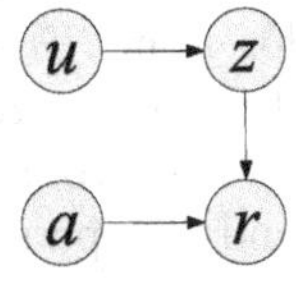

Fig. 2. 3-way aspect model

Hofmann models the probability density function $p(r|a, z)$ with a Gaussian mixture model and develops an Expectation Maximization (EM) method to learn mixture coefficients $P(z|u)$ and $p(r|a, z)$. Note that, due to Gaussian modeling, estimating $p(r|a, z)$ becomes estimating $p(r; \mu_{a,z}, \sigma_{a,z})$.

In the end, the learned model includes $P(z|u)$s for each user and for each state of Z, and values of μ and σ for each item and each state of Z.

Prediction for the target (user, item) pair is simply the weighted average of the means of a_t for each state z. That is,

$$\hat{R}_{u_t,a_t} = \sum_z P(z|u_t)\mu_{a_t,z} \tag{1}$$

Note that the model size grows linearly with the number of users; in fact, it is $O(m + n) \simeq O(n)$, if $n \gg m$. Furthermore, since $P(z|u)$'s are precomputed in the model, recommending to the new users pose a challenge. Hofmann proposes to perform a limited EM iteration in this situation.

SVD

Singular Value Decomposition (SVD) is a matrix factorization technique that can produce three matrices given the rating matrix A: $SVD(A) = U \times S \times V^T$. Details of SVD can be found in [6]; however, suffice it to say that the matrices U, S, and V can be reduced to construct a *rank-k* matrix, $X = U_k \times S_k \times V_k^T$ that is the closest approximation to the original matrix.

SVD requires a complete matrix to operate; however, a typical CF rating matrix is very sparse (see table 2). To circumvent this limitation of the CF datasets, [25] proposed using average values in the empty cells of the rating matrix. An alternate method proposed by Srebro et al. [27] finds a model that maximizes the *log-likelihood* of the actual ratings by an EM procedure. The EM procedure is rather simple and is stated below:

E-step: Missing entries of A are replaced with the values of current X. This creates an *expected* complete matrix A'.

M-step: Perform $SVD(A')$. This creates un updated X.

This EM process is guaranteed to converge. Upon convergence, the final X represents a linear model of the rating data, and the missing entries of the original A are filled with predicted values.

Personality Diagnosis

Personality Diagnosis [19] is a probabilistic CF algorithm that lies in between *model-based* and *memory-based* approaches. In this CF algorithm, each user is assumed to have a *personality type* that captures their true, internal preferences for items. However, the true personality type is unobservable, since users rate items by adding a *Gaussian* noise to their true preferences on the items.

The probability that the target user u_t's rating on an item a_t is x, given u_t and u_i's personality types are same, is defined by equation 2.

$$P(R_{u_t,a_t} = x|type_{u_t} = type_{u_i}) = e^{-(x-R_{u_i,a_t})^2/2\sigma^2} \qquad (2)$$

The authors derive the probability that two users' personalities are of the same type as follows.

$$P(type_{u_t} = type_{u_i}|\mathbf{R}_{u_t}) = 1/n \prod_{a \in \mathcal{I}} P(R_{u_t,a} = x_a|type_{u_t} = type_{u_i}) \qquad (3)$$

where $\mathbf{R}_{u_t}$ is the set of ratings reported by the target user.

Finally, the prediction on the target item a_t for u_t is computed as

$$\hat{R}_{u_t,a_t} = \operatorname*{argmax}_x P(R_{u_t,a_t} = x|\mathbf{R}_{u_t}) \qquad (4)$$

$$= \operatorname*{argmax}_x \sum_i P(R_{u_t,a_t} = x|type_{u_t} = type_{u_i})$$

$$.P(type_{u_t} = type_{u_i}|\mathbf{R}_{u_t}) \qquad (5)$$

User-based KNN

This algorithm belongs to the *memory-based* class of CF algorithms. Predictions under this algorithm are computed as a two step process. First, the similarities between the target user and all other users who have rated the target item are computed — most commonly using the Pearson correlation coefficient [8,20]. That is,

$$w_{u_i u_t} = \frac{\sum_{a \in \mathcal{I}}(R_{u_i,a} - \overline{R}_{u_i})(R_{u_t,a} - \overline{R}_{u_t})}{\sqrt{\sum_{a \in \mathcal{I}}(R_{u_i,a} - \overline{R}_{u_i})^2 \sum_{a \in \mathcal{I}}(R_{u_t,a} - \overline{R}_{u_t})^2}} \qquad (6)$$

where $\mathcal{I}$ is the set of items rated by both of the users.

Then the prediction for the target item a_t is computed using at most k closest users found from step one, and by applying a weighted average of deviations from the selected users' means:

$$\hat{R}_{u_t,a_t} = \overline{R}_{u_t} + \frac{\sum_{i=1}^k (R_{u_i,a_t} - \overline{R}_{u_i})w_{u_i,u_t}}{\sum_{i=1}^k w_{u_i,u_t}} \qquad (7)$$

Note that we follow a number of improvements suggested in [8], including dividing similarities by a constant if the two users have not co-rated enough items.

Item-based KNN

This algorithm is also an instance of a *memory-based* approach. Predictions are computed by first computing item-item similarities. [23] proposed adjusted cosine measure for estimating the similarity between two items a, and b:

$$w_{a,b} = \frac{\sum_{u_i \in \mathcal{U}} (R_{u_i,a} - \overline{R}_{u_i})(R_{u_i,b} - \overline{R}_{u_i})}{\sqrt{\sum_{u_i \in \mathcal{U}} (R_{u_i,a} - \overline{R}_{u_i})^2 \sum_{u_i \in \mathcal{U}} (R_{u_i,b} - \overline{R}_{u_i})^2}} \tag{8}$$

Where, $\mathcal{U}$ denotes the set of users who have rated both a and b.

Once the *item-item* similarities are computed, the rating space of the target user u_t is examined to find all the rated items similar to the target item a_t. Then equation 9 is used to perform the weighted average that generates the prediction. Typically, a threshold of k similar items are used rather than all.

$$\hat{R}_{u_t,a_t} = \frac{\sum_{all\_similar\_items,d} (w_{a_t,d} * R_{u_t,d})}{\sum_{all\_similar\_items,d} (|w_{a_t,d}|)} \tag{9}$$

CBSMOOTH

In their paper [31], the authors present a framework to address two issues of the recommender systems: rating sparseness and algorithm scalability. We briefly discuss the framework as the following steps:

- Step 1: Cluster users into a pre-determined number of groups. Authors use the k-MEANS clustering algorithm and Pearson correlation coefficient as the similarity function.
- Step 2: Replace the missing ratings of each user using the cluster a user belongs to. If a user u_t has not rated an item a, a *smoothed* rating is injected as a combination of the average rating of u_t and the average deviation of ratings on a by all users in u_t's cluster who rated a. That is, $\overline{R}_{u_t} + \sum_{u_i \in \mathcal{C}(u_t,a)} (R_{u_i,a} - \overline{R}_{u_i})/|\mathcal{C}(u_t,a)|$, where $\mathcal{C}(u_t,a)$ indicates all the users of u_t's cluster who rated a.
- Step 3: Find the most similar clusters of each user by computing the similarity between a user and the centroids of the clusters. Pre-select the users of the closest clusters of the target user so that neighbors are sought only from these pre-selected users.
- Step 4: Recompute the similarity between the active user and the pre-selected users by weighting each pre-selected user's ratings based on whether the rating is actual or *smoothed*. A parameter λ, where $0 \leq \lambda \leq 1$, is used to provide a weight of $(1 - \lambda)$ for an actual rating, and a weight of λ for a smoothed rating. Step 5: Let us denote these weights by w_λ.
- Compute recommendations for a user by selecting top K most similar users found in step 4, and by applying an equation similar to 7, however, incorporate w_λs for neighbors' ratings.

Table 1. Comparison of time-complexities of the selected CF algorithms

CF algorithm	Offline	Online	Scalable?
pLSA	$O(mn)$	$O(m)$	Yes
SVD	$O(n^2m + m^2n)$	$O(m)$	Yes, expensive offline
Personality Diagnosis	-	$O(mn)$	No
ClustKnn	$O(mn)$	$O(m)$	Yes
User-based KNN	-	$O(mn)$	No
Item-based KNN	-	$O(mn)$	No; yes with precomputation
CbSmooth	$O(mn)$	$O(mn)$ or $O(m)$	Yes; needs $O(n^2)$ memory

Authors say that a number of different algorithms can emanate from this framework by including or not including some of the steps, such as smoothing missing rating and neighbor pre-selection. However, their flagship algorithm is what authors call SCBPCC, which includes all of the steps above. We denote this algorithm by CbSmooth (Cluster-based Smoothing) in this paper.

CbSmooth addresses the rating sparsity problem by introducing smoothed ratings (step 2 above). However, CbSmooth is not scalable. Authors advocate to pre-select about 30% of all users for each user. This means that the computations still remain $O(mn)$ and are reduced by a constant factor only. CbSmooth can be made scalable if the neighbor pre-selections are performed during the offline phase. However, this imposes an additional memory requirement of $O(n^2)$, which can be prohibitive in many systems.

Comparison of time-complexity

Table 1 shows the time complexities of all the CF algorithms we address in this paper including ClustKnn.

We have collected the complexity-values directly from the respective papers where they were introduced, without formally deriving them here. We, however,

Table 2. Properties of the datasets

Property	Ml1m	MlCurrent
Number of users	6,040	21,526
Number of movies	3,706	8,848
Number of ratings	10,00,209	29,33,690
Minimum $|u_i|$, $\forall i$	20	15
Average rating	3.58	3.43
Sparsity	95.5%	98.5%
Rating distribution		

translate the values into the notations we follow in this paper. For an example, Hofmann [11] shows that the offline time complexity of pLSA is $O(kN)$, where k is the number of states of Z and N is the total number of ratings in the system. Since in the worst case, $N = nm$, we use the offline complexity to be $O(mn)$.

From the table it is clear that CLUSTKNN is one of the cheapest CF algorithms presented, considering both the offline and online time complexities. Since CLUSTKNN produces recommendations for a user in $O(m)$ time, it effectively transforms the User-based KNN into a highly scalable version by reducing the online time from $O(mn)$ to linear in m. Note that although the time complexities of pLSA and CLUSTKNN are identical, CLUSTKNN is much simpler and operates on an intuitive basis.

5   Empirical Analysis

5.1   Datasets

We derived our datasets from MovieLens, a research recommender site maintained by the GroupLens project[4]. Although the registered users of MovieLens can perform activities like adding tags, adding and editing movie-information, engaging in forum discussions, and so forth, the main activity taking place is rating movies so that they can receive personalized movie recommendations. As of this writing, MovieLens has more than 105,000 registered members, about 9,000 movies, and more than 13 million ratings.

We use two datasets in this paper. The first dataset is publicly available. The second dataset has been created by taking the latest 3 million ratings and the corresponding users and movies. We denote the former dataset as ML1M and the latter as MLCURRENT throughout the paper. Table 2 summarizes the number of users, number of movies, number of ratings, minimum number of ratings of each user, *sparsity*, and rating distribution of each dataset. Sparsity of a dataset is defined as the percent of empty cells (that is, no rating) in the *user × movie* matrix.

One key difference between the two datasets is in the rating scale. In ML1M, the rating scale is 1 star to 5 stars, with an increment of 1 star; however, for the last couple of years MovieLens has enabled half-star ratings. As a result, in MLCURRENT, the rating scale is 0.5 star to 5.0 stars, in 0.5 star increments.

Furthermore, note from the average ratings and the rating distributions that, the distributions are skewed toward higher rating values. This is perhaps a common phenomenon since people typically consume products they think they might like. Therefore, their reports on products (movies, in this context) are mostly on what they enjoyed. Another reason for positive skewness might be the user interface itself—if the products presented to the users are ordered by the likelihood that the users would like them, they may only focus on these products when submitting ratings.

---

[4] *http://www.cs.umn.edu/Research/GroupLens/*

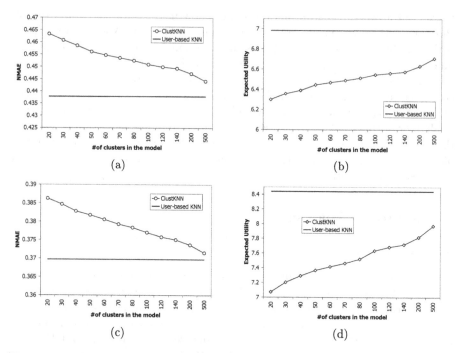

Fig. 3. Prediction performance of CLUSTKNN: (a)-(b) on ML1M, and (c)-(d) on ML-CURRENT dataset. Results of user-based KNN are shown for comparison.

5.2   Evaluation Metrics

In this section we briefly review the metrics we use to evaluate the quality of recommendations produced by the CF algorithms. The first two to follow are to evaluate rating-predictions, and the last category is to evaluate top-N recommendations.

NMAE

Mean Absolute Error (MAE) is the most commonly applied evaluation metric for CF rating predictions. MAE is simply the average of the absolute deviation of the computed predictions from the corresponding actual ratings. Formally,

$$MAE = \frac{1}{N} \sum_{j=1}^{N} |R_{u_j} - \hat{R}_{u_j}| \tag{10}$$

where N represents the total number of predictions computed for all users.

According to this metric, a better CF algorithm has a lower MAE.

Other similar metrics such as Mean Squared Error (MSE) or Root Mean Squared Error (RMSE) are sometimes used for CF evaluation as well. Here, we only report MAE, as one general result from past work is that most evaluation metrics correlate well [25,9].

In [7], the authors wondered about how good the CF algorithm MAEs are over purely random guessing. They proposed using the Normalized Mean Absolute Error (NMAE) that is computed by dividing the MAE of a CF algorithm with the expected MAE from random guessing. In this paper, we use the version of NMAE proposed in [15]. Formally,

$$NMAE = MAE/E[MAE] \qquad (11)$$

Since the ML1M dataset has a rating scale of 1-5, $E[MAE]$ $= \frac{1}{25}\sum_{i=1}^{5}\sum_{j=1}^{5}|i-j| = 1.6$, assuming both ratings and predictions are generated by a uniform distribution. Similarly, for the MLCURRENT dataset, $E[MAE] = 1.65$.

Note that an NMAE value less than 1.0 means the approach is working better than random. An added benefit of using NMAE is that evaluation of CF datasets of different rating scales become comparable.

Expected Utility (EU)

A limitation of MAE is that it treats the same values of error equally across the space of the rating scale. For example, MAE would find no difference between the two $(\hat{R}, R)$ pairs $(5.0, 2.0)$ and $(2.0, 5.0)$. However, depending on the underlying product-domain, the users may be unhappy more about the former pair than the latter.

In order to overcome this limitation, we propose the Expected Utility (EU) metric, a variant of which can be commonly found in *Decision Theory*.

For this accuracy metric, we arrange a 10×10 matrix for a CF algorithm, where rows represent predictions, and the columns represent actual ratings. The (i, j)-th cell of this matrix gives the count of occurrence of the pair $(\hat{R}_i, R_j)$. We also construct a static 10×10 utility table where each entry corresponding to $(\hat{R}_i, R_j)$ is computed using the following utility formula: $U(\hat{R}_i, R_j) = R_j - 2|\hat{R}_i - R_j|$. Notice that the utility equation tries to penalize *false positives* more than *false negatives*. For example, $U(\hat{R}_i = 5, R_j = 2) = -4$, $U(\hat{R}_i = 2, R_j = 5) = -1$, $U(\hat{R}_i = 5, R_j = 5) = 5$, and $U(\hat{R}_i = 1, R_j = 1) = 1$. The interpretation is that not seeing a movie you would not like is no cost or value, not seeing a movie you would have liked is low cost (because there are many other good movies to see), seeing a movie you did not like is expensive and a waste of time, and seeing a movie you like is a good experience.

Based on these two matrices, the expected utility is computed as follows:

$$EU = \sum_{\substack{1\leq i\leq 10 \\ 1\leq j\leq 10}} U(\hat{R}_i, R_j)P(\hat{R}_i|R_j) \qquad (12)$$

Note that many cells of the 10×10 matrix are zeros or contain very small values; therefore, we estimate probabilities using an an m-estimate [3] smoothing. The m-estimate can be expressed as the following:

$$p = \frac{r + m * P}{n + m} \qquad (13)$$

where n is the total number of examples, r is the number of times the event we are estimating the probability for occurs, m is a constant, and P is the prior probability. We have used $m = 2$ for our calculations.

Note that according to EU, the higher the EU of a CF algorithm, the better the performance is.

Precision-Recall-F1

Precision and recall [5] have been in use to evaluate information retrieval systems for many years. Mapping into recommender system parlance, precision and recall have the following definitions regarding the evaluation of top-N recommendations. Precision is the fraction of the top-N recommended items that are *relevant*. Recall is the fraction of the *relevant* items that are recommended. A third metric, F1, is the harmonic mean of precision and recall, and combines precision and recall into a single metric. Formally,

$$F1 = \frac{2 * precision * recall}{(precision + recall)} \tag{14}$$

Since the metrics involve the notion of relevancy, it is important to define what the relevant items are to a user. Furthermore, it is safe to say that users almost never enter preference information into the system on all the *relevant* items they have ever consumed—making the recall measure questionable in the CF domain. A good source of discussion on these and other CF evaluation metrics can be found in [9].

Researchers have tried a variety of ways to incorporate precision and recall into CF evaluation [1,24]. In this paper, we follow an approach similar to Basu et al [1]. In particular, for our datasets, we consider the target user's *relevant* items known to us as the ones she rated 4.0 or above. Furthermore, since our experiment protocol involves dividing the data into training and test sets, we focus on the test set to find the actual *relevant* items of the target user and to compute the top-N list for her. Specifically, the top-N list only contains items that are in the target user's test set. Similarly, a list of *relevant* items are also constructed for the target user from her test set items. Based on the *relevant* list of and the top-N list for the target user, the usual precision-recall-F1 computation ensues.

5.3   Results

Most of our empirical investigation involves taking a five-fold cross-validation approach over each dataset. In other words, we randomly partition our data into five disjoint folds and apply four folds together to train a CF algorithm, and use the remaining fold as a test set to evaluate the performance. We repeat this process five times for each dataset so that each fold is used as a test set once. The results we present are averages over five folds.

First we demonstrate the rating-prediction performance of CLUSTKNN. Figure 3 plots the predictive performance of CLUSTKNN both for the metrics

Table 3. Comparison of rating-prediction quality of the selected CF algorithms. (The best results in each column and the results of CLUSTKNN are shown in bold face.)

CF algorithm	MAE		NMAE		EU	
	ML1M	MLCURRENT	ML1M	MLCURRENT	ML1M	MLCURRENT
SVD	**0.69**	-	**0.43**	-	6.81	-
User-based KNN	0.70	0.61	0.44	0.37	**6.98**	8.44
Item-based KNN	0.70	**0.60**	0.44	**0.36**	6.93	**8.48**
CLUSTKNN (k=200)	**0.72**	**0.62**	**0.45**	**0.37**	**6.63**	**7.82**
pLSA	0.72	0.61	0.45	0.37	6.57	7.95
Personality Diagnosis	0.77	0.66	0.48	0.40	5.00	3.19
CBSMOOTH	0.71	0.62	0.44	0.37	6.86	8.24

NMAE and EU, and for both of the datasets. Since CLUSTKNN can be regarded as approximating user-based KNN with the two becoming equivalent when k equals the number of users in the system (assuming non-empty clusters), we have also included the predictive performance of user-based KNN in the plots — to consider it as an upper bound for CLUSTKNN. As depicted in figure 3, the performance of CLUSTKNN with a moderate value of k, both by MAE and EU, is nearly as good as the user-based KNN. For example, on the MLCURRENT dataset, which has more than 21,500 users, a CLUSTKNN model with 200 clusters gives an NMAE of 0.37 and EU=7.82 — very close to the corresponding user-based KNN results: NMAE=0.36 and EU=8.44. Furthermore, a trend evident from the graph is that as k gets higher, accuracy keeps improving.

Table 3 compares prediction qualities of the ratings produced by the selected CF algorithms. Note that each algorithm requires a few parameters to be set which can be crucial for its better performance. For example, number of z in pLSA, σ in personality diagnosis, and so forth. We followed the suggestions and specifications found in the respective papers to tune the algorithms so that they perform their best.

We see from table 3 that SVD produced the best quality rating-predictions according to both NMAE and EU on the ML1M dataset. We did not have enough computational resources available to run our particular MATLAB implementation of SVD on the MLCURRENT dataset. User and item-based KNN produce the next best quality predictions. CLUSTKNN with k=200 performs very well, and it is at least as accurate as pLSA and CBSMOOTH, and much better than the other hybrid model- and memory-based CF algorithm, personality diagnosis. Interestingly, paying a close attention to the NMAE and EU columns, the finding of [25,9] that CF evaluation metrics correlate, becomes evident. Indeed, the correlation coefficient between MAE and EU on ML1M dataset is -0.94, and on MLCURRENT dataset it is -0.97. Note that negative correlations are due to the fact that the directions of MAE and EU are opposite, i.e., MAE is an *error* metric and EU is a *value* metric. Next we turn into top-N recommendation results.

Figure 4 shows the interplay between precision and recall, and the resulting F1 for CLUSTKNN as N varies. The pattern present in the figure is consistent across each of the CF algorithms we studied. Note that more than 50% of the

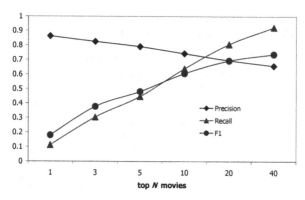

Fig. 4. ClustKnn ($k = 200$) top-N recommendation performance on Ml1m dataset with varying values of N

Table 4. Comparison of top-N recommendation quality of the selected CF algorithms.

CF algorithm	top-3			
	Precision		F1	
	Ml1m	MlCurrent	Ml1m	MlCurrent
SVD	**0.8399**	-	**0.379**	-
User-based KNN	0.833	**0.6693**	0.379	**0.4086**
Item-based KNN	0.819	0.657	0.374	0.407
ClustKnn ($k{=}200$)	**0.825**	**0.659**	**0.377**	**0.407**
pLSA	0.817	0.656	0.375	0.406
Personality Diagnosis	0.789	0.622	0.366	0.391
CbSmooth	0.816	0.645	0.372	0.399

CF algorithm	top-10			
	Precision		F1	
	Ml1m	MlCurrent	Ml1m	MlCurrent
SVD	**0.7564**	-	**0.6131**	-
User-based KNN	0.750	**0.5953**	0.610	0.556
Item-based KNN	0.749	0.592	0.610	0.556
ClustKnn ($k{=}200$)	**0.743**	**0.589**	**0.606**	**0.553**
pLSA	0.739	0.587	0.604	0.552
Personality Diagnosis	0.723	0.565	0.595	0.537
CbSmooth	0.742	0.584	0.605	0.549

users have only 12 or fewer *relevant* items in the test sets of Ml1m, and 6 or fewer in the test sets of MlCurrent. Therefore, recall values quickly ramp up and higher values of N provide less valuable information if we want to compare the algorithms.

Table 4 shows the comparative top-N recommendation results of the algorithms for $N{=}3$ and 10. The results closely follow the results in the rating-predictions. Further, ClustKnn displays good top-N performance, as good as pLSA and CbSmooth, and much better than personality diagnosis.

6   Discussion

Scalability and other features. From the discussion thus far we see that CLUSTKNN is highly scalable—the online prediction time varies linearly with the number of items in the system. CLUSTKNN is *intuitive*. Its foundation rests on a neighborhood-based algorithm that embraces the *collaborative filtering* philosophy, i.e., recommend based on the neighbors' opinions. However, since there can be far too many users from which to find neighbors, CLUSTKNN creates a constant number of pseudo users by grouping real users. The accuracy of this hybrid *memory* and *model-*based algorithm is very good—the best algorithm in our collection is better by only a tiny percentage. The sensitivity of recommender system users to changes in algorithm accuracy has not been studied, but it is reasonably unlikely that users will notice an MAE change of less than 1%. The learned cluster model can be used to find various customer segments and their general characteristics.

Memory Footprint. The memory footprint of this algorithm is very small once the model is learned. The Memory required to generate recommendations for the target user is only $O(km + m)$, where m is the number of items in the system—$O(km)$ for the model and $O(m)$ to store the target user's profile. As a result, this algorithm is ideal for platforms with low storage and processing capabilities.

Recommendations on Handheld Devices. One such platform is handheld computers. These devices are far slower and can store much less data than their desktop counterparts. Furthermore, many devices in use today are not continuously connected to networks. Deployment of recommender systems on handheld devices is an active area of research today [17], and CLUSTKNN provides one possible way to implement a self-contained recommender system on a handheld device. CLUSTKNN can also be useful in high-usage systems where recommendation throughput is an important factor.

Finally, we conclude our discussion with an alternate approach we could have taken regarding clustering and collaborative filtering.

Is it better to focus on the best-matched cluster to find neighbors, or to scan all of the cluster-centers? CLUSTKNN computes recommendations for the target user by seeking the closest neighbors from the cluster centers. However, another possibility is to first find the best-matched cluster for the target user, and then search for the best neighbors within the selected cluster only. We now provide three reasons to avoid this approach. First, this approach might hurt the *coverage* of the recommender, i.e., there can be more items with fewer personalized recommendations. The reason is that the users in the chosen cluster may not have rated a large fraction of the items that people in other clusters rated. Second, this approach might incur high computational cost similar to the regular user-based KNN, since the selected cluster can be a very large one. Third, as figure 5 shows, a large fraction of the closest neighbors may reside in other clusters than the one the target user belongs to. As a result, using a single cluster can easily lead to using less similar neighbors and thereby reducing

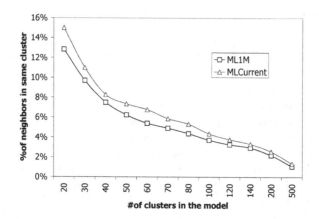

Fig. 5. Percent of top 20 neighbors that can be found in the same cluster

accuracy. Note also from the figure that this problem gets worse as the number of clusters grows.

7   Conclusion

In this paper we have explored clustering to address scalability, a fundamental challenge to collaborative filtering recommender algorithms. In particular we have studied CLUSTKNN, a hybrid *memory-* and *model-*based collaborative filtering algorithm that is simple, intuitive, and highly scalable. The method achieves recommendation quality comparable to that of several other well-known CF algorithms. Further, the operator of the recommender system can tune a parameter in the model to trade off speed and scalability.

In the future, we plan to extend this approach to mitigate the so called *cold-start* problem [26] in CF. That is, a collaborative filtering recommender cannot produce personalized recommendations on newly introduced items lacking any or sufficient user-opinions on those items. By clustering on the space of item feature information, we hope to investigate the implications of building a *hybrid* recommender that works as a CF-based recommender on items with enough preference information, and as a content-based recommender otherwise.

Acknowledgments

We appreciate many helpful comments provided by Sheng Zhang of Dartmouth College in properly implementing SVD-based CF. Dan Cosley of GroupLens research was very helpful in giving feedback on early drafts of this paper. Shilad Sen's pLSA code was of great help. This work was supported by grants from the NSF(IIS 03-24851 and IIS 96-13960).

References

1. Basu, C., Hirsh, H., Cohen, W.: Recommendation as classification: using social and content-based information in recommendation. In: AAAI 1998. Proceedings of the 1998 National Conference on Artificial Intelligence, pp. 714–720 (1998)
2. Breese, J.S., Heckerman, D., Kadie, C.: Empirical analysis of predictive algorithms for collaborative filtering. In: UAI 1998. Proceedings of the 14th Conference on Uncertainty in Artificial Intelligence, pp. 43–52 (July 1998)
3. Cestnik, B.: Estimating probabilities: A crucial task in machine learning. In: Proc. Ninth European Conference on Artificial Intelligence, pp. 147–149 (1990)
4. Chee, S.H.S., Han, J., Wang, K.: RecTree: An efficient collaborative filtering method. In: Kambayashi, Y., Winiwarter, W., Arikawa, M. (eds.) DaWaK 2001. LNCS, vol. 2114, Springer, Heidelberg (2001)
5. Cleverdon, C., Mills, J., Keen, M.: Factors Determining the Performance of Indexing Systems: ASLIB Cranfield Research Project. Volume 1: Design. In: ASLIB Cranfield Research Project, Cranfield (1966)
6. Deerwester, S.C., Dumais, S.T., Landauer, T.K., Furnas, G.W., Harshman, R.A.: Indexing by latent semantic analysis. Journal of the American Society of Information Science 41(6), 391–407 (1990)
7. Goldberg, K., Roeder, T., Gupta, D., Perkins, C.: Eigentaste: A constant time collaborative filtering algorithm. Inf.Retr. 4(2), 133–151 (2001); ID: 187
8. Herlocker, J., Konstan, J., Borchers, A., Riedl, J.: An algorithmic framework for performing collaborative filtering. In: SIGIR 1999. Proceedings of the 1999 Conference on Research and Development in Information Retrieval (August 1999)
9. Herlocker, J., Konstan, J., Terveen, L., Riedl, J.: Evaluating collaborative filtering recommender systems. ACM Transactions on Information Systems 22(1), 5–53 (2004)
10. Hofmann, T.: Probabilistic latent semantic analysis. In: UAI 1999. Proc. of Uncertainty in Artificial Intelligence, Stockholm (1999)
11. Hofmann, T.: Latent semantic models for collaborative filtering. ACM Trans. Inf. Syst. 22(1), 89–115 (2004)
12. Jain, A.K., Murty, M.N., Flynn, P.J.: Data clustering: a review. ACM Comput. Surv. 31(3), 264–323 (1999)
13. Kelleher, J., Bridge, D.: Rectree centroid: An accurate, scalable collaborative recommender. In: Cunningham, P., Fernando, T., Vogel, C. (eds.) Procs. of the Fourteenth Irish Conference on Artificial Intelligence and Cognitive Science, pp. 89–94 (2003)
14. Linden, G., Smith, B., York, J.: Amazon.com recommendations: Item-to-item collaborative filtering. IEEE Internet Computing 7(1), 76–80 (2003)
15. Marlin, B.: Modeling user rating profiles for collaborative filtering. In: NIPS (2003); crossref: DBLP:conf/nips/2003
16. Melville, P., Mooney, R.J., Nagarajan, R.: Content-boosted collaborative filtering for improved recommendations. In: Eighteenth national conference on Artificial intelligence, American Association for Artificial Intelligence, pp. 187–192 (2002); ID: 179
17. Miller, B., Albert, I., Lam, S.K., Konstan, J.A., Riedl, J.: Movielens unplugged: Experiences with a recommender system on four mobile devices. In: HCI 2003. Proceedings of the 17th Annual Human-Computer Interaction Conference, British HCI Group, Miami, FL (September 2003)

18. Nasraoui, O., Pavuluri, M.: Complete this puzzle: A connectionist approach to accurate web recommendations based on a committee of predictors. In: Mobasher, B., Nasraoui, O., Liu, B., Masand, B. (eds.) WebKDD 2004. LNCS (LNAI), vol. 3932, Springer, Heidelberg (2006)

19. Pennock, D.M., Horvitz, E., Lawrence, S., Giles, C.L.: Collaborative filtering by personality diagnosis: A hybrid memory and model-based approach. In: UAI 2000. Proceedings of the 16th Conference on Uncertainty in Artificial Intelligence, Stanford, CA, pp. 473–480. Morgan Kaufmann Publishers Incl., San Francisco (2000)

20. Resnick, P., Iacovou, N., Suchak, M., Bergstrom, P., Riedl, J.: GroupLens: An open architecture for collaborative filtering of netnews. In: CSCW 1994. Proceedings of the 1994 ACM Conference on Computer Supported Cooperative Work, Chapel Hill, North Carolina, United States, pp. 175–186. ACM Press, Chapel Hill, North Carolina, United States (1994)

21. Salton, G., McGill, M.J.: Introduction to Modern Information Retrieval. McGraw-Hill, New York (1986)

22. Sarwar, B.M., Karypis, G., Konstan, J., Riedl, J.: Recommender systems for large-scale e-commerce: Scalable neighborhood formation using clustering. In: ICCIT 2002. Fifth International Conference on Computer and Information Technology (2002)

23. Sarwar, B., Karypis, G., Konstan, J., Riedl, J.: Item-based collaborative filtering recommendation algorithms. In: WWW 2001. Proceedings of the 10th International Conference on World Wide Web, Hong Kong, pp. 285–295. ACM Press, Hong Kong (2001)

24. Sarwar, B.M., Karypis, G., Konstan, J.A., Riedl, J.: Analysis of recommender algorithms for e-commerce. In: ACM E-Commerce 2000, pp. 158–167. ACM Press, New York (2000)

25. Sarwar, B.M., Karypis, G., Konstan, J.A., Riedl, J.: Application of dimensionality reduction in recommender system – a case study. In: ACM WebKDD 2000 Web Mining for E-Commerce Workshop, Boston, MA, USA, ACM Press, New York (2000)

26. Schein, A.I., Popescul, A., Ungar, L.H., Pennock, D.M.: Methods and metrics for cold-start recommendations. In: SIGIR 2002. Proceedings of the 25th annual international ACM SIGIR conference on Research and development in information retrieval, Tampere, Finland, pp. 253–260. ACM Press, New York, NY, USA (2002)

27. Srebro, N., Jaakkola, T.: Weighted low rank approximation (2003)

28. Steinbach, M., Karypis, G., Kumar, V.: A comparison of document clustering techniques (2000)

29. Swearingen, K., Rashmi, S.: Interaction design for recommender systems. In: Designing Interactive Systems 2002, ACM Press, New York (2002)

30. Ungar, L., Foster, D.: Clustering methods for collaborative filtering. In: Proceedings of the Workshop on Recommendation Systems, AAAI Press, Menlo Park California (1998)

31. Xue, G.-R., Lin, C., Yang, Q., Xi, W., Zeng, H.-J., Yu, Y., Chen, Z.: Scalable collaborative filtering using cluster-based smoothing. In: SIGIR 2005. Proceedings of the 28th annual international ACM SIGIR conference on Research and development in information retrieval, Salvador, Brazil, pp. 114–121. ACM Press, New York, NY, USA (2005)

32. Yu, K., Xu, X., Tao, J., Ester, M., Kriegel, H.-P.: Instance selection techniques for memory-based collaborative filtering. In: SDM (2002)

Detecting Profile Injection Attacks
in Collaborative Filtering:
A Classification-Based Approach*

Chad A. Williams[1], Bamshad Mobasher[2], Robin Burke[2], and Runa Bhaumik[2]

[1] Department of Computer Science
University of Illinois at Chicago
Chicago, Illinois, USA
cwilliam@cs.uic.edu
[2] Center for Web Intelligence, DePaul University
School of Computer Science, Telecommunication, and Information Systems
Chicago, Illinois, USA
{mobasher,rburke,rbhaumik}@cs.depaul.edu

Abstract. Collaborative recommender systems have been shown to be vulnerable to profile injection attacks. By injecting a large number of biased profiles into a system, attackers can manipulate the predictions of targeted items. To decrease this risk, researchers have begun to study mechanisms for detecting and preventing profile injection attacks. In prior work, we proposed several attributes for attack detection and have shown that a classifier built with them can be highly successful at identifying attack profiles. In this paper, we extend our work through a more detailed analysis of the information gain associated with these attributes across the dimensions of attack type and profile size. We then evaluate their combined effectiveness at improving the robustness of user based recommender systems.

1 Introduction

Due to the open nature of collaborative systems, there is little to prevent attackers from inserting fake profiles in an attempt to bias the system in their favor. These attacks where a malicious user enters biased profiles in order to influence the system's behavior have been termed "shilling" or "profile injection" attacks. In theory, an attacker could swamp an unprotected system with enough profiles to control its recommendations completely. As a result, the vulnerabilities and robustness of collaborative recommender systems have been the subject of recent research [1,2,3,4]. While there are techniques to increase the effort required to create profiles like requiring users to respond to a captcha[1] before an account is created, such measures also discourage participation thus

---

* This research was supported in part by the National Science Foundation Cyber Trust program under Grant IIS-0430303.

[1] www.captcha.net/

O. Nasraoui et al. (Eds.): WebKDD 2006, LNAI 4811, pp. 167–186, 2007.

decreasing the collaborative user base. As long as profiles are accepted without extraordinary measures to ensure their authenticity, it is possible for an attacker to launch such an attack. However this does not mean defending against such attacks is impossible.

Recent efforts have focused on reducing the impact of profile injection attacks through detecting and discounting suspected attack profiles. Chirita et al. [5] proposed several metrics for analyzing rating patterns of malicious users and evaluated their potential for detecting such attacks. Su, et al. [6] developed a spreading similarity algorithm for detecting groups of very similar attackers, which was shown to be effective for a simplified attack scenario. O'Mahony et al. [7] developed several techniques to defend against the attacks described in [3] and [4], including new strategies for neighborhood selection and similarity weight transformations. In our prior work we introduced an attack model-specific approach to profile classification and explored its effectiveness at detecting random, average, and segment push attacks [8,9]. In [10] we showed our attack model-specific approach to be more effective at detecting smaller, more difficult to detect attacks than the technique described in [5].

In this paper we extend the work in [11] through a deeper analysis of the impact the dimensions (or characteristics) of an attack can have on the effectiveness of a profile classification approach to detection. Prior work has examined the value of detection attributes almost exclusively with respect to the attribute's effectiveness at detecting a particular attack model. As this work demonstrates, this level of analysis is insufficient and a more in depth analysis is required to properly determine the value of an attribute. In our results below, we examine the information gain of two detection attributes in detail across the dimensions of attack type, profile size, and attack size and show that each of these dimensions must be considered to ensure sufficient detection coverage. In addition, we analyze the impact of these detection schemes on the robustness of a kNN recommender system. In particular, we measure the robustness via change in the predicted rating of a target item before and after attack. We show that such a detection scheme can improve the stability of a recommender system, keeping its predicted ratings steady under most attack scenarios.

Our approach to detecting attacks via pattern classification uses known attack models to build a training set of authentic and attack profiles, where standard data mining techniques are then applied to build a classifier. With such an approach, the closer an attacker imitates a known attack model, the greater the chance of detection. Of course, the attacker may build profiles that deviate from these models and thereby evade detection. However, our most effective attack models (described below) were derived by reverse engineering the recommendation algorithms to maximize their impact. We hypothesize, therefore, that they are optimal in the sense of providing maximum impact on the recommender system with the least amount of effort from the attacker.

Our detection model is based on constructing a set of attributes that are calculated for each profile in the database. Supervised learning methods are then used to build classifiers based on these attributes, which are trained to

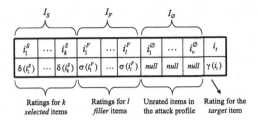

Fig. 1. The general form of an attack profile

discriminate between genuine profiles and those that are part of an attack. In this work we apply nearest-neighbor classification using kNN. Once attack profiles have been detected, they are eliminated to reduce the bias introduced by the attack. Ideally all attack profiles would be ignored and the system would function as if no bias had been injected. For a system to be considered robust, it should be able to withstand a direct attack on an item with minimal prediction shift.

2   Attack Models

For our purposes, a profile injection attack against a recommender system consists of a set of *attack profiles* inserted into the system with the aim of altering the system's recommendation behavior with respect to a single target item i_t. An attack that aims to promote i_t, making it recommended more often, is called a *push attack*, and one designed to make i_t recommended less often is a *nuke attack* [4].

An attack model is an approach to constructing the attack profiles, based on knowledge about the recommender system, its rating database, its products, and/or its users. The general form of an attack profile is depicted in Figure 1. The attack profile consists of an m-dimensional vector of ratings, were m is the total number of items in the system. The profile is partitioned in four parts. The null partition, $I_\emptyset$, are those items that have not been rated in the profile. The single target item i_t will be given a rating as determined by the function γ, generally this will be either the maximum or minimum possible rating, depending on the attack type. As described below, some attacks require identifying a group of items for special treatment during the attack. This special set I_S receives ratings as specified by the function δ. Finally, there is a set of filler items I_F whose ratings are added to complete the profile. Their ratings are provided by the function σ. It is the strategy for selecting items in I_S and I_F and the functions γ, σ, and δ that define an attack model and give it its character.

Two basic attack models, introduced originally in [3] are the *random* and *average* attacks. Both of these models involve the generation of attack profiles using randomly assigned ratings given to some filler items in the profile. In the random attack, the assigned ratings are based on the overall distribution of user ratings in the database. In our formalism, I_S is empty, the contents of I_F are selected randomly, and the function σ generates random ratings centered on the overall average rating in the database. The average attack is very similar, but the rating for each filler item is computed based on more specific knowledge of the individual mean for each item.

Of these attacks, the average attack is by far the more effective, but it may be impractical to mount, given the degree of system-specific knowledge of the ratings distribution that it requires. Further, as we show in [12], it is ineffectual and hence unlikely to be employed against an item-based formulation of collaborative recommendation. Our own experiments yielded three additional attack models: the bandwagon, segment and love/hate attacks described below. See [1,2,12] for additional details.

The *bandwagon attack* is similar to the random attack, but it uses a small amount of additional knowledge, namely the identification of a few of the most popular items in a particular domain: blockbuster movies, top-selling recordings, etc. This information is easy to obtain and not dependent on any specifics of the system under attack. The set I_S contains these popular items and they are given high ratings in the attack profiles. In our studies, the bandwagon attack works almost as well as the much more knowledge-intensive average attack.

The *segment attack* is designed specifically as an attack against the item-based algorithm. Item-based collaborative recommendation generates neighborhoods of similar items, rather than neighborhoods of similar users. The goal of the attack therefore is to maximize the similarity between the target item and the *segment items* in I_S. The segment items are those well-liked by the market segment to which the target item i_t is aimed. The items in I_S are given high ratings to increase the similarity between them and the target item; the filler items are given low ratings, to decrease the similarity between these items and the target item. This attack proved to be highly effective against the item-based algorithm as expected, but it also works well against user-based collaborative recommendation.

Our experiments also showed that the segment attack worked poorly as a nuke attack, as it was difficult to construct variants of it that were effective. The dislikes of a market segment are much more dispersed than its preferences, thus it is more difficult to construct a set I_S of items disliked by the target audience than to construct one that is generally liked. Our final attack model, the *love/hate attack* is a simple one that, nonetheless, is quite effective against both item-based and user-based algorithms as a nuke attack. It associates a low rating with the target item and high ratings with the filler items I_F (I_S is not used).

3   Attack Profile Classification

Our aim is to learn to label each profile as either being part of an attack or as coming from a genuine user. As described above, our approach is classification learning based on attributes derived from each individual profile. These attributes come in two varieties: generic and model-specific. The generic attributes are basic descriptive statistics that attempt to capture some of the characteristics that will tend to make an attacker's profile look different from a genuine user. The model-specific attributes are implemented to detect characteristics of profiles generated by known attack models.

3.1 Generic Attributes

We hypothesize the overall statistical signature of attack profiles will differ significantly from that of authentic profiles. This difference comes from two sources: the ratings given to the target item and I_S segment, and the distribution of ratings among the filler items. As many researchers in the area have theorized [3,5,4,13], it is unlikely if not unrealistic for an attacker to have complete knowledge of the ratings in a real system. As a result, generated profiles will deviate from rating patterns seen for authentic users. This variance may be manifested in many ways, including an abnormal deviation from the system average rating, or an unusual number of ratings in a profile. As a result, an attribute that captures these anomalies is likely to be informative in identifying attack profiles.

Prior work in attack profile classification has focused on detecting the general anomalies in attack profiles. Chirita et al. [5] introduced several attributes for detecting these differences often associated with attack profiles. One of these attributes, *Rating Deviation from Mean Agreement* (RDMA), was intended to identify attackers through examining the profile's average deviation per item, weighted by the inverse of the number of ratings for that item. We propose two variants of the RDMA attribute which we have found to be valuable as well when used in a supervised learning context.

First, we propose a new attribute *Weighted Deviation from Mean Agreement* (WDMA) that is strongly based on RDMA, but which we have found to provide higher information gain. Let U be the universe of all users u in the database. Let P_u be a profile for user u, consisting of a set of ratings $r_{u,i}$ for some items i in the universe of items to be rated. Let n_u be the size of this profile in terms of the numbers of ratings. Let l_i be the number of ratings provided for item i by all users, and $\overline{r_i}$ be the average of these ratings. The WDMA attribute can be computed in the following way:

$$WDMA_u = \frac{\sum\limits_{i=0}^{n_u} \frac{|r_{u,i} - \overline{r_i}|}{l_i^2}}{n_u}$$

This attribute places higher weight on rating deviations for sparse items than the original RDMA attribute.

The second variation of the RDMA measure which we call *Weighted Degree of Agreement* (WDA) uses only the numerator of the RDMA equation and can be computed as follows:

$$WDA_u = \sum\limits_{i=0}^{n_u} \frac{|r_{u,i} - \overline{r_i}|}{l_i}$$

This captures the sum of the differences of the profile's ratings from the item's average rating divided by the item's rating frequency.

In addition to rating deviations, some researchers have hypothesized that attack profiles are likely to have a higher similarity with their closest neighbors than real users would, because they are all being generated using the same process whereas genuine users have preferences that are more dispersed [5,14]. This hypothesis was confirmed in our earlier experiments, which found that the most effective attacks are those in which a large number of profiles with very similar characteristics are introduced. This intuition is captured in the *Degree of Similarity with Top Neighbors* (DegSim) feature, also introduced in [5].

The DegSim attribute is based on the average similarity of the profile's k nearest neighbors and is calculated as follows:

$$DegSim_u = \frac{\sum\limits_{v \in neighbors(u)} W_{u,v}}{k}$$

where $W_{u,v}$ is the similarity between users u and v calculated via Pearson's correlation, and k is the number of neighbors.

One well-known characteristic of correlation-based measures is their instability when the number of data points is small. Since it is the number of items co-rated by two users that determines their similarity, this factor can be taken into account and similarity decreased when two users have few items that they have co-rated. This feature is computed as follows. Let $I_{u,v}$ be the set of items i such that ratings exist for i in both profiles u and v, that is $r_{u,i}$ and $r_{v,i}$ are defined. $|I_{u,v}|$ is the size of this set. The similarity of profiles u and v is adjusted as follows:

$$W'_{u,v} = W_{u,v} \frac{|I_{u,v}|}{d}, \text{if } |I_{u,v}| < d$$

The co-rate factor can be taken into account when calculating $DegSim$, producing a slightly different attribute $DegSim'$.

A third generic attribute that we have introduced is based on the number of total ratings in a given profile. Some attacks require profiles that rate many if not all of the items in the system. If there is are large number of possible items, it is unlikely that such profiles could come from a real user, who would have to enter them all manually, as opposed to a soft-bot implementing a profile injection attack. We capture this idea with the measure *Length Variance* (LengthVar) which measures of how much the length of a given profile varies from the average length in the database.

$$Length Var_u = \frac{|n_u - \overline{n_u}|}{\sum\limits_{u \in U} (n_u - \overline{n_u})^2}$$

where $\overline{n_u}$ is the average length of a profile in the system.

3.2   Model-Specific Attributes

In our experiments, we found that the generic attributes are insufficient for distinguishing true attack profiles from eccentric but authentic profiles. This is especially true when the profiles are small, containing fewer filler items. Such attacks can still be successful in influencing recommendation results, so we seek to augment the generic attributes with some that are designed specifically to match the characteristics of known attack models.

As shown in Section 2, attacks models can be defined based on the characteristics of the attack profile partitions i_t (the target item), I_S (selected items), and I_F (filler items). Model-specific attributes are those that aim to recognize the distinctive signature of a particular attack model. These attributes are based on partitioning each profile in such a way as to maximize the profile's similarity to one generated by a known attack model. Statistical features of the ratings that make up the partition can then be used as detection attributes. One useful property of partition-based features is that their derivation can be sensitive to additional information (such as time-series or critical mass data) that suggests likely attack targets.

Our detection model discovers partitions of each profile that maximizes its similarity to a known attack model. To model this partitioning, each profile is split into two sets. The set $P_{u,T}$ contains all items in the profile with the profile's maximum rating (or minimum in the case of a nuke attack); the set $P_{u,F}$ consists of all other ratings in the profile. Thus the intention is for $P_{u,T}$ to approximate $\{i_t\} \cup I_S$ and $P_{u,F}$ to approximate I_F. (We do not attempt to differentiate i_t from I_S.) It is these partitions, or more precisely, their statistical features that we use as detection attributes.

Average Attack Detection Model. The average attack model divides the profile into three partitions: the target item given an extreme rating, the filler items given other ratings (determined based on the attack model), and unrated items. The model essentially just needs to select an item to be the target and all other rated items become fillers. By the definition of the average attack, the filler ratings will be populated such that they closely match the rating average for each filler item. We would expect that a profile generated by an average attack would exhibit a high degree of similarity (low variance) between its ratings and the average ratings for each item except for the single item chosen as the target.

The formalization of this intuition is to iterate through all the highly-rated items, selecting each in turn as the possible target, and then computing the mean variance between the non-target (filler) items and the overall average. Where this metric is minimized, the target item is the one most compatible with the hypothesis of the profile as being generated by an average attack, and the magnitude of the variance is an indicator of how confident we might be with this hypothesis. More formally, we compute $MeanVar$ for a profile P_u twice; once for push attacks, and once for nuke attacks. This metric can be computed as follows, where we define the set of ratings that are potential targets $P_{u,T} = \{i \in P_u, \text{such that} r_{u,i} = r_{max}\}$ (or r_{min} for nuke attacks.). $P_{u,F}$ is the rest of the profile: $P_u - P_{u,T}$.

$$MeanVar_u = \frac{\sum\limits_{j \in P_{u,F}} (r_{u,j} - \overline{r_u})^2}{|P_{u,F}|}$$

Whichever of the calculations yields the lowest value, we consider this the optimal partitioning for $P_{u,T}$ and $P_{u,F}$, and the value so computed we use as the *Filler Mean Variance* feature for classification purposes. We also compute *Filler Mean Difference*, which is the average of the absolute value of the difference between the user's rating and the mean rating (rather than the squared value as in the variance.)

Finally, in an average attack, we would expect that attack profiles would have very similar within-profile variance: they would have more or less similar ratings for the filler items and an extreme value for the target item. So, our third model-derived feature is *Profile Variance*, simply the variance associated with the profile itself.

Segment Attack Detection Model. For the segment attack model, the partitioning feature that maximizes the attack's effectiveness is the difference in ratings of items in the $P_{u,T}$ set compared to the items in $P_{u,F}$. Thus we introduce the *Filler Mean Target Difference* (FMTD) attribute. The attribute is calculated as follows:

$$FMTD_u = \left| \left(\frac{\sum_{i \in P_{u,T}} r_{u,i}}{|P_{u,T}|} \right) - \left(\frac{\sum_{k \in P_{u,F}} r_{u,k}}{|P_{u,F}|} \right) \right|$$

Target Focus Detection Model. All of the attributes thus far have concentrated on inter-profile statistics; target focus, however, concentrates on intra-profile statistics. Here we are seeking to make use of the fact that often many attack profiles are required to insert the desired bias. Only a substantial attack containing a number of targeted profiles can achieve this result. It is therefore profitable to examine the density of target items across profiles. One of the advantages of the partitioning associated with the model-based attributes described above is that a set of suspected targets are identified for each profile. For our *Target Model Focus* attribute (TMF), we calculate the degree to which the partitioning of a given profile focuses on items common to other attack partitions, and therefore measures a consensus of suspicion regarding each profile. To calculate TMF for a profile, first we define F_i, the degree of focus on a given item, and then select from the profile's target set the item that has the highest focus and use its focus value. Specifically,

$$TMF_u = \max_{j \in P_T} F_j, \text{ where}$$
$$F_i = \frac{\sum_{u \in U} \Theta_{u,i}}{\sum_{u \in U} |P_{u,T}|}, \text{ and}$$
$$\Theta_{u,i} = \begin{cases} 1, & \text{if } i \in P_{u,T} \\ 2, & \text{otherwise} \end{cases}$$

Although the TMF attribute focuses on model target density; it is easy to see how a similar approach could be used to incorporate other evidence of suspicious profiles for example from time series data or unsupervised detection algorithms. This type of attribute could significantly reduce the impact a malicious user could make by constraining the number of profiles they could inject before they risk the detection of their entire attack effort.

4   Methodology

The results in this paper were generated using the publicly-available Movie-Lens 100K dataset[2]. This dataset consists of 100,000 ratings on 1682 movies by 943 users. All ratings are integer values between one and five where one is the lowest (disliked) and five is the highest (most liked). Our data includes all the users who have rated at least 20 movies.

The attack detection and response experiments were conducted using a separate training and test set by partitioning the ratings data in half. The first half was used to create training data for the attack detection classifier used in later experiments. For each test the second half of the data was injected with attack profiles and then run through the classifier that had been built on the augmented first half. This approach was used since a typical cross-validation approach would be overly biased since the same movie being attacked would also be the movie being trained for.

For these experiments we use 15 detection attributes:

- 6 generic attributes: WDMA, RDMA, WDA, Length Variance, DegSim (k = 450), and DegSim' (k = 2, d = 963);
- 6 average attack model attributes (3 for push, 3 for nuke): Filler Mean Variance, Filler Mean Difference, Profile Variance;
- 2 segment attack model attributes (1 for push, 1 for nuke): FMTD; and,
- 1 target detection model attribute: TMF.

The training data was created by inserting a mix of the attack models described above for both push and nuke attacks at various filler sizes that ranged from 3% to 100%. Specifically the training data was created by inserting the first attack at a particular filler size, and generating the detection attributes for the authentic and attack profiles. This process was repeated 18 more times for additional attack models and/or filler sizes, and generating the detection attributes separately. For all these subsequent attacks, the detection attributes of only the attack profiles were then added to the original detection attribute dataset. This approach allowed a larger attack training set to be created while minimizing over-training for larger attack sizes due to the high percentage of attack profiles that make up the training set (10.5% total across the 19 training attacks).

The segment attack is slightly different from the others in that it focuses on a particular group of items that are similar to each other and likely to be popular among a similar group of users. In our experiments, we have developed several user segments defined by preferences for movies of particular types. In these experiments, we use the Harrison Ford segment (movies with Harrison Ford as a star) as part of the training data and the Horror segment (popular horror movies) for attack testing.

---

[2] http://www.cs.umn.edu/research/GroupLens/data/

4.1   Generating Recommendations

To generate recommendations, we use the standard kNN collaborative filtering algorithm based on user-to-user similarity [15]. (The scope of this paper precludes consideration of item-based algorithms.) In selecting neighbors, we use Pearson's correlation coefficient for user-user similarities and a neighborhood size $k = 20$. We also filter out all neighbors with a similarity of less than 0.1 to prevent predictions being based on very distant or negative correlations. After identifying a neighborhood, we use the following formula (from [13]) to compute the prediction for a target item i and target user u:

$$p_{u,i} = \bar{r}_u + \frac{\sum\limits_{v \in V} sim_{u,v}(r_{v,i} - \bar{r}_v)}{\sum\limits_{v \in V} |sim_{u,v}|}$$

where V is the set of k similar neighbors to a target user u; $r_{v,i}$ is the rating of i for neighbor v; $\bar{r}_u$ and $\bar{r}_v$ are the average ratings over all rated items for u and v, respectively; and $sim_{u,v}$ is the Pearson correlation.

Chirita, et al. [5] used their measure of the probability of a profile being part of an attack to discount the similarity computation used in prediction and neighborhood formation. For our attack classifier, we found that best results were obtained by completely eliminating profiles labeled as attacks.

4.2   Evaluation Metrics

There has been considerable research in the area of recommender systems evaluation [16]. Some of these concepts can also be applied to the evaluation of the security of recommender systems, but in evaluating security, we are interested not in performance, but rather in the changes induced by an attack. Our goal is to measure the effectiveness of an attack - the "win" for the attacker. The desired outcome for the attacker in a "push" attack is of course that the pushed item be more likely to be recommended after the attack than before. We follow the lead of [4] in measuring an algorithm's stability via prediction shift, which measures the change in the predicted rating of an item before and after attack. Let $p(u, i)$ be the rating predicted by the system for a given user/item pair, and let $p'(u, i)$ be the prediction for the same pair after the system has been attacked.

$$PredShift(u, i) = p'(u, i) - p(u, i)$$

This quantity is then averaged over all of the test users to arrive at an average prediction shift for that item. These values are averaged once again over all items to derive a measure of the effectiveness of the attack.[3]

---

[3] Note that we do not use the absolute value of the change. A push attack is intended to create a positive change of predicted rating, taking the absolute value of the shift would hide changes that occur in the opposite direction.

For measuring classification performance, we use the standard measurements of precision and recall. Since we are primarily interested in how well the classification algorithms detect attacks, we look at each of these metrics with respect to attack identification. Thus precision is calculated as:

$$precision = \frac{\#\ true\ positives}{(\#\ true\ positives\ +\ \#\ false\ positives)}$$

$$recall = \frac{\#\ true\ positives}{(\#\ true\ positives\ +\ \#\ false\ negatives)}$$

where *# true positives* is the number of attack profiles correctly identified as attacks, *# false positives* is the number of authentic profiles that were misclassified as attacks, and *# false negatives* is the number of attack profiles that were misclassified as authentic.

4.3   Experimental Setup

Based on the training data described above, kNN with $k = 9$ was used to make a binary profile classifier with $PA_u = 0$ if classified as *authentic* and $PA_u = 1$ if classified as *attack*. To classify unseen profiles, the k nearest neighbors in the training set are used to determine the class using one over Pearson correlation distance weighting. All segment attack results reflect the average over the 6 combinations of Horror segment movies. Classification results and kNN classifier were created using Weka [17].

In all experiments, to ensure the generality of the results, 50 movies were selected randomly that represented a wide range of average ratings and number of ratings. Each movie was attacked individually and the average is reported for all experiments. For prediction shift experiments, we used a neighborhood size of $k = 20$ in the k-nearest-neighbor algorithm, and a sample of 50 users mirroring the overall distribution of users in terms of number of movies seen and ratings provided. The results reported below represent averages over the combinations of test users and test movies.

The Chirita et al. algorithm was also implemented for comparison purposes (with $\alpha = 10$), and run on the test set described above. Comparative results are shown in the next section. It should be noted that there are a number of methodological differences between the results reported in [5] and those shown here. The attack profiles used in [5] used 100% filler size and targeted 3 items simultaneously. In the experiments below, we concentrate on a single item and vary the filler size. Also their results were limited to target movies with low average ratings and few ratings, the 50 movies we have selected represent both a wider range of average ratings and variance in rating density.

5   Experimental Results

Average Information Gain Analysis

Below we present a detailed analysis of the information gain associated with the attributes discussed above. As our results below show, the information gain

Table 1. Information gain for the detection attributes against push attacks

Attribute	Random		Average		Bandwagon		Segment	
	Info Gain	Rank	Info Gain	Rank	Info Gain	Rank	Info Gain	Rank
DegSim (k=450)	0.161	6	0.116	9	0.180	5	0.180	12
DegSim' (k=2, d=963)	0.103	9	0.177	7	0.101	9	0.213	10
WDA	0.233	4	0.229	3	0.234	4	0.246	5
LengthVariance	0.267	1	0.267	1	0.267	1	0.269	3
WDMA	0.248	2	0.238	2	0.248	2	0.229	8
RDMA	0.240	3	0.229	4	0.240	3	0.239	7
FillerMeanDiff*	0.064	13	0.084	13	0.064	13	0.244	6
MeanVar*	0.099	10	0.093	12	0.100	10	0.222	9
ProfileVariance*	0.083	12	0.109	10	0.086	12	0.274	2
FMTD*	0.130	7	0.189	5	0.131	7	0.276	1
FMV*	0.094	11	0.126	8	0.095	11	0.263	4
TMF*	0.194	5	0.185	6	0.174	6	0.176	13

varies significantly across several dimensions. First we present the information gain associated with each attribute across attack models. This is followed by an analysis of the effect of filler size and attack size on the information gain of an attribute.

For our experiments each attack was inserted targeting a single movie at 5% attack size and a specific filler size. Each of the test movies was attacked at filler sizes of 3%, 5%, 10%, 20%, 40%, 60%, 80%, and 100% and the results reported are averaged over the 50 test movies and the 8 filler sizes. Table 1 shows the average information gain (info gain) for each attribute, and its relative rank for each of the push attacks described above. The model-specific attributes as indicated with an '*'. The LengthVar attribute is very important for distinguishing attack profiles, since few real users rate more than a small percentage of the items. The attributes with the next highest gain for average, random, and bandwagon attack are those using the "deviation from mean agreement" concept from [5]: WDMA, RDMA, and WDA. For segment attack, however, the model specific attribute FMTD, which captures the mean rating difference between the target and filler items, is the most informative. The next most informative is profile variance, which follows intuition since segment attack gives all items the same rating except the segment items. Interestingly, TMF, which uses our crude measure of

Table 2. Information gain for the detection attributes against nuke attacks

Attribute	Random		Average		Love/Hate	
	Info Gain	Rank	Info Gain	Rank	Info Gain	Rank
DegSim (k = 450)	0.161	6	0.111	10	0.155	11
DegSim' (k = 2, d = 963)	0.104	10	0.176	5	0.213	9
WDA	0.234	4	0.229	4	0.253	5
LengthVariance	0.267	1	0.267	1	0.267	3
WDMA	0.248	2	0.238	2	0.244	8
RDMA	0.240	3	0.229	3	0.249	7
FillerMeanDiff*	0.084	12	0.094	12	0.249	6
MeanVar*	0.109	9	0.103	11	0.200	10
ProfileVariance*	0.095	11	0.121	8	0.095	12
FMTD*	0.138	8	0.154	7	0.276	1
FMV*	0.077	13	0.069	13	0.276	1
TMF*	0.190	5	0.162	6	0.267	4

which items are under attack, also has strong information gain. This suggests that further improvements in detecting likely attack targets could yield even better detection results.

The results displayed in Table 2 were obtained following the same methodology, but the model-specific attributes (indicated with an '*') were created to look for nuke attacks. The table depicts the average information gain for each attribute, and its relative rank for each of the nuke attacks described above. For average and random attacks, the relative information gain of the attributes is pretty consistent between push and nuke attacks. A closer inspection of the information gain reveals that the informativeness of the generic attributes is nearly identical. For the model based attributes, the FillerMeanDiff, MeanVar, and ProfileVariance (single target) attributes all become slightly more informative, whereas the FMTD and FMV (multiple target) attributes generally become less informative. Conceptually the reason this occurs is due in part to the distribution characteristics of the data. In our dataset, there are more high ratings than low ratings as the system mean of a 3.6 rating reflects. Since the information gain of the single target attributes improves with correct selection of the actual target item, for the average and random model-specific attributes, the probability of identifying the correct target item increases. On the other hand, since the group attack model-specific attributes select all items with the user's minimum rating as the suspected target, the models also mask some of the more extreme variability in real user ratings thus decreasing the information gain for detecting nuke attacks targeting a single item.

The attribute information gain shows some interesting differences between the love/hate attack and the other nuke attacks. Due to the simplicity of this attack, a single minimum rating and all other ratings given the system maximum, it is not surprising that the variance and similarity based attributes are far more informative. The most similar attack is the segment attack without the addition of the target segment (I_S). A comparison of the information gain of the attributes detecting the segment push attack and the love/hate nuke attack reflects this intuition with the only major differences occurring in the ProfileVariance, and TargetModelFocus attributes. ProfileVariance becomes less informative due primarily to the same rating distribution reasons given earlier. The TargetModelFocus attribute on the other hand becomes more informative since it is very easy to identify the actual nuke attack target with these profiles.

Information Gain Surface Analysis

To understand the informativeness of the attributes in greater depth, we experimented with the dimensions of filler size and attack size on the information gain of each attribute for each attack model. For this set of experiments, the 50 test movies were attacked at a number of combinations of filler sizes and attack sizes. The information gain surfaces below are based on the average information gain across the 50 sampled movies at filler sizes of 3%, 5%, 10%, 20%, 40%, 60%, 80%, and 100% across attack sizes of .5%, 1%, 5%, and 10%.

Our results showed that across all attributes the information gain increased with the attack size at least up to a 10% attack size, as would be expected since

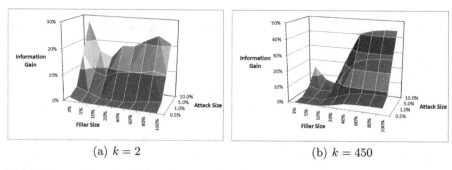

(a) $k = 2$ (b) $k = 450$

Fig. 2. Comparison of information gain vs. filler size and attack size for random push attacks

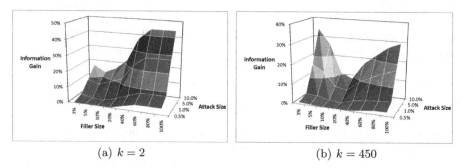

(a) $k = 2$ (b) $k = 450$

Fig. 3. Comparison of information gain vs. filler size and attack size for average push attacks

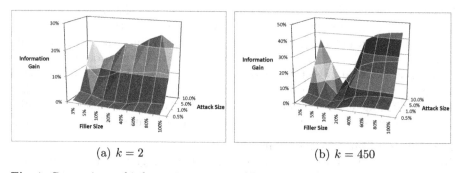

(a) $k = 2$ (b) $k = 450$

Fig. 4. Comparison of information gain vs. filler size and attack size for bandwagon push attacks

a small attack might look like an eccentric profile, whereas a large number of these profiles targeting the same item appear more like a malicious group. The more interesting aspect of these results is the impact filler size on the amount of information gain and how this affect differs across attack type. Below we illustrate this impact through a detailed examination of the informativeness of

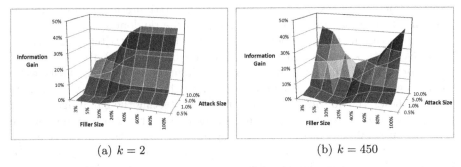

(a) $k = 2$ (b) $k = 450$

Fig. 5. Comparison of information gain vs. filler size and attack size for segment push attacks

the DegSim ($k = 450$) and DegSim' ($k = 2, d = 963$) attributes across the various push and nuke attack types. A similar analysis was performed for all of the attributes and all of the models (results not included for brevity).

Figure 2 shows the information gain of the DegSim attribute using $k = 450$ and DegSim' using $k = 2, d = 963$ across the dimensions of filler size and attack size, thus creating the information gain surface for these attributes at detecting random push attacks. As the surface shows, while the tables above provide some insight into the benefit of each of these attributes across attack models, the informativeness of each attribute will vary greatly based on filler size and attack size as well. As the figure shows while a k of 450 may provide higher average information gain, the attribute based on $k = 2, d = 963$ is also needed since it is more informative for filler sizes less than 20%.

Figure 3 shows the information gain surface for the same two attributes for average push attack. Like the surface for random attack, across all filler sizes the information gain increases with attack size. Also like random attack both attributes have areas where they superior, however, the areas where each of these attributes is most informative compared to each other has flipped. For random attack the smaller k was more informative at lower filler sizes and less informative by comparison for large filler sizes, as the information gain surfaces depict for average attack the opposite is true. The reason for this change is due to the differences in how similar the resulting profiles are of each of these attacks to real profiles. Intuitively an average attack profile should be far more similar to real profiles than random attack profiles. As a result, for low filler sizes the average attack is difficult to differentiate from real profiles looking only at the 2 closest neighbors. However its degree of similarity with a high number of neighbors is higher than usual since there are no eccentric ratings thus the reason for the higher information gain of the $k = 450$ attribute. Random attack shows the reverse for the same reasons. Specifically for lower filler sizes, the amount of eccentricity associated with random ratings when weighted by the number of ratings makes the low degree of similarity with its closest neighbors stand out and makes the DegSim' attribute more informative. At higher filler sizes, the attack profiles have enough overlap with a large number of profiles to make the additional neighbors associated with the DegSim attribute more informative at detecting the lack of correlation associated with the random attack.

Next we examine the detection characteristics of these attributes against the bandwagon attack depicted in Figure 4. Recall from Section 2, that this attack model uses a small number of widely popular items to increase similarity while populating filler ratings in a manner similar to the random attack model. As Figure 4 shows, the information gain surface for detecting the bandwagon attack reflects detection characteristics similar to the earlier attacks depending on the filler size. At small filler sizes the "bandwagon" items make the information gain surface of detecting the attack profiles similar to that of the average attack for small filler sizes, but as the filler size grows to 40% or larger the random filler ratings dominate making detection more like that of random attack.

As described in Section 2, the segment attack targets a group of popular movies from a segment giving them the highest rating along with the target item, and gives the lowest rating to all filler items. Figure 5 displays the information gain surface of the two DegSim based attributes for detecting segment attack profiles. As the figure shows, like the bandwagon attack, the segment items make detection of the attack similar to that of average or bandwagon attack for low filler sizes, but the lack of variability of the filler items makes the DegSim' attribute the most informative for larger filler sizes.

As these results have shown, to properly evaluate detection attributes it is insufficient to look at just a single attack model or filler size. The attributes described above were selected based on their characteristics as a whole at providing coverage across these dimensions.

Classification Performance Analysis

Figure 6 compares the detection capabilities of our algorithm using model-specific features with the Chirita algorithm for the basic attacks: random and average. For both precision and recall, the model-specific algorithm is dominant. Precision is particularly a problem for the Chirita algorithm: many false positive identifications are made. However, as the authors point out, this is probably not too significant since discarding a few real users will not generally impact the system's recommendation performance, and our experiments showed that generally this was true. We also see that the model-specific version has better recall especially a low filler sizes: recall that the Chirita algorithm was tuned for 100% filler sizes, so this is not surprising.

Figure 7 extends these results to examine the bandwagon and segment attacks. Again a similar pattern is seen. Precision is a bit lower, especially for the segment attack, but recall is extremely high for the model-specific algorithm. Chirita again suffers at low filler sizes. There is an interesting dip at 3% filler size. This occurs because the average number of user ratings is around this number. The *LengthVar* attribute is not useful at this point because the attack profiles do not differ in length from a typical user.

Nuke attack results are shown in Figure 8. Three attacks are shown: average, random and love/hate. Again, precision is low for the Chirita algorithm and

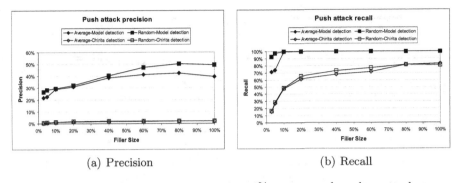

(a) Precision   (b) Recall

Fig. 6. Classification statistics against 1% average and random attacks

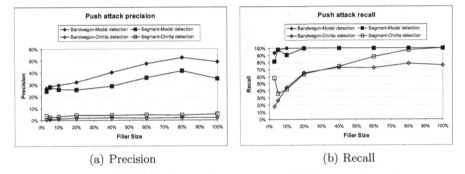

(a) Precision   (b) Recall

Fig. 7. Classification statistics against 1% bandwagon and segment attacks

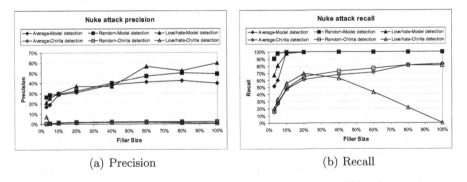

(a) Precision   (b) Recall

Fig. 8. Classification statistics for both classifiers against 1% nuke attacks

recall results are similar to those seen for the push attacks, except that the love/hate attack proves to be difficult for Chirita to detect at high filler sizes.

Robustness Analysis

The results above show that both detection schemes have some success in identifying attack profiles. While this is promising, the real proof of the concept is

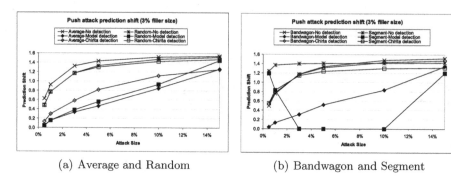

(a) Average and Random   (b) Bandwagon and Segment

Fig. 9. Prediction shift for push attacks with and without attack detection

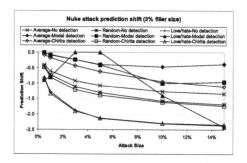

Fig. 10. Prediction shift for nuke attacks with and without detection

its impact on the recommender system itself. Can using a detection algorithm reduce the impact of an attack, forming a successful defense?

We measure the robustness of the system with the *Prediction Shift* metric discussed above on the recommendation algorithm as described in Section 4.1. We used the troublesome 3% filler size to maximize the difficulty of detection and varied the attack size, expressed here as a percentage of the original profile database: a 1% attack equals 9 attack profiles inserted into the database.

Figure 9a shows the average prediction shift for the recommendation algorithm, with and without attack profile detection, for both our model-specific as well as Chirita detection methods against the average and random attacks. Lower prediction shifts signify a more robust system. Large attacks have a strong effect if no detection is employed. At 5% attack, the attacked item is already rated 1.4 points higher, enough to move a middling movie (3.6 is the system average) all the way to the maximum of 5. The Chirita algorithm, despite its lower recall in the detection experiments, still has a big impact on system robustness against the average attack, cutting the prediction shift by at least half for low attack sizes. It does less well for the random attack, for which it was not designed. Our classification approach improves on Chirita except at the very largest attack sizes. At these sizes, the attack profiles begin to alter the statistical properties of the ratings corpus, so that the attacks start to look "normal."

Figure 9b continues this analysis to the bandwagon and segment attacks. We see how significant the threat posed by the segment attack is here. At very low attack sizes, it is already having an impact equivalent to the average attack at 5% attack size. At these lower sizes, the model-based approach is actually inferior to Chirita. At 3%, the targeted attributes kick in and the segment attack is virtually neutralized until it becomes very large. Chirita shows more or less the same pattern as against the random attack.

Figure 10 shows nuke attacks. The low-knowledge love/hate attack is quite effective, almost as good as the average attack. Either of these attacks can reduce the predicted score of a highly-favored item (5.0 prediction) all the way to below the mean, with just a 3% attack size. The model-based approach does very well at defending against average and random attacks. It does less well with the love/hate attack, for which it must be said it has no model-specific features. Chirita again is somewhere in the middle, doing better against the love/hate attack at low and very high attack sizes, but not elsewhere.

6   Conclusion

Profile injection attacks are a serious threat to the robustness and trustworthiness of collaborative recommender systems and other open adaptive systems. An essential component of a robust recommender system is a mechanism to detect profiles originating from attacks so that they can be quarantined and their impact reduced. We have demonstrated that the information gain associated with detection attributes can vary greatly not just across attack types, but also based on filler size and attack size. In addition, we show that classifiers built using these features can be quite effective at detecting attacks, and that this detection can improve the stability of the recommender, keeping its predicted ratings steady under most attack scenarios. The segment and love/hate attack models prove to be the wiliest opponents. They can strongly impact prediction even at low attack sizes and it is precisely at these small sizes that they are difficult to detect. We are still studying the problem of detection for these attack types.

References

1. Burke, R., Mobasher, B., Zabicki, R., Bhaumik, R.: Identifying attack models for secure recommendation. In: Beyond Personalization: A Workshop on the Next Generation of Recommender Systems, San Diego, California (January 2005)
2. Burke, R., Mobasher, B., Bhaumik, R.: Limited knowledge shilling attacks in collaborative filtering systems. In: Proceedings of the 3rd IJCAI Workshop in Intelligent Techniques for Personalization, Edinburgh, Scotland (August 2005)
3. Lam, S., Riedl, J.: Shilling recommender systems for fun and profit. In: Proceedings of the 13th International WWW Conference, New York (May 2004)
4. O'Mahony, M., Hurley, N., Kushmerick, N., Silvestre, G.: Collaborative recommendation: A robustness analysis. ACM Transactions on Internet Technology 4(4), 344–377 (2004)

5. Chirita, P.-A., Nejdl, W., Zamfir, C.: Preventing shilling attacks in online recommender systems. In: WIDM 2005. Proceedings of the 7th annual ACM international workshop on Web information and data management, Bremen, Germany, ACM Press, New York (2005)

6. Su, X.-F., Zeng, H.-J., Chen., Z.: Finding group shilling in recommendation system. In: WWW 2005. Proceedings of the 14th international conference on World Wide Web (May 2005)

7. O'Mahony, M.P., Hurley, N.J., Silvestre, G.: Utility-based neighbourhood formation for efficient and robust collaborative filtering. In: EC 2004. Proceedings of the 5th ACM Conference on Electronic Commerce, pp. 260–261. ACM Press, New York (2004)

8. Burke, R., Mobasher, B., Williams, C., Bhaumik, R.: Detecting profile injection attacks in collaborative recommender systems. In: CEC/EEE 2006. Proceedings of the IEEE Joint Conference on E-Commerce Technology and Enterprise Computing, Palo Alto, CA, IEEE Computer Society Press, Los Alamitos (2006)

9. Mobasher, B., Burke, R., Williams, C., Bhaumik, R.: Analysis and detection of segment-focused attacks against collaborative recommendation. In: Nasraoui, O., Zaïane, O., Spiliopoulou, M., Mobasher, B., Masand, B., Yu, P.S. (eds.) WebKDD 2005. LNCS (LNAI), vol. 4198, pp. 96–118. Springer, Heidelberg (2006)

10. Burke, R., Mobasher, B., Williams, C., Bhaumik, R.: Classification features for attack detection in collaborative recommender systems. In: KDD 2006. Proceedings of the ACM SIGKDD Conference on Knowledge Discovery and Data Mining, Philadelphia, ACM Press, New York (2006)

11. Williams, C., Bhaumik, R., Burke, R., Mobasher, B.: The impact of attack profile classification on the robustness of collaborative recommendation. In: KDD 2006. Proceedings of the 2006 WebKDD Workshop, held at ACM SIGKDD Conference on Data Mining and Knowledge Discovery, Philadelphia, ACM Press, New York (August 2006)

12. Burke, R., Mobasher, B., Williams, C., Bhaumik, R.: Segment-based injection attacks against collaborative filtering recommender systems. In: ICDM 2005. Proceedings of the International Conference on Data Mining, Houston (December 2005)

13. Mobasher, B., Burke, R., Bhaumik, R., Williams, C.: Effective attack models for shilling item-based collaborative filtering systems. In: SIGKDD 2005. Proceedings of the 2005 WebKDD Workshop, held in conjuction with ACM, Chicago, Illinois, ACM Press, New York (2005)

14. Resnick, P., Iacovou, N., Suchak, M., Bergstrom, P., Riedl, J.: Grouplens: an open architecture for collaborative filtering of netnews. In: CSCW 1994. Proceedings of the 1994 ACM conference on Computer supported cooperative work, Chapel Hill, NC, pp. 175–186. ACM Press, New York (1994)

15. Herlocker, J., Konstan, J., Borchers, A., Riedl, J.: An algorithmic framework for performing collaborative filtering. In: SIGIR 1999. Proceedings of the 22nd ACM Conference on Research and Development in Information Retrieval, Berkeley, CA, ACM Press, New York (1999)

16. Herlocker, J., Konstan, J., Tervin, L.G., Riedl, J.: Evaluating collaborative filtering recommender systems. ACM Transactions on Information Systems 22(1), 5–53 (2004)

17. Witten, I.H., Frank, E.: Data Mining: Practical machine learning tools and techniques, 2nd edn. Morgan Kaufmann, San Francisco, CA (2005)

Predicting the Political Sentiment of Web Log Posts Using Supervised Machine Learning Techniques Coupled with Feature Selection

Kathleen T. Durant and Michael D. Smith

Harvard University, Harvard School of Engineering and Applied Sciences,
Cambridge MA, USA
{Kathleen,Smith}@eecs.harvard.edu

Abstract. As the number of web logs dramatically grows, readers are turning to them as an important source of information. Automatic techniques that identify the political sentiment of web log posts will help bloggers categorize and filter this exploding information source. In this paper we illustrate the effectiveness of supervised learning for sentiment classification on web log posts. We show that a Naïve Bayes classifier coupled with a forward feature selection technique can on average correctly predict a posting's sentiment 89.77% of the time with a standard deviation of 3.01. It significantly outperforms Support Vector Machines at the 95% confidence level with a confidence interval of [1.5, 2.7]. The feature selection technique provides on average an 11.84% and a 12.18% increase for Naïve Bayes and Support Vector Machines results respectively. Previous sentiment classification research achieved an 81% accuracy using Naïve Bayes and 82.9% using SVMs on a movie domain corpus.

Keywords: Sentiment Classification, Blogs, Web Logs, Naïve Bayes, Support Vector Machines, WEKA, feature selection.

1 Introduction

In December 2004, a Gallup Poll reported that over the last two years the only news and related information source showing an increase in daily use was the Internet. Every other news source decreased, and local TV news, local newspapers and network news magazine shows reached new lows. The percentage of Americans getting their news on the Internet every day has increased in Gallup polls from 3% in 1995 to 20% in 2004 [2]. Out of the 94 million Americans using the Internet in September 2005, 46% of them use the Internet daily to read news. It is the third most popular activity on the Internet, surpassed only by ubiquitous activities such as processing email and using a search engine [19].

The number of web logs, also referred to as *blogs*, has increased dramatically in the last few years. An estimated 59.6 million blogs now exist in cyberspace, up from just 100,000 in 2002 [6]. According to Technorati, an authority on blogs, the number of web logs doubles every 6 months with 75,000 new web logs coming into existence every day. The daily posting volume of web log posts is 1.2 million or 18 posts a

O. Nasraoui et al. (Eds.): WebKDD 2006, LNAI 4811, pp. 187–206, 2007.

second. In November 2004, a Pew Poll reported the number of readers accessing information on web logs had increased by 58% over the course of the year [4]. 10% of all Internet users either have a web log or have posted their opinion to a newsgroup or some other online journal. In February 2004, 17% of the Internet users had used the Internet to read someone else's web log; by September 2005, that figure has increased to 27% [16, 17]. In February 2004, 5% of the polled Internet users had used the Internet to create a web log; by September 2005, that figure has jumped to 9% [16, 17]. Using web logs to share ideas and opinions is growing rapidly in popularity and has become an integral part of our online culture.

Web logs provide a mechanism for people to express their ideas and opinions with the world. They allow a writer to share his first-hand experience, thoughts and opinions with anyone in the world that has access to the Internet. The compendium of web logs can be viewed as a plethora of people's opinions. Our research applies sentiment classification to the voluminous collection of opinions found in web logs. Sentiment classification is the ability to judge a passage of text as positive or negative given a particular domain or topic. More specifically, sentiment classification is the ability to label a passage according to its general sentiment $p \in \{-1, 1\}$, where -1 represents unfavorable and 1 represents a favorable description. It divides a collection of opinions into two opposing camps.

We limit our web logs to political web logs; this is a new domain area for sentiment classification research. Previous sentiment classification studies used news articles as its domain [20, 10, 7]. Others used movie reviews [10, 1, 14, 15]. Nasukawa and Yi used camera reviews as their domain [13], and Turney and Littman's corpus was composed of 410 reviews from Epinions randomly sampled from four different domains: automobiles, banks, movies and travel destinations [22]. Das and Chen's research was applied to Yahoo's stock message boards [3].

We believe political web log posts to have different characteristics than the domains in previous studies. Web logs are highly opinionated and rich in sentiment. Predicting the sentiment of a political web post (i.e., predicting that the post came from a liberal or conservative blogger) is more difficult than predicting sentiment of traditional text (e.g., newspaper articles). Nonprofessional writers usually author web logs; the writing takes on a less formal conversational style of documentation. The language used in web logs is quite rich and has many forms of speech such as cynicism and sarcasm. Many times the complete concept of a post can only be determined by the interplay of the text and a picture posted with the text. Other times the sarcasm is so heavy, readers misinterpret the meaning of a post. Hyperlinks also play an important role in the meaning of a web log post. Most web logs contain many hyperlinks; enabling a reader to follow the evolution of a topic from web log to web log. The information from the hyperlinks often enhances the meaning of a post. Our domain can be characterized quite differently than traditional prose and even other online opinionated data; yet we show that a standard machine learning technique perform almost as well in our domain as in other domains and if coupled with a feature selection algorithm can surpass previous results.

We have chosen to create a topic-specific corpus. Our topic is people's opinion on President George W. Bush's management of the Iraq War. Corpuses from previous studies are only domain specific not topic specific [1, 7, 10, 13, 14, 15, 22]. Engström showed machine learning classification to be highly topic-dependent [5]. If given a topic-specific corpus a machine classifier takes advantage of topic-specific terms and in general produces higher results than if given a nonspecific topic corpus. However, we found an opposite result. Our classifiers trained on our topic specific data using the same standard feature set representation performed slightly worse than a classifier trained on a nonspecific topic corpus [14]. We believe this degradation is due to the characteristics of our web log corpus.

The ability to judge sentiment would be extremely useful when applied to the vast number of opinions found in the growing number of on-line documents such as web logs and editorial pages of news feeds. Predicting and tagging sentiment of a web log post could improve the process of web logging. It could help organize the information and allow users to find and react to opposite or similar opinions thus improving and simplifying the process of sharing and discussing opinions in web logs. In this paper we investigate three aspects of our web log corpus that need to be understood in order to pre-tag the sentiment of web log posts: applicable machine learning techniques, feature selection, and class constituency. We recognize time as an influential aspect of our data and use a simple segmentation scheme but do not investigate other solutions.

We chose to partition our slightly greater than two years of data by the month; thus creating twenty-five partitions. We predict the sentiment of political web posts for each of the 25 different time segments. We believe our data and many of our terms to be time-specific so we keep our data time-ordered. We chose our time interval to be a month because we needed an interval large enough to ensure enough postings to create good-sized datasets yet small enough to limit the number of events discussed within the interval.

We vary dataset creation along two dimensions: class constituency and feature set collection. We also investigate the use of different machine learning techniques such as Naïve Bayes and Support Vector Machines. We wish to determine if existing technology can be successfully applied in our domain. Since we wish to take advantage of all our data, we measure the accuracy of different datasets that consist of balanced and imbalanced categorical compositions. In our first collection we gather as many posts as we can from the web. This approach led to an imbalanced category makeup within our datasets. This imbalance is expected, since the topic may be discussed more ardently in one camp than the other. One camp could be inflamed on a topic; while the other camp ignores the topic. Our second collection balances the constituency of our datasets by randomly discarding posts of the majority class, the class that outnumbered the other class. This approach led to smaller datasets. Smaller datasets tend to produce lower accuracies than larger datasets; however we show balanced datasets produce similar yet unbiased accuracy results. We then considered three different approaches to feature selection. Our first approach limits the features to the terms occurring at least five times within the corpus, a representation used in a previous study [14]. We then added features found within log posts for the current month but were not part of the dataset, yielding on average feature sets 1.75 times larger. The added features did not improve the accuracy of our datasets. Lastly, we applied a forward search feature selection algorithm to determine our features; this technique drastically decreased the number of features. It also improved our results significantly; on average an 11.84% and a 12.18% increase for Naïve Bayes and Support Vector Machines respectively.

2 Previous Work in Sentiment Classification

Previous work can be categorized by the approach used to perform sentiment classification. The knowledge-based approach uses linguistic models or some other form of knowledge to glean insight into the sentiment of a passage. Later approaches apply statistical or machine learning techniques for achieving sentiment classification. A brief history of both approaches follows.

2.1 Knowledge-Based Sentiment Classification

Both Hearst [8] and Sack [20] categorized the sentiment of entire documents based on cognitive linguistics models. Other researchers such as Huettner and Subasic [10], Das and Chen [3], and Tong [20] manually or semi-manually constructed a discriminate word lexicon to help categorize the sentiment of a passage. Hatzivassiloglou and McKeown [7], and Turney and Littman [22] chose to classify the orientation of words rather than a total passage. They used the semantic orientation of individual words or phrases to determine the semantic orientation of the containing passage. They preselected a set of seed words or applied linguistic heuristics in order to classify the sentiment of a passage. Beineke, Hastie and Vaithyanathan extend Turney and Littman's research using a pseudo-supervised approach [1]. They address the problem of the limited number of labeled data by using both labeled and unlabeled data. They defined anchors of sentiment as pairs of words that co-occur frequently and support a positive or negative sentiment. Other words found to occur more frequently with the anchor words are then chosen to be anchor words. They use the anchor words as their feature set and apply a Naïve Bayes classifier to the dataset.

Nasukawa and Yi [13] take a completely different approach to sentiment analysis. They see a topic as an item containing many different parts or features. They wish to identify the sentences that contain opinions concerning the features of the topic. Sentiment analysis involves the identification of sentiment expressions, polarity and strength of the expression, and their relationship to the subject. They choose a particular topic of interest and manually define a sentiment lexicon for identification. The classification of each review was manually determined by a judge rather than the author of the review. They believe this approach provides not just a sentiment class but an analysis of the opinions found within a review. This approach is useful when measuring customer satisfaction of a particular product. It allows a product to be reviewed as a sum of its parts. Many consumers update on-line product web logs; being able to organize and sort positive and negative comments benefits the supplying corporation of a product as well as consumers.

2.2 Statistical Sentiment Classification

Pang, Lee, and Vaithyanathan have successfully applied standard machine learning techniques to a database of movie reviews [14]. They chose to apply Naïve Bayes, Maximum Entropy and Support Vector Machines to a domain specific corpus of movie reviews. They represented the reviews in eight different formats, the simplest being a unigram representation. The accuracy of their most successful representation, the unigram feature set representation, and their most successful machine learning induction method, Support Vector Machines, produced an accuracy of 82.9%. Their Naïve Bayes classifier with a unigram feature set representation achieved an accuracy of 81.0%. They continued their research by defining a scheme that addresses the nature of a review. They argue a review consists of both objective and subjective sentences, where the objective sentences describe the plot of the movie and the subjective sentences expresses the reviewer's opinion of the story. They created extracts from the reviews that contained the sentences identified as the most opinionated. They achieved some success in this approach creating extracts 60% the size of the original review with accuracy better than or at least as accurate as the accuracy of the full text review [15].

3   From Blogs to Datasets

The website, themoderatevoice.com, is a political web log that lists and categorizes over 250 web logs as *left voices, right voices* or *moderate voices*. The list was created by the journalist Joe Gandelman, who classifies himself as a political moderate. Gandelman's categorization of each blog is the information we attempt to predict. We allow postings from a blog to inherit the categorization of the blog and attempt to classify a post as originating from a left voice or a right voice.

We harvested the posts from the left-voice and right-voice blogs for the time period of March 2003 to March 2005. We apply a topic selection filter over the posts. Our filter identifies the posts that contain our specific topic from the selected posts. The following sections discuss the details of the posts collected to create our dataset of political blogs. This discussion is then followed by a description of our chosen feature set representation and values.

3.1   A Description of the Web Data

Out of the 99 left-voice blogs and the 85 right-voice blogs listed in March 2005 on themoderatevoice.com, 84 left-voice blogs and 76 right-voice blogs were included within our study. The other 24 blogs were eliminated because they were political cartoons, lacked archives, were broken links, or were an online magazine that contained no original posts. For a complete list of the contributing web logs please refer to Appendix A. The total size of the right-voices' web files is slightly less than 775 Megabytes; while the total size of the left-voices' web files is slightly over 1.13 Gigabytes. From the 1.875 Gigabytes of web files we were able to extract 399 Megabytes of political web log posts.

Since Gandelman's listing was dated March 2005, many of the web logs did not exist as far back as March 2003. Because of this the earlier datasets are in general smaller than the later dated datasets. Also, interest in our topic waxed and waned across the two-year period, affecting the sizes of the datasets.

3.2   Extracting Web Log Posts on Topic

We have chosen to limit the postings to a particular topic. It is the opinion of this topic we plan to identify. The topic we chose is people's opinion on how well President George W. Bush is handling the Iraq War. The topic of the posting is determined by the terms: President Bush and Iraq War. Let $t_1, t_2, t_3 \dots t_n$ be the terms found within a posting p. The posting p is eligible for extraction if there exists t_i, t_j, t_k, t_l such that :

```
((t₁ =~ "^President" || t_j =~ "^Bush") &&
 (t_k =~ "^Iraq" || t₁ =~ "^War")).                          (1)
```

The extraction rule is a perl regular expression that requires two concepts to be found within the extracted blog posting: President George W. Bush and the Iraq War. The rule allows either prefix terms *President* or *Bush* to represent the concept President George W. Bush. The Iraq War can be represented by prefix terms *Iraq* or *War*.

From the 399 Megabytes of web log posts, our topic selection filter determined 38,789 posts were deemed on-topic comprising 147 Megabytes, while 216,904 posts were deemed off-topic (252 Megabytes). As demonstrated by Table 1, the liberal bloggers consistently wrote more postings on-topic than the conservative bloggers; in some months the liberal posts outnumbered the conservative posts 2 to 1.

3.3 Dataset Representation

The datasets are represented by the most prevalent single word terms or *unigrams* occurring within the posts for the month. No stemming is performed on the terms. The features of the datasets are the unigrams occurring at least five times within the posting corpora. The values for the features represent presence versus absence of the feature within the post; we call this representation the *Boolean Presence feature set representation*. A value of 0 means the unigram was not found within the posting. Correspondingly, a value of 1 means the unigram was found within the posting. We chose the Boolean presence representation because it yielded a higher accuracy than the standard frequency feature representation in previous related research [14].

Since a unigram does not convey the context of a word, we used Das and Chen's technique to capture the polarity of the word's environment [3]. The idea is to negate words in the post that are found after a negative word such as *not*, or *no*. Since we are interested in sentiment, it is important we differentiate when words in a post are used to express the opposite meaning of the word. Unigrams are marked as negative if they are preceded by a negative term. The negative clause ends at the next punctuation mark. On average, this improves predictability between 2 to 4%.

We use a standard bag-of-features framework to represent our blog postings. Let $\{f_1,\dots, f_m\}$ be a predefined set of m features that may appear in a post. Let $f_i(d)$ be equal to 1 if the feature f_i appears in the post d and equal to 0 if the feature f_i does not appear in post d. Then each post d is represented by the post vector:

$$d = (f_1(d), f_2(d), \dots, f_m(d)).   (2)$$

Table 1 lists the number of posts and the size of the feature sets for each month. The full feature set is created from all the posts within the month; while the reduced feature set is created from a randomly created category-balanced group of posts. The feature selection subset is determined by a forward feature selection algorithm that analyzes the utility of each feature. The selection algorithm seeks to remove redundant features.

Table 1. The percentage of postings on-topic, the number of postings, and the number of features for each month

Month	Percentage of Postings on Topic		Number of Postings		Number of Features		
	Right-voice	Left-voice	Right-voice	Left-voice	Full	Reduced	Feature Selection Subset
2003-03	16.92	24.48	258	400	9487	6150	133
2003-04	13.92	21.52	176	238	7059	4694	111
2003-05	9.46	18.02	113	208	6036	3501	105
2003-06	9.54	23.56	156	318	8023	4364	104
2003-07	11.60	29.79	207	464	9828	5264	120
2003-08	8.55	19.65	157	321	8792	4511	101
2003-09	13.45	25.71	257	424	10908	6149	141
2003-10	11.81	25.10	250	448	11028	6252	139
2003-11	15.62	25.33	276	410	10971	6602	142
2003-12	17.21	22.88	302	456	11884	6736	130
2004-01	14.30	23.21	352	636	13079	7574	157
2004-02	14.29	26.28	286	729	12318	6535	169
2004-03	15.43	26.48	370	819	13396	7994	123
2004-04	17.36	30.67	496	879	15729	9505	159
2004-05	15.41	29.98	440	1027	16767	9092	185
2004-06	16.95	27.32	417	902	16130	8697	219
2004-07	17.91	26.25	522	876	16565	9778	201
2004-08	17.84	27.62	615	1135	18819	11151	158
2004-09	21.53	32.75	784	1305	20644	12455	220
2004-10	23.55	31.83	972	1611	23009	14341	171
2004-11	15.95	20.84	467	807	17401	9408	197
2004-12	11.14	20.29	288	736	16254	6859	165
2005-01	13.77	22.12	506	971	18237	10245	209
2005-02	12.58	18.61	453	775	16285	9404	235
2005-03	12.26	15.69	336	633	14060	7822	149
Average	14.73	24.63	378	701	13708	7803	158

Table 1 provides some insights into the evolution of our topic over the two years. One striking statistic is the higher level of interest this topic has among the liberal bloggers than the conservative bloggers. Not only do we have more on-topic posts from the liberal bloggers, they also tend to post more often on this topic than the conservative bloggers. Also the number of posts on-topic varies from month to month. Some of this variation can be blamed on fewer blogs existing in March 2003 than in March 2005. However, the level of interest the liberal and conservative bloggers had in the current events of the war also accounted for the imbalance. On average, we had twice as many liberal posts as conservatives.

4   Machine Learning Techniques

We gauged the effectiveness of known sentiment classification technology on our novel collection of political web posts. We considered two different machine learning techniques: Naïve Bayes and Support Vector Machines and measured their applicability in our domain.

4.1   Naïve Bayes Classifier

A Naïve Bayes classifier is a probabilistic classifier based on probability models that incorporate strong independence assumptions among the features. Our Naïve Bayes classifier assigns a given web log post d the class $c*$

$$c* = \text{Argmax}_c \, P(c \mid d); c \in \{\text{right-voice, left-voice}\}. \tag{3}$$

A document of length n is represented as an m-dimensional vector, where f_i is the ith dimension in the vector and m is the number of features, as described in Section 3.3. We derive the Naïve Bayes (NB) classifier by first observing that by Bayes' rule

$$P(c \mid d) = \frac{P(c)P(d \mid c)}{P(d)} \tag{4}$$

$P(d)$ plays no role in assigning $c*$. To estimate the term $P(d \mid c)$, Naïve Bayes decomposes the estimate by assuming all the f_i's are conditionally independent given d's class. Term $n_i(d)$ is the presence of term i in document d (value 0 or 1).

$$P_{NB}(c \mid d) = \frac{P(c)(\prod_{i=1}^{m} P(f_i \mid c)^{n_i(d)})}{P(d)} \tag{5}$$

We chose to use a Naïve Bayes classifier because of its simplicity, its quick computation time compared to other machine learning techniques and its performance using the Boolean presence feature set representation in a previous study [14]. The Naïve Bayes assumption of attribute independence performs well for text categorization at the word feature level. When the number of features is large, the independence assumption allows for the parameters of each feature to be learned separately, greatly simplifying the learning process. The celerity of the Naïve Bayes modeling process makes it a favorable candidate for application to our fast-growing web log domain. Our experiments use the Naïve Bayes implementation from the WEKA machine-learning toolkit, version 3.4 [23]. We chose to use the Naïve Bayes' multinomial event-driven model.

4.2   Support Vector Machines

Support Vector Machines (SVMs) identify a hyperplane that separates two classes or categories of data. The chosen hyperplane creates the largest separation or margin between the two classes; hence it is a large margin classifier. Our search for the hyperplane is a constrained optimization problem. Assume we have n log posts to be categorized. Our collection C of web log posts is represented as Formula 6 where x_i represents the features of the post; and c_i represents the categorization of that post, either a *left voice* or a *right voice*.

$$C = \{(x_1,c_1), (x_2,c_2),(x_3,c_3)...(x_n,c_n)\} \tag{6}$$

The dividing hyperplane of our two classes is defined to be $w \cdot x - b = 0$. The parallel hyperplane for one category is defined as $w \cdot x - b = 1$ and for the other category is $w \cdot x - b = -1$. The space between the two parallel hyperplanes is the margin we wish to optimize. Not all of the data being classified is used in identifying the dividing hyperplane, only the closest points to the margin or the points that lie on the two parallel hyperplanes are used. These points are the contributing support vectors of the hyperplane. To include non-contributing points into the equations of the parallel hyperplanes, we rewrite the equations as inequalities, $w \cdot x - b \geq 1$ for one category and $w \cdot x - b \leq -1$ for the other category. The non-contributing data points will vary in distance from the corresponding hyperplane. Our two inequalities can be rewritten as Formula 7 since our c_i's represent the category values (1, -1) of our web posts. The quadratic optimization problem is to minimize the length of w given the constraint in Formula 7. This will identify the largest margin between our left and right voices.

$$c_i(w \cdot x_i - b) \geq 1 \quad \text{for } 1 < i < n. \tag{7}$$

We use the SMO kernel implementation from the WEKA machine-learning toolkit version 3.4 [23]. SMO, sequential minimal optimization, breaks the large quadratic optimization problem into the smallest quadratic optimization problems that can be solved analytically. We chose to use a SVM classifier because it outperformed other techniques in a previous study [14]. It also takes a different approach to classification than Naïve Bayes.

4.3 Validation Technique

We chose to use the same validation technique for all classifiers, stratified 10-fold cross-validation. In stratified 10-fold cross-validation, a dataset is randomly divided into 10 sets with approximately equal size and category distributions. For each *fold*, the classifier is trained using all but one of the 10 groups and then tested on the remaining group. This procedure is repeated for each of the 10 groups. The cross-validation score is the average performance across each of the ten runs.

4.4 Feature Selection

We investigated improving the collection of sentiment classifier's accuracy results by applying off-the-shelf feature selection to our datasets. In particular we have applied a forward search technique that evaluates the predictive ability of each feature individually and the redundancy among the features. The technique, *CfsSubsetEval* implemented in WEKA 3.4 [23], chooses a subset of the given features and aims to reduce the number of features while improving the accuracy results. We have chosen to search the feature set using a *BestFirst* search, starting from an empty subset and proceeding until the results of the current subset cannot be improved. The technique chooses features that are highly correlated with the predicting class but have low intercorrelation. We chose this technique since we believe reducing redundancy within our features will support the Naïve Bayes assumption of independent features.

5 Experiments

In order to evaluate existing technology, we create seven different *collections of classifiers*, five containing Naïve Bayes classifiers and two containing Support Vector Machines. Each collection allows us to evaluate the effectiveness of one known aspect of the sentiment classification technology on our domain. Our goal is to achieve high accuracy on the results of the total dataset as well as on each of the two categories. We wish to keep our datasets small while still retaining high accuracies.

Our first collection of classifiers is created from *all* available posts from the left-voices and right-voices blogs. This collection contains datasets with different numbers of left-voices and right-voices log posts. We refer to it as our *unbalanced collection of classifiers*.

Our second collection of classifiers contains an equal number of left-voices and right-voices web log posts, but its feature set is determined by the full, unbalanced collection of datasets. We refer to it as our *balanced inflated collection of classifiers*. By comparing the results of our balanced inflated collection and our unbalanced collection, we can quantify the importance of balanced categories within our datasets.

Our third collection contains an equal number of left-voices and right-voices web log posts and its feature set is determined by this balanced dataset of posts. We refer to this collection as our *balanced collection of classifiers*. By comparing the results of our balanced collection to our balanced inflated collection, we can evaluate the two different feature set representations. It will reveal if more features on-topic improves the accuracy of the datasets.

Our fourth collection contains an unequal number of left-voices and right-voices posts. The categorical makeup is equivalent to the categorical makeup of the unbalanced collection of classifiers; however, the number of elements in each dataset is equivalent to the corresponding dataset in the balanced collection of classifiers. We refer to this collection as the *small unbalanced collection of classifiers*. We compare the results of these datasets to the results of the unbalanced collection of classifiers to consider the effects of unbalanced class constituency and dataset size to the accuracy results of left-voices and right-voices.

Our last Naïve Bayes collection contains an equal number of left-voices and right-voices posts. The feature set is determined by a subset feature selection technique described in Section 4.4. We refer to this collection as the *Naïve Bayes feature selection collection of classifiers*. We compare the results of this collection with the collection of balanced Naïve Bayes collection to consider the effects of our feature selection algorithm on our Naïve Bayes classifiers.

Our first Support Vector Machine collection contains an equal number of left-voices and right-voices posts, with the feature sets determined by the contributing posts and SVM classifiers. We refer to it as our *SVM collection of classifiers*. Comparing our balanced collection to our SVM collection of classifiers allows us to evaluate the effectiveness of our two machine learning techniques on our chosen domain.

Our next Support Vector Machines collection also contains an equal number of left-voices and right-voices posts; with the feature set determined by the *CfsSubsetEval* algorithm [23] described in Section 4.4. We refer to this collection as our *SVM feature selection collection of classifiers*. By comparing our SVM collection of classifiers to our SVM feature selection collection allows us to evaluate the effectiveness of our feature selection algorithm on our Support Vector Machine classifiers. We also compare our Naïve Bayes feature selection collection to the SVM feature selection collection to consider the effects of feature selection on our two chosen machine learning algorithms.

6 Results

Using our seven collections, Section 6.1 shows that Naïve Bayes performs well and SVMs perform adequately when predicting the sentiment of political blog posts even though the domain of our data is quite different from traditional text. In Section 6.2, we show increasing the feature set to contain topic-specific terms not selected by our feature selection algorithm does not improve the accuracy of the datasets; however decreasing the feature set to remove redundant features does improve the results of Naïve Bayes and Support Vector Machines. In particular on average it improves our Naïve Bayes results by 11.18% and our SVM results by 12.18%. We also show reducing the average size of the datasets by 30% in order to balance the categories does not have a negative effect on the total accuracy. It actually has the positive effect on the category makeup of the misclassified posts.

6.1 Comparing Different Machine Learning Techniques

Our first set of experiments compares two machine learning techniques: Naïve Bayes and Support Vector Machines on two collections of balanced datasets. In Figure 1, on average, SVMs correctly predicted the category of web log posts 75.47% of the time with a standard deviation of 2.64. Our Naïve Bayes classifiers outperformed Support Vector Machines, on average, by correctly predicting a posting's political category 78.06% of the time with a standard deviation of 2.39. We performed a paired samples t-test on our results, pairing our classifiers month-by-month. Our t-test showed Naïve Bayes outperforms SVMs at a 99.9% confidence level, with a confidence interval of [1.425, 3.488]. Previous research was able to achieve an 81.0% accuracy using Naïve Bayes and 82.9% using SVMs on a nonspecific corpus using the Boolean presence feature set representation [14]. SVMs are doing a poor job predicting the sentiment of our topic-specific web log posts compared to its success on a non-specific topic movie review corpus [14]. One potential cause for this is in our topic-specific corpus the number of terms in common between our two categories will be higher than in a nonspecific topic corpus. These common terms make it more difficult to identify the hyperplane separating the two categories; this finding contradicts Engström's results [5].

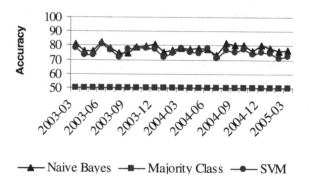

Fig. 1. Sentiment classification results of a collection of Naïve Bayes classifiers and SVM classifiers. Both sets contain the same data elements and feature sets.

6.2 Comparing Different Feature Sets

In Figure 2 we compare the collection of balanced classifiers to the collection of Naïve Bayes feature selection classifiers. In these sets of experiments the number of elements, the class composition, and the classifier, Naïve Bayes, remain constant. Only the feature set varies. As shown in Figure 2 the Naïve Bayes feature selection classifiers outperform the Naïve Bayes classifiers containing our baseline features. In Figure 3 we do the same comparison as in Figure 2, the only difference is the machine learning technique considered. We see improvement results in the SVM feature selection classifiers. In particular, our Naïve Bayes classifier collection coupled with a forward feature selection technique on average correctly predict a posting's sentiment 89.77% of the time with a standard deviation of 3.01. Our SVMs collection coupled with a forward feature selection technique on average correctly predicts a posting's sentiment 87.66% of the time with a standard deviation of 2.22. Naïve Bayes significantly outperforms Support Vector Machines at the 95% confidence level with a confidence interval of [1.5, 2.7]. On average, we gain an 11.84% increase for Naïve Bayes and a 12.18% increase for SVMs. These results show reducing the number of features by removing redundant features yields higher results for Naïve Bayes and SVM classifiers.

In Figure 4 we compare the collection of balanced classifiers to the collection of inflated balanced classifiers. In these sets of experiments the number of elements in the datasets is constant and the classifier is Naïve Bayes; only the number of features is varied. Our accuracy range for the collection of balanced inflated classifiers is 72.97% to 81.69%. The average predictability value is 78.06% with a standard deviation of 2.39. Our range for predictability for the collection of balanced classifiers is 73.16% to 82.67%, with an average predictability value of 77.93% and a standard deviation of 2.41. There is no improvement in accuracy with the inflated feature set even though the added features are relevant to the current month's data. The results for the two collections are indistinguishable. These results shows increasing the feature set with topic-related terms does not improve our results.

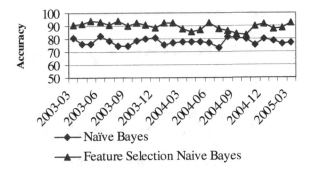

Fig. 2. Sentiment classification results of balanced Naïve Bayes classifiers vs. Feature Selection Naïve Bayes. The feature selection Naïve Bayes classifiers significantly outperform the Naïve Bayes classifiers.

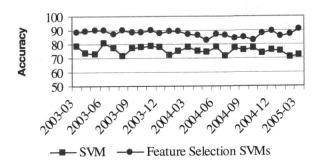

Fig. 3. Sentiment classification results of balanced Support Vector Machine classifiers vs. Feature Selection SVMs. The feature selection SVM classifiers significantly outperform the SVM classifiers.

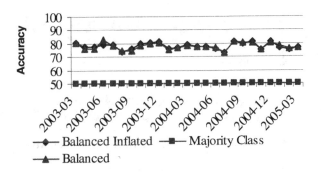

Fig. 4. Sentiment classification results of two sets of balanced Naïve Bayes classifiers vs. the Majority class. The difference between the two balanced sets is the number of features used.

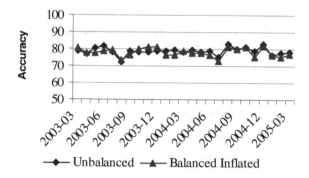

Fig. 5. Sentiment classification results of a set of balanced inflated classifiers and a set of unbalanced classifiers. The sets have identical feature sets.

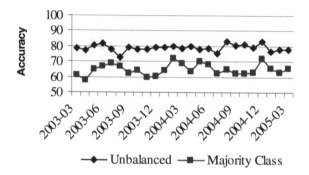

Fig. 6. Sentiment Classification results of a set of unbalanced Naïve Bayes classifiers compared to the actual percentage of the dataset belonging to the Majority Class

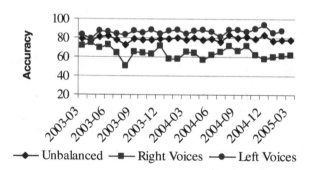

Fig. 7. Sentiment Classification results by category of a set of unbalanced Naïve Bayes Classifiers by category

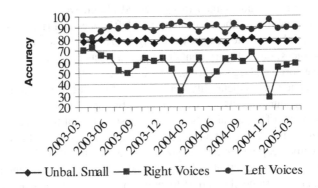

Fig. 8. Sentiment classification results by category of a set of smaller, unbalanced Naïve Bayes classifiers. Note the change in range of the y axis from the above graphs.

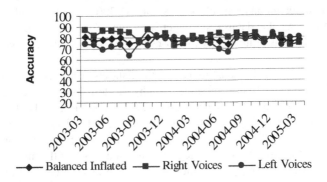

Fig. 9. Sentiment classification results by category of a set of balanced inflated Naïve Bayes classifiers. To ease comparison to Figure 8, this graph has an extended y axis range.

6.3 Comparing Different Categorical Constituencies

Figure 5 compares the results of the balanced inflated classifiers to the unbalanced classifier results. In these sets of experiments the collections contain Naïve Bayes classifiers with identical feature sets. Our unbalanced collection of classifiers contains all on-topic log posts that were available for the given months. Even though the sizes of the balanced datasets are on average only 70% the size of the corresponding unbalanced datasets, Figure 5 illustrates that the total accuracy of the two sets are strikingly similar; they are within fractions of each other.

Yet Figure 6 shows the unbalanced classifiers in many months are barely outperforming the Majority class found within the datasets. We wanted to explain the poor results from our unbalanced classifiers. We believe the answer lies in the constituency of the correctly classified instances rather than in a category that is intrinsically more difficult to predict. To understand this observed effect, we begin by comparing the success in predictability of the two categories (left-voices and right-voices) to the accuracy of the total population as shown in Figure 7. Clearly, we are doing a poor job on our right-voices; our category containing fewer posts. The left-voice category consistently outperforms the right-voice category.

The discrepancy in predictability between our two categories can be attributed to the imbalance in our datasets, as we can show by the following two sets of experiments. The first set of experiments keeps the constituency of the datasets constant and varies the size of the datasets. Our next set of experiments varies the constituency of the datasets while keeping the dataset size constant. Both sets of experiments contain the same Naïve Bayes induction technique and the same feature set representation.

The results of our same class constituency and smaller dataset size experiments are displayed in Figure 8. These smaller datasets performed worse on predicting the right-voice postings than the original unbalanced classifiers. The average accuracy for the right-voice category in the larger unbalanced dataset was 64.34%, for the smaller unbalanced dataset 56.71%. The average accuracy for our left-voice category in the collection of larger unbalanced classifiers was 86.30%, for the smaller unbalanced dataset 89.58%. As the dataset size decreases the effect of the imbalanced class makeup of the datasets dramatically increases the bias found within the correctly classified posts.

In Figure 9, we vary the constituency of the datasets, while keeping the size constant. As shown in the figure, in some months the left-voices are easier to predict while in other months the right-voices are predicted more accurately. The overall average for the left-voices category is 75.09% for the right-voices category is 80.82%. We generated the overall average of the individual month's percentage of misclassifications per category; the left-voice category constitutes 56% of the misclassified posts while the right-voice category constitutes 44%. When given a uniform distribution in the datasets, right-voices are easier to predict than left-voices. This is especially true for the early segment of the time spectrum, or the first months of the war from March 2003 to November 2003. In this section the left-voice category constitutes 64% of the misclassified posts while the right-voice category constitutes 36%.

Figure 8 and 9 together demonstrate reducing the average size of the datasets by 30% in order to balance the categories did not have a negative effect on the total accuracy. It actually had the positive effect on the category makeup of the misclassified posts.

7 Conclusions and Future Work

We have investigated the utility of Naïve Bayes and SVMs on a novel collection of datasets created from political web log posts. We showed a Naïve Bayes classifier significantly outperforms Support Vector Machines at a confident level of 99%, with a confidence interval of [1.425, 3.488]. We show applying feature selection to our results can improve our results significantly, in particular it improves our Naïve Bayes results by 11.84% and our SVM results by 12.18%. We show a Naive Bayes classifier is sensitive to the class makeup of the dataset. Not having a balanced composition of the classes introduces a bias within the results; the majority class is more likely to be classified correctly than the minority class. As the databases decrease in size, the bias effect due to the unbalanced composition of the datasets magnifies.

We also showed our baseline feature set representation works as well as a similar feature set representation that was on average 1.75 times larger than our representation. The larger feature set was generated from all the on-topic web log posts for the current month. The added features were all from left-voices web posts. However, the added features did not improve the accuracy of the classification of the left-voices posts.

We have shown we can predict the political leanings of a posting on the Iraq War at an average accuracy of 78.6% for a two-year period without feature selection technique and 89.77% on average with a forward search feature selection technique. Even though we have not tried another topic we believe we would attain similar results on another topic since there is nothing particular in our sentiment classification system approach that is particular to our chosen topic.

There are many interesting questions we can explore with our current dataset, including different time partitions, different representations for our postings, different representations for the feature sets, and different values for those features. We can explore the effects of size posting on predictability. Finally, we would like to further our research by exploring the ability to track changes within people's opinions on a particular topic and explore the time dependency of our data. We want to be able to classify the data within months as stable (consistent with previous data), or trendy (not pertaining to previous discussions). We are also interested in identifying the length of trends within the data.

Acknowledgements. We thank Stuart M. Shieber for his insightful comments on this work. This research was supported in part by a research gift from Google.

References

[1] Beineke, P., Hastie, T., Vaithyanathan, S.: The Sentimental Factor: Improving Review Classification via Human-Provided Information. In: ACL 2004. Proceedings ACL: Association of Computational Linguistics, Barcelona, pp. 263-270 (2004)

[2] Carroll, J.: Local TV and Newspapers Remain Most Popular News Sources, Increased use of Internet news this year. The Gallup Poll. poll.gallup.comcontent/default.aspx?CI=14389 (December 2004)

[3] Das, S., Chen, M.: Yahoo! for Amazon: Extracting Marketing Sentiment from Stock Message Boards. In: APFA 2001. Proceedings of the 8th Asia Pacific Finance Association Annual Conference (2001)

[4] Dube, J.: Blog Readership up 58% in 2004. CyberJournalist.net (January 2005), www.cyberjournalist.net/news/001819.php

[5] Engström, C.: Topic Dependence in sentiment classification. Master's thesis, St Edmunds's College, University of Cambridge (2004)

[6] Gard, L.: The Business of Blogging. Business Week Online (December 2004)

[7]   Hatzivassiloglou, V., McKeown, K.: Predicting the Semantic Orientation of Adjectives. In: Proceedings of the ACL-EACL 1997 Joint Conference: 35th Annual Meeting of the Association for Computational Linguistics and 8th Conference of the European Chapter of the Association for Computational Linguistics, pp. 174–181 (1997)

[8]   Hearst, M.: Direction-based text interpretation as an information access refinement. In: Jacobs, P. (ed.) Text-Based Intelligent Systems, Lawrence Erlbaum Associated (1992)

[9]   Hu, M., Liu,B.: Mining and Summarizing Customer Reviews. In: Proceedings of the ACM SIGKDD International Conference on Knowledge Discovery & Data Mining KDD 2004, pp.168-174 (2004)

[10] Huettner, A., Subasic, P.: Fuzzy typing for document management. In: ACL 2000 Companion Volume: Tutorial Abstracts and Demonstration Notes, pp. 26–27 (2000)

[11] Kushal, D., Lawrence, S., Pennock, D.: Mining the Peanut Gallery: Opinion Extraction and Semantic Classification of Product Reviews. In: WW W 2003. Proceedings of the Twelfth International World Wide Conferences, pp. 519–553 (2003)

[12] Madden, M.: Online Pursuits: The Changing Picture of Who's Online and What They Do. Pew Internet and the American Life Project Report (2003), www.pewinternet.org/PPF/r/106/report_display.asp

[13] Nasukawa, T., Yi, J.: Sentiment Analysis: Capturing Favorability Using Natural Language Processing. In: Proceedings of the K-CAP-03, 2nd International Conference on Knowledge Capture, pp. 70–77 (2003)

[14] Pang, B., Lee, L., Vaithyanathan, S.: Thumbs up? Sentiment Classification using Machine Learning Techniques. In: Conference on Empirical Methods in Natural Language Processing (EMNLP), pp. 79-86 (2002)

[15] Pang, B., Lee, L.: A Sentimental Education: Sentiment Analysis Using Subjectivity Summarization Based on Minimum Cuts. In: Proceedings of the 42nd ACL, pp. 271-278 (2004)

[16] Pew Internet and the American Life Project (2004), www.pewinternet.org/trends/Internet%20Activities_12.21.04.htm

[17] Pew Internet and the American Life Project (2005), www.pewinternet.org/trends/Internet_Activities_12.05.05.htm

[18] Rainie, L.: The State of Blogging. Pew Intenet and the American Life Project Report (2005), www.pewinternet.org/PPF/r/144/report_display.asp

[19] Rainie, L., Shermak J.: Search engine use shoots up in the past year and edges towards email as the primary internet application. Pew Internet and the American Life Project Report in conjunction with comScore Media Metrix (2005), www.pewinternet.org/pdfs/PIP_SearchData_1105.pdf

[20] Sack, W.: On the computation of point of view. In: Proceedings of the Twelfth American Association of Artificial Intelligence (AAAI), pp. 1488. Student Abstract (1994), www.pewinternet.org/pdfs/PIP_SearchData_1105.pdfv

[21] Tong, R M.: An Operational System for Detecting and Tracking Opinions in On-line Discussion. In: SIGIR 2001 Workshop on Operational Text Classification (2001)

[22] Turney, P.D., Littman, M.L.: Unsupervised Learning of Semantic Orientation from a Hundred-billion-word Corpus. Technical Report EGB-1094, National Research Council Canada (2002)

[23] Witten, I.H., Frank, E.: Data Mining Practical Learning Tools and Techniques with Java Implementations. Academic Press, San Diego, CA (2000)

Appendix A: Web Logs Used in this Research

Liberal Web Logs	Conservative Web Logs
aboutpolitics.blogspot.com	atrainwreckinmax-
allspinzone.blogspot.com	well.blogspot.com
www.americablog.org	acepilots.com
www.reachm.com/amstreet	www.alarmingnews.com
angrybear.blogspot.com	www.alittlemoretotheright.com
atrios.blogspot.com	alwaysright.blogs.com
www.bopnews.com	always_right
www.bullmooseblog.com	americandigest.org
www.burntorangereport.com	anticipatoryretaliation
www.busybusybusy.com	armiesofliberation.com
cernigsnewshog.blogspot.com	asmallvictory.net
corrente.blogspot.com	www.balloon-juice.com
www.crookedtimber.org	betsyspage.blogspot.com
www.cursor.org	www.blogsforbush.com
www.dailykos.com	www.blogsofwar.com
www.davidsirota.com	www.bobhayes.net
demagogue.blogspot.com	bogusgold.blogspot.com
www.democraticunderground.com	www.calblog.com
demwatch.blogspot.com	coldfury.com
digbysblog.blogspot.com	command-post.org
dneiwert.blogspot.com	commonsense-
emergingdemocraticmajoritywe-	runswild.typepad.com
blog.com	www.littlegreenfootballs.com
donkeyrising/index.php	mypetjawa.mu.nu
donkeywonk.blogs.com/mrleft	northeastdilemma.blogspot.com
nielsenhayden.com/electrolite	pikespeak.blogspot.com
ezraklein.typepad.com/blog	www.thepoliticalteen.net
farleft.blogspot.com	talesofawanderingmind
geffen.blogspot.com	www.slantpoint.com
	www.slingsnarrows.com/blog
www.heartsoulandhumor.blogspot.com	www.qoae.net
www.hoffmania.com	www.redlinerants.com
jackotoole.net	redmindbluestate.blogspot.com
jameswolcott.com	rightmoment.blogspot.com
www.joeterrito.com	www.right-thinking.com
www.juancole.com	rightwingnews.com
kbonline.typepad.com/random	sayanythingblog.com
kirghizlight.blogspot.com	www.sgtstryker.com
www.kudzufiles.com	www.shotinthedark.info
lastonespeaks.blogspot.com	southernappeal.blogspot.com
www.leanleft.com	principledobjection.blogspot.com
www.liberaloasis.com	www.thewaterglass.net
www.liquidlist.com	varifrank.com
markschmitt.typepad.com	volokh.com
maxspeak.org/mt	wizbangblog.com
mediamatters.org	xrlq.com
www.michaeltotten.com	youngpundits.blogspot.com
moderateleft.blogspot.com	themarylandmoder-
www.mydd.com	ate.blogspot.com

www.nathannewman.org/log	therapysessions.blogspot.com
newleftblogs.blogspot.com	www.danieldrezner.com/blog
wpblog.ohpinion.com	www.davidlimbaugh.com
www.oliverwillis.com	demrealists.blogspot.com
www.pandagon.net	www.diggersrealm.com
www.patridiots.com	www.donaldsensing.com
www.pennywit.com/drupal/index.php	www.eddriscoll.com/weblog.php
presidentboxer.blogspot.com	www.erickerickson.org
profgoose.blogspot.com	www.fringeblog.com
www.prospect.org/weblog	www.gaypatriot.org
www.richardsilverstein.com	www.hughhewitt.com
rittenhouse.blogspot.com	www.hundredpercenter.com
rogerailes.blogspot.com	incite1.blogspot.com
rogerlsimon.com	www.indcjournal.com
roxanne.typepad.com/rantrave	www.indepundit.com
samueljohn-	www.instapundit.com
son.com/blog/otherblog.html	www.inthebullpen.com
seetheforest.blogspot.com	www.iraqnow.blogspot.com
stevegilliard.blogspot.com	www.jquinton.com
suburbanguerrilla.blogspot.com	justoneminute.typepad.com
www.tbtmradio.com/geeklog	lashawnbarber.com/index.php
www.talkingpointsmemo.com	libertariangirl.blogspot.com
www.talkleft.com	www.gregpiper.com
tbogg.blogspot.com	conservativeeyes.blogspot.com
thatcoloredfellasweblog.bloghorn.com	www.dailynewsbrief.com
www.the-hamster.com	dailypundit.com
www.theleftcoaster.com	www.danegerus.com/weblog
www.thetalentshow.org	www.calicocat.com
www.thetalkingdog.com	cbcbcbcb.blogspot.com
thinkprogress.org	chrenkoff.blogspot.com
www.thismodernworld.com	
www.tompaine.com/blogs	
www.unspun.us	
usliberals.about.com	
wampum.wabanaki.net	
warandpiece.com	
www.washingtonmonthly.com	
xnerg.blogspot.com	

Analysis of Web Search Engine Query Session and Clicked Documents

David Nettleton[1], Liliana Calderón-Benavides[1,2],
and Ricardo Baeza-Yates[1,3]

[1] Web Research Group, University Pompeu Fabra
Passeig de Circumval-lació 8, 08003, Barcelona, Spain
[2] Information Technology Research Group
University Autónoma of Bucaramanga
Street 48 # 39 - 234, Bucaramanga, Colombia
{david.nettleton,liliana.calderon}@upf.edu
[3] ICREA & Research Profesor
Yahoo! Research Barcelona
Ocata 1, 08003 Barcelona, Spain
ricardo@baeza.cl

Abstract. The identification of a user's intention or interest by the analysis of the queries submitted to a search engine and the documents selected as answers to these queries, can be very useful to offer more adequate results for that user. In this Chapter we present the analysis of a Web search engine query log from two different perspectives: the query session and the clicked document. In the first perspective, that of the query session, we process and analyze web search engine query and click data for the query session (query + clicked results) conducted by the user. We initially state some hypotheses for possible user types and quality profiles for the user session, based on descriptive variables of the session. In the second perspective, that of the clicked document, we repeat the process from the perspective of the documents (URL's) selected. We also initially define possible document categories and select descriptive variables to define the documents.

We apply a systematic data mining process to click data, contrasting non- supervised (Kohonen) and supervised (C4.5) methods to cluster and model the data, in order to identify profiles and rules which relate to theoretical user behavior and user session "quality", from the point of view of user session, and to identify document profiles which relate to theoretical user behavior, and document (URL) organization, from the document perspective.

1   Introduction

Web search log data analysis is a complex data mining problem. This is not essentially due to the data itself, which is not intrinsically complex, and typically comprises of document and query frequencies, hold times, and so on. The complexity arises from the sheer diversity of URL's (documents) which can be found, and of the queries posed by users, many of which are unique. There is also the question of the data volume, which tends to be very large, and requires careful preprocessing and sampling. The analyst may also have the impression that there is a certain random aspect to the searches

O. Nasraoui et al. (Eds.): WebKDD 2006, LNAI 4811, pp. 207–226, 2007.

and corresponding results, given that we are considering a generalist search engine (TodoCL[1]), as opposed to a specialized domain search engine (such as Medline) or a search engine contained within a specific website (for example, in a University campus homepage). Given this scenario, in order to extract meaning from the data, such as user behavior categories, we consider different key elements of the user's activity, such as: (i) the query posed by the user, (ii) the individual documents selected by the user, and (iii) the behavior of the user with respect to the documents presented by the search engine. Recent work, such as that of Ntoulas et al [1] has evaluated the predictability of page rank and other aspects in the web over different time periods. They found a significant change in the web over a period of 3 months, affecting page rankings. In [2], Baeza-Yates and Castillo traces the user's path through web site links, relating the user behavior to the connectivity of each site visited. Baeza-Yates et al [3] evaluates different schemes for modeling user behavior, including Markov Chains. In [4], Nettleton et al proposes different techniques for clustering of queries and their results. Also, Sugiyama et al [5] has evaluated constructing user profiles from past browsing behavior of the user. They required identified users and one day's browsing data. In the current work, the users are anonymous, and we identify behavior in terms of "query sessions". A query session is defined as one query made by a user to the search engine, together with the results which were clicked on, and some descriptive variables about the user behavior (which results were clicked on, the time the pages are "held" by the user, etc.). Finally, Lee et al [6] have developed an approach for the automatic detection of user 'goals' in web search. They used a reduced set of 50 pre-selected queries from which ambiguous queries had been eliminated, to get a set of 30 queries. The results were promising, but were based on a very small set of queries that were biased to computer science and that were not too ambiguous.

Advantages of Our Approach. In this work we propose a systematic data mining approach to cluster and identify user types and profiles of clicked query documents, an area which is still relatively new in the web mining field. We also define a novel set of "quality" indicators for the query sessions and a set of document categories for the clicked URL's in terms of the most frequent query for each URL. For both cases we analyze the clusters with respect to the defined categories and the input variables, and create a predictive model. Our approach has the advantage of not requiring a history log of identifiable users, and defines profiles based on information relating non-unique queries and selected documents/URL's.

Structure of the Chapter. The Chapter has the following structure: in Section 1 we present the hypothetical user type, quality profiles and document categories which we propose to identify and predict in the data; in Section 2 we describe the data processing algorithms, Kohonen SOM and C4.5; in Section 3 we describe the data capture and preparation process; in Section 4 we describe the data analysis phase, and in Section 5 we present the data clustering work; finally, Section 6 describes the predictive modeling with C4.5 rule and tree induction, using the user type and quality profiles as predictive values for query modeling; and the document category labels as predictive values for document modeling.

---

[1] TodoCl http://www.todocl.com

1.1   User Profiles

We can define as hypothesis, three main user search behavior categories defined by Broder [7], which can be validated from the data analysis. We have to add that this classification is very coarse, therefore the real data does not have to exactly fall into these categories. Broder's three categories are:

- **Navigational:** this user type typically accounts for approx. 25% of all queries. The user is searching for a specific reference actually known by him, and once he finds it, he goes to that place and abandons the query session. For example, a user searches for "white house", finds the corresponding URL reference, and then goes to that reference and conducts no further searches. This user would typically use a lower number of clicks and a minimum hold time (the time the user takes to note the reference he is looking for).
- **Informational:** this type typically accounts for approx. 40% of all queries. The user is looking for information about a certain topic, visiting different Web pages before reaching a satisfactory result. For example, a user searches for "digital camera", finds several references, and checks the prices, specifications, and so on. This user would spend more time browsing (higher document hold time) and would make more document selections (greater number of clicks).
- **Transactional:** this type typically accounts for approx. 35% of all queries. The user wants to do something, such as download a program or a file (mp3, .exe), make a purchase (book, airplane ticket), make a bank transfer, and so on. This user would make few document selections (clicks) but would have a higher hold time (on the selected page). We can confirm the transactional nature by identifying the corresponding document page (for example, an on-line shopping web page for purchasing a book, a page for downloading a software program, etc.).

In this study, we are interested in applying a methodological data mining approach to the data, in order to identify profiles and rules, which are related to the three main user types defined by Broder [7], and the "session quality" profiles which we will now present in Section 1.2. Also, we wish to inter-relate the two visions of query-session and document, and identify useful features from the overall perspective by analyzing the resulting clusters and profiles. We propose that this is an effective approach for identifying characteristics in high dimensional datasets.

1.2   Quality of Query Sessions

In this section we define four hypothetical categories that indicate query session "quality", and which will be validated in Sections 5 and 6 from the data analysis. We define two categories to indicate a "high" quality query session, and two categories to indicate a "low" quality session. The quality of the query sessions can be affected on the one hand by the ability of the user, and on the other hand by the effectiveness of the search engine. The search engine is effective when it selects the best possible documents for a given user query. There are other related issues, such as response time and computational cost, although these aspects are out of the scope of the current study. In the

Table 1. Hypothetical user quality profiles

Profile (Quality of query session)	high1	high2	low1	low2
Average hold time of selected documents		high		low
Ranking of documents chosen	high		low/medium	
Number of clicks	low		high	high

case of user queries, we have chosen some variables which describe the activity: number of search results clicked on; ranking of the search results chosen (clicked) by the user; duration of time for which the user holds a clicked document. From these variables, we can define some initial profiles which can be used to classify (or distinguish) the user sessions in terms of "quality". As a first example, we could say that a good quality session would be one where the user clicks on a few documents which have a high ranking (e.g. in the first five results shown), given that it is reasonable (though not definitive) to assume the ranking of the results is correct with respect to what the user is looking for and has expressed in the corresponding query. With reference to Table 1, this profile corresponds to "high1". Contrastingly, if the user looks a long way down the list of results before clicking on a document, this would imply that the ranking of the results is not so good with respect to the query. Another profile for a good quality query session would be a high hold time, which implies that the user spends a longer time reading/visualizing the clicked document (profile "high2" of Table 1).

In the case of low hold times, we cannot assume low quality, because the user may be a "navigational" type, and therefore finds what he wants and leaves the current session. In the case of an "informational" or "transactional" user type, a lower hold time would indicate that the user has not found the content interesting. If we combine this with a high number of clicks, it would indicate that the user has found it necessary to check many results. This profile would correspond to "low2" of Table 1. If the user selects many low ranking documents this would also identify that the ordering of the results does not correspond well with the query (profile "low1" of Table 1). In order to distinguish the user types in this way, we would need to analyze the content of the documents, which is outside the scope of this study. Therefore, we will limit ourselves to quality profiles which can be detected without the need for document content analysis. Table 1 summarizes the key variable value combinations together with an indicator of query session quality. Later, we use these "profiles" to evaluate the query session quality in the clustering results, and as category label for a rule induction predictive model. The corresponding numerical ranges for the "low", "medium" and "high" categories were assigned by inspection of the distribution of each variable, together with consultation with the "domain" expert. The ranges for "low", "medium" and "high", respectively, for each of the variables of Table 1 are as follows: "average hold time of selected documents for a given query", (0-40, 41-60, >60); "average number of clicks for a given query", (1-2, 3, >3). In the case of "average ranking of documents chosen for a given query", the corresponding labels have an inverse order, that is, "high", "medium" and "low, with corresponding ranges of (1-3, 4-5, >5). These ranges are also used for identifying the "Broder" user search behavior categories, as described previously in Section 1.1.

1.3   Document Categories

In this section we define the document categories we have used to classify the clicked URLs and which will be validated in Sections 5 and 6 from the data analysis.

Table 2. Hypothetical document categories (ODP + 2 new categories)

ODP Categories	Arts, Games, Education, Reference, Shopping, Business, Health, News, Society, Computers, Recreation, Science, Sports, World, Home
New Categories	Sex, Various

The Open Directory Project[2] defines general categories (see Table 2) which can be used to classify search queries. We manually assigned the categories to 1800 documents, using the most frequent query as the classifier. That is, for each document, we identify the most frequent query for that document, and then classify the query using the ODP topics. Therefore, the document is classified in terms of its most frequent query. We defined a new topic "Education" which substituted "Kids and Teens", this latter topic being the original ODP topic. We also defined a class "Various" for documents which did not seem to classify into any of the other available topics and the class "Sex" which is not directly defined in ODP.

Document Descriptive Variables. The variables used to characterize the clicked documents were: click hour (0 to 24), click day (1 to 7), click month (1 to 4), hold time (seconds), ranking of the clicked document in the results page and frequency of the document in the dataset. We also derived the frequency of the most popular query associated with the document.

2   Data Processing Algorithms

In this section, we briefly present the algorithm steps and the distance measure for the Kohonen SOM clustering algorithm, and the partition algorithm and criteria used by C4.5 rule/tree induction. They represent two techniques with a completely different approach: the SOM accumulates cases at each 'lattice node' starting with the complete dataset and progressively reducing the local areas (neighborhood) of update; on the other hand, C4.5 starts with a small training subset, testing it on the whole dataset, and progressively increases the size of the subset to include more cases, partitioning the cases based on the values of selected input variables. In general, the Kohonen SOM can be used as a first phase of data mining in order to achieve homogeneous clusters from high dimensional data. Then C4.5 can be used to create classifier models for each cluster created by the SOM. This is confirmed by the results we present in Section 6 of this Chapter, in which C4.5 produces higher accuracy on individual clusters, and lower accuracy given the whole dataset without clustering as input. Also, the Kohonen

---

[2] ODP at http://dmoz.org

SOM presents a "machine learning" solution as an alternative to the traditional statistical approach of k-Means clustering, often used for clustering term-document data and queries. We could add that the neural network approach of the SOM is adequate for clustering complex datasets with noise and high dimensionality.

2.1   Kohonen SOM

The Kohonen SOM [8] is a set of processors which organize themselves in an autonomous manner, only requiring the original inputs and an algorithm to propagate changes in the net. The state of the net resides in the weights (coefficients) assigned to the interconnections between the units. It has two layers: layer one contains inputs nodes and layer two contains 'output' nodes. The modifiable weights interconnect the output nodes to the common input nodes, in an extensive manner.

2.2   C4.5 Decision Tree Algorithm

C4.5 [9] is an induction algorithm which generates rules from subsets (windows) of cases extracted from the complete training set, and evaluates their goodness using criteria based on the precision in classifying the cases. The main heuristics used (see below) are:

- The information value that a rule provides (or tree branch) calculated by *info*.
- The global improvement that a rule/branch causes, calculated by *gain*.

C4.5 is based on the classic method of 'divide and conquer' [10].

3   Data Capture and Preparation

In this section, we describe the original data used, which is organized in a relational data mart structure. We also describe the preprocessing realized to obtain the two datasets, one from the point of view of the user query, and the other from the point of view of the document/Url.

3.1   Data Mart

In order to conduct the different tests proposed in this study, we used a set of web search logs, from the Chilean search engine, TodoCl.com, captured over a 92 day period from 20th April to 20th July 2004. The data contained in this log file was pre-processed and stored in a relational data base, which enabled us to carry out different analyses on the search behavior of the users of this search engine. From the log file, we have initially selected a total of 65282 queries and 39998 documents.

Before proceeding, we first present some of the concepts used by Baeza-Yates in [3], necessary to understand the data structures used:

- **Query** is a set of one or more keywords that represent a user information need formulated to a search engine.
- **Query instance** is a single query submitted to a search engine in a defined point of time.

- **Query Session** consists of a sequence of "query instances" by a single user made within a small range of time.
- **Click** is a document selection that belongs to a query session.
- **Document** is an "URL" Internet address reference.

We indicate that the data analyzed was captured by a team from the Center for Web Research[3], Department of Computer Science, University of Chile [3]. The data mart we use consists of a series of relational tables which hold transactional and descriptive data about the queries made by the users and the documents clicked by the user from the search results presented to him. The "Click" table is the most disaggregated of the tables, and contains one line per click by the user. The URL (document) reference is included, together with the time and date of the click, the time the URL was held on screen by the user (hold time), and the ranking of the URL clicked in the list of URL's found. The "Query" table contains an index to the queries made by the users, including the query terms, number of terms and query frequency. Finally, the "QuerySession" table links the "Query" table to the "Click" table, and aggregates the user sessions from the "Click" table.

"A Priori" and "A Posteriori" Data. Often, in data mining, we consider the descriptive variables in terms of two groups: (i) "a priori", which are known before an event occurs (such as the launch of a search query) and (ii) "a posteriori", which are only known after the event has occurred. In the present study, we only have a few "a priori" variables, such as the number of terms and the terms themselves, to describe a user query. On the other hand, we have a significant number of relevant "a posteriori" variables, such as 'hold times for documents selected', 'ranking of documents selected', 'number of clicks', and so on. Therefore, we decided to use both "a priori" and "a posteriori" variables in the predictive model of Section 6, but calculated exclusively for the given 'training' and 'test' time periods. That is, the 'training' data used 'a posteriori' variables calculated exclusively from the first 2 months of data, and the 'test' data consists of variables calculated exclusively from the 3rd month of data. This is important for the predictive model of Section 6. On the other hand, the unsupervised clustering of Section 5 does not have to be restricted to 'a priori' variables or data, given that it represents the 'exploration phase'.

3.2   Data Preprocessing

Using the data mart described in Section 3.1 as a starting point, we preprocess to produce two datasets: a "query" dataset, derived from tables "Query", "QuerySession" and "Click", and a "documents" dataset, derived principally from the table "Click". The resulting data structures are shown in Figure 1.

With reference to Figure 1, the "Query" table contains a series of statistics and aggregated values for the queries. "AholdTime" is the average hold time for the URL's clicked which correspond to the query and "Arank" is the average ranking of those URL's. "freqQ" is the number of times the query has been used (in the click data), and "numTerms" is the number of terms of the query. "Anumclicks" is the average number

---

[3] Center for Web Research http://www.cwr.cl

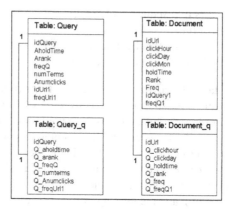

Fig. 1. Dataset definition for queries and documents with associated tables of quantiles for selected variables

of clicks made corresponding to the given query in the click table. Finally, "idUrl1" represents the URL whose frequency was greatest for the corresponding query (from the click data) and "freqUrl1" is its corresponding frequency relative to the given query. These data variables have been selected to create a "profile" of the "query" in terms of the statistical data available, which will serve for posterior analysis of the characteristics of search behavior in terms of the queries.

The "Document" table contains a series of statistics and aggregated values for the URLs referenced in the click table. "clickHour" is the average hour (0 to 23) in which the document was clicked, "clickDay" is the average day (1 to 7, corresponding to monday - sunday) on which the document was clicked and "clickMon" is the average month (1 to 4, corresponding to april - july) in which the document was clicked. "holdTime" and "Rank" correspond to the average hold time in the click data and the average ranking of the document in the click data. 'Freq' is the number of times the document appears in the click data. Finally, "idQuery1" represents the query whose frequency was greatest for the corresponding URL, and "freqQ1" is its frequency relative to the corresponding URL. These data variables have also been selected to create a "profile" of the "document" in terms of the statistical data available, which will serve for posterior analysis of the characteristics of search behavior in terms of the documents.

Finally, with reference to Figure 1, we observe two additional tables in the lower row, which contain the quantiles of selected variables from the corresponding tables in the upper row. The quantiles have been generated automatically using the SPSS program, and all the variables have been transformed into 10 quantiles, with the following exceptions: "clickhour", 5 quantiles, "clickday", 4 quantiles, and "numterms", 4 quantiles. The number of quantiles was chosen by a previous inspection of the distribution and number of values for each variable. The quantile versions of the variables were used as inputs to the Kohonen clustering algorithm.

With reference to the query data variables, the quantile ranges are as follows: "Q_a holdtime" 2(0), 3(1-7), 4(8-17), 5(18-29), 6(30-45), 7(46-48), 8(69-105), 9(106-188), 10(189-16303); "Q_arank" 1(1), 2(2), 3(3), 4(4), 6(5-6), 7(7), 8(8-9), 9(10-13), 10(14-119); "Q_freqQ" 3(2), 7(3), 8(4), 9(5-6), 10(7-284); "Q_numterms" 1(1), 2(2), 3(3),

4(4-12); "Q_Anumclicks" 2(1), 5(2), 7(3), 8(4), 9(5-6), 10(7-80). In the case of the variable "Q_aholdtime", we observe that the last quantile has captured some large non-representative values.

With reference to the document data variables, the quantile ranges are as follows: "Q_clickhour" 1(0-11), 2(12-14), 3(15), 4(16-17), 5(18-23); "Q_clickday" 1(1-2), 2(3-4), 3(5-7). "Q_holdtime" 1(0), 2(0.14-4.4), 3(4.5-10.5), 4(10.53-18.5), 5(18.57-29.25), 6(29.27-44), 7(44.07-65.91), 8(66-104.8), 9(105-198.5), 10(198.67-40732); "Q_rank" 1(1), 2(1.03-1.98), 3(2-2.97), 4(3-3.97), 5(4-4.98), 6(5-6.39), 7(6.4-8.32), 8(8.33-11), 9(11.04-17.25), 10(17.33-200); "Q_freq" 3(2), 7(3), 8(4), 9(5-6), 10(7-210).

In the case of the variables in each dataset which were not used in the clustering, but were used for cross referencing across datasets, their quantiles were as follows. For the query dataset: "Q_freqURL1" 2(1), 6(2), 8(3), 9(4), 10(5-166); for the document dataset: "Q_freqQ1" 3(1), 7(2), 9(3), 10(4-166).

3.3 Data Sampling

Random samples were selected from the queries and documents datasets, respectively, to create two new datasets of 1800 records each. These datasets were used as input to the Kohonen SOM. The filtered source datasets had the following number of records: documents 39998; queries 11981.

The queries selected must have a frequency greater than 1 (occur more than once) in the click data table. Also the documents (URL's) must also have a frequency greater than 1 in the click data file. The requirement of frequency > 1 for queries and documents, avoids including "once off" or unique queries and documents in the datasets, as these queries tend not to have any interrelations and create a great dispersion. Finally we filtered records whose hold time was greater than 900 seconds, given that this is a reasonable maximum for normal user sessions.

4 Data Pre-analysis

In this section we explain the initial analysis of the datasets, using correlation and graphical techniques. We also applied k-Means to perform an initial clustering to confirm the initial hypothesis of their being coherent clusters in the data. In this manner we can identify at this stage any errors in the data or problems due to preprocessing.

With reference to Table 3, we can observe a promising degree of correlation between key variable pairs for the complete query dataset comprising of 11981 different queries. In particular, we can indicate the following correlations: 0.706 for "average hold time" with respect to "average number of clicks"; 0.642 for "frequency of the query" with respect to "frequency of the URL which is recovered most often by this query"; 0.461 for "Average ranking of the documents clicked after running the query" with respect to "average number of clicks made after running the query".

In the same way that we did for the query dataset, we did an analysis for the document dataset in which we observe the degree of correlation between key variable pairs for the complete document dataset consisting of 39998 different documents. In particular, we can indicate the following correlations: 0.535 for "frequency of document" with respect

Table 3. Query dataset: Pearson Correlation values for variable quantiles (**Number of cases= 11981)

	Quantiles avg. hold time	Quantiles avg. rank	Quantiles query frequency	Quantiles num. terms	Quantiles avg. num clicks	Quantiles freq of Url1
Quantiles avg. hold time	1.000	**.399**	**.299**	-.061	**.706**	**.309**
Quantiles avg. rank	.399	1.000	.188	-.170	**.461**	.049
Quantiles query frequency	.299	.188	1.000	**-.233**	.202	**.642**
Quantiles num. terms	-.061	-.170	-.223	1.000	-.050	-.173
Quantiles avg. num clicks	.706	.461	.202	-.050	1.000	.383
Quantiles freq. of Url 1	.309	.049	.642	-.173	.383	1.000

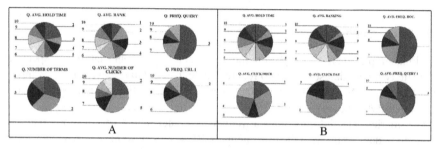

Fig. 2. Sector diagrams for selected quantiles of key variables in the query (A) and document datasets (B)

to "frequency of most popular query associated with the document"; -0.119 for "ranking of the document" with respect to "frequency of most popular query associated with the document"; 0.170 for "hold time of the document" with respect to "frequency of the document"; 0.109 for "avg. hold time of document" with respect to "frequency of most popular query associated with the document.

In Figure 2 we can see the sector diagrams generated for the quantiles of the key variables in the query (Figure 2-A) and document (Figure 2-B) datasets.

For query dataset (Figure 2-A) we observe that in the case of "q. freq query" (quantiles of freq. of query), aprox. 55% of the values are in quantile 3, and the second largest proportion is that of quantile 7. For "Avg. number of clicks", quantile 5 has the largest proportion followed by quantile 2. For the correspondences of quantiles to original value ranges, refer to Section 3.2.

For document dataset (Figure 2-B) we observe that in the case of "q. avg. freq. doc" (quantiles of avg. freq. of doc), aprox. 55% of the values are in quantile 3, and the second largest proportion is that of quantile 7. For "q. Avg. ranking", quantile 1 has the largest proportion followed by quantiles 3 and 6, respectively. For the correspondences of quantiles to original value ranges, refer to Section 3.2

In Figure 3 we see the frequencies of document categories in the dataset used for clustering. From the total number of 1800 documents, we observe that 616 (34%) are category "Reference". An example of a "Reference" document would be: "http://www.

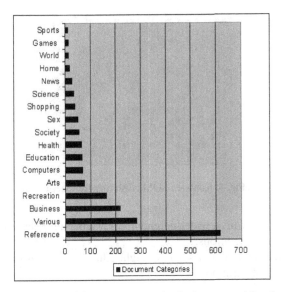

Fig. 3. Frequencies of document categories in dataset used for clustering

navarro.cl/trabajo/datos-historico/mensaje-precidencial-sc-2.htm" and its most frequent associated query is "articulo 171 del codigo del trabajo" (in English, "article 171 of the labor code"). We also see that 217 (12%) of the documents are defined as the "Business" category. An example of a "Business" document is "http://www.paritario.cl/lista_comites.htm" and its most frequent associated query is "zanartu ingenieros consultores s.a.".

5   Data Clustering

In this section, we explain the clustering process applied to the query dataset using the Kohonen SOM technique, and the following analysis of the data groupings with respect to the user type and quality profiles defined in Section 1. The input variables to the query clustering were: Q_aholdtime, Q_arank, Q_freqQ, Q_numterms and Q_Anumclicks. We also detail the clustering process and results for the document data. With respect to the document, the input variables to the clustering were: Q_clickhour, Q_clickday, Q_holdtime, Q_rank, Q_freq. See Section 3 for the descriptions of the variables.

5.1   Clustering of the Data in Homogeneous Groups

The Kohonen SOM algorithm was used as the clustering method for each dataset, using only the quantile values of the selected variables as inputs. The Kohonen SOM was configured to produce an output lattice of 15 x 15, giving 225 clusters, for each dataset. The cluster quality was verified in a post-processing phase, by inspection of activation values and standard deviations. As recommended by Kohonen in [8], we trained the Kohonen net in two stages:

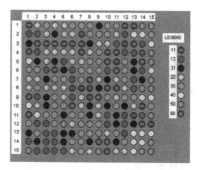

Fig. 4. Kohonen SOM clustering for Queries

- An ordering stage with a wider neighborhood value, a higher learning rate, and a smaller number of iterations.
- A convergence stage with a smaller neighborhood value, lower learning rate and greater number of iterations.

With reference to Figures 4 and 5, we can see the graphic output of the Kohonen SOM at the end of the (convergence stage) training run (5000 iterations) for query data and document data, respectively. The original Kohonen SOM output was color coded, and we have assigned corresponding cluster id's (column 1 of Tables 4 and 5) to represent the color scheme. For example, in the case of the queries data, cluster 11 corresponds to dark purple, 12 to light purple, 21 to dark blue, and so on, to 60 which corresponds to red, following the sequence of the spectrum. In this manner we have maintained the information with respect to the sequential ordering of the cluster groups.

All the training runs were run to complete convergence, that is, when the Kohonen SOM no longer altered the clustering assignments and the patterns (see Figures 4 and 5) became fixed, which occurred within the 5000 iterations, for both datasets. In Figure 4 (Queries), we observe that the Kohonen SOM has created three major cluster groups, labeled "11", "12" and "30". In terms of the number of cases assigned (as opposed to the number of cluster nodes), by individual inspection we find that the distribution of cases to the query cluster groups of Figure 3 is more equal than that of the document cluster groups of Figure 5. In Figure 5 (Documents), we observe three main groups of clusters, labeled "21", "22" and "30". We also observe four minor cluster groups indicated by labels "11", "12", "40" and "50". Therefore, we state that the Kohonen clustering has identified three major and four minor groupings of clusters. We can now inspect the corresponding data in each of these cluster groups, in order to identify distinguishing characteristics in terms of the input variables.

Tables 4 and 5 list the level 1 cluster groupings generated by the Kohonen SOM 15x15 lattice for the query and documents datasets, respectively. Each of the cluster groups consists of a number of lattice nodes (individual clusters), and these are later detailed in Section 5.2.

Analysis of the Queries Clustering. In Table 4, we note that row 1 of the cluster data indicates that cluster group 11 has 191 corresponding queries, and its confidence

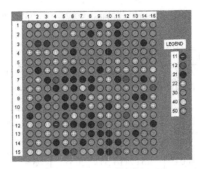

Fig. 5. Kohonen SOM clustering for Documents

Table 4. Kohonen clustering of Queries data: averages of input variables for 'level 1' cluster groups

Queries							Confidence	
Cluster Group*	Avg. number of terms	Avg. query freq.	Avg. hold time	Avg. ranking	Avg. number of clicks	Number of Queries	Avg. activation	Stdev. activation
11	3.16	**2.63**	30.87	4.94	1.92	191	8.77	2.60
12	2.24	3.53	103.66	6.86	1.92	214	11.07	2.91
21	1.94	**6.84**	126.59	6.97	2.57	205	11.73	**3.40**
22	2.51	4.59	125.01	5.70	3.28	306	11.86	3.21
30	1.93	4.34	**128.78**	**9.86**	**6.88**	449	14.18	2.82
40	2.04	2.95	**4.16**	**4.42**	**11.00**	189	**6.44**	2.61
50	**3.45**	2.69	69.24	4.53	1.11	153	7.84	**2.35**
60	**1.53**	4.56	111.03	4.73	2.00	89	9.78	2.97

(activation) value was on average 8.77 with a standard deviation of 2.60. The activation value refers to the neuron activation in the lattice and may be considered as a "quality" or "confidence" indicator for the corresponding cluster. With respect to the variable values, we observe that cluster group 11 has the minimum value (2.63) for "average query frequency" (shown in bold). Cluster group 30 has the maximum values for "average ranking of clicked results" (9.86), "average number of clicks" (6.88), and "average hold time" (128.78). Finally, cluster group 50 has the maximum value for "average number of terms" (3.45), the second lowest value for "average query frequency" (2.69) and the second lowest value for "average number of clicked results" (1.11). We can say that these values are mutually coherent for cluster group 50, given that less frequent queries would tend to have a higher number of terms and as they are more specific, the user would click on less of the shown results.

Analysis of the Documents Clustering. With reference to the document cluster group data in Table 5, we observe that cluster group 12 has the lowest average hold time for documents (34.84), the second lowest value for the average ranking of the documents (6.05), and the highest value for document frequency (6.96), that is, the average

Table 5. Kohonen clustering of Document data: averages of input variables for 'level 1' cluster groups

Documents (Url's)							Confidence	
Cluster Group*	Avg. hold time	Avg. ranking	Avg. docum. freq	Avg. click hour	Avg. click day	Number of Docs.	Avg. activation	Stdev. activation
11	**241.17**	**14.7**	2.93	**12.33**	3.19	54	10.67	2.78
12	**34.84**	6.05	**6.96**	12.90	2.69	48	10.43	2.34
21	131.29	7.34	5.20	15.46	3.19	408	**11.23**	2.64
22	77.35	**6.01**	4.51	14.37	3.57	330	10.10	**3.08**
30	97.65	7.46	2.70	14.26	**4.32**	759	9.49	2.76
40	118.35	9.11	**2.15**	13.50	1.88	82	**9.64**	**2.33**
50	57.67	9.00	2.39	**18.13**	**1.87**	119	**9.64**	2.29

number of times that the corresponding documents have been clicked in our dataset. It is coherent that the most popular documents (high frequency) have a high ranking (where position "1" would be the highest ranked), although the low hold time would need further explanation. The low hold time could be due to the corresponding pages being of a "navigational" type, therefore the users navigate to them but then disconnect. In the case of cluster group 40, we observe the lowest document frequency (2.15).

We recall that the document categories were initially presented and defined in Section 1.1 of the Chapter. The document categories were not given as input to the clustering. Therefore, given the incidence of greater frequencies of given document categories in specific clusters, we can infer that the input variables given as inputs to the clustering have a relation to the document categories, in the measure that is evidenced.

5.2   Analysis of Resulting Clusters for Query Sessions: User Types and Quality Profiles

User Types. Now we make some interpretations of the level 1 query clustering results, in terms of the user categories presented in Section 1.

- **Navigational:** the query-sessions grouped in level 1 query cluster 40 (see Table 4) has a low hold time and a low number of clicks, which has a direct relation with Broder's proposal [7] with respect to the number of documents visited and time spent browsing as a consequence of a query of this type. One example of a "navigational" type query in cluster group 40 is "chilecompra" (chilepurchase) with corresponding URL "http://www.chilecompra.cl", average hold time of 0 and average number of clicks equal to 1. Another example of a typical query in this cluster group is "venta de camisetas de futbol en chile" (sale of football shirts in chile) with corresponding URL: "http://www.tumejorcompra.tst.cl/-futbol.php", average hold time of 0 seconds and average number of clicks equal to 1.
- **Informational:** in query cluster group 30 (see Table 4), it can be clearly seen that clusters were generated which grouped the query-sessions whose number of clicks and hold time is high. One example of an informational type query in this

cluster group is "cloroplasto" with principal corresponding URL "http://ciencias. ucv.cl/biologia/mod1/-b1m1a007.htm", average hold time of 731 seconds and average number of clicks equal to 7. Another example is the query "software ingenieria structural" with principal corresponding URL "http://www.pilleux.cl/-mt771/", average hold time of 1062 seconds and average number of clicks equal to 8.

- **Transactional:** in query cluster group 12 (see Table 4) we can observe medium to high hold times and a low number of clicks, which coincides with our hypothesis for this type of users, although the characteristics are not as strong as for the "navigational" and "informational" user types. Given that we have the queries submitted to the search engine, and we have the documents (web pages) that the user selected from those retrieved by the search engine, we can confirm individual results as being transactional by visual inspection of the query and of the web page selected. For example, in cluster group 12, cluster 11,14 we have the following query: "compra y venta de autos" (purchase and sale of automobiles) with principal corresponding URL "http://autos.123.cl/registracion.asp", with a hold time of 580 seconds and average number of clicks equal to 3. In this case the transaction involves filling in a form.

Quality Profiles. We now interpret the clusters with reference to the session quality profiles presented in Section 1 (Table 1). High1: in all of cluster group 40 we can see a high clicked document ranking (low values) and a low number of clicks (all equal to 1), which corresponds to the hypothetical Profile 1 which indicates "high" quality. High2: cluster 30 has the highest average hold time (see Table 4), which is indicative of this quality type. Low1: cluster group 30 shows a low/medium clicked document ranking and a high number of clicks, which indicates a problem of low quality according to our definition. On the other hand, we also identified cluster group 30 as having profile High2, which is defined in terms of average hold time. This is not necessarily contradictory, given that the queries can show good quality in some aspects, and low quality in other aspects. We would have to investigate the individual level 2 clusters and samples of individual queries and their clicked documents, in order to confirm the problem areas. Low2: from the summary statistics of the query clustering, we have not clearly identified this profile among the clusters. We recall that profile Low2 corresponds to a "low" quality profile, indicated by a low average hold time, together with a high number of clicks.

5.3   Analysis of Resulting Clusters and Subclusters: Documents

Once the Kohonen SOM had generated satisfactory clusters, we selected specific cluster groups by observation, which exhibited potentially interesting data value distributions. For each selected cluster group, we calculated statistics for the corresponding individual cluster nodes of the Kohonen lattice. The selected cluster groups for the documents dataset, cluster groups 12 and 40, whose statistics are summarized in Table 6.

With reference to Table 6, Cluster Group 12, we observe a relatively high ranking (column 3, 1=highest), and relatively high document frequency (column 4). For Cluster Group 40, we also observe some general characteristic values/tendencies, such as a low document frequency (column 4) and (click day (column 6). We recall that the days

Table 6. Average values for key variables used for clustering of document data (corresponding to clusters groups in Table 4, and one comparative variable not used in clustering (Freq of query 1)

Cluster*	Average values (for each cluster)						Confidence	Query
	Hold time	Ranking	Freq. doc.	Click hour	Click day	Number of docs.	Avg. activation	Freq. of query 1
Level 2 Document clusters (for level 1 Cluster 12)								
9,12	27.74	**6.11**	**14.7**	10.90	**3.00**	10	11.55	3.10
4,7	**5.93**	5.65	7.57	15.00	2.86	7	10.26	2.86
6,15	58.93	**1.70**	**6.33**	**9.67**	2.83	6	11.14	**4.67**
15,8	**81.47**	4.93	7.14	9.83	**3.00**	6	12.36	3.33
12,7	68.72	5.07	3.00	**17.83**	**2.17**	6	11.11	**2.33**
Level 2 Document clusters (for level 1 Cluster Group 40)								
1,1	**166.25**	**13.55**	2.00	11.90	1.90	10	11.43	1.40
4,4	**11.11**	8.44	2.00	13.56	1.78	9	8.12	1.22
3,12	76.94	**2.61**	2.00	12.33	1.89	9	7.97	1.22
15,6	18.07	0.57	2.00	15.71	1.71	7	5.54	**1.57**
4,1	28.92	21.75	2.00	**10.83**	**2.00**	6	10.7	**1.17**

of the week were coded as 1=Monday, 2=Tuesday, , 7=Sunday. Individual clusters, such as (6,15) show specific characteristics such as high ranking (1.70), high document frequency (6.33), and low click hour (9.67), which are also primary or secondary characteristics of cluster group 12. With reference to Table 6, columns 2 to 8 represent the same variables as those of Table 5. In column 1 we see the cluster id corresponding to the Kohonen lattice and for the corresponding cluster group, of the first 5 clusters ordered by number of documents assigned. Therefore, in Table 6 we observe the summary statistics for individual clusters (9,12; 4,7; 6,15; 15,8; 12,7) assigned to cluster group 12.

Finally, in the last column of Table 6, "Freq of query 1" is a variable which was not used as input to the document clustering, and which represents the quantile of the frequency of the query which most coincides with the given document, in the click data.

6   Tree and Rule Induction Using C4.5

In this section now we use C4.5 to generate a decision tree/ruleset from the two perspectives taken in this analysis: Queries and Documents.

6.1   Rule and Tree Induction on Query Dataset

First we create a model with the user type label defined in Section 1.1 as the classifier category. Secondly, we use the quality label defined in Section 1.2 to create a second predictive model. We try to train a model on the whole dataset, in order to identify individual rules of high precision which can be useful for user and session classification. The input variables were: "number of terms in query"; "query frequency in the historical data"; "average hold time for query", "average ranking of results selected for query", "average number of clicks for query", "frequency of the document/URL most retrieved by the query in the historical data", "average hour day for running of query (0 to 24)", "average day for running of query (1 to 7)". We note that the original variables have been used as input, not the quantile versions used as input to the Kohonen clustering. This was done to simplify the interpretation of the results in terms of the real data values. We used as training set the first two months click data, and as the test set we used the third consecutive month. See Section 3.1 for a description of the original data captured. All the statistical variables (averages, sums) were calculated exclusively for the corresponding time periods, in order to guarantee that only "a priori" information was used to train the models. The queries used in the training and test datasets were selected using the following criteria: the same query must occur in the training (months 1 and 2) and in the test data (month 3); frequency of query greater than 1 in the training data, and in the test data; frequency of the most frequent document corresponding to the query greater than 1, in the training dataset and in the test dataset. This selection is carried out in order to eliminate "unique" queries and documents, and obtained a total of 1845 queries for the training and test datasets to predict "user type". In the case of the "quality label" model, we obtained a total of 1261 queries for the training and test datasets.

$$
\begin{aligned}
Rule1 &: Qholdtime \leq 40 \\
&\Rightarrow class\,nav\,[69.9\%] \\
Rule2 &: Qholdtime \\
&\quad\ Qnumclicks \leq 2 \\
&\Rightarrow class\,tra\,[50\%] \\
Rule3 &: Qnumclicks > 2 \\
&\Rightarrow class\,inf\,[56.4\%] \\
Default\,&class : nav
\end{aligned}
\tag{1}
$$

In (1) we see the resulting rules induced by C4.5 on the training dataset with the user categories as output. We observe that in order to classify 'nav' type users, C4.5 has used exclusively the 'hold time', whereas for 'tra' type users C4.5 has used 'hold time' and 'number of clicks'. Finally, in the case of 'inf' type users, C4.5 has used exclusively 'number of clicks'. This is coherent with our hypothetical definitions of these user types: 'nav' users have shorter hold times, 'inf' users have many clicks, and 'tra' users have greater hold times and fewer clicks. We could also say that the variables that best differentiate 'inf' users from 'nav' users are the hold time and the number of clicks, respectively.

The ruleset was evaluated on the test data (1845 items), which overall gave 686 errors (37.2%). The accuracy for the individual rules is pressented in Table 7.

Table 7. Accuracy for individual rules evaluated on the test data

Rule	Used	Errors	Label
1	946	285 (30.1%)	nav
2	228	109 (47.8%)	tra
3	671	292 (43.5%)	inf

We observe that "nav" (navigational) is the easiest user type to predict, followed by "inf" (informational), whereas "tra" (transactional) seems to be more ambiguous and difficult to predict.

We also trained a model using the quality categories as the output label. The pruned decision tree generated by C4.5 for the quality categories is shown in (2):

$$
\begin{aligned}
&Qnumclicks \leq 3: \\
&|\ Qrank > 3 \Rightarrow high2\ (171.0) \\
&|\ Qrank \leq 3: \\
&|\ |\ Qnumclicks \leq 2 \Rightarrow high1\ (523.0) \\
&|\ |\ Qnumclicks > 2 \Rightarrow high2\ (25.0) \\
&Qnumclicks > 3: \\
&|\ Qholdtime \leq 40 \Rightarrow low2\ (108.0) \\
&|\ Qholdtime > 40: \\
&|\ |\ Qrank \leq 3 \Rightarrow high2\ (24.0) \\
&|\ |\ Qrank > 3 \Rightarrow low1\ (410.0)
\end{aligned}
\tag{2}
$$

This tree was tested on 1261 unseen cases, which gave an overall error of 44%. We observe that "high1" and "low1" are the easiest quality classes to predict, followed by "high2" and "low2" which gave significantly lower predictive accuracies. One possible cause of this could be the range assignments which we defined in Section 1.2, or due to ambiguities between the different classes.

The overall precision on the whole dataset was not high for the rule induction model, although we did identify several rule "nuggets", which was our stated objective. One example of a good precision rule was "$Qrank \leq 3$ and $Qnumclicks \leq 2 \Rightarrow$ class high1" which had only a 31% error on the complete test dataset. It was also found that the user types were easier to predict than the quality classes. One further course of action would be to revise the ranges we assigned to the quality labels in Section 1.2, reassign the labels and rerun C4.5 on the data. Also we could try to train on selected clusters from the Kohonen clustering, although we would have to retrain the clustering only on the first two months data, and test the rules on the third (unseen) month.

6.2 Rule and Tree Induction on Document Dataset

First we create a model with the document category label, as defined in Section 1.1, as the classifier category. In Section 6.1 we try to train a model in order to identify individual rules of high precision which can be useful for document and user behavior classification. The input variables were: "avg. click hour"; "avg. click day"; "avg. hold time", "avg. rank", "avg. frequency of the document" "freq. of the most popular query related to the document". We note that the original variables have been used as input, not the quantile versions used as input to the Kohonen clustering. This was done to simplify the interpretation of the results in terms of the real data values.

We used as training set the first two months click data, and as the test set we used the third consecutive month. All the statistical variables (averages, sums) were calculated exclusively for the corresponding time periods, in order to guarantee that only "a priori" information was used to train the models. The documents used in the training and test datasets were selected using the following criteria: the same document must occur in the training (months 1 and 2) and in the test data (month 3); frequency of document greater than 1 in the training data, and in the test data; frequency of the most frequent query corresponding to the document greater than 1, in the training dataset and in the test dataset. This selection is carried out in order to eliminate "unique" documents and queries, and obtained a total of 1775 documents. We used a split of approximately 60/40 for the training and test datasets, giving 1058 training cases and 717 test cases. The predictive label (output) was the "document" category.

In (3) we can see a section of the decision tree induced by C4.5 on the training data, with the document categories as output. For example, the decision path:

$$
\begin{aligned}
&holdTime > 60: \\
&| \quad clickDay = 2: \\
&| \quad | \quad holdTime \leq 123: \\
&| \quad | \quad | \quad rank \leq 4: 8\,(27/14)
\end{aligned}
\tag{3}
$$

indicates that document category 8 (Business) corresponds to documents with a hold time greater than 60 seconds and less than 123 seconds, clickDay equal to 2 (Tuesday), and ranking equal to or less than 4. There were 27 documents which were correctly classified by this rule from the training data, and 14 documents were misclassified. This gives a precision for this decision path of $1 - (14/(27 + 14))100 = 65.85\%$.

By reviewing the complete tree generated, we observe that the C4.5 algorithm has employed all five of the input variables (holdTime, clickDay, rank, clickHour and freq). We note that "clickDay" was defined as a categorical type variable, whereas the remaining variables were defined as numerical. The most general criteria chosen by C4.5 was "holdTime", followed by "clickDay". The most "specific" criteria used were "click-Hour", "rank" and "freq". We can see extensive use of "clickDay" and "clickHour", which agrees with other authors who have identified a strong relation between the type of documents selected, the day of the week and the time of day. For example, "Business" (category 8), tends to be selected on a weekday [clickDay = 5:], and in the working hours: [clickHour $\leq$ 16 : 8 (11/5)]. On the other hand, the "Home" (category 11) tends to be selected at the weekend: [clickDay = 7: 11 (11/6)]. This tree was tested on the test dataset consisting of 717 unseen cases, which gave an overall error of 34.9%. We reiterate that the objective of the tree and rule induction was to identify specific higher precision rules, rather than to achieve a high precision global model. Several examples of high precision decision paths are:

$$
\begin{aligned}
&holdTime > 60: \\
&| \quad clickDay = 4: \\
&| \quad | \quad rank > 1: \\
&| \quad | \quad | \quad holdTime \leq 66: 9\,(11/4)
\end{aligned}
\qquad
\begin{aligned}
&holdTime > 60: \\
&| \quad clickDay = 3: \\
&| \quad | \quad clickHour > 13: \\
&| \quad | \quad | \quad rank > 4: 2\,(27/8)
\end{aligned}
$$

| Decision path 1 | Decision path 2 |

The decision path 1 correctly classified 11 documents and misclassified 4 documents of category 9 (Health), which gives a precision of $1 - (4/(11 + 4))100 = 73.33\%$. In the second example of a high precision decision path 2, correctly classified 27 documents and misclassified 8 documents of category 4 (Reference), which gives a precision of $1 - (8/(27 + 8))100 = 77.14\%$.

7 Conclusions

In this Chapter we have contrasted two different techniques, Kohonen SOM clustering and C4.5 rule/tree induction, for mining web query log data. We have also studied the web log data from two perspectives: query session and documents. This extends previous results done using other techniques such as k-means. We have detailed all the data mining steps, from initial data preparation, pre-analysis/inspection, transformation (quantiles, outliers), sampling, unsupervised and supervised learning algorithms, and analysis of results. In Section 1 of the Chapter we made some initial hypotheses about the user types, the user session quality profiles and the document categories, and in Sections 5 and 6 we have proceeded to analyze the results in order to identify characteristics which correspond to these user types, profiles and document categories. The use of machine learning techniques to identify the user categories allows us to confirm the user type "mix" for specific data sets, and to define new user types. In this manner we can classify, on one side, our users and query sessions, and on the other side, the documents and the user behavior with respect to them, in a way which helps us to quantify current user and search engine behavior, enabling us to adapt our system to it, and anticipate future needs.

Acknowledgements. This work was partially funded by MEC Grant TIN 2006-15536-C02-01.

References

1. Ntoulas, A., Cho, J., Olston, C.: What's new on the web?: the evolution of the web from a search engine perspective. In: 13th international conference on WWW, pp. 1–12. ACM Press, New York, NY, USA (2004)
2. Baeza-Yates, R., Castillo, C.: Relating web structure and user search behavior (extended poster). In: 10th International Conference on WWW, Hong Kong, China (2001)
3. Baeza-Yates, R., Hurtado, C., Mendoza, M., Dupret, G.: Modeling user search behavior. In: LA-WEB 2005, p. 242. IEEE Computer Society Press, Los Alamitos (2005)
4. Nettleton, D.F., Baeza-Yates, R.: Busqueda de información en la web: técnicas para la agrupación y selección de las consultas y sus resultados. In: CEDI LFSC, Granada, Spain (2005)
5. Sugiyama, K., Hatano, K., Yoshikawa, M.: Adaptive web search based on user profile constructed without any effort from users. In: 13th international conference on WWW, pp. 675–684. ACM Press, New York (2004)
6. Lee, U., Liu, Z., Cho, J.: Automatic identification of user goals in web search. In: 14th international conference on WWW, Chiba, Japan, pp. 391–400. ACM Press, New York (2005)
7. Broder, A.: A taxonomy of web search. SIGIR Forum 36(2), 3–10 (2002)
8. Kohonen, T.: Self organization and associative memory. Springer Series in Information Sciences, vol. 8. Springer, Heidelberg (1988)
9. Quinlan, J.R.: C4.5: programs for machine learning. Morgan Kaufmann Publishers Inc., San Francisco, CA, USA (1993)
10. Hunt, E.B.: Artificial Intelligence. Academic Press, New York (1975)

Understanding Content Reuse on the Web: Static and Dynamic Analyses

Ricardo Baeza-Yates[1], Álvaro Pereira[2,*], and Nivio Ziviani[2]

[1] Yahoo! Research &
Barcelona Media Innovation Centre
Barcelona, Spain
rbaeza@acm.org
[2] Department of Computer Science
Federal University of Minas Gerais
Belo Horizonte, Brazil
{alvaro,nivio}@dcc.ufmg.br

Abstract. In this paper we present static and dynamic studies of duplicate and near-duplicate documents in the Web. The static and dynamic studies involve the analysis of similar content among pages within a given snapshot of the Web and how pages in an old snapshot are reused to compose new documents in a more recent snapshot. We ran a series of experiments using four snapshots of the Chilean Web. In the static study, we identify duplicates in both parts of the Web graph – reachable (connected by links) and unreachable components (unconnected) – aiming to identify where duplicates occur more frequently. We show that the number of duplicates in the Web seems to be much higher than previously reported (about 50% higher) and in our data the duplicated in the unreachable Web is 74,6% higher than the number of duplicates in the reachable component of the Web graph. In the dynamic study, we show that some of the old content is used to compose new pages. If a page in a newer snapshot has content of a page in an older snapshot, we say that the source is a parent of the new page. We state the hypothesis that people use search engines to find pages and republish their content as a new document. We present evidences that this happens for part of the pages that have parents. In this case, part of the Web content is biased by the ranking function of search engines.

1 Introduction

The Web grows at a fast rate and little is known about how new content is generated. At the same time, a large part of the Web is duplicated. Other pages are created by using older pages, such as by querying a search engine, selecting a few highly ranked pages and copying selected paragraphs from them. In this paper we present static and dynamic studies involving the analysis of similar

---

* This work was partially done when at Yahoo! Research Barcelona as a Ph.D. intern.

O. Nasraoui et al. (Eds.): WebKDD 2006, LNAI 4811, pp. 227–246, 2007.

content among pages within a given snapshot of the Web and how pages in an old snapshot are reused to compose new documents in a more recent snapshot.

For the static study, we present an algorithm to find duplicate and near-duplicate documents in a Web collection. Considering each collection independently (statically), we obtained the frequency of duplicates in a set of documents that can be reached by following links. Our aim is to identify where duplicates occur more frequently on the Web graph and what the impact on coverage is when only crawling documents from the reachable set of the Web graph. We show that the Web has many more duplicates than previously acknowledged in the literature, because we had access to most of the unconnected part of the Web graph. For instance, the work in [1] used collections crawled by following links on the Web. In this case the sample of the Web is biased because most of the documents are crawled from the reachable set of the Web graph.

Considering the collections in an evolutionary way (dynamically), we show how old content is used to create new content. At first, we looked for original sources, if any, of the content of a new page. We can say that each source is a *parent* of a new page and hence we can study how old content evolves in time, that is, which pages are really new and do not have parents and which ones have parents. Additionally, we state the hypothesis that when pages have parents, most of the time there was a query that related the parents and made possible for a person to create the new page. If this is the case, some Web content is biased by the ranking function of some search engine.

We ran a series of experiments using four snapshots of the Chilean Web Considering our data set: i) we analyze if duplicates occur more or less frequently according to reachable and unreachable sets of the Web graph; ii) we present a study about the influence of old content in new pages; iii) we present evidence that search engine ranking algorithms are biasing the content of the Web; and iv) we show that the number of copies from previously copied Web pages is indeed greater than the number of copies from other pages.

This paper is organized as follows. Section 2 presents definitions and the Web collections used in the experiments. Section 3 presents an algorithm to detect duplicates and a static study on Web content reuse. Sections 4 and 5 present a dynamic study of our Web collections. Section 4 presents a study of the relation of search engines with the Web content evolution. Section 5 shows how much old content is used to compose new documents. Section 6 presents related work. Finally, Section 7 presents the conclusions of our work.

2   Conceptual Framework

In this section we present some definitions and the Web collections used in the experiments.

2.1   Definitions

The definitions are the following:

Definition 1. Shingle Paragraph: *A shingle paragraph is a sequence of three sentences of the document, where a sentence is a sequence of words ended by a period.* It is a way of measuring the content similarity among documents, using the concept of shingles [2]. If a period is not found until the 150th character, then the sentence is finished at that point and a new sentence begins at the 151th character. This limitation is due to the fact that some documents have no period (for example, some program codes). In this work we used two types of shingle paragraphs: **with overlap** of sentences and **without overlap** of sentences. As an example, suppose we have a document containing six sentences $s_1. s_2. s_3. s_4. s_5. s_6$, where s_i, $1 \leq i \leq 6$, is a sentence of the text. The shingle paragraphs with overlap of sentences are: "$s_1. s_2. s_3.$", "$s_2. s_3. s_4.$", "$s_3. s_4. s_5.$", "$s_4. s_5. s_6.$". The shingle paragraphs without overlap of sentences are: "$s_1. s_2. s_3.$", "$s_4. s_5. s_6.$".

Definition 2. Cluster: *For a given collection, it is a set of documents with exactly the same shingle paragraphs, without overlap of sentences. Each document in a collection is either (i) **clustered**, if it belongs to a cluster, or (ii) **unique**, otherwise.*

Definition 3. Duplicate Document: *It is any clustered document with exception of the original document that initiated the cluster.* Finding the original document is not important, we only need to consider that it exists in order to calculate the number of duplicates in a given collection. We can say that two documents of the same cluster are duplicates one of the other. **Near-Duplicate:** *It is a document with a given minimal percentage of identical shingle paragraphs of another document in the collection.* This percentage is related to the number of shingle paragraphs of both documents.

Definition 4. Reachable Component: *For a given collection, it is a set of documents that can be reached by following links, from a given initial document.* **Unreachable Component:** *It is the set of documents that are not in the reachable component.* The initial document is randomly chosen. If less than 50% of the documents are reached by following links from a given initial document, another document must be used as the initial document. The objective is to simulate a Web crawler following links (navigational and external links) and composing a Web database. Considering the macro structure of the Web proposed by Broder [3], the reachable component comprises the "central core" (the strongly connected component [4]). If the initial document belongs to the "in" component, a part of this component will also be included in the reachable component just defined. As well, the last reachable documents found belong to the "out" component.

Definition 5. Minimal Number of Identical Paragraphs: *It is a minimal threshold of the number of identical paragraphs to consider a new document (in a more recent collection) as a partial copy of an old document (in an older collection).*

Definition 6. New Similar Document: *It is a new document composed by at least one paragraph existent in an old document.*

Definition 7. Answer Set: *For a given query, it is the document set returned by the query processor of a search engine.* **Total Answer Set:** *for a given query log, it is the document set composed by the union of the answer sets of all queries.*

Definition 8. Equivalent Documents: *Two documents in two distinct Web collections are equivalent if their URLs are identical.* In this case, a document in an older collection remains existing in a more recent collection.

Definition 9. Document Relationship: *A new document has a **parent** if it shares a minimal number of identical shingle paragraphs with the parent document and they are not equivalent. An old document has a **child** on the basis that it shares a minimal number of identical paragraphs with the child document and they are not equivalent.* These definitions are recursive if more than two collections are considered. Thus, for three collections it is possible to identify grandparents and grandchildren, considering the newest and the oldest collections, respectively.

2.2   Web Collections

For the experiments we used four collections of pages of the Chilean Web that were crawled in four distinct periods of time. Table 1 presents the main characteristics of the four collections.

Table 1. Characteristic of the collections

Collection	Crawling date	# of docs (millions)	Size (Gbytes)
2002	Jul 2002	1.04	2.3
2003	Aug 2003	3.11	9.4
2004	Jan 2004	3.13	11.8
2005	Feb 2005	3.14	11.3

In our experiments we considered only documents with more than 450 characters and at least three shingle paragraphs with overlap of sentences (see Definition 1). In order to consider two documents as similar, previous experiments show that it is necessary to have a minimal degree of similarity between them to avoid finding too many false matches. This is the case when only one or two popular shingle paragraphs are identical. Following these restrictions, the number of documents considered from the collections presented in Table 1 is reduced to approximately 75% in our experiments.

Every collection was crawled by the Web search engine TodoCL[1]. To crawl the collections, the complete list of the Chilean Web primary domains were used to start the crawling, guaranteeing that a set of pages under almost every

---

[1] www.todocl.cl or www.todocl.com

Chilean domain (.cl) was crawled, once the crawls were pruned by depth. These characteristics are fundamental for studying the evolution of the Web content.

3 Duplicate Study

In this section we present the duplicate study. Section 3.1 presents the algorithm we used to find duplicate and near-duplicate documents (see Definition 3) and Section 3.2 presents the results about duplicates for our collections.

3.1 Algorithm for Duplicate Detection

The algorithm works by clustering duplicate documents [5]. Since our collections are not large (see Table 1), the algorithm uses the whole text of the documents for comparison, improving the precision of the results.

The comparison step of the algorithm uses shingle paragraphs without overlap of sentences (see Definition 1). Collection C (with n documents) is divided into m subcollections S_i, $0 \leq i < m$. The algorithm runs in m steps. For each subcollection S_i, $0 \leq i < m$, the shingles of the documents in S_i are first inserted into a hash table.

Next, the shingles of C are searched in the hash table. A duplicate is detected if all shingles of a document in C have a match in a document of S_i and both documents have the same number of shingles. At the end of each iteration i, the subcollection S_i is excluded from C ($C = C - S_i$).

For each new duplicate pair found, a new cluster (see Definition 2) is created and the duplicate pair is inserted into the new cluster. For that, a cluster identifier is associated with each document. If one of the documents of the pair was previously inserted into a given cluster, then the other document of the pair is inserted into this cluster. At the end, the algorithm returns a set of clusters, with each cluster containing a list of clustered documents.

Figure 1 illustrates the main steps of the algorithm using a sample test collection C containing $n = 20$ documents. In the example, collection C is divided into $m = 10$ subcollections, each one containing two documents. Sentences in each document are represented by letters, as shown in documents 1, 2, 19 and 20. Every document contains four shingle sentences (for instance, document 1 has the shingles "a. a. a.", "b. b. b.", "c. c. c.", "d. d. d.").

Following Figure 1, in the first iteration, the documents 1 and 2 (from subcollection S_0) are inserted into the hash table. Next, the shingles of the documents of C (documents 1 to 20) are searched in the hash table. Therefore, it is possible to see that document 19 is a duplicate of document 2. In the second iteration, documents 3 and 4 (from subcollection S_1) are inserted into the hash table and the shingles of the documents of collection C (documents 3 to 20) are searched in the hash table. Next iterations occur similarly.

When using this algorithm, false matches occur when two documents have the same number of identical shingle paragraphs, but with some repeated shingle. For example, suppose that the document 3 in Figure 1 has the following sentences:

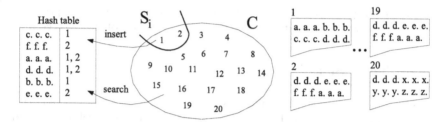

Fig. 1. Process for duplication analysis

e. e. e. d. d. d. e. e. e. d. d. d (the shingles are "*e. e. e.*", "*d. d. d.*", "*e. e. e.*" and
"*d. d. d.*"). Once every shingle of the document 3 is found in the hash table for
the document 2 and both documents have four shingle paragraphs, then they
are considered duplicates. As this situation seems to occur with a very small
probability, the percentage results are not biased by false matches.

3.2   Results About Duplicates

In this section we present the results about duplicates and near-duplicates. Table 2 presents statistical results for the collections used. According to the table,
the number of clustered documents (that is, the number of clusters in addition
to the number of duplicates) represents more than 50% of the documents for
collections 2003 and 2004. For collection 2004, only 48.9% of the documents are
unique (i.e., do not belong to a cluster).

In turn, Table 3 shows the number of near-duplicates compared to the number
of duplicates for each collection. We considered three values of minimal percentage of identical shingle paragraphs: 90%, 70% and 50% (see Definition 3).

Table 2. General statistics about duplicates

Collection	# of docs	# of clusters	# of dup.	% of dup.
2002	614,000	76,000	196,000	31.9%
2003	2,067,000	252,000	804,000	38.9%
2004	2,033,000	266,000	876,000	43.1%
2005	2,175,000	256,000	778,000	35.8%

Table 3. Data about near-duplicates

Collection	% of dup.	90% near.	70% near.	50% near.
2002	31.9	33.4	35.7	39.9
2003	38.9	40.8	46.1	52.8
2004	43.1	44.5	47.9	53.4
2005	35.8	37.0	43.2	49.9

The percentage of near-duplicates for 90% of similarity is slightly greater than the percentage of duplicates. For instance, for collection 2003, only 1.9% of the documents share at least 90% of their shingles paragraphs and are not duplicates. On the other hand, for the same collection, 7.1% of the documents share at least 70% of their shingles paragraphs and are not duplicates, and 13.9% of the documents share at least 50% of their shingle paragraphs and are not duplicates.

Again, the analysis of Table 2 reveals that collection 2002 has the smallest percentage of duplicates (31.9%) whereas collection 2004 has the highest percentage (43.1%). These figures are higher than the figures found in the literature (Shivakumar and Garcia-Molina [6] reports 27% and Fetterly, Manasse and Najork [7] reports 22%).

Our hypothesis was that the difference occurs because our collections were crawled based on a list of primary domains, which includes URLs that cannot be reached following links obtained from other pages. Most of the Web crawlers work following links, considering only documents from the connected component of the Web graph. Duplicates do not have the same inlinks as the original document (the source of the duplicates).

To study this hypothesis we place the documents of each collection in either reachable or unreachable component, according to Definition 4. According to the number of documents, the reachable component represents 54.0%, 51.6%, 56.8% and 63.9% of the collections 2002, 2003, 2004 and 2005, respectively. Table 4 presents the number and percentage of duplicates for the complete collection, for the reachable component and for the unreachable component.

Observing Table 4 for the collection 2002 we see that the real number of duplicates for the complete collection is 68.8% higher than the number of duplicates found for the reachable component. On average this percentage is 50.9%, considering the four collections. The number of duplicates found for the unreachable component is on average 74.6% higher than the number of duplicates for the reachable component. These expressive percentages show that most duplicates occur in the unreachable component of the Web graph. We also verify that the absolute real number of duplicates is about two or three times the absolute number of duplicates in the reachable component. One reason for this results is that text spam might be more common in the unreachable part and one well used technique is to mix paragraphs from other pages.

Table 4. Percentage of duplicates for the complete collection and, the reachable and unreachable components

Collection	Complete		Reachable		Unreachable	
	number	perc. (%)	number	perc. (%)	number	perc. (%)
2002	196,000	31.9	62,000	18.9	108,000	38.2
2003	804,000	38.9	277,000	25.9	430,000	43.0
2004	876,000	43.1	339,000	29.3	443,000	50.4
2005	778,000	35.8	361,000	26.0	323,000	41.1

To support our results we analyze the number of duplicates in a Brazilian Web collection [8] crawled in 1999 by the TodoBR search engine[2]. For this collection a list of domains was **not** used to start the crawler. It means that new pages are normally found only when a link to these pages are added from an existing page in an older snapshot. The percentage of duplicates for this collection is very similar to what is acknowledged in the literature: 24.9% of the documents are duplicates. This supports our conclusion that including the disconnected component (such as for the Chilean collections), the Web has more duplicates than previously acknowledged in the literature.

Returning to the Chilean Web collection, now we study the relations between duplicate and cluster sizes. For collection 2004, nine clusters have more than 10,000 documents, in which two of them have more than 20,000 documents. The duplicates belonging to these clusters represent 7.1% of the documents of the collection. This explains the high number of duplicates for collection 2004 in relation to the other collections studied, as shown in Table 2.

For collection 2003, 95.7% of the clusters have ten or less documents. Documents in these small clusters represent 63.3% of clustered documents and only 40.5% of duplicate documents. The same figures were found for the other collections, which means that large clusters have more influence in the number of duplicates than small clusters.

Clusters with two documents (with only one duplicate) are very frequent. Collections 2002, 2003, 2004 and 2005 have 52,000, 158,000, 167,000, 160,000 clusters containing only two documents, respectively. In every case these values represent about 63% of the clusters, but only approximately 19% of the duplicates.

Our results on duplicates have an important impact for search engine Web crawlers. Once the Web grows at a very fast rate, is extremely dynamic and has many replicated content, search engines have to heuristically decide which pages to crawl. In this section we have shown that the reachable component of our Web graphs contain a representative portion of the Web, in terms of coverage. In order to design a Web crawler, many different aspects must be considered. Considering the coverage and elimination of duplicates, Web crawlers designers may choose to crawl only pages reached by links, instead of listing every found directory and crawling every document in a directory.

4   Log-Based Content Evolution Study

In this section we present an algorithm and experiments related to the log-based content evolution study. In this part of the work we mine data with the objective of supporting the hypothesis that people use search engines to find pages and republish their content as a new document. Section 4.1 presents a description of the algorithm. Section 4.2 presents the setup procedure to perform the experiments. Section 4.3 presents the experimental results for this study.

---

[2] TodoBR is a trademark of Akwan Information Technologies, which was acquired by Google in July 2005.

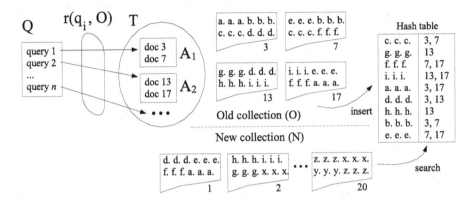

Fig. 2. Method to find new similar documents

4.1   Algorithm Description

In this section we describe a log-based algorithm to study the evolution of the Web content. The algorithm is composed of two stages. The objective of the first stage is to find new similar documents (see Definition 6), which are candidates of being copies. The objective of the second stage is to filter the new similar documents found in the first stage and find (with a high probability) new documents with content of old documents returned by queries. By finding those documents, we present evidence that states the initial hypothesis. The two stages are described in this section.

Finding New Similar Documents. We use Figure 2 as an example to explain the method to find new similar documents, with the purpose of finding candidates to be filtered in the second stage of the algorithm. For this, we consider pairs of old–new Web collections, referring to the older collection as *old* (O) and to the more recent collection as *new* (N). We explain the method dividing it into three main steps.

Firstly, a set Q of queries (a query log) is used to simulate a user performing a query on the search engine. The query processor of the search engine TodoCL is used as the ranking function and is applied to each query as well as to the old collection. An answer set A_i (see Definition 7) is returned for each query performed. In the example of Figure 2 the ranking function returns the documents 3 and 7 for the query 1 and the documents 13 and 17 for the query 2. The content of these documents are shown in the figure.

Secondly, each document from the total answer set T (see Definition 7) has its shingle paragraphs extracted and inserted into a hash table. We use shingle paragraphs with overlap of sentences (see Definition 1). With the purpose of comparison, shingles are normally used in samples, as a randomized technique that allows false positives. In this part of the work we consider **all** the shingle paragraphs of the documents, with the advantage of improving the precision.

Thirdly, each document from the new collection N has its shingle paragraphs searched in the hash table. A new similar document is detected when at least one shingle of the new document is found in the hash table. While new documents are being compared a table is constructed containing important data for the next stage: the new similar document identifier, the old document identifier, and the query identifier.

In the example of Figure 2 the new collection has 20 documents (documents 1, 2 and 20 are shown). Document 1 is a new similar document, since one or more shingles of this document are found in the hash table. Document 1 has shingle paragraphs from documents 3, 7, 13 and 17. Document 2 is also a new similar document.

An important goal of this algorithm stage is the possibility of repeating the search engine operation in a given period of time. We are able to repeat what had been done in the past by users of the search engine TodoCL, recovering the same Web documents that were recovered on that period of time. This is possible because:

- We know the periods of time (with a good approximation) that every collection was indexed and used in the search engine (see Table 1).
- We used the same query processor used by the search engine in each period of time between every collection pair.
- We used the most frequent performed queries, aiming to increase the probability of finding a query used for copying by at least one of the users that performed that query in the past.

Filtering New Similar Documents. At this stage the new similar documents found in the first stage are filtered. Besides the data returned from the previous stage, the conditions to filter also use data about duplicates returned by the duplicate detection algorithm (see Section 3), and data with the URLs of the documents for every collection. The conditions to filter are the following:

1. Consider a minimal number of identical paragraphs (see Definition 5). We studied six minimal values: 5, 10, 15, 20, 25 and 30 identical shingle paragraphs. This condition is important to eliminate a false match, with only a few identical shingle paragraphs, that occurs because some documents have, for example, an identical prefix or suffix automatically generated by an html editor.
2. The new document must be composed by pieces of two old documents returned by the same query. It is intuitive that, in many cases, if the new document has some content of documents returned by the same query, a user might have performed that query before composing the new document. We think that in many cases a user performed a query and used only one query result to compose a new page. This situation cannot be captured by our algorithm. If we considered this situation, we could not infer that the user found that page because he/she previously performed the query in the search engine.

3. The new document must contain at least two **distinct** shingle paragraphs from each old document, in order to ensure that the old content used in the new document is not the same amongst both of the two old documents.
4. The new document URL cannot exist in the old collection. This condition guarantees that the new document was not published in the old collection, improving the precision of the results.
5. When a new document matches all the previous conditions, any duplicate of this document cannot be considered a new match. With this condition we eliminate duplicates among new documents.
6. When two old documents match all the previous conditions, any duplicate of one of these old documents cannot be considered as a new match. For example, consider that two old documents A and B are used to compose a new document. If later B and C are candidates to compose another new document and, if C is a duplicate of A, the new match is not considered. With this condition we eliminate duplicates among old documents.

Notice that with all these conditions we may incorrectly filter documents. For example, maybe a document with an old URL has a new content copied from old documents (see condition 4 above). Maybe a user really used queries to find documents to copy but the user copied only few shingle paragraphs (see condition 1). Maybe a user used only one document returned from a query to compose the new document (see conditions 2 and 3). We do not care about these situations. We are concerned in reducing as many as possible of the false matches, i. e., to avoid finding a new document that was not composed because a user performed a query.

4.2   Experimental Setup

In the experiments we used sets of the most frequent queries performed in a given period. We selected the most frequent queries because if more users performed that query, then it is more probable that one of the users has done it to compose a new document. We sorted the queries by their frequencies, eliminated the top 1,000 queries (they are many times navigational queries or related to pornography) and considered the following 15,000 top queries. For every query log these 15,000 queries represent approximately 14% of the user requisitions in the search engine.

Table 5 presents the meta data related to the three query logs used. In some experiments we used this log, as we present in Section 4.3.

Table 5. Characteristics of the logs

Query log	Log period	Most freq.	Least freq.
2002	Aug/02 – Jun/03	640	71
2003	Sep/03 – Dec/03	168	23
2004	Feb/04 – Jan/05	449	51

The log periods are related to the period that the collections presented in Table 1 had been used as data in the search engine. We did not consider one month of log before and after each crawl, once we do not know exactly when the new database was indexed and refreshed in the operating search engine. For example, the collection 2002 was crawled in July, 2002 and the collection 2003 was crawled in August, 2003. The query log 2002 considers the period between August, 2002 and June, 2003.

4.3   Experimental Results

This section presents the experimental results related to the log based content evolution study. The experiments are in general based on the following criteria: compare the number of documents returned by the algorithm presented in Section 4.1 (Figure 2) that obey all the six conditions shown in Section 4.2, using: (i) the real log for a given period, and (ii) a log of another period. For example, if we use the collection pair 2003–2004 as data set, in the situation *(i)* above we would use the query log 2003 shown in Table 5. This is the real query log for the period from 2003 to 2004. The query log 2002 (or 2004) could be used for the situation *(ii)* above, that is a query log of a period distinct of 2003–2004, the period which the collection was used in the search engine. To support our hypothesis, more documents must be returned for the situation *(i)* (using query log 2003), that simulate real query requisitions occurred between 2003 and 2004.

In general our collections have been crawled in a very distant period one from another. Table 1 in Section 2 presents the period of each crawl. From collection 2002 to 2003, there is an interval of 13 months, equivalently from collection 2004 to 2005. The period from collection 2003 to 2004 is the shortest: six months.

In order to choose the collection pair to be used in the experiments we observed the average lifespan of Web documents. The lifespan of a document is the difference between the date that it was deleted and the date that it was created [9]. Junghoo Cho [10] found that the average lifespan of Web documents is between 60 and 240 days, considering a sample of 720,000 documents from popular sites. Brewington et al. [11] found that the average lifespan is approximately 140 days for a data set of 800 million documents. Other works [12,13,14] present similar values, also considering other measures besides the average lifespan.

If we choose an old–new collection pair crawled 390 days longer one apart from another, it is likely that many new documents composed using old documents are no more detected in the new collection, due to the lifespan of the new document. For this reason we choose the collection pair 2003–2004 as old and new collections for the first experiment set.

Our first experiment set consists of the three frequent query logs presented in Table 5 for the collection pair 2003–2004, using the algorithm presented in Figure 2. Our hypothesis is that some users performed queries in collection 2003 for composing new documents, that were published in the collection 2004.

Figure 3 presents three curves for the query logs 2002, 2003 and 2004, from 5 to 30 minimal number of identical paragraphs (see Definition 5). For the query log 2003 the algorithm returned much more documents than for the other logs for

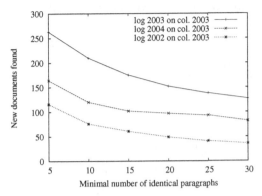

Fig. 3. Query logs 2002, 2003 and 2004 used for the collection pair 2003–2004 for different minimal number of identical paragraphs

any minimal number of identical paragraphs considered. It represents an evidence that people make searches to find a content and create a new document.

According to Figure 3, the use of the query logs 2002 and 2004 also returned some new documents. More documents are returned using the query log 2004 than the query log 2002. We highlight some possible reasons for these figures:

- It is possible that the query log 2003 has more similar queries to the query log 2004 than to the query log 2002.
- It is possible that queries that returned new documents with the query log 2004 were not in the set of the 15,000 frequent queries considered in the query log 2003, but occurred in another part of the query log 2003.
- It is possible that some documents returned with the query log 2004 (or also with the query log 2002) were composed by old documents returned in two or more different queries performed by the user in a session.
- It is possible that the old documents were returned together by other queries in another search engine.

In the second experiment set we used parts of the logs shown in Table 5. We divided the query logs 2002 and 2004 into five bimonthly logs. For example, in log 2004 we considered the months February and March as being the bimonthly log 1, the months April and May as being the bimonthly log 2, and so on, until the months October and November as being the bimonthly log 5. We preferred not to use the remaining month in the log, December, since this log would have queries with about half of the frequency of the bimonthly logs, what probably would bias the results.

For each bimonthly log we sorted the queries by their frequencies, eliminated the top 1,000 queries and considered the 5,000 top queries. We used fewer queries than the previous logs (in which we used 15,000 queries) because now the period is shorter (two months) and we are not interested in less frequent queries. Table 6 presents information about the bimonthly logs. The average values considered in the table are related to the five bimonthly logs used for each year.

Table 6. Characteristics of the bimonthly logs

Query log	Log period	Average most freq.	Average least freq.
2002	Aug/02 – May/03	98	27
2004	Feb/04 – Nov/04	149	27

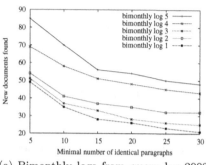 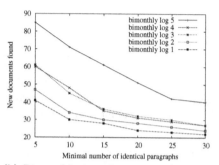

(a) Bimonthly logs from query log 2002, used for collection pair 2002–2003.

(b) Bimonthly logs from query log 2004, used for collection pair 2004–2005.

Fig. 4. Bimonthly logs study

Figure 4 presents the number of documents returned when a) the five 2002 bimonthly logs are used for the collection pair 2002–2003, and b) the five 2004 bimonthly logs are used for the collection pair 2004–2005. Bimonthly log 5 is the most recent bimonthly log and bimonthly log 1 is the oldest bimonthly log.

According to the figures, the most recent bimonthly logs returned more documents than older bimonthly logs. This would be expected, considering that many documents composed by documents returned by queries in the oldest bimonthly logs do not exist any more in the more recent collection of the pair, due to the lifespan of the documents.

Considering that the average lifespan of a Web document is about 140 days [11], equivalently 4.5 months, the fact of finding a great number of documents for the two most recent bimonthly logs from both query logs 2002 and 2004 is another evidence that users performed queries in the search engine before composing their new pages with old content.

The third experiment set uses the bimonthly logs 4 and 5 (the most recent bimonthly logs) from both query logs 2002 and 2004 for both collection pairs 2002–2003 and 2004–2005. We expect better results running the bimonthly logs from 2002 for the collection pair 2002–2003 and the bimonthly logs from 2004 for the collection pair 2004–2005, since they are the real simulation of users performing queries in the past.

Figure 5 presents the number of documents returned when a) bimonthly logs 4 and 5 from 2002 and 2004 are used for collection pair 2002–2003 and b) bimonthly logs 4 and 5 from query logs 2002 and 2004 are used, for collection pair 2004–2005. When the real data is used (logs 2002 in pair 2002–2003 and logs 2004

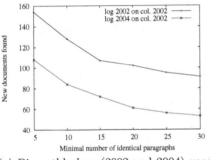

(a) Bimonthly logs (2002 and 2004) used for collection pair 2002–2003.

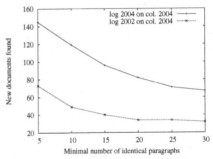

(b) Bimonthly logs (2002 and 2004) used for collection pair 2004–2005.

Fig. 5. Distinct bimonthly log sets used in the same collection

in pair 2004–2005) the result is substantially better. The comparison of the two curves in each plot provides another piece of evidence towards the consistency of our hypothesis.

As a conclusion, we have presented evidence for arguing that the stated hypothesis is valid, in various ways, considering our data set. We clearly discard the possibility that all the results found and shown in this section are just coincidences.

5 Web Content Evolution Study

In this section we study how old content is used to compose new documents. Section 5.1 presents our algorithm to find the parents and children. Section 5.2 presents the results for the Chilean Web, using distinct old–new collection pairs.

5.1 Algorithm Description

In this section we describe our algorithm to study the content evolution of the Web. Similarly to the algorithm presented in Section 4.1, this algorithm is composed of two stages. The objective of the first stage is to find new similar documents (see Definition 6). The objective of the second stage is to select parents from a candidate set.

The first stage of the algorithm consists of randomly selecting a sample of old documents (from an old collection O), inserting their shingles into a hash table, and searching for the shingles of each new document (from a new collection N) in the hash table. With exception of how the old documents are selected, this step is similar to the first step of the algorithm of the log-based content evolution study presented in Section 4.1.

Figure 6 presents the second stage of the algorithm. N_i is the new similar document, O_j is the correspondent old document with some similarity with N_i and $minNum$ is the minimal number of identical paragraphs.

The algorithm of Figure 6 initially filters the new similar documents with the minimal number of identical paragraphs equals to 10. This condition is applied to

1 For each document pair (N_i, O_j)
2   If $minNum > 10$
3   If it is the first time that O_j is a parent and O_j URL is found in new col.
4   Increment the number of equivalents;
5   Else
6   If it is the first time that N_i or a duplicate of N_i is a child
7   Increment the number of children;
8   If it is the first time that O_j is a parent
9   Increment the number of parents;

Fig. 6. The second stage of the algorithm to study content evolution of the Web

eliminate false matches, since we manually verified that many old–new document pairs with short overlap have only formatting in common, that was not cleaned by the crawler system.

The algorithm verifies if O_j is found in the new collection (step 3). If it is found, the number of equivalent documents (see Definition 8) is incremented. If it is not the first occurrence of O_j, it is not searched again.

After verifying if the documents are equivalent, the algorithm verifies if N_i is a child of O_j. The condition represented in step 6 of the algorithm is a way of eliminating duplicates in the new collection. Consider that a document A has thousands of duplicates in both collections old and new. It is probable that if we randomly choose about 5% of the old collection, one of the duplicates of A will be chosen. If we allow duplicates in the new collection, every duplicate of A in the new collection will be considered as a child, introducing noise in the results.

Finally, if the condition of the step 6 is true, N_i is a child of O_j. The child is classified and the number of parents is incremented, what happen only if N_i is the first child of O_j.

5.2   Chilean Web Content Evolution

We study the content evolution for the Chilean Web by randomly choosing documents from collections 2002, 2003 and 2004, and observing the occurrence of parts of these documents in the most recent collections. Table 7 presents the number of parents in collection 2002 that generate children, grandchildren and great-grandchildren, respectively in collections 2003, 2004 and 2005. The random sample contains 120,000 documents from collection 2002.

Table 7. Number of equivalent documents and parents in collection 2002 that generated descendants

collection pairs	2002–2003	2002–2004	2002–2005
# of parents	5,900	4,900	4,300
# of children	13,500	8,900	9,700
# of equivalents	13,900	10,700	6,800

According to Table 7, 5,900 documents of the collection 2002 are parents of 13,500 documents in the collection 2003 for the sample considered. We see that 8,900 documents in the collection 2004 are grandchildren of documents in the collection 2002, and that 9,700 documents in the collection 2005 are great-grandchildren of documents in the collection 2002.

Table 8, in turn, presents the number of parents in collection 2003 that generate children and grandchildren, respectively in collections 2004 and 2005 (for a random sample of 120,000 documents from collection 2003). In relation to the collection 2003, 5,300 documents are parents of documents in the collection 2004 and 5,000 are grandparents of documents in the collection 2005. The sample considered in collection 2003 generated content in 33,200 documents of the collection 2004 and 29,100 documents of the collection 2005.

Table 8. Number of equivalent documents and parents in collection 2003 that generated descendants

collection pairs	2003–2004	2003–2005
# of parents	5,300	5,000
# of children	33,200	29,100
# of equivalents	19,300	10,500

The collection 2003 generated many more children than collection 2002. We suppose this is due to the fact that the Chilean Web of 2002 was not crawled in a large part to create collection 2002 (see Table 1). Thus, many documents in the most recent collections were composed by documents existent on the Web in 2002 but not existent in the collection 2002.

Observing Tables 7 and 8 we see that the number of children is always considerably greater than the number of parents. For the collection pair 2003–2004 there are, on average, more than six children for each parent. Thus, few documents are copied many times, so the number of documents that do not generate a child is smaller than the number of documents that do not have parents.

Now we observe the evolution of the number of children and the number of equivalent documents in these years. From collection pair 2003–2004 to collection pair 2003–2005 the number of children reduced only 12.5%, while the number of equivalent documents reduced 45.5%. From collection pair 2002–2004 to collection pair 2002–2005 the number of children increased.

We conclude that the number of copies from previously copied documents is indeed greater than the number of documents copied from random old documents. An open question is: do the search engines contribute to this situation, since they privilege popular documents [15,16] and people use search engine to compose new documents? (according to the evidences previously presented in this paper). We recently finished a deeper study that gives strong evidence that this hypothesis is true [17].

6   Related Work

In this section we present works related to finding and eliminating duplicates and near-duplicates on the Web, and works related to the dynamics of the Web content.

Broder et al. [1] used shingle to estimate the text similarity among 30 million documents retrieved from a walk of the Web. The similarity was evaluated using a sample of fixed size (a fingerprint) for each document. Considering a resemblance of 50%, they found 2.1 million clusters of similar documents, a total of 12.3 million documents.

Shivakumar and Garcia-Molina [6] crawled 24 million Web documents to compute the overlap between each pair of documents. Pieces of the documents are hashed down to a 32-bits fingerprint and stored into a file. A similarity is detected if two documents share a minimal number of fingerprints. The number of replicas is estimated as approximately 27%. Cho, Shivakumar and Garcia-Molina [5] combined different heuristics to find replicated Web collections. They used 25 million Web documents and found approximately 25% of duplicates.

Fetterly, Manasse and Najork [7] extended the work by Broder et al. [1] in terms of the number of compared documents and investigated how clusters of near-duplicate documents evolve with the time. They found that clusters of near-duplicate documents are fairly stable and estimated the duplicates as approximately 22%.

Ntoulas, Cho and Olston [12] crawled all pages from 154 sites on a weekly basis, for a period of one year, studying some aspects of the Web evolution, such as birth, death, and replacement of documents. They found that every week 8% of the pages are replaced and about 25% are new created links. With respect to the pages that do not disappear over time, about 50% do not change at all, even after one year. Additionally, those that do change, only undergo minor changes in their content, and even after a whole year 50% of the changed pages are less than 5% different from their initial version. In a similar work using the same data set, Ntoulas et al. [18] found that after a year, about 60% of the documents and 80% of the links on the Web are replaced.

Cho and Roy [15] studied the impact of search engines on the popularity evolution of Web documents. Given that search engines currently return popular documents at the top of search results, they showed that newly created documents are penalized because these documents are not very well known yet. Baeza-Yates, Castillo and Saint-Jean [16] showed that Pagerank [19] is biased against new documents, besides obtaining information on how recency is related with the Web structure. This fact supports our findings, given that we show that ranking algorithms are biasing the content of the Web. From the perspective of a search engine user, the Web does not evolve too much, considering that the new content is partially composed by the content of old popular documents.

Mitzenmacher [20] introduced a dynamic generative user model to explain the behavior of file size distributions (not only Web text documents). He showed that files that are copied or modified are more likely to be copied or modified subsequently.

Our work differs from the above mentioned papers in four main aspects: i) we study duplicate documents in collections where all sites under a given domain (.cl, from Chile) were crawled, which represents accurate and representative subsets of the Web; ii) we compare the number of duplicates for the complete collection and for the reachable and unreachable components; iii) we associate the search engine ranking algorithms with the Web content evolution; and iv) we study how old content is used to create new content in new documents.

7   Concluding Remarks

In this paper we have presented a study about duplicates and the evolution of the Web content. We have shown that the Web has many more duplicates than previously acknowledged in the literature. Other works use collections crawled by following links on the Web. The number of duplicates found for the unreachable component is on average 74.6% higher than the number of duplicates for the reachable component. Once we have used accurate and representative subsets of the Web, we believe that our conclusions can be extended to other Web collections.

We have shown that a significant portion of the Web content has evolved from old content. We have also shown that this portion is partly biased by the ranking algorithm of Web search engines, as people use a query to select several sources to apply a cut and paste to create part or all the content of a new page.

Additionally, we have demonstrated that the number of copies from previously copied Web pages is indeed greater than the number of copies from other pages. An open question is: do the search engines contribute to this situation, since they privilege popular documents and people use search engine to compose new documents? If the answer is true, then search engines contribute to slow down the evolution of the Web.

As future work it would be interesting to study the characteristics of the documents in the unreachable component of the Web (most of the times they are more recent documents [3]). Maybe it is heuristically possible to separate the interesting new documents from other documents that are many times replications of documents in the reachable component of the Web graph.

Acknowledgements

This work was partially funded by Spanish Education Ministry grant TIN2006-15536-C02-01 (R. Baeza-Yates and A. Pereira) and by Brazilian GERINDO Project–grant MCT/CNPq/CT-INFO 552.087/02-5 (N. Ziviani and A. Pereira), and CNPq Grants 30.5237/02-0 (N. Ziviani) and 14.1636/2004-1 (A. Pereira). We also would like to thank Karen Whitehouse for the English revision.

References

1. Broder, A., Glassman, S., Manasse, M., Zweig, G.: Syntactic clustering of the Web. In: Sixth International World Wide Web Conference, pp. 391–404 (1997)
2. Broder, A.: On the resemblance and containment of documents. In: SEQUENCES 1997. Compression and Complexity of Sequences, pp. 21–29 (1998)

3. Broder, A., Kumar, R., Maghoul, F., Raghavan, P., Rajagopalan, S., Stata, R., Tomkins, A., Wiener, J.: Graph structure in the web. In: WWW 2000. Ninth International World Wide Web Conference, Amsterdam, Netherlands, pp. 309–320 (May 2000)
4. Cormen, T.H., Leiserson, C.E., Rivest, R.L.: Introduction to algorithms. MIT Press/McGraw-Hill, San Francisco, CA (1990)
5. Cho, J., Shivakumar, N., Garcia-Molina, H.: Finding replicated Web collections. In: ACM International Conference on Management of Data (SIGMOD), pp. 355–366. ACM Press, New York (2000)
6. Shivakumar, N., Garcia-Molina, H.: Finding near-replicas of documents on the Web. In: Atzeni, P., Mendelzon, A.O., Mecca, G. (eds.) The World Wide Web and Databases. LNCS, vol. 1590, pp. 204–212. Springer, Heidelberg (1999)
7. Fetterly, D., Manasse, M., Najork, M.: On the evolution of clusters of near-duplicate Web pages. In: First Latin American Web Congress, Santiago, Chile, pp. 37–45 (November 2003)
8. Calado, P.: The WBR-99 collection: Data-structures and file formats. Technical report, Department of Computer Science, Federal University of Minas Gerais (1999), http://www.linguateca.pt/Repositorio/WBR-99/wbr99.pdf
9. Castillo, C.: Effective Web Crawler. PhD thesis, Chile University, Ch. 2 (2004)
10. Cho, J.: The evolution of the web and implications for an incremental crawler. In: VLDB. 26th Intl. Conference on Very Large Databases, Cairo, Egypt, pp. 527–534 (September 2000)
11. Brewington, B., Cybenko, G., Stata, R., Bharat, K., Maghoul, F.: How dynamic is the web? In: Ninth Conference on World Wide Web, Amsterdam, Netherlands, pp. 257–276 (May 2000)
12. Ntoulas, A., Cho, J., Olston, C.: What's new on the Web? the evolution of the Web from a search engine perspective. In: WWW 2004. World Wide Web Conference, New York, USA, pp. 1–12 (May 2004)
13. Douglis, F., Feldmann, A., Krishnamurthy, B., Mogul, J.C.: Rate of change and other metrics: a live study of the world wide Web. In: Symposium on Internet Technologies and Systems USENIX, Monterey, CA, pp. 147–158. (December 1997)
14. Chen, X., Mohapatra, P.: Lifetime behaviour and its impact on Web caching. In: WIAPP 1999, San Jose, CA, pp. 54–61. IEEE Computer Society Press, Los Alamitos (July 1999)
15. Cho, J., Roy, S.: Impact of search engine on page popularity. In: WWW 2004. World Wide Web Conference, New York, USA, pp. 20–29 (May 2004)
16. Baeza-Yates, R., Castillo, C., Saint-Jean, F.: Web dynamics, structure and page quality. In: Levene, M., Poulovassilis, A. (eds.) Web Dynamics, pp. 93–109. Springer, Heidelberg (2004)
17. Baeza-Yates, R., Pereira, A., Ziviani, N.: Genealogical trees on the web: A search engine user perspective (submitted) (2007)
18. Ntoulas, A., Cho, J., Cho, H.K., Cho, H., Cho, Y.J.: A study on the evolution of the Web. In: Korea, U.– (ed.) Conference on Science, Technology, and Entrepreneurship (UKC), Irvine, USA, pp. 1–6 (2005)
19. Page, L., Brin, S., Motwani, R., Winograd, T.: The pagerank citation ranking: Bringing order to the Web. Technical Report CA 93106, Stanford Digital Library Technologies Project, Stanford, Santa Barbara (January 1998)
20. Mitzenmacher, M.: Dynamic models for file sizes and double pareto distributions. Internet Mathematics 1(3), 305–333 (2003)

Author Index

Lecture Notes in Artificial Intelligence (LNAI)

Vol. 4660: S. Džeroski, L. Todorovski (Eds.), Computational Discovery of Scientific Knowledge. X, 327 pages. 2007.

Vol. 4659: V. Mařík, V. Vyatkin, A.W. Colombo (Eds.), Holonic and Multi-Agent Systems for Manufacturing. VIII, 456 pages. 2007.

Vol. 4651: F. Azevedo, P. Barahona, F. Fages, F. Rossi (Eds.), Recent Advances in Constraints. VIII, 185 pages. 2007.

Vol. 4648: F. Almeida e Costa, L.M. Rocha, E. Costa, I. Harvey, A. Coutinho (Eds.), Advances in Artificial Life. XVIII, 1215 pages. 2007.

Vol. 4635: B. Kokinov, D.C. Richardson, T.R. Roth-Berghofer, L. Vieu (Eds.), Modeling and Using Context. XIV, 574 pages. 2007.

Vol. 4632: R. Alhajj, H. Gao, X. Li, J. Li, O.R. Zaïane (Eds.), Advanced Data Mining and Applications. XV, 634 pages. 2007.

Vol. 4629: V. Matoušek, P. Mautner (Eds.), Text, Speech and Dialogue. XVII, 663 pages. 2007.

Vol. 4626: R.O. Weber, M.M. Richter (Eds.), Case-Based Reasoning Research and Development. XIII, 534 pages. 2007.

Vol. 4617: V. Torra, Y. Narukawa, Y. Yoshida (Eds.), Modeling Decisions for Artificial Intelligence. XII, 502 pages. 2007.

Vol. 4612: I. Miguel, W. Ruml (Eds.), Abstraction, Reformulation, and Approximation. XI, 418 pages. 2007.

Vol. 4604: U. Priss, S. Polovina, R. Hill (Eds.), Conceptual Structures: Knowledge Architectures for Smart Applications. XII, 514 pages. 2007.

Vol. 4603: F. Pfenning (Ed.), Automated Deduction – CADE-21. XII, 522 pages. 2007.

Vol. 4597: P. Perner (Ed.), Advances in Data Mining. XI, 353 pages. 2007.

Vol. 4594: R. Bellazzi, A. Abu-Hanna, J. Hunter (Eds.), Artificial Intelligence in Medicine. XVI, 509 pages. 2007.

Vol. 4585: M. Kryszkiewicz, J.F. Peters, H. Rybinski, A. Skowron (Eds.), Rough Sets and Intelligent Systems Paradigms. XIX, 836 pages. 2007.

Vol. 4578: F. Masulli, S. Mitra, G. Pasi (Eds.), Applications of Fuzzy Sets Theory. XVIII, 693 pages. 2007.

Vol. 4573: M. Kauers, M. Kerber, R. Miner, W. Windsteiger (Eds.), Towards Mechanized Mathematical Assistants. XIII, 407 pages. 2007.

Vol. 4571: P. Perner (Ed.), Machine Learning and Data Mining in Pattern Recognition. XIV, 913 pages. 2007.

Vol. 4570: H.G. Okuno, M. Ali (Eds.), New Trends in Applied Artificial Intelligence. XXI, 1194 pages. 2007.

Vol. 4565: D.D. Schmorrow, L.M. Reeves (Eds.), Foundations of Augmented Cognition. XIX, 450 pages. 2007.

Vol. 4562: D. Harris (Ed.), Engineering Psychology and Cognitive Ergonomics. XXIII, 879 pages. 2007.

Vol. 4548: N. Olivetti (Ed.), Automated Reasoning with Analytic Tableaux and Related Methods. X, 245 pages. 2007.

Vol. 4539: N.H. Bshouty, C. Gentile (Eds.), Learning Theory. XII, 634 pages. 2007.

Vol. 4529: P. Melin, O. Castillo, L.T. Aguilar, J. Kacprzyk, W. Pedrycz (Eds.), Foundations of Fuzzy Logic and Soft Computing. XIX, 830 pages. 2007.

Vol. 4520: M.V. Butz, O. Sigaud, G. Pezzulo, G. Baldassarre (Eds.), Anticipatory Behavior in Adaptive Learning Systems. X, 379 pages. 2007.

Vol. 4511: C. Conati, K. McCoy, G. Paliouras (Eds.), User Modeling 2007. XVI, 487 pages. 2007.

Vol. 4509: Z. Kobti, D. Wu (Eds.), Advances in Artificial Intelligence. XII, 552 pages. 2007.

Vol. 4496: N.T. Nguyen, A. Grzech, R.J. Howlett, L.C. Jain (Eds.), Agent and Multi-Agent Systems: Technologies and Applications. XXI, 1046 pages. 2007.

Vol. 4483: C. Baral, G. Brewka, J. Schlipf (Eds.), Logic Programming and Nonmonotonic Reasoning. IX, 327 pages. 2007.

Vol. 4482: A. An, J. Stefanowski, S. Ramanna, C.J. Butz, W. Pedrycz, G. Wang (Eds.), Rough Sets, Fuzzy Sets, Data Mining and Granular Computing. XIV, 585 pages. 2007.

Vol. 4481: J. Yao, P. Lingras, W.-Z. Wu, M.S. Szczuka, N.J. Cercone, D. Ślęzak (Eds.), Rough Sets and Knowledge Technology. XIV, 576 pages. 2007.

Vol. 4476: V. Gorodetsky, C. Zhang, V.A. Skormin, L. Cao (Eds.), Autonomous Intelligent Systems: Multi-Agents and Data Mining. XIII, 323 pages. 2007.

Vol. 4460: S. Aguzzoli, A. Ciabattoni, B. Gerla, C. Manara, V. Marra (Eds.), Algebraic and Proof-theoretic Aspects of Non-classical Logics. VIII, 309 pages. 2007.

Vol. 4457: G.M.P. O'Hare, A. Ricci, M.J. O'Grady, O. Dikenelli (Eds.), Engineering Societies in the Agents World VII. XI, 401 pages. 2007.

Vol. 4456: Y. Wang, Y.-m. Cheung, H. Liu (Eds.), Computational Intelligence and Security. XXIII, 1118 pages. 2007.

Vol. 4455: S. Muggleton, R. Otero, A. Tamaddoni-Nezhad (Eds.), Inductive Logic Programming. XII, 456 pages. 2007.

Vol. 4452: M. Fasli, O. Shehory (Eds.), Agent-Mediated Electronic Commerce. VIII, 249 pages. 2007.

Vol. 4451: T.S. Huang, A. Nijholt, M. Pantic, A. Pentland (Eds.), Artifical Intelligence for Human Computing. XVI, 359 pages. 2007.

Vol. 4442: L. Antunes, K. Takadama (Eds.), Multi-Agent-Based Simulation VII. X, 189 pages. 2007.

Vol. 4441: C. Müller (Ed.), Speaker Classification II. X, 309 pages. 2007.

Vol. 4438: L. Maicher, A. Sigel, L.M. Garshol (Eds.), Leveraging the Semantics of Topic Maps. X, 257 pages. 2007.

Vol. 4434: G. Lakemeyer, E. Sklar, D.G. Sorrenti, T. Takahashi (Eds.), RoboCup 2006: Robot Soccer World Cup X. XIII, 566 pages. 2007.

Vol. 4429: R. Lu, J.H. Siekmann, C. Ullrich (Eds.), Cognitive Systems. X, 161 pages. 2007.